THE
613
MITZVOT

THE
613
MITZVOT

A Contemporary Guide to the Commandments of Judaism

Ronald L. Eisenberg

Schreiber Publishing
Rockville, MD

Schreiber Publishing
Post Office Box 4139
Rockville, MD 20849 U.S.A.

Library of Congress Cataloging-in-Publication Data

Eisenberg, Ronald L.
   The 613 mitzvot: a contemporary guide to the commandments of
judaism /Ronald
L. Eisenberg.-- 1st ed.
      p. cm.
   Includes bibliographic references.
   ISBN 978-0-88400-333-5 (pbk.)
1. Commandments, Six hundred and thirteen. I. Title: Six hundred
thirteen mitzvot. II. Title: Contemporary guide to the commandments of
Judaism. III. Title.
   BM520.8.E34 2008
   296.1'8--dc22

                                                      2008000573

Printed in the United States of America

10 9 8 7 6 5 4 3

For Zina Schiff

and

For Avlana Kinneret and Cherina Carmel,
beautiful daughters of the commandments

קַדְּשֵׁנוּ בְּמִצְוֹתֶיךָ

Sanctify us with Your commandments

וּבְמִצְוֹתֶיךָ תִּרְדוֹף נַפְשִׁי

And let my soul pursue Your commandments

THE COMMANDMENTS

Positive Commandments

Negative Commandments

PREFACE

THE 613 MITZVOT are a basic cornerstone of Judaism. However, many Jews are unaware of the biblical sources, rabbinic and medieval interpretations, and modern applications of the commandments. Using the epic *Sefer ha-Mitzvot* of Maimonides as the foundation, this book develops a new approach to detail all of the 248 positive and 365 negative mitzvot in an easily readable style. For each mitzvah, there is a citation of its biblical source according to Maimonides, as well as a discussion in narrative text of its essential features, the views of major commentators, and current applications.

A unique feature of this book is the frequent combining of several mitzvot into one section to eliminate unnecessary repetition. For example, the 10 commandments dealing with the additional (*musaf*) offering for Sabbath and festivals are joined in a single short section, which explains how these sacrifices are now mentioned in the *Musaf Amidah* in modern synagogues. Similarly, the 13 mitzvot related to the laws of offerings and the 16 forbidden relationships are combined into individual sections that make these arcane topics understandable to the modern reader. Extensive cross-referencing between those positive and negative commandments dealing with the same subject enables the reader to rapidly survey the entire topic without duplication.

The introductory material opens with a discussion of how Maimonides enumerated and grouped the mitzvot. Then there is a listing of the rabbinic commandments, which were not specifically based on Torah verses, as well as the basic Noahide laws that are binding on all human beings and constitute the fundamental precepts required for the establishment of a civilized society. This is followed by an analysis of the *ta'amei ha-mitzvot*, the reasons for observance of the commandments offered during the biblical, talmudic, and medieval periods. There is also a discussion of the performance of the mitzvot, including such concepts as glorifying the mitzvah, love and joy in the mitzvah, conscious purpose (*kavanah*), and what to avoid when performing the mitzvot. The final section deals with the controversial issue of the obligation of women to perform the commandments.

The appendix contains a detailed listing of all the commandments and their biblical sources. This is followed by a listing of the commandments by *parshiyot*, so that they can be more easily studied in conjunction with the weekly Torah portion. Finally, there are two alternative categorizations of the mitzvot offered by Maimonides.

The 613 Mitzvot is designed both for observant Jews, to provide a deeper understanding of the development of the mitzvot that they routinely observe, and for less observant Jews who are interested in learning about their traditions and who may be inspired to more extensively practice their religion and thus accept "the yoke of the commandments."

I want to thank my dear wife, Zina Schiff, for her valuable suggestions in revising the manuscript, and publisher Morry Schreiber, for his constant encouragement and friendship.

ENUMERATION OF
THE MITZVOT

THE FIRST MENTION of a precise number of commandments appears in a talmudic statement (Mak. 23b) by R. Simlai, a fourth-century sage in the Land of Israel, who observed that "six hundred and thirteen commandments were communicated to Moses; three hundred and sixty five negative commandments [*mitzvot lo ta'aseh*], corresponding to the number of days [in the solar year], and two hundred and forty eight positive commandments [*mitzvot aseh*], corresponding to the number of parts of the human body." In Hebrew, the commandments are termed the *Taryag Mitzvot*, since the numerical value of these letters equals 613 (*tav* = 400; *resh* = 200; *yud* = 10; *gimel* = 3). These 613 mitzvot can also be viewed as the sum of the 611 Scriptural commandments, which were announced to the people directly by Moses—the word "Torah" in Hebrew has a numerical value of 611 (*tav* = 400; *resh* = 200; *vav* = 6; *hei* = 5)—plus the first two of the Ten Commandments, which were spoken directly to the people by God (Mak. 23b-24a).

During the Talmudic period, there was no attempt to precisely enumerate each individual commandment. The first effort in this direction was made in the Gaonic period (second half of the 8th century) by Simon Kayyara (or Kairo) in his *Halachot*

Gedolot (Great Laws). However, he cited a different division of commandments (265 positive and 348 negative) and included some mitzvot that were established only by rabbinic ordinance.

The major monumental work listing and elucidating the meaning of the commandments was the *Sefer ha-Mitzvot* (Book of the Commandments) of Maimonides (1135-1204). Known popularly as the Rambam (acronym for Rabbi Moses ben Maimon), this central figure in the world of halachah (Jewish law) and Jewish philosophy probably completed this work while already settled in Egypt in 1170, two years following the completion of his *Commentary on the Mishnah*. Ironically, Maimonides originally had envisioned merely listing in introductory prefaces those commandments found in each of the 14 volumes of his *Mishneh Torah*, his massive compendium encompassing all of Jewish law. However, observing that his predecessors had followed no definite principles in their selection of the 613 commandments and often had treated multiple aspects of a single commandment as individual mitzvot, Maimonides decided to write a special treatise on the Taryag Mitzvot. The first part of *Sefer ha-Mitzvot* is devoted to the Fourteen Principles underlying his decisions regarding which commandments should be included among the 613. These principles were defined with rigorous logic combined with a profound insight into the subtleties of rabbinic law. The remainder of the book consists of a detailed presentation of the 248 positive and 365 negative commandments, with extensive discussions of the degree of punishment incurred in transgressing them. Unlike the *Mishneh Torah*, in which Maimonides simply states the law without citing sources or presenting the arguments that led him to arrive at his conclusions, *Sefer ha-Mitzvot* is richly annotated and allows the reader an insight into Maimonides' intricate reasoning process.

Numerous other sages have attempted to classify the commandments. The most extensive criticism of Maimonides' list was provided by Nachmanides (1195-1270), also known as the Ramban (acronym for Rabbi Moses ben Nachman). This Spanish talmudist and kabbalist, who combined the rationalist approach with a search for hidden meanings in his *Commentary on the Torah*, argued that 17 positive and 17 negative commandments should replace an equal number in Maimonides' list. *Sefer ha-Chinuch* (Book of Education), which is attributed to the 13th-century Aaron Ha-Levi of Barcelona, arranged the commandments according to the order in which they appear in the Torah, so that they could be studied along with the weekly Torah reading in the synagogue. For each commandment, this work analyzed its nature (Torah source and rabbinic explanation), rationale, related specific laws, and conditions (where and to whom it applied and the punishment for transgressing it). In the 19th century, the Chafetz Chaim (Israel Meir Ha-Cohen) wrote the *Sefer ha-Mitzvot ha-Katzar* (Short Book of the Commandments), which includes a listing of those positive and negative commandments that are still applicable today.

Organization of the mitzvot according to Maimonides

As noted by many subsequent commentators, Maimonides organized the positive commandments in the following ten groups:

1. Belief in One God and our duties toward God (1-19)
2. Sanctuary, priesthood, and sacrifices (20-95)
3. Sources of ritual uncleanness and modes of purification (96-113)
4. Gifts to the Temple, the poor, the Kohanim, and Levites; the Sabbatical and Jubilee Years; and the preparation of food (114-152)
5. Holy days and the observances connected with them (153- 171)

6. Proper functioning of the Jewish State (172-193)
7. Duties toward our fellow human beings (194-209)
8. Duties attached to family life (210-223)
9. Enforcement of the criminal law (224-231)
10. Laws relating to real and personal property (232-248)

Similarly, Maimonides organized the negative commandments into ten groups:

1. Idolatry and related subjects (1-59)
2. Duties to God and the Sanctuary (60-88)
3. Sacrifices, priestly gifts, Kohanim, Levites, and related subjects (89-171)
4. Prohibitions affecting food (172-209)
5. Cultivation of land (210-228)
6. Duties toward our fellow human beings, the poor, and employees (229-270)
7. Administration of justice, authority of the courts, and related issues (271-319)
8. Sabbath and Festivals (320-329)
9. Forbidden degrees of marriage and related subjects (330-361)
10. Head of the Jewish State and its officers (362-365)

Rabbinic commandments:

The Rabbis established seven mitzvot that were not based on any verses in the Torah. These include:

1. Washing hands before eating (Eduy. 5:6)
2. Lighting Sabbath candles (Shab. 20b)
3. Reciting the Hallel psalms of praise (Ps. 113-18) on festival days (Ber, 14a; Pes. 117a)
4. Lighting Hannukah candles (Shab 23a)
5. Reading the Scroll of Esther on Purim (Meg. 7a)
6. Making an "eruv" (to alleviate some Sabbath restrictions con-

cerning the limitation of movement and transfer of objects) (Er. 21b)

7. Saying a blessing of thanksgiving before experiencing pleasure in worldly items (such as for specific foods) (Ber. 35a)

Like the performance of mitzvot based on Torah verses (d'oraita), the observance of rabbinic (d'rabbanan) commandments is preceded by reciting a blessing of sanctification. Nevertheless, there are substantial differences in the manner in which these two types of commandments are observed. Commandments based on Torah verses must be observed with the greatest possible strictness; the mitzvah must be repeated if there is any doubt whether it has already been performed. Thus, if uncertain whether one has recited the *Shema*, a person must recite it, on the assumption that he had not already previously said it. In contrast, a similar uncertainty as to whether one has fulfilled a rabbinic commandment would not obligate the individual to repeat the mitzvah. According to Jewish law, conscious purpose (*kavanah*) is an unequivocal requirement for discharging most Scriptural commandments, but is not strictly necessary (though strongly recommended) in the case of rabbinic mitzvot.

Noahide Laws

The Rabbis derived seven basic laws that were binding on all human beings and constituted the fundamental precepts required for the establishment of a civilized society. They are termed the "Noahide laws" since they are to be observed by all people on earth, whom the Torah describes as descended from the three sons of Noah (Gen. 9:19). The Noahide laws include (1) the establishment of courts of justice and the prohibition of (2) idolatry, (3) blasphemy, (4) murder, (5) incest and adultery, (6) robbery, and (7) eating flesh cut from a live animal (before it is killed).

Although Israelites in the Land were obliged to carry out all of the Torah commandments, observance of the seven Noahide laws was all that was required of non-Jews who lived among the Israelites or attached themselves to the Jewish community. In this way, non-Jews could assure themselves a place in the World to Come.

REASONS FOR OBSERVANCE
OF THE COMMANDMENTS
(Ta'amei ha-Mitzvot)

Why should Jews observe the commandments? Are they to be obeyed merely because they represent the will of God, or because they possess some intrinsic meaning designed to spiritually improve the person who performs them, or for both reasons? Throughout the centuries, the answers to these questions have varied among the classical Jewish texts. Some have argued that we should not search for reasons for the mitzvot since they transcend our understanding, while others have maintained that every effort should be made to discover their underlying meanings. Abraham Joshua Heschel observed that "in doing more than we understand, we come to understand more than we do"—of ourselves, the Tradition, and the world.

Biblical

The Torah offers specific reasons for relatively few of the commandments. A classic example is the prohibition against oppressing a stranger (Neg. Comm. 252), which is repeated 36 times in the Torah and is based on the verse "for you were strangers in the land of Egypt" (Exod. 22:10). Having suffered greatly as strangers in the land of Egypt, the Israelites learned first hand the need to be sensitive to the plight of strangers in their midst. Broad reasons given for observing the entire gamut of positive and negative commandments include: (a) ensuring the holiness of the nation; (b) upholding the everlasting legal covenant; (c) sustaining the love relationship between God and Israel; (d) the concept of reward and punishment; (e) sanctifying the Name of God; and (f) leading a wise and moral life.

As the Israelites stood at the foot of Mount Sinai, God offered them the opportunity to be "a kingdom of priests and a holy nation" (Exod. 19:6). The root of the Hebrew word for "holy" is "*kadosh*" (lit. "separate"). Therefore, by observing the commandments the Israelites would become a unique nation, God's "most beloved treasure among all the peoples" (Exod. 19:5).

The relationship between God and the Jewish people can be seen as both an everlasting legal covenant (*brit*) and a passionate love affair. In exchange for strict observance of the Divine commandments, God promised the Israelites physical prosperity, a homeland, and a unique spiritual relationship. The Israelites formally ratified this agreement when they stated as one, "All that God has commanded, we will do and we will obey" (Exod. 24:7). This covenant was understood to continue through the generations, for as Moses declared almost 40 years later: "It was not with our ancestors that God made this covenant, but with us, we who are here, all of us who are alive today" (Deut. 5:3). Thus all Jews are obligated to fulfill the terms of the covenant just as if they had personally stood at the foot of Mt. Sinai. Similarly, in every generation all Jews are to regard themselves as having been personally redeemed from bondage in Egypt.

The relationship between God and Israel can also be seen as a marriage contract signifying the intense and unquenchable love between two parties. Israel is described as a "beloved people," Divinely selected not because of its size but rather "because of God's love for you" (Deut. 7:6-8). Describing the Divine love for Israel, Hosea (2:21-22) relates God as saying "And I will wed you forever; and I will betroth you with righteousness and justice, and with goodness and mercy, and I will wed you with faithfulness. Then you shall be devoted to God." These prophetic words of consecration are recited each morning by traditional Jews as they wrap the tefillin (Pos. Comm. 12-13) around their hands, symbolizing the daily renewal of the marital relationship established between God and the Israelites at Mount Sinai.

A constant theme in the Torah is that one receives a reward for observing the commandments and punishment (either divine or human) for disobeying them. The second paragraph of the *Shema* (Deut. 13-21) stresses that the prosperity of the Israelite nation is dependent on its faithfully obeying the Divine mitzvot. If the Israelites heed the commandments, God will "supply your land with rain at the proper season ... so that you will have ample harvest of grain and wine and oil. And I will provide grass in the field for your cattle, and you will eat and be satisfied." Conversely, in response to forsaking the commandments God will "close up the heavens and there will be no rain and the earth will not yield its produce; and you will soon perish from the good land which God is giving you."

The classic descriptions of reward and punishment relating to whether the Israelites followed or disobeyed the commandments are the two elaborate lists of blessings and curses (Lev. 26:3-39; Deut 28:1-68). Following a recital of the blessings that will accrue to the nation for fulfilling the commandments, there is a chilling prophecy detailing an extensive list of the dire consequences that would befall the people (termed the "Tochachah," or Admonition) if they spurned God and the mitzvot in the Torah.

The Torah requires that many of the commandments are to be enforced by human courts. Extensive regulations define the four types of capital punishment (Pos. Comm. 226-230), the cities of refuge for those who have committed involuntary manslaughter (Pos. Comm. 182, 225), monetary compensation of inflicting injuries (Pos. Comm. 236), the legal remedies for negligence (Pos. Comm. 237-238; 240-241), and the restitution required for various types of theft (Pos. Comm. 239).

Observing the commandments serves to sanctify God's Name (Pos. Comm. 9), enhancing God's reputation and honor among the nations. Conversely, disobeying the mitzvot, especially those prohibitions relating to maltreatment of non-Jews, can bring shame on the entire House of Israel and profane the Name of God (Neg. Comm. 63).

The Bible considered the performance of the commandments to be essential for leading a life of wisdom and morality. They represent the true standard of how to lead an ethical life, since they are the commandments of a completely moral God. "The teaching of God is perfect, renewing life; the decrees of God are enduring, making the simple wise. The commandments of the Lord are just, rejoicing the heart; the instruction of God is clear, making the eyes light up. The fear of God is pure, abiding forever; the judgments of God are true, righteous altogether" (Ps. 19:7-9). As created in the image of God, the embodiment of such virtues as holiness, compassion, and justice, human beings are commanded to walk in God's ways (Pos. Comm. 8), to imitate God and the Divine pattern of actions as much as can be done by mere mortals.

Talmudic

The predominant view of the Rabbis of the Talmud is that one should obey the commandments because they come directly from God and reflect the Divine will. This view maintains that God the Creator has a certain plan for the universe and humans beings. God's will has been revealed in Scriptures, the meaning of which is interpreted by the Tradition. Because of the supranatural origin of the commandments, it is pointless to try to find rational or natural reasons to justify them. Therefore, the duty of the Jew is simply to obey them.

Ironically, attempting to discover the underlying reasons for the commandments might actually lead to people *not* observing them. A person might decide that the reason was valid, but that it did not apply in his or her specific case. Similarly, the reason may have been valid when the commandment was issued, but was no longer applicable because social, economic, or other conditions had changed. One who is a true believer does not need reasons to observe the mitzvot; conversely, one who does not observe the commandments will not necessarily be convinced if a reason is given.

Nevertheless, the rabbis offered several specific reasons for observing the mitzvot in addition to affirming those given in the Bible. Various texts state that the commandments were given "only to refine God's creatures," "to preserve My world, since if it were not for the Law the world would again become without form and void," and as a way to maintain the identity of the Jewish People despite their dispersion among the nations. "If it were not for My Law which you accepted, I should not recognize you, and I would not regard you more than any of the idolatrous nations of the world." Interpreting the verse "You are beautiful, my love", Song of Songs Rabbah (1:15) notes that, "You [Israel] are beautiful through the commandments, both positive and negative. You are beautiful through loving deeds, beautiful in your House with the heave offerings and tithes, beautiful through the commandments about gleaning, the forgotten sheaf and the second tithe ... beautiful in prayer, the reading of the *Shema*." In summary, the reason offered by the rabbis for observing the commandments was to help the Jewish People transform themselves and the world into the kind of community that God wanted them to become.

Middle Ages

The dominant medieval view (philosophers, mystics, musar movement) was that the commandments are not ends in themselves, but rather are a means to the end of human self-development and perfection. The Talmudic rabbis were primarily concerned with *what* actions were required to perform those commandments detailed and explicated in the Written and Oral Law, viewing the mitzvot as a way of fulfilling God's will, which is the ultimate purpose of human existence. In contrast, the medieval mind focused on *why* and *how* the mitzvot should be observed.

Philosophers

According to the Jewish philosophers of the Middle Ages, unreflective faith in observance of the commandments is necessary but not sufficient. To have complete faith, one must reflect on the reasons for the mitzvot and the proper way in which to perform them, based on the intense text study that they viewed as a major religious obligation for Jews. However, this effort was to be limited to an intellectual and spiritual elite and not available to the unlettered masses. If certain knowledge were given to those who were not prepared for it, they would misunderstand and misuse it, ending up observing the commandments even less than before.

Saadia Gaon, the first of the great medieval Jewish philosophers, argued that unless one really understood the ideological, conceptual, and theological underpinnings of one's beliefs, religious observances have no foundation, are meaningless, and simply mechanical. He divided the commandments into those that are rational (*sichliyot*), such as the prohibitions against murder (Neg. Comm. 289) and stealing (Neg. Comm. 244), and those that are irrational and could only be given through revelation (*shimiyot*), such as *sha'atnez* (Neg. Comm. 42) and the red heifer (Pos. Comm. 113).

The preeminent medieval philosopher was Maimonides (Rambam), who argued that all of the commandments had rationales and useful purposes, even if these could not yet be understood by the human mind. The general explanation for the mitzvot was they were a means for improving human character – the development of correct thinking and behavior, as well the instilling of moral virtue and the dispelling of moral vice. Theologically, the essence of the commandments was to affirm the Oneness of God and polemicize against idolatry. For example, Maimonides maintained that the prohibition against combining milk and meat was an attack against an idolatrous practice of a fertility cult during the Biblical period. A problem not addressed by Maimonides was that, if a commandment was based on what was done long ago, why should it still be observed when that reason no longer exists? In essence, he considered the commandments as a means of moving people from a state of moral, intellectual and spiritual potentiality to actualizing their human perfection. Indeed, living a moral life and developing the virtues was one way to make the transition from a human being to being human. According to Maimonides, the only truly "happy" individuals were not those who attained pleasure, but rather those who fulfilled their potential.

Mystics

For the Jewish mystics and practitioners of Kabbalah, the goal of life was communion with the Divine (*deveikut*, or cleaving to God). Observance of the commandments, along with the development of a proper moral and ethical character, were prerequisites, for God does not want to come into an intimate relationship with an immoral person. The Zohar developed the concept that what humans do on earth has an effect not only on ourselves, society, and the cosmos, but also on the inner life of God. Fulfilling the mitzvot restores union and harmony in the spiritual realm of the sefirot; in turn, this ultimately channels positive Divine energy into our material world. According to this theurgical approach, not only does God redeem man, but we redeem God.

Musar

The musar movement, popularized by Israel Salanter in mid-19th century Lithuania, stressed that one should have the proper motivation when observing the commandments. Efforts were made to identify and hopefully inculcate the right attitude that would strengthen observance, so that one did not do the right thing for the wrong reasons. Centuries earlier, in his discussion of the meaning of "holiness," Nachmanides had argued that there must be more than merely observing the commandments— a person can observe all the laws but, if done for the wrong motivation, can still be a moral degenerate ("a scoundrel with the permission of the Torah"). Bahya ibn Pekuda stressed the distinction between the "duties of the limbs" (actions) and the "duties of the heart" (internal spiritual motivation). One who physically fulfills the commandments without the right intention and attitude misses the entire point of performing the mitzvot.

In his mystical writings, Nachmanides pointed out the similarity between the Hebrew words *mitzvot* and *midot* (moral values), showing that they are differentiated only by a little tail on a letter and thus can be considered to be the same. He argued that the purpose of a human being is to become a *baal midot* (virtuous person) by fulfilling the mitzvot, which can be understood as vehicles for the formation of proper character.

Performance of the Mitzvot

The rabbis focused much attention on the psychological and spiritual aspects of performing the commandments (*shemirat ha-mitzvot*). They stressed that religious observance in Judaism is not merely a mechanical performance nor the discharge of a burdensome obligation, but rather an infinitely rich and rewarding experience within the reach of every individual. Instead of being a thoughtless matter of routine, religious observance requires constant and careful consideration, since the greater the devotion with which the mitzvot are carried out, the greater the reward and spiritual satisfaction.

Glorifying the Mitzvah (hiddur mitzvah)

By going beyond the call of duty in fulfilling a mitzvah, a Jew can reflect glory upon the One who commanded its observance. Based on the verse "This is my God and I will glorify Him" (Exod. 15:2), the Talmud (BK 9b) suggests that one should spend up to an extra third of the cost of a mitzvah on its adornment. Thus, on Sukkot the Jew should purchase the best etrog possible and bedeck the sukkah with the most beautiful decorations. Other examples of glorifying the mitzvah include buying the most beautiful tefillin, shofar, and tallit, as well as employing the finest clear ink, best quality pen, and most skilled scribe with superb script in the writing of a Torah scroll. However, one must always be wary of focusing too much concentration on the means for performing a commandment and not paying sufficient attention to the meaning of the mitzvah itself.

Love of the Mitzvah (chivuv mitzvah)

The classic example of manifesting love of the mitzvah is not to bargain over the price when buying something pertaining to a mitzvah, but rather to pay at once whatever the seller asks. This is done to show that the love of God is greater than any attachment to material goods. Similarly, one demonstrates love of the mitzvah by performing a commandment personally, even when the law permits it to be delegated to others. The Torah relates that when leaving Egypt, the Israelites carried the un-leavened bread and bitter herbs bound up in their clothes upon their own shoulders (Exod. 12:34), rather than placing them on their beasts of burden. In preparation for the Sabbath, the distinguished rabbis of the Talmud showed their love of the mitzvah by performing such menial tasks as fanning the fire, salting fish, cutting up beet roots, chopping wood, and carrying heavy loads in and out of the house (Shab. 119a).

Joy in the Mitzvah (simchah shel mitzvah)

Performing a mitzvah should be considered a privileged opportunity to serve God and never as a burden. Consequently, the mitzvot should be performed with enthusiasm and an uplifted heart. "One should not stand up and say prayers while immersed in sorrow, or idleness, or laughter, or chatter, or frivolity, or idle talk, but only while still rejoicing in the performance of some religious act" (Ber. 31a). Related to this is the excited anticipation one should feel for an approaching festival, treating it as an honored guest that will soon arrive.

Although difficult to accomplish, the Talmud (Ber. 60b) teaches that the meaning of the Mishnah, "It is incumbent on a man to bless God for the evil in the same way as for the good," is that one must recite the blessing for evil with the same joy and absolute devotion as one says for the good. Similarly, the verse, "I will sing of kindness and justice" (Ps. 101:1), was interpreted as requiring that one praise God with the same joy whether the recipient of Divine mercy or in strict accordance with the principles of justice. For the Rabbis, the ultimate experience was achieved by R. Akiva, who as his martyred soul was departing his body, had such profound belief in the perfect goodness of God that he was able to perform with a joyful heart *Kiddush ha-Shem*, (Sanctification of the Name), the highest mitzvah in Judaism (see Pos. Comm. 9).

Alertness (zerizut)

The performance of a mitzvah should never be postponed, but rather always accomplished at the earliest possible moment, based on the verse, "I have hastened, and not delayed, in the observance of Your commandments" (Ps. 119:60). Thus, the mitzvah of circumcision, which could be performed at any time of the day, is carried out in the morning. When Abraham was ordered to journey to Mount Moriah to sacrifice his son, Isaac, the Patriarch is described as setting out early in the morning to accomplish this grievous task.

Observing that the words "*mitzvot*" and "*matzot*" are identical when written in the unvocalized Hebrew text of the Bible, the Mehilta interpreted the verse "And you shall watch the unleavened bread" (Exod. 12:17) as meaning that, "Just as one should not be slow when making unleavened bread, lest it leaven, so one should not be slow to perform a mitzvah. If a mitzvah comes your way, perform it immediately."

Conscious Purpose (kavanah)

When a mitzvah entails the performance of a specific act (such as the eating of unleavened bread), one who merely performs the act without conscious purpose generally fulfills his obligation. However, where no specific act is required, there must be a conscious awareness fulfilling one's duty. In a talmudic example (RH 27b): "If a man is passing behind a synagogue, or if his house adjoins the synagogue, and he hears the sound of the shofar, or of the reading of the Scroll of Esther, then if he listens with attention he fulfills his obligation, but otherwise he does not." The blessing recited before performing a mitzvah not only offers praise to God, but also reminds the individual of the importance of the sanctified act.

Mitzvot should be performed for their own sake (*lishmah*), without any ulterior motive or expectation of a reward. Instead, the Jew must completely subjugate his or her own personal desires to the service of God as written in the Psalms (40:9), "To do Your will, O my God, I have desired, and Your law is in my very heart."

What to Avoid in Performing Mitzvot

A commandment may not be treated with disrespect (*bizui mitzvah*). Thus it is forbidden to use a sacred object for a secular purpose, such as the express talmudic prohibition of counting money by the light of the Hannukah candles (Shab 22a). Attending to one's own affairs before fulfilling a mitzvah is also considered a form of disrespect, so that one should not eat before reciting the morning prayers (Ber. 10b). The use of inferior material in the performance of a mitzvah constitutes disrespect, so that one should not employ poor-quality wool for weaving tzitzit or hold a Torah scroll without a covering.

Objects that have been used to perform a mitzvah must be treated with respect, even when they have become too old or worn for this purpose. Thus religious items that can no longer be used (tallit, tefillin, Torah scroll) must not be thrown away.

Instead, they must be buried to prevent their desecration. In past centuries, old or worn religious items were hidden from sight in a *genizah*, such as the famous one in Cairo.

A mitzvah must never be performed with the "fruits of sin" (*mitzvah haba'ah b'averah*) (Suk. 30a). As the Talmud (Sanh 6b) observes, "If one has stolen a measure of wheat and has ground, kneaded and baked it, and set apart the challah, how can he recite a blessing over it? It would not be a blessing, but rather a blasphemy!"

OBLIGATIONS OF WOMEN TO PERFORM THE COMMANDMENTS

The great majority of mitzvot apply equally to men and women. Obvious exceptions are those mitzvot that are gender-based, such as circumcision and laws regarding menstruation. According to the Mishnah (Kid. 29a), women are obligated to observe virtually all the negative commandments. The three exceptions are trimming the locks and the beard (Neg. Comm. 43, 44), from which women are exempt for biological reasons, and avoiding contact with a corpse (Neg. Comm. 166), which applies only to male Kohanim since women pass on the priestly lineage but do not have any priestly functions. With respect to the positive commandments, both men and women are required to perform all those that are independent of time. However, for commandments that are time-bound, "men are obligated and women are exempt." The most common explanation for this distinction is that it reflects the traditional domestic role of women in society. Imposition of time-bound mitzvot would be an unreasonable burden on a busy wife and mother.

The Talmud lists five specific time-bound positive commandments for which women are not obligated – dwelling in a sukkah and taking up the lulav (Four Species) on Sukkot (Pos. Comm. 168, 169), hearing the shofar on Rosh Hashanah and Yom Kippur (Pos. Comm. 170), wearing tzitzit (fringes; Pos. Comm. 14), and putting on tefillin (Pos. Comm. 12, 13). (Elsewhere, women are also exempted from counting the omer

[Pos. Comm. 161] and from reciting the *Shema* [Pos. Comm. 10]; nevertheless, they still have an obligation to pray in private at their own time.) Conversely, women are exempt from some positive commandments that are not time-bound, such as the study of Torah (Pos. Comm. 11), procreation (Pos. Comm. 212), and the redemption of the firstborn son (Pos. Comm. 80).

Because the Mishnah uses the term "exempt" in describing the time-bound positive commandments that were not obligatory for women, the question arises of whether women "may" perform these mitzvot if they so choose. Although most rabbinic authorities permit women to voluntarily assume these halachic obligations, even considering it a meritorious act, there is controversy concerning whether women are allowed to recite the appropriate blessing before performing an optional commandment. Maimonides maintained that a woman cannot recite a blessing including the phrase, "Who has sanctified us with His commandments and commanded us to ..." in conjunction with a mitzvah that she is not obligated to perform. He further ruled that a woman's performance of such a mitzvah is not equal to that of a man, based on the concept that fulfilling a mitzvah that one has been commanded to perform has greater merit than assuming obligations that are not required. Rabbenu Tam championed the opposing view, maintaining that women could recite the blessings because performance of the commandments reflected the obligation of the Jewish people as a whole.

Another controversial issue is whether a woman who assumes a given mitzvah as her duty (such as reading the Torah) can perform this commandment on behalf of men. Except for a few recent opinions, the traditional consensus has been that women may not discharge men's obligations for mitzvot they have taken upon themselves because they are fulfilling them voluntarily rather than as a Divinely mandated responsibility. According to the concept of *"kevod ha-tzibbur,"* which literally

means "the honor of the community," having a woman discharge a mitzvah for men would cast doubt on the education
and piety of the male members of the congregation, putting
them to shame by implying that none of them was capable of
performing this function. This is similar to a talmudic teaching
(Ber. 20b) that permits a woman to recite the grace after meals
on behalf of her husband under certain circumstances, though
the rabbis add that "a curse light on the man whose wife and
children have to say the grace for him" (since he would appear insufficiently knowledgeable or pious to do it for himself).
In liberal synagogues, women are permitted to read from the
Torah and lead prayer services.

POSITIVE
COMMANDMENTS

Belief in the Existence of God (1)

The fundamental essence of Judaism is a belief in God, who is omniscient, omnipresent, omnipotent, and the Creator of everything in existence. This is clearly stated in the first of the Ten Commandments, *"I am the Lord your God, who brought you out of the land of Egypt..."* (Exod. 20:2). Belief in One God is a prerequisite for the acceptance of all of the other commandments, because a denial of the existence of God would render observance of the other Divinely mandated commandments irrelevant. The existence of God is the first of the Thirteen Principles of Faith of Maimonides, who maintained that any Jew denying this belief is an apostate who does not merit a portion in the World to Come.

Other commentators have disagreed. For Abravanel, this was merely an introductory statement to the subsequent commandments, so that the Israelites gathered around the base of Mount Sinai would know Who was addressing them. Hasdai Cresca insisted that because a commandment can only apply to matters of free will and free choice, belief cannot be commanded. The talmudic rabbis viewed this as a summons to accept the yoke of Divine sovereignty and recognize God as the Supreme Authority—the prerequisite for God to transmit the laws and decrees that shaped the Jewish people.[1]

Why does the first commandment describe God as the Redeemer from Egypt, rather than the Creator of the universe? Ibn Ezra maintained that the Exodus from Egypt was an event that hundreds of thousands of Israelites actually witnessed, unlike the creation of world that occurred well before the advent of human beings, thus enabling them and subsequent generations to believe in a personal God who is involved with His people in their time of need. Nachmanides added that the miraculous deliverance from Egypt reinforced the concept of God's omnipotence. According to *Sefer ha-Chinuch*, the Exodus reaffirmed freedom as a Divine gift and the fulfillment of God's promise to the Patriarchs.

Unity of God (2)

The principle of monotheism is founded on the verse, *"Hear, O Israel: the Lord is our God, the Lord is One"* (Deut. 6:4). The *Shema* is a core of the morning and evening prayers, part of the mezuzah (Pos. Comm. 15) and tefillin (Pos. Comm. 12, 13), and the final words on the lips of countless martyrs throughout the centuries who gave their lives for the sanctification of God's name (*Kiddush ha-Shem*). In the Torah scroll, the *ayin* of the word *Shema* and the *daled* of the word *echad* are written larger than the other letters. Together they form the word *eid* (witness), indicating that the Jew who pronounces the *Shema* bears witness to the unity of God and declares it to all the world. The unity of God implies that God cannot be divided or fragmented and thus must be a purely spiritual, non-physical, Being. This unity and incorporeality of God constitute two of Maimonides' Thirteen Principles of Faith.

The final word of the *Shema* can also be translated as "unique," totally different from the pagan gods and beyond all human understanding. Indeed, God is truly a Supreme Being, entirely unlike anything in the Divinely created universe. Maimonides argued that humans cannot describe the essence of an incomparable God, and thus are forced either to say what God is not (negative attributes) or to refer to the manifestations of God that are evident in our world (attributes of action). Ba'al ha-Turim noted that the various and often contradictory aspects of God (strict, stern judge vs. merciful, compassionate parent) might lead the unwitting to believe that there is more than one God, but stressed the importance of understanding that these are only manifestations of the same One God. For the mystical Zohar, the *En Sof* represented the infinite, concealed God (what God really is, beyond both our comprehension and any human relationship), while the 10 *Sefirot* (emanations) reflected the revealed or manifested God with whom some relationship is possible.

In the Messianic Age, all people will finally recognize God as supreme throughout the world, as noted in the conclusion of the *Aleinu* prayer, "For on that day, God will be One and His Name One" (Zech. 14:9).

Love of God (3)

"And you shall love the Lord your God..." (Deut. 6:5) means performing His commandments out of pure love, with an intense desire to fulfill the Divine will and achieve the highest level in man's relationship with God, rather than because of fear of punishment or the inducement of a reward. People who are motivated by fear may abandon a task if it becomes too difficult to perform, whereas those who act based on love are prepared to make substantial sacrifices for the objects of their affection.[2, 3]

The Mishnah (Ber. 9:5; 54a) explains that a person should serve God with all one's emotions and desires ("with all your heart"), even to the point of giving up one's life for God ("with all your soul"), and even at the cost of one's wealth ("with all your might/resources").[4] Noting that the word *le-vavecha* (your heart) has an extra *vav*, the Rabbis deduced that this required Jews to serve God not only with their noble impulses but even with the base and selfish desires of their hearts—both the *yetzer ha-tov* (inclination to do good) and the *yetzer ha-ra* (inclination to do evil). Thus it is necessary to turn our appetites, our physical lusts, and our egocentricity to the service of God by sanctifying the way we eat, act sexually, and earn and spend our money.[5] The Rabbis interpreted the similarity between the words *middah* (measure) and *me'odecha"* (resources/might) as indicating that Jews should be willing to give up everything for God and must willingly accept whatever God has allotted for them.

How can one be commanded to love? The Sefat Emet taught

that every human soul has an instinctive wish to love God, its Creator. However, this natural inclination may be blocked by a variety of impediments, which are removed by performing the mitzvot and focusing one's efforts on the study and teaching of Torah (as noted in the next few verses).[6, 7] Maimonides noted that by meditating on God's great and wondrous deeds and creations, and seeing in them His incomparable and infinite wisdom, one will immediately come to love and praise God and be filled with longing to know Him.

The mutual love of the people of Israel and God was metaphorically described by the prophets Isaiah, Jeremiah, and Hosea as the love between a bride and groom. They warned of the dire consequences that would occur if the bride (Israelites) ever betrayed the trust of her bridegroom (God). The Song of Songs was interpreted as an allegory of the love between God and the Jewish people, which begins with the Exodus from Egypt on Passover and is "consummated" with their "marriage" — the giving of the Torah at Mount Sinai seven weeks later, which is celebrated on the festival of Shavuot.[8]

Maimonides wrote of the rabbinic concept that the love of God also includes the obligation for service and faith. Just as one praises and extols a person one loves and calls upon others to love the object of your affection, so the attainment of true love for God will inspire one to "call upon the foolish and ignorant to seek knowledge of the truth which you have already acquired."

Fear of God (4)

In the verse, *"You shall fear the Lord your God"* (Deut. 6:13; 10:20), the phrase *yirat ha-Shem* can be translated as "fear" or "awe" of God. After the commandment to love God (Pos. Comm. 3), Moses added the complementary obligation to fear Him. According to Nachmanides, love motivates people to serve; fear prevents them from sinning.

Maimonides related this commandment to the rabbinic doctrine of reward and punishment, an integral part of traditional Judaism and the eleventh of his Thirteen Principles of Faith. Human beings must always be aware of their insignificance in the cosmos and the extent of their lack of understanding in comparison to the omnipotence and omniscience of the Divine. Consequently, when about to sin a person should immediately sense that his thoughts and actions are both evident and displeasing to God. This fear of the "Ever-present Eye" and of Heavenly punishment should be sufficient to prevent the person from sinning.[9]

Abraham Joshua Heschel preferred to translate *yirat ha-Shem* as "awe" (or "reverence") of God. The realization that God is the foundation of the world leads to an overwhelming sense of awe and the holiness of God. For Heschel, "awe" of God was a term almost equivalent to our word "religion," for which there is no true Hebrew equivalent.

Regardless of the precise translation of *yirat ha-Shem*, the Psalms (111:10) and Proverbs (9:10) call it "the beginning of wisdom." After grimly concluding that his lifetime of amassing possessions was merely "emptiness and chasing after wind, of no profit under the sun" (1:11), the author of Ecclesiastes ends his book with the affirmation that there is an ultimate purpose to life—"Fear God and obey His commandments, for this is the whole of man" (12:13). Indeed, the term *yirat ha-Shem* has come to define the pious Jew, who is convinced that by performing God's commandments he or she is fulfilling the Divine will.

Serving (Worshiping) God (5)

The command to "serve" God is repeated several times in the Torah (e.g., Exod. 23:25; Deut. 6:13; 11:13; 13:5). After the destruction of the Second Temple, in which the sacrificial rite was termed *"avodah"* (service), the Rabbis substituted as its

replacement prayer (*avodah she-b'lev* [lit. "service of the heart"];
Taan. 2a). As R. Eleazar observed, "prayer is more efficacious
than good deeds ... [and] than sacrifices" (Ber. 32b).

The Rabbis decreed that Jews pray three times a day and
suggested two major reasons for this practice (Ber. 26b). According to one opinion, the three services correspond to the daily
sacrifices in Temple times—the morning and afternoon prayers to
the *Shacharit* and *Mincha* offerings; the evening (*Ma'ariv*) prayers
to the nighttime burning on the Altar of all the fat and organs
of the daily offerings. The other attributes the establishment of
the three daily services to the patriarchs, based on three biblical
references—Abraham "rose up early in the morning and hurried
to the place where he had stood [in the presence of the Lord]"
(Gen. 19:27), and "standing" always means "praying;" Isaac went
out "to meditate in the field toward evening" (Gen. 24:63); and
Jacob prayed before he went to sleep on his stone pillow and
dreamt of angels ascending and descending the ladder connecting the earth to heaven (Gen. 28:11).

Maimonides stressed the importance of *kavanah* in prayer.
This Hebrew word can be translated as "proper devotion" or
"concentration," but more literally means "direction of the
heart." For Maimonides, a person who prayed without *kavanah*
was obligated to recite the prayers over again. True devotion
required freeing one's mind from extraneous thoughts and a
conscious awareness of standing in the presence of God. He
noted that the pious folk of old used to wait for an hour before engaging in prayer (the source of the preparatory *Pesukei
de-Zimra* portion of the morning service today) and remain
for an hour afterwards, in order to achieve and maintain the
proper frame of mind.[10] Maimonides was convinced of the
power and efficacy of prayer, based on the verse, "The Lord
is near to all who call Him, to all who call Him in truth"
(Ps. 145:18).[11]

Cleaving to God (6)

"*To God shall you cleave*" (Deut. 10:20) raises the question of how it is possible to cling to a purely spiritual, incorporeal God. The rabbis suggested that the way to cleave to God is by imitating the Divine attributes, which can best be learned by studying with knowledgeable and pious teachers. They also used this text to conclude that one has a duty to marry a wise man's daughter, or to give one's own daughter in marriage to a wise man, as well as to bestow gifts to wise men and to conduct business relations with them.

Maimonides interpreted this as a command to seek out and associate with wise individuals, those closest to God, "to join with them in every possible manner of fellowship: in eating, drinking, and business affairs, to the end that we may succeed in becoming like them in respect of their actions and in acquiring true opinions from their words." As is written in *Pirkei Avot* (1:4), "Let your house be a meeting place for the wise; sit amid the dust of their feet and drink in their words with thirst."

The mystics developed the idea of "*devekut*" (cleaving to God) as the highest rung on the spiritual ladder. This intimate communion with God could only be achieved by mastering the ability to love and fear God (Pos. Comm. 3, 4). In the most intense form of this approach, the human being reaches the goal of a mystical union with God (*unio mystica*), which the kabbalists likened to a drop of water being absorbed in a great sea or to a ray of light in the sun. *Devekut* may be viewed as the expression or culmination of the love between God and human beings, which can be based on the attraction of (a) like to like or (b) opposites. The former implies that there is something in the essence of the human being (e.g., soul, intellect) that is like God and enables *devekut* to occur between them. Thus for Maimonides, based on Aristotle, communion with God occurs directly through the "rational faculty of the human soul" and the "Active Intellect." This could only be achieved by a few members of the elite, who combined extensive scholarship with intense preparation. If the love between God and man is viewed as the attraction of opposites (material human beings and spiritual God), there are problems regarding how they can truly achieve communion (e.g., fire and water) and the potential danger (i.e., how can one cleave to a God who is described as a "burning fire," and the possible disaster of an annihilation reaction when "material" and "anti-material" try to combine). The solution of the kabbalists was the need for an indirect communion through an "intermediary," a synthesis of the opposites into something that has qualities of each of them. Among the suggested intermediaries are the religious commandments (a spiritual act in physical form); the sacred word (Torah scroll [physical] and sacred text [spiritual]); prayer; ethical actions (helping others); and even a human being (e.g., Hasidic master; tzadik).[12] According to the Hasidic tradition, *devekut* should be a constant state of mind, even when dealing with the mundane concerns of everyday life, not merely an experience that can only be achieved during intense meditation and prayer.

Swearing in God's Name (7)

"In God's name you shall swear" (Deut. 6:13; 10:20) means that when a person is required to confirm or deny something, he or she should only do it in God's name (and not by any created objects such as angels or the stars). The rabbis believed that taking an oath was strong motivation toward fulfilling promises. However, they were troubled by this verse, both because of the likelihood that God's name might become frequently used in conjunction with frivolous oaths, and because of the serious consequences related to taking a false oath. The Talmud

indicates that all transgressions can be forgiven, except those involving a false oath (Shev. 39a). Consequently, they eliminated the practice of swearing by God's name before Jewish courts of law, substituting other forms of oaths instead.

Maimonides supported the use of God's name when taking an oath, arguing that it added to the weight that could be attached to a person's declaration. As he observed, "Just as one is forbidden to take an oath for which there is no necessity (Neg. Comm. 62), so we are commanded to take an oath when necessary." Nachmanides disagreed, maintaining that it was only the rare individual who possessed the appropriate degree of holiness and piety to warrant being able to invoke the name of God with proper reverence. He argued that this commandment was rather a prohibition against swearing in the name of an idol.[13]

Walking in God's Ways (8)

The verse *"What does God ask of you? Only to fear the Lord your God, to walk in all of His ways…"* (Deut. 10:12) has been interpreted to mean that we are commanded to be like God as much as possible given the limitations of our mortal state. Because man was made in the Divine image, Maimonides argued that the supreme duty of human beings is to pattern their actions after those of God. As the Talmud (Sot. 14a) observed, we should clothe the naked just as God clothed Adam and Eve (Gen. 3:21), visit the sick as God visited Abraham after his circumcision (Gen. 18:3), comfort the mourners as God did for Isaac (Gen. 25:11), and bury the dead as God buried Moses (Deut. 34:6).

This duty of imitating God is a fundamental teaching of Judaism. Its classic expression is found in the verse, "You shall be holy, for I the Lord your God am holy" (Lev. 19:2). Unlike paganism, which portrayed its gods in the physical image of man, in Judaism it is man who is made in the image of God (Gen. 1:27).

Ibn Ezra focused on the words "to walk," indicating that the command is to translate God's ways and attributes into actions designed to improve the world, rather than being satisfied with mere belief in God. Abravanel noted that literally "walking" in the ways of a totally spiritual God would require life-threatening abstention from food, drink, and other bodily functions. He argued that the command implies that we must imbue with holiness our daily mundane functions, rather than simply follow our primitive and animalistic instincts.

Sanctifying God's Name
(*Kiddush ha-Shem*) (9)

The last half of the verse *"You shall not profane My holy name, rather I should be sanctified among the children of Israel"* (Lev. 22:32) is the basis for the commandment to sanctify God's Name. Although originally addressed to the priesthood, obligating them to fulfill their duties to God as guardians of the Sanctuary, the command to sanctify God's Name was later extended to the entire Jewish people, who were to be "a kingdom of priests and a holy nation" (Exod. 19:6).

Each Jew, great or small, has the privilege and responsibility of sanctifying the Name of God through his or her behavior (whether among Jews or gentiles)—by studying Torah and performing the commandments, and by treating others kindly, considerately, and honestly. Thus, people would say, "Fortunate are the parents and teachers who raised such a person." Conversely, there is no greater degradation for a Jew than to act in a way that would make people say the opposite (Yoma 86a).

Maimonides observed that this commandment makes us "duty bound to proclaim this true religion to the world, undeterred by fear of injury from any source." Unfortunately, this has too often led to martyrdom (*Kiddush ha-Shem*), the ultimate expression of sanctifying the Name of God, as Jews have given up their lives rather than desecrate the Name of God (*Chillul ha-Shem*;" Neg. Comm. 63).

According to the rabbis, if a Jew is forced to transgress any of the commandments (except three) at pain of death, he may violate the law rather than surrender his life. This is in accordance with the principle of "You shall therefore keep My statutes, and My ordinances, which if a man do *he shall live by them*" (Lev. 18:5). However, it is incumbent on the Jew to sacrifice his life rather than be guilty of the three cardinal sins – idolatry, adultery and murder. As *Sefer ha-Chinuch* noted, just as a good servant is willing to give up his life for his master, how much more so should we, the servants of God, be prepared to forfeit our lives in obedience to the command of the King of kings.

Martyrdom is not the only way in which one can sanctify the Name of God. Israel sanctifies God's Name in the liturgy, when Jews recite the *Kaddish* and exclaim "Magnified and sanctified be His great Name," and when the congregation recites the *Kedushah* and affirms "We will sanctify Your Name in the world even as they sanctify it in the highest heaven." However, it is more important to hallow the Name of God by moral action, especially by performing acts of justice and compassion in the sight of gentiles, for people judge Judaism by the conduct of Jews. Maimonides[14] stressed that living properly in accordance with the highest Jewish standards is considered an act of *Kiddush ha-Shem*. For example, "the scholar who is scrupulous in his own conduct, speaks gently to his fellows, shows concern for their welfare, receives them with a cheerful countenance, accepts humiliation at their hands without humiliating them, shows honor even to those that slight him, is faithful in his dealings, does not waste his time in the company of ignorant men and their affairs, is always engaged in the study of the Law...so that all may be disposed to praise him and love him and be desirous of emulating his deeds—such a one sanctifies the Lord."

Reading the *Shema* (10)

"You shall speak of them ... when you lie down and when you rise up" (Deut. 6:7) is the commandment to recite the *Shema* twice each day. In addition to "Hear O Israel: the Lord is our God, the Lord is One" (Deut. 6:4)—the basic declaration of faith of the Jewish people in the Unity and Oneness of God—the *Shema* also includes three other Torah portions (Deut. 6:4-9, Deut. 11:13-21, and Num. 15:37-41) that are read every morning and evening. As a time-based commandment, reading the *Shema* was not obligatory for women.

Sefer ha-Chinuch says that the *Shema* must be recited in the morning and evening so that one can acceptance of God's sovereignty ("the yoke of the Kingdom of Heaven") at all times. In this way, Jews are reminded that God is always watching them and guarding them from committing sins. Nachmanides considered each of the two daily readings of the *Shema* as distinct commandments, since the observance of one is independent of the other.

The Rabbis considered these three selections to represent the entire Torah. They taught that reciting them twice daily during prayer services fulfilled the command to study Torah "day and night" (Men. 99b). However, they never told this to the people, lest it decrease their commitment to study. The *Shema* was also viewed as representing the acceptance of the yoke of both the kingship of Heaven (*kabbalat ol malchut shamayim*) and of the commandments (*kabbalat ol ha-mitzvot*). It effectively became a "pledge of allegiance" and a repetition of the ceremony at Mount Sinai, where the Israelites took an oath of loyalty to God the King and pledged to obey the royal laws.[15]

The *Shema* should be recited with full concentration on the meaning of the words. To prevent distractions, it is customary to follow the practice of Judah the Prince (Ber. 13b) and place the right hand over the eyes while saying the first verse.[16] The

Shema should be recited loud enough to be heard by the ear, since it is written *"Hear,* O Israel" (Ber. 15a). Any language can be used (Sot. 32b)—because it is crucial that the worshiper understand what he or she is affirming—as long as one enunciates the words clearly. In the Talmud (Ber. 1:3), there is a debate concerning how the *Shema* should be read. Beit Shammai took the words "when you lie down and when you rise up" literally, ruling that the evening *Shema* should be recited while reclining while in the morning it should be said standing upright. Beit Hillel argued persuasively that the verse merely referred to the times of the readings, and that no special posture was required.

Unlike the *Amidah,* which must be said while standing, the *Shema* may be recited while standing or sitting, or even while traveling (stopping only to recite the first verse). According to Maimonides,[17] "Everyone may read the *Shema* in the ordinary postures—standing, walking, lying down, or riding on an animal. It is forbidden to recite the *Shema* in a prone position (with one's face to the ground) or in a supine position (on one's back looking straight up), but one may read it while lying turned to one side." For a long time, the Jews in Israel stood up for the *Shema,* both because of its importance and because it was an act of witnessing God (and testimony in a Jewish court is always given while standing). In ninth-century Babylonia, however, the Karaites argued that standing for the *Shema* meant that that the Jews considered only these three passages (and the Ten Commandments) to be fundamental tenets of the faith and of Divine origin. To counteract such views, the rabbis ruled that the *Shema* be recited while seated, and this remains the prevailing custom today.[18]

There also was much debate during the tannaitic period as to the times for reciting the *Shema.* The Rabbis (Ber. 1:1-2) eventually ruled that the evening *Shema* can be recited from nightfall until dawn, though ideally it should be said before midnight.

The morning *Shema* can be recited from the first traces of the dawn until the end of the third "hour" after sunrise (one-fourth of the day).[19]

The first line of the *Shema* has traditionally been the final prayer of Jewish martyrs throughout the ages, as they died sanctifying God's Name. With the last breath, the Jew is to pronounce this affirmation of faith, timing it so that the final word he utters in life is *Echad* (One).

Teaching and Studying the Torah (11)

The command to teach and study the Torah (*Talmud Torah*) is derived from the verse *"And you shall teach them diligently to your children..."* (Deut. 6:7). Variations of this commandment occur frequently—"And you shall *teach* them" (Deut. 11:19), and "*do* them" (Num. 15:39); "that they may *learn*" (Deut. 31:12). Rashi explained that "to your children" also refers to one's students, since the Torah considers students to be like children.[20] "Diligently" was interpreted to mean that one should be so fluent in words of Torah that one can answer any question at once without hesitation. According to Abravanel, the Hebrew word *v'shinantem* (you shall teach) derived from the word *shnayim* (two), implying that Torah instruction requires repetition to be truly understood.

The Rabbis elevated the study and teaching of the Torah to the highest degree of religious devotion and experience. For example, Maimonides said that "He who occupies himself in the study of the Torah for its own sake ....is deserving of the whole world. He is called friend, beloved (of God), lover of God, lover of mankind; it clothes him with humility and reverence and fits him to become righteous, saintly, upright, and faithful; it keeps him far from sin and brings him near to virtue, and from him men enjoy counsel and sound knowledge, understanding and might..."[21] In discussing the varies activities for which "a man enjoys the fruits in this world while the principal remains for him the in the World to Come," the Talmud (Pe'ah 1:1) notes that "the study of the Torah is equal to them all." Maimonides observed that without wisdom there cannot be any good act or any true knowledge, maintaining that a defining characteristic of the Messianic Age will be the freedom to study Torah forever without oppression or interference.[22]

Traditionally, women were not considered bound by the commandment to study Torah because the verse was translated as "And you shall teach them to your *sons*." Instead, they were taught the various laws pertaining to women, which include almost all the negative commandments and many positive ones. Jewish women were generally well versed in the laws of the Sabbath, kashrut, family purity, blessings, and (in ancient times) the laws of purity (*taharah*) and impurity (*tumah*).[23] However, most modern translations use the word "*children*," so that the commandment to study Torah applies equally to both men and women.

Wearing Tefillin (12-13)

"You shall bind them for a sign upon your hand, and they shall be for frontlets between your eyes" (Deut. 6:8) is the commandment for Jews to wear tefillin on the head (**12**) and arm (**13**). Often translated by the Greek term "phylacteries" (amulets), tefillin are small black leather boxes containing parchments on which are written the four sets of biblical verses that mention this commandment: (a, b) Exod. 13:1-10 and 11-16, which speak of the Exodus from Egypt; and (c, d) Deut. 6:4-9 and 11:13-21, the first two passages of the *Shema*, which express the Jewish belief in One God, the acceptance of Divine kingship, the concept of reward and punishment, and the responsibility to observe all the commandments.

Once donned all day and removed at night, tefillin now are worn only during each weekday morning service. They are not worn on the Sabbath or on festivals because, like the Sabbath (Exod. 31:17) and circumcision (Gen. 17:11), tefillin are designated by the term *ot*—a "sign" of the covenant between God and Israel, the Divinely chosen people. Therefore, wearing tefillin would be considered superfluous in view of these days also being symbols of holiness.

Tefillin are put on after the tallit (Pos. Comm. 14). The tefillin of the arm is wrapped in seven rings, coiled in a descending spiral around the person's weaker forearm (for most people, the left arm closest to the heart). These rings may symbolize the seven branches of the Menorah, the seven benedictions recited at the marriage ceremony, or the seven Hebrew words in the verse from Psalms (145:16), "You open Your hand and satisfy every living creature with favor." One reason for wearing the tefillin on the weaker arm is that this commandment is immediately followed in the Torah by the one to "write them on the doorposts of your house [mezuzah]" (Pos. Comm. 15), which led the Rabbis to conclude that the hand that writes must be the same hand that wraps (i.e., the stronger hand). (Left-handed people wear the tefillin on their "weaker" right arm; Men. 37a). After the tefillin of the head is put on, three rings are wound around the middle finger and then around the back and palm of the hand, while reciting the verses from Hosea (2:21-22) in which the word "betrothal" is used three times in the description of Israel's spiritual engagement to God. Jews who follow the Sephardic and Hasidic practice wind the tefillin around the arm in an overhand (clockwise) fashion, while Ashkenazim use a counterclockwise motion.

The Rabbis declared that, "Whoever has the tefillin on his head, the tefillin on his arm, tzitzit on his garment, and the mezuzah on his doorpost is completely protected from sinning" (Men. 43b), based on the verse "And a threefold cord [refer-ring to the three precepts enumerated] is not rapidly broken" (Eccl. 4:12). According to Nachmanides, the tefillin on the arm is a symbol of God's power, as well as our determination to devote our hearts and might to the Divine will. The tefillin on the head reflects our resolve to also dedicate our thoughts to God.[24] Maimonides[25] noted that the presence of tefillin on one's head and arms ensures that "a man is modest and God-fearing, being drawn neither into laughter nor into idle talk—shunning all thoughts of evil and rather directing his heart to words of truth and righteousness." For Abravanel, tefillin are visual reminders of the need to bind ourselves in dedication to God, so that we obey the Divine commandments rather than follow our evil inclination.[26] Lau observes that tefillin relate to the three parts of the body that most characterize the individual—the head (intellect), arm (physical strength), and heart (opposite the tefillin of the arm and the seat of the emotions)—all of which must be used to fulfill God's wishes.[27]

Maimonides considered the wearing of tefillin on the head and arm as two distinct commandments, based on a Talmudic ruling (Men. 38a) that if a person has only a single tefillin, he should wear whichever one he has (thus at least fulfilling that commandment). Traditionally, these commandments were not obligatory for women. This was based on the verse "so that the Law of the Lord is always in your mouth" (Exod. 13:9), in which tefillin are associated with the study of Torah, which the Rabbis did not consider a female obligation. However, according to a *baraita* (Er. 96a), Michal, the daughter of Saul and wife of King David, "wore tefillin and the Sages did not protest." Moreover, the daughters of the great medieval scholar Rashi also wore tefillin. In modern times, some women have begun to wear traditional tefillin or those of their own design.

Fringes (Tzitzit) (14)

"Make fringes on the corner of your garments throughout the generations" (Num. 15:38) is the verse from which is derived the

wearing of the tallit (prayer shawl) in the synagogue. Because
the explicit purpose of the tzitzit is "that you may see them
[and recall all the commandments of the Lord and obey them,
so that you do not go astray after your own heart and eyes]"
(Num. 15:39), the tallit is only worn during the day. The sole
exception is Yom Kippur, when the *Kol Nidrei* service actually
starts just before evening and the tallit adds sanctity to the occasion. Wearing a tallit is obligatory for Jewish males thirteen
or older, though some Orthodox synagogues follow the Eastern
European tradition in which a tallit is worn only by married
men. This is based on the fact that the phrase "If a man marries
a wife" immediately follows the repetition of the commandment concerning tzitzit (Deut. 22:12). However, all men wear
a tallit whenever they are leading the congregation in prayer
or are called up for an *aliyah* to the Torah.

When reciting the phrase "O bring us in peace from the four
corners of the earth" in the second blessing before the *Shema*,
the worshiper gathers the four fringes of the tallit together in
the left hand. During the third paragraph of the *Shema* (Num.
15:37-41), the fringes are kissed on the three occasions when the
word tzitzit is read. When called to the Torah, the custom is
to touch the tzitzit to the first word of the passage to be read,
and then kiss them before reciting the Torah blessing. After the
Torah reading, one touches the tzitzit to the last word read and
kisses them before reciting the second blessing.

In addition to the tallit worn during prayer services, some Jews
also wear fringes on a *tallit katan*, a light undergarment that is
fitted over the neck and shoulders so that the tzitzit are visible.

The last half of the Torah verse commanding the wearing of
tzitzit adds, "and they shall put with the fringe of each corner a
thread of blue (*techelet*)" (i.e., one blue thread and seven white
ones). This blue was made from a precious dye that was extracted
from a sea snail (*chilazon*) by a few families on the Mediterranean

coast (Men. 42b). After the destruction of the Second Temple, the secret of obtaining this exact shade was lost, and the use of the blue thread in the fringes was discontinued. Recently, some have claimed to discover a close relative of the snail, and *tallitot* with blue fringes made from its due are now available. The blue stripes woven into many *tallitot* symbolize this ancient *techelet*.

Various commentators have suggested reasons for the blue threads. The Rabbis (Sot. 17a) maintained that they help its wearer focus on his duty to God, since blue resembles the [color of the] sea, the sea resembles the heavens, and the heavens resemble the Throne of Glory. For the K'li Yakar, the blue threads of the fringes also symbolize the waters of the sea. Just as the ocean must be kept within defined boundaries lest flooding and disaster occur, so must each Jew live within the defined bounds of the commandments.[28]

In each collection of eight threads, one is longer than the rest and is wound around the remaining seven threads in either of two different ways. Among Ashkenazic Jews, there are four series of rings of 7, 8, 11, and 13 windings, respectively. The sum of these numbers equals 39, the numerical value of the Hebrew words *YHVH Echad* (God is One). Thus, when looking at the fringes, one is constantly reminded of the fundamental Jewish principle of monotheism. Among Sephardic Jews, the pattern of windings is 10, 6, 5, 6, numbers that respectively represent the letters *YHVH*. The Rabbis noted that the numerical value of the Hebrew word tzitzit (fringes) is 600. When combined with the eight threads and five knots on each fringe, this adds up to 613—the precise number of mitzvot in the Torah. Thus, by looking at the fringes we are to "remember all the Lord's commands and obey them" (Num. 15:39).[29]

Women have traditionally been exempt from the commandment to wear tzitzit, because it is a time-bound mitzvah. Moreover, garments with four corners on which fringes were hung were originally considered to be male attire, and the Bible forbids a

woman from wearing a man's clothing (and vice versa; Neg.
Comm. 39, 40). Nevertheless, some women are known to have
worn *tallitot* during talmudic and later times. For example, Judah
the Prince is described as having personally attached fringes
to his wife's apron (Men. 43a). Maimonides[30] maintained that a
woman may wear tzitzit, but should not recite the blessing. In
non-Orthodox synagogues, some women have begun wearing
tallitot for worship, either at their Bat Mitzvah or later as adults.
Although *tallitot* for women are not specifically prohibited by
Jewish law, many women feel uncomfortable wearing one.[31, 32]

Affixing a Mezuzah (15)

The commandment to affix a mezuzah comes from the verse
"And you shall write them upon the doorposts of your house" (Deut.
6:9, 11:20). The mezuzah is the distinctive mark of a Jewish
home. It contains a small roll of parchment on which a scribe
has written the first two paragraphs of the *Shema* (Deut. 6:4-9
and 11:13-21), which include the commandment concerning the
mezuzah. The parchment is enclosed in a case that is fastened to
the upper third of the doorpost on the right side of the outside
door as well as the door to every room in the house (except a
bathroom, storeroom, or kitchen). It is placed at eye level, to
remind us to always be aware of and reach up toward God.

The mezuzah is slanted so that the upper end of the case is
pointed inward. The Hebrew word *"Shaddai"* is written on the
back of the parchment and can be seen through a small opening
near the top of the container. According to the Zohar, the reason
why this Name of God is used in the mezuzah is that its three
Hebrew letters (*shin, daled, yud*) are the first letters in the phrase
Shomer Daltot Yisrael (Guardian of the Doors of Israel). A Jew
who moves into a new home is expected to put a mezuzah on
the outer door immediately, or at least within the first thirty days.
A Jew who sells or rents a home to a fellow Jew is required to

leave the *mezuzot* in place, but must remove them if the purchaser or lessee is a non-Jew. Traditional Jews observe the custom of kissing the mezuzah (either by touching it with a fingertip and then kissing the finger, or by kissing the finger before touching the mezuzah) both on entering and leaving the house.

A mezuzah is generally placed at the entrance to a synagogue or other Jewish community building, though this is not strictly required unless it contains an apartment and thus qualifies as a dwelling (Yoma 11b). The commandment to affix a mezuzah applies only to permanent structures and not to temporary or casual places, such as a sukkah, a camping tent, or an automobile.

The Rabbis (Men. 43b) said that a person who has tefillin on his head and arm, fringes on his garments, and a mezuzah on his doorway will commit no transgressions, since these reminders are like guardian angels saving him from sin (Ps. 34:8). Some have considered the mezuzah as a protective device to prevent evil spirits from entering the house, with its name deriving from a combination of the two Hebrew words *"mavet"* and *"zaz,"* meaning "Death, go away." Maimonides attacked those who believed the mezuzah to be a mere amulet to ward off evil spirits as ignorant people who failed to appreciate that its true purpose was to keep Jews constantly aware of the Unity of God and the need to fulfill their moral duties

Some modern Jews wear a mezuzah (lacking the inner parchment) around the neck as a good luck charm, or as an affirmation of Jewish identity. Beautifully designed and decorated mezuzah cases have become superb examples of Jewish art.

The Assembly During the Feast of Tabernacles (16)

"Assemble the people, the men and the women and the children" (Deut. 31:12) is the commandment for the entire nation to come together at the Temple on the second day of the Sukkot festival

in the Sabbatical Year to listen to the king read from the Book of Deuteronomy. The specific portions read were (a) from the beginning of the book to the end of the first paragraph of the *Shema* (1:1-6:9), (b) the second paragraph of the *Shema* (11:13-21), and (c) verses 14:22 through 28:69. These passages deal with allegiance to God, the covenant between God and the Jewish people, and reward and punishment.[33] For Maimonides,[34] the reason for this commandment was to stress the primacy of the Torah in Jewish life, and therefore it was fitting that all Israelites (men, women, and children) should gather together to hear it read.[35]

The second half of the verse explains that the purpose of this practice was "that they may hear, and so learn (to fear the Lord your God), and observe all the words of this law." The Rabbis interpreted this to mean that merely "to hear" a portion of the Torah read once every seven years in a public assembly was not sufficient. It must also be "learned" as an object of study and "observed" by every Jew embodying its laws into his or her own life.

Expanding on this commandment, the Rabbis divided the entire Torah into 154 portions that were read consecutively on each Sabbath in the synagogue, so as to cover the entire Torah in three years (Meg. 29b). In effect, what now is considered the weekly Torah portion (called *parashah* by Ashkenazim and *sidrah* by Sephardim) was read over three consecutive weeks. The large and influential community of Jews in Babylonia developed the custom of completing the whole Torah in a single year, and this rule eventually became the generally accepted practice throughout the world. Some Conservative synagogues have returned to the triennial cycle, though they read one third of each *parashah* every year so that the entire Torah is read every three years. This practice has become increasingly popular, though it has the distinct disadvantage that the Torah is no longer read consecutively, so that narratives and bodies of biblical legislation are interrupted.

In addition to reading the Torah, the custom developed of also reading a thematically related selection from the Prophets (haftarah) on each Sabbath, festival, and fast day. Most scholars believe this dates back to the days before the Hasmonean revolt of 167 B.C.E, when Antiochus Epiphanes issued a decree banning the public reading of the Torah. Since other public readings in the synagogue were still permitted, the Rabbis added the reading of prophetic verses that related directly or indirectly to the topic of the Torah reading scheduled for that week.

A King to Write a Scroll of Law (17)

The commandment *"When he sits on the throne of his kingdom, he shall write for himself a copy of the law"* (Deut. 17:18) was designed to serve as a check on the secular authority of the king and to impress upon him the supremacy of Divine Law as revealed in the Torah (*Sefer ha-Chinuch*).

Rashi translates this verse as meaning that the king was commanded to write *two* copies of the Torah, one to be stored in his treasury (where the king might be overwhelmed with hubris by his vast quantities of material wealth) and the other to be kept with him at all times (to exert a positive influence on his activities). He was required to read from it daily, so that he would not deviate from its precepts, fall victim to excessive pride, and become a tyrant who oppressed the people. According to Maimonides, if the king inherited a Torah scroll from his father, he still must write (or commission someone else to write) one for himself. Otherwise, the king was responsible for writing two scrolls of the Law.[36]

Writing a Torah Scroll (18)

"Now, therefore, write this song for you ..." (Deut. 31:19) was originally a Divine command to Moses and Joshua to write down the final farewell hymn of joy that Moses spoke to the

children of Israel just before his death (Deut. 32:1-43). The
Rabbis derive from this verse that every Jew is commanded
to write a Torah scroll. Even if given a Torah scroll by one's
parents, each individual is still obliged to write one, since the
verse contains the words "for you."

Realizing the tremendous challenge and difficulty involved
in actually writing one's own Torah scroll, Maimonides stated
that "if he cannot write it himself, he is obliged to purchase one,
or to hire a scribe to write it for him." Based on the talmudic
statement (Men. 30a), "Even if he corrected but one letter [in
a *sefer Torah*] he is regarded as if he had written it [the entire
Torah]," in recent centuries the custom has developed for the
scribe who completes the writing of a Torah scroll to merely
trace the outline of the letters of the first verses in Genesis
and the last verses in Deuteronomy. At a festive celebration
(*siyyum*), members of the congregation, often selected by auction, dedicate letters and thus symbolically participate in the
writing of a Torah scroll. *Sefer ha-Chinuch* maintained that this
commandment can be fulfilled by purchasing religious texts
that expound on the Torah.

A Torah scroll must be handwritten on sheets of parchment
that are specially prepared from the skins of a kosher animal
and then sewn together. The writing is a sacred task entrusted to
a professional scribe (*sofer*), who is both devoutly religious and
skilled in his craft. The scribe must have before him a finished
copy from which he reads, pronouncing every word before
inscribing it. Although some authorities disagree, the accepted
rule is that a woman may not write a Torah scroll; if she does,
the scroll is invalid for public use. This is based on a talmudic
dictum (Sof. 1:13), "a person who cannot serve as the representative of the public in religious matters is not permitted to write
a scroll of the Torah," and women in post-talmudic times were
not permitted to read the Torah before a congregation.[37]

As the holiest object in the Jewish ritual, the Torah scroll is accorded the profoundest respect, and all are required to rise and remain standing when the Torah is taken from the ark and carried in a procession around the synagogue before and after being read. Members of the congregation honor the passing Scroll by touching the covering mantle with the fingers, a tallit, or a prayer book and then kissing that object.

As the last of the 613 commandments in the Torah, the obligation to write a Torah scroll assures the continuity of the tradition, so that future generations will have access to all the commandments and be able to study and fulfill them.

Grace after Meals (*Birkat ha-Mazon*) (19)

"You shall eat and be satisfied, and bless the Lord your God" (Deut. 8:10) is the commandment to recite the grace after meals. It consists of four blessings and is recited after a meal at which one has eaten bread of an amount at least equivalent to the size of an olive (*ke-zayit*), approximately one ounce by volume. The first blessing praises God for providing food for all creatures; the second expresses thanks for the good land of Israel that God has given us, the redemption from Egypt, the covenant of circumcision, and the Revelation of the Torah; the third is a plea for God's mercy, the rebuilding of Jerusalem, and the restoration of the ancient Temple and the Davidic kingdom; and the fourth offers thanks for God's eternal goodness to us and includes a request for sending Elijah the Prophet, as well as blessings upon the house in which one has eaten and upon all who shared the meal. The last blessing also includes a number of general supplications beginning with the word *ha-Rachaman* (May the Merciful One) and ends with the same prayer for peace (*Oseh Shalom*) that concludes the full *Kaddish*—for only when at peace is it possible to truly enjoy all the other Divine blessings. On Sabbath and festivals, the *Birkat ha-Mazon* is preceded by the

singing of *Shir ha-Ma'alot* (Psalm 126), a prophetic description of the return of the Israelites from Babylonian captivity and the ultimate restoration of Zion.

According to the Talmud (Ber. 48b), the four blessings arose from different sources. The first is attributed to Moses upon receiving *manna* from heaven; the second was composed by Joshua when he conquered the land of Canaan; and the third was written by David and Solomon because of their respective roles in making Jerusalem the capital of the Israelite state and building the Temple. The core of the fourth blessing (*ha-Tov v'ha-Meitiv*; "Who is good and Who does good") was added by the Rabbis after the unsuccessful rebellion led by Bar Kochba in the second century C.E., in gratitude both for the corpses at Betar not decaying and spreading disease and for the Romans finally granting the Jews permission to bury them.

When bread is not eaten, there are two other forms of the Grace after Meals depending on the type of food consumed. After eating food prepared from the five species of grain (wheat, barley, rye, oats, and spelt) not in the form of bread, wine, or fruits (grapes, figs, olives, pomegranates, and dates) that are indigenous to the Land of Israel, one recites a short summary of the *Birkat ha-Mazon* in a single benediction with insertions for the type of food eaten and for special occasions such as the Sabbath or festival. For any other food, the Grace after Meals consists of a brief benediction generally known by its first two words, *Borei nefashot* (Who creates living things).

It is customary not to recite the grace after meals until all utensils (especially knives) have been removed from the table. This reflects the comparison of the dining table to the Temple Altar, which was constructed of stones that were not hewn with tools that also could be used as weapons.

The grace *after* meals is the only blessing explicitly commanded by the Torah itself. The rabbis later extended this obligation to reciting various blessings over food and drink *before* consuming them.

Maimonides accused the person of committing a sacrilege by enjoying a meal (or other Divine gift) without offering a blessing and thus failing to express his gratefulness to God for food as well as for past favors bestowed on the Jewish people. He decried those who take their blessings for granted and emulate Esau, of whom the Bible says: "He ate and drank, and he rose and went away. Thus did Esau spurn the birthright" (Gen. 25:34).[38]

Building a Sanctuary (*Mishkan*) (20)

"They shall make a Sanctuary for Me" (Exod. 25:8) commanded the Israelites to build a portable tent-like structure for the Divine Presence, "so that I may dwell among them." It consisted of an outer court, enclosed by curtains, and the Sanctuary proper, which was divided into two chambers by a hanging curtain (*parochet*). The outer chamber contained the table of Show-bread (Pos. Comm. 27), the Menorah (Pos. Comm. 25), and the Golden Altar for incense (Pos. Comm. 28). The inner chamber (Holy of Holies) was entered only once a year by the High Priest on Yom Kippur, the Day of Atonement. The sole object within the Holy of Holies was the Ark of the Covenant, which held the two stone tablets inscribed with the Ten Commandments.

Sefer ha-Chinuch stated that the Sanctuary, rather than a dwelling place for God, was a central focus where the people could worship God and receive Divine inspiration.[39] For Nachmanides, the Sanctuary was symbolic of the historic experience on Mount Sinai, as it was ringed by the tribes and topped by the cloud of God's Presence. Ibn Ezra remarked that the Sanctuary was a permanent place among the people for God's Glory that had rested on Sinai, so that Moses would not be required to ascend the mountain whenever God wanted to communicate with him. Several commentators have maintained that the

Sanctuary was a manifestation of God's forgiveness, a place for the Jewish people to again enter into the Divine Presence after having almost irrevocably sundered their intimate relationship with God by building and worshiping the golden calf.

The portable Sanctuary was replaced by a permanent structure when King Solomon built the First Temple (housing the Ark of the Covenant) in Jerusalem. After the destruction of the First Temple by the Babylonians in 586 B.C.E. and the Second Temple by the Romans in 70 C.E., the centrality of God's Presence became shifted to the synagogues and study halls.

Does God need a special sanctuary? According to the Kotzker Rebbe, the answer to the question "Where does God dwell?" is simply "Wherever you let God in."

Revering the Sanctuary (21)

"You shall have reverence for my Sanctuary" (Lev. 19:30) is the commandment to show respectful behavior and maintain a feeling of awe when in God's holy place. Visiting the Temple was not to be a casual activity, but rather a deep emotional experience of attempting to commune with God.[40] The rabbis defined reverence as meaning "One may not enter the Temple Mount with his staff, or his sandals, or his wallet, or with the dust upon his feet, nor may he make of it a short cut; still less may he spit there" (Ber. 54a). When leaving the Temple, the worshiper always moved toward the exit walking backward, so as never to turn his back on the Holy of Holies.

Even almost two millennia after its destruction, the site of the Temple has retained its sanctity. A Jew is forbidden from entering those portions of the Temple Mount that were exclusively reserved to the Kohanim and Levites. Moreover, since all are now judged ritually impure, Orthodox rabbis have prohibited every Jew from entering the Temple Mount.

Based on the words of Ezekiel (11:16)—"Thus says the Lord

God: Although I have removed them far off among the nations, and although I have scattered them among the countries, yet I have been to them as a 'little sanctuary' (*mikdash me-at*) in the countries where they have gone" — the Talmud (Meg. 29a) applied the term "little sanctuary" to the synagogue, a substitute for the ancient Temple. As such, the command to revere the sanctuary – to maintain a feeling of awe and comport oneself with appropriate dignity and etiquette – also extends to current houses of worship.

Guarding the Sanctuary (22)

The injunction to the Levites to keep guard over the Sanctuary and patrol it throughout the night is derived from two verses: "*And you and your sons with you shall be before the Tent of the Testimony*" (Num. 18:2), and "*And they shall safeguard the Tent of Meeting*" (Num. 18:4). There were three inner stations manned by the Kohanim and 21 outer stations guarded by the Levites.[41]

According to Maimonides,[42] the constant guarding of the Sanctuary was to accord it "respect and honor," as well as to prevent "laymen, the [ritually] unclean, and mourners" from entering it.

Levitical Services in the Sanctuary (23)

Certain services related to the Sanctuary were the exclusive province of the Levites, based on the verses: "*But the Levites alone shall do the service (of the Tent of Meeting)*"(Num. 18:23), and "*He shall serve in the Name of the Lord his God, as do all his fellow Levites*" (Deut. 18:7).

According to the Talmud (Ar. 11b), all the Levites in Israel were divided into two groups that were responsible either for opening and closing the gates of the Sanctuary or for chanting during the offering of the sacrifices. Young Levites were not permitted to perform any Sanctuary service until they had completed a five-year period of initiation or preparation.[43]

Although the actual chanting in the Sanctuary was reserved to the Levites themselves, the accompaniment of musical instruments might also be performed by Kohanim and members of the noble families of Israel. Those Levites whose voices had lost their strength or sweetness were disqualified from participating in the service.[44]

Ablutions of the Kohanim (24)

Before entering the Sanctuary to perform the service, the Kohanim were commanded to wash their hands and feet in accordance with the verse *"And Aaron and his sons shall wash their hands and feet when they go into the Tent of Meeting"* (Exod. 30:19). Failure to comply with this commandment desecrated the holiness of the Sanctuary and invalidated the service of any ministering Kohen.

Even in the absence of the Temple, observant Jews ceremonially wash their hands before beginning any prayer service (which the Rabbis have declared to be the current equivalent of the sacrificial rite). Traditional Jews also ritually wash their hands and recite the appropriate blessing before meals, since the dining table is compared to the Altar upon which the sacrificial service was performed.

Kindling the Menorah In the Sanctuary (25)

"Aaron and his sons shall set it in order" (Exod. 27:21) is the commandment that the Kohanim tend the lights of the Menorah in the Sanctuary (and later, in the Temple in Jerusalem). The lamps were to be lit in the evening; in the morning it was the duty of the Kohen to remove the burnt wick, replace it with a fresh one, and fill the lamp with absolutely pure

oil (Exod. 30:7). This procedure also was performed on the Sabbath, just as burnt offerings also were brought on that day, although kindling of other fire was forbidden.[45] According to tradition, only the center lamp was left burning all day because no sunlight fell into the Sanctuary. This ancient lamp is represented in modern synagogues by the *ner tamid* (perpetual, or eternal, light), which is left continually burning and usually hangs near or above the Ark. This symbolizes the Divine Presence, which dwells among the congregation of Israel (Shab. 22b), and the spiritual enlightenment that is forever emanating from the Torah.

The Rabbis interpreted the Menorah as a symbol of Israel and its mission to be "a light to the nations" (Isa. 42:6). Maimonides and *Sefer ha-Chinuch* considered the Menorah as enhancing the glory of the Sanctuary through its illumination. Abravanel took a more symbolic approach to the Menorah, seeing the lamp of God as the soul of man (Prov. 20:27), with its seven branches representing the seven degrees of wisdom found in the Divine law. The lamps all turned inward toward the Holy of Holies, indicating that true wisdom must be consistent with the fundamentals of the Torah, which was housed in the Ark of the Covenant. The pure gold of the Menorah implied that wisdom must not be polluted by alien ideas. Sforno noted that the unity of the people of Israel was stressed by the fact that the entire seven-branched Menorah was fashioned from a single block of gold.[46]

The emblem of the State of Israel combines the Menorah, the symbol of light, with two olive branches, the symbol of peace. A large sculptured menorah portraying significant incidents in Jewish history stands outside the Knesset (Parliament) building in Jerusalem, a symbol of the miraculous rebirth of the Jewish people after almost 2,000 years of exile.

Priestly Blessing (26)

"You shall bless the children of Israel, saying unto them: May God bless you and keep you; may God shine His face on you and be gracious to you; may God lift up His countenance on you and grant you peace" (Num. 6:23-26) are the words that the Kohanim were commanded to use in their daily blessing of the people. According to Bahya ibn Pekuda, these short blessings of three, five, and seven words, respectively, are to remind us of the foundation of all blessings—the three Patriarchs, the Five Books of Moses, and the seven Heavens. The verses progress from a request for material blessing and protection to a petition for spiritual blessing, and finally to a plea for the highest of Divine blessings, the gift of peace.[47]

Each morning and evening immediately after the daily offerings in the Temple, the Kohanim would ascend a special raised platform (*duchan*), place their *tallitot* over their heads, raise their arms, spread out their fingers in a special fan-like gesture (forming the Hebrew letter *shin*, the first letter of *Shaddai*, one of the Names of God), and pronounce these three blessings that included the four-letter Name of God (Tetragrammaton). The Talmud stressed that this did not mean that the Kohanim had any independent power to confer or withhold blessings—only God can assure people of success, abundance, and happiness; instead, the Kohanim only served as the channel through which the blessing was conveyed.

In many Orthodox synagogues today, the Kohanim remove their shoes (as they did when performing the Temple ritual), wash their hands, and ascend the platform in front of the Ark. Facing the congregation and with their tallitot covering their faces, the Kohanim repeat the priestly blessing in a haunting and mysterious tone, word for word after the prayer leader. They stretch both arms and hands out at shoulder height with their hands touching at the thumbs and their palms forward. The first two fingers of each hand are separated from the other two to produce a fan-like appearance. This custom appears to derive from a commentary on the verse from Song of Songs (2:9), "My beloved [Israel] is like a gazelle or a young deer who stands behind our wall, gazing in at the windows, looking through the lattice." The Rabbis considered this to be an allusion to the Kohen as he blessed the people, with the "windows" representing the Kohen's shoulders and arms and the "lattice-work" his fingers. In a later period, outstretched hands became symbolic of the Kohanim, and it is common to find this representation engraved on tombstones of members of the priestly family. The Talmud (Hag. 16b) forbids a person from looking at the hands of the Kohanim while they are pronouncing the priestly benediction, lest their "eyes become dimmed," and in many communities a father draws his children to himself and covers them with his tallit.

In many synagogues, the Priestly Blessing is now often read by the rabbi or cantor (not necessarily a Kohen) as a closing benediction at the end of the service. It also is recited as a special blessing by the officiating rabbi on other occasions, such as Bar and Bat Mitzvah ceremonies, weddings, and circumcisions.

Congregants initially listened silently while the prayer leader recited the Priestly Blessing, but then began to say appropriate biblical quotations to themselves (Sot. 40a). Today, it is customary to respond *Amen* after each of the three sections when said by the Kohanim, but with *Kein yehi ratzon* (So may it be Your will) when recited by the prayer leader.

On Sabbath eve, it is a custom for parents to bless their children with the priestly blessing, preceded by either "May God make you like Ephraim and Menasheh" (for sons) or "May God make you like Sarah, Rebecca, Rachel, and Leah" (for daughters).

The Show-bread (27)

"You shall always set the Show-bread upon the Table before Me" (Exod. 25:30) is the command to continually place the Show-bread (*lechem panim*; lit., the "bread of the Presence") before God in the Sanctuary. The Show-bread are described (Lev. 24:5-9) as consisting of twelve large flat, oblong loaves of wheat flour (corresponding to the number of the tribes of Israel) that were placed in equal two rows on the Table each Sabbath and left there until the next Sabbath, when they were removed (miraculously still fresh) and eaten by the Kohanim.

Most commentators understood the Show-bread as an expression of the continual thankfulness of the Israelites to God for providing them with the daily necessities of existence.[48] According to Nachmanides, bread was selected as the object of this commandment since it was universally recognized as the staff of life.

Abravanel thought that the arrangement of the Show-bread into two rows of six loaves each was intended to recall the manna that fell from heaven to feed the Children of Israel in the wilderness. For six days of the week (not on the Sabbath), each person received one portion in the morning and another in the evening (though on Friday they actually were double portions!), adding up to twelve. Just as God provided food for the Israelites during their wanderings, the Show-bread reinforced the faith among Jews that God would continue to sustain them with all their needs in their own day.[49]

Burning of the Incense (28)

"On it Aaron shall burn incense of sweet spices" (Exod. 30:7) is the source of the commandment for the Kohanim to sprinkle incense (made of eleven different ingredients) on the hot glowing coals of the Golden Altar twice a day, morning and night.

The burning of the incense was one of the most desired services in the Sanctuary, and lots were cast to choose the Kohen who was to perform the task. The preparation of the incense was said to be done to the beat of a special chant, since working in rhythm to music was deemed to result in improved mixing of its various components (Abravanel).[50]

Sweet incense was used in the Temple, either for the practical purpose of counteracting the slaughterhouse smell of the burning flesh and blood of the sacrifices, or to symbolically provide a "sweet savor" to the Lord. The cloud of aromatic incense in the Tabernacle was later perceived as a reminder of the invisible Presence of God, as was the cloud that accompanied the Israelites during the Exodus and their wanderings in the wilderness. For the Rabbis, incense became a metaphor for fervent and contrite prayer. They explained that the four letters of the Hebrew word for incense (*ketoret*) stood for holiness (*kiddushah*), purity (*tahorah*), pity (*rachamim*) and hope (*tikvah*)—a summary of the prerequisites of prayer and its spiritual results for the worshipper.[51]

The fragrance of incense and spices survives today in the Havdalah ceremony, which separates the departing Sabbath from the rest of the week. A spice box is passed around for everyone to smell the fragrant spices that refresh and revive the spirit and dispel the sadness accompanying the end of the special Sabbath day. A more mystical reason is that the spices either provide spiritual compensation for the additional soul that each Jew figuratively possesses on the Sabbath day,[52] which Rashi defined as a unique feeling of rest and contentment, or that they symbolize the spiritual farewell "feast" for that extra soul.[53]

The Altar (29-30)

One commandment (29) instructs the priests to keeping a fire constantly burning on the Altar (*"A perpetual fire shall remain burning on the Altar;"* Lev. 6:6), while another (30) requires them to remove the ashes from it (*"The Kohen shall put on his linen garment ... and he shall take up the ashes;"* Lev. 6:3).

The Kohanim were required to place wood on the fire every day, in the morning and at dusk, so that a perpetual fire was kept burning on the Altar (see Neg. Comm. 81). For the Israelites, the perpetual fire was a witness to their continuing desire to serve God, which pervaded their entire existence and was not limited to specific times and places.[54]

Removing the ashes from the Altar completed the sacrifice of the previous day and was the first act in the daily service in the Sanctuary. According to tradition, the ashes of the burnt offering were deposited on the east side of the incline leading to the Altar. When they accumulated, the ashes were carried outside the camp.[55]

The Midrash observed that a fire burned continuously on the Altar of Moses' Sanctuary for 116 years, yet its thin copper layer never melted and its wooden structure was never charred (Lev. R. 7:5).

The Rabbis explained the special symbolism of the Altar by devising an acronym from the consonants of its Hebrew name (MiZBe'aCh). *"Mechilah"* (forgiveness) portrayed the Altar as the channel through which the Israelites could seek atonement from God, from whom they had become estranged by sin. *"Zechut"* (merit) signified that the Altar offered an outlet for the qualities of thanksgiving, humility, and contrition, through which merit was acquired. *"Brachah"* (blessing) indicated that by faithfully obeying the teachings focusing on the Altar, one both earns Divine blessings and becomes a blessing to others. Finally, *"Chaim"* (life) meant that the Altar symbolized that the way to achieving eternal life in the World to Come was to devote one's temporal life to truth, righteousness, and holiness.[56]

Removing the Ritually Unclean (31)

The injunction to remove ritually unclean persons from the camp is found in such verses as: *"(Command the children of Israel), that they shall expel from the camp everyone with* tzara'at, *everyone who has a flux, and everyone contaminated by a human corpse"* (Num. 5:2), and *"You shall you put them outside the camp"* (Num. 5:3).

After the erection of the Tabernacle, the Israelites were required to free their camp of all ritual contamination (*tumah*) so that the Divine Presence (*Shechinah*) could dwell within it. Three classes of ritually unclean persons were to be excluded from varying portions of the camp. One afflicted with *tzara'at* (Pos. Comm. 101), a skin condition often mistranslated as "leprosy," was excluded from the entire camp. Those afflicted with fluxes (issues) (Pos. Comm. 104) were excluded from the Sanctuary proper and the Levite encampment around it. A person who had become ritually unclean through contact with the dead (Pos. Comm. 107) was only excluded from the Sanctuary itself.

The Kohanim (32-38)

Members of the priestly caste (Kohanim), the descendants of Aaron, were to be shown honor and deference (**32**) because they were consecrated to God and offered the sacrifices to the Lord (Lev. 21:8). However, the Talmud accords more honor to those who attained extensive learning through their own efforts than to those who fortuitously were born into the priestly class. "If a *mamzer*[57] is a scholar [learned in the Law] and the High Priest an ignoramus, the learned *mamzer* takes precedence" (Hor. 13a).

This biblical verse is the source of the custom in traditional synagogues to give the Kohen the first aliyah to the Torah. Today, Reform and liberal Conservative congregations have abolished the distinction between Kohen, Levite, and Israelite, both because it is difficult to be certain of the lineage of any Jew (though a gene characteristic of Kohanim has been documented) and because of a belief in equality for all their members.

The Kohanim arrayed themselves in garments of special splendor and beauty when they ministered in the Sanctuary (**33**). The

vestments of the priests (Exod. 28:4-42) distinguished them from
the rest of the Israelites and added to the solemnity and awe
of the Sanctuary service. The garments of the ordinary Kohen
were the tunic, breeches, girdle, and turban. The *Kohen Gadol*
(High Priest) also wore the *breastplate* (with its twelve precious
stones, each engraved with the name of one of the tribes of
Israel), the *robe* (blue with a hem adorned with pomegranate-
shaped balls and golden bells), the *ephod* (an upper garment
with two onyx stones, each engraved with the names of six
of the tribes), and the *frontlet* (with the golden plate engraved
with the words "holy to the Lord").

One of the duties of the Kohanim was to bear the Ark on
their shoulders when it was transported from place to place
(**34**). Although this commandment was initially addressed only
to the Levites (Num. 7:9), according to Maimonides the responsibility for this task later was extended to the Kohanim. The
staves inserted into the four rings of the Ark were not allowed
to be removed (Neg. Comm. 86).

When the *Kohen Gadol* assumed his position, oil of anointment (**35**) of a specific composition was poured over his head
(Lev. 21:10). This was prepared from a mixture of myrrh, sweet
cinnamon, sweet calamus, and cassia in an olive oil base.[58] It
was forbidden to duplicate this oil for secular purposes (Neg.
Comm. 83) or to use it to anoint anyone other than the *Kohen
Gadol* or a king (Neg. Comm. 84).

The *Kohen Gadol* was commanded to marry, but (**38**) he could
only wed a virgin (Lev. 21:13-14). The common Kohen was not
bound by this latter restriction. As the individual responsible for
performing the most sacred duties in the Sanctuary, in which
he served as the intermediary between God and Israel, it was
critical that the *Kohen Gadol* be in a good mood and have a
positive affect. The Rabbis deduced the requirement to marry
based on the talmudic statement that, "One who does not have

a wife lives without joy, without blessing, and without good-ness," as well as without Torah, protection, and peace (Yev. 62b). Similarly, the *Kohen Gadol* was prohibited from observing mourning, even for his father and mother (Neg. Comm. 167). (For limitations on whom a Kohen was permitted to marry see Neg. Comm. 158-162.)

Contact with the dead was considered ritually defiling (Num. 19), and thus temporarily rendered a Kohen unfit to perform his duties. Therefore, a Kohen was generally obliged to avoid corpses and cemeteries (Neg. Comm. 166-168). However, in the case of the unattended dead body of a man whose relatives were unknown, everyone, even the *Kohen Gadol*, had to assist with the burial process (Neg. Comm. 166).

The prohibition against Kohanim having any contact with the dead was qualified (37) in the verse *"except for the rela-tives who are closest to him: his mother, father, son, daughter, and brother; also for his virgin sister who has no husband"* (Lev. 21:2-3). These were concessions to the natural feelings of the Kohen as a human being. The wife was not mentioned since the Torah regarded man and wife as "one flesh" (Gen. 2:24), and her presence in this list was thus automatically implied. The mother was named before the father, because there usu-ally is a deeper attachment between her and the son, and his desire to be with her at the end would be more intense. The "virgin sister who has no husband" refers to one who was betrothed but not yet married.[59]

According to the Torah (Deut. 18:6), it can be inferred that most of the tribe of Levi were scattered among the other tribes so that only a small portion actually lived in Jerusalem at any given time. The Kohanim (and Levites) were divided into 24 groups, each of which ministered in the Sanctuary for one week at a time. During the three Pilgrimage Festivals (Passover, Shavuot, Sukkot), all the groups were in attendance simultaneously. Maimonides counted having the Kohanim "ministering in courses" as a positive commandment (36). Nachmanides disagreed, arguing that this was only an oral tradition and not an obligatory rule of the Torah.[60]

Daily Offerings (39-40)

Burnt Offering (39)

"(This is what you shall offer on the Altar for the Lord: two year-ling lambs without blemish), each day as a continual burnt offering" (Num. 28:3-4; Exod. 29:38-39) is the commandment to bring the daily burnt offerings in the morning and at dusk. (Nachmanides viewed these as two distinct commandments.)

The burnt offering was totally consumed on the Altar (Pos. Comm. 63). Because its Hebrew name (*olah*) means "that which ascends," modern scholars and translators often prefer the term "elevation-offering." The morning offering in the Temple was a festive event, with the Levites singing the Song of the Day accompanied by music (today recited at the end of the daily morning service). At every pause during the psalm, there was a blast of the horn and all prostrated themselves on the ground (Tamid 33b).[61]

The daily burnt offerings (*tamid*), the core of the sacrificial system, were brought on behalf of the entire nation and were a central feature of the regular public services in the Jerusalem Sanctuary. They were purchased with the half shekels contributed by all Israelites, both rich and poor (Pos. Comm. 121). Even though members of the general public could not perform any of the priestly or levitical duties, they were represented at the Temple during the offering of the daily sacrifices by the *ma'amadot*. Just as the priests "ministered in 24 courses" (Pos. Comm. 36), the entire country was divided into 24 districts, each of which sent a delegation of eminent and pious Israelites to represent it at the daily public offerings for one week every six months. These men were known as the *Anshei Ma'amad* (Men of Standing), because their task was to *stand by* and observe the Temple ritual. They also joined together to recite prayers and read from Genesis. Those *Anshei Ma'amad* unable to travel to Jerusalem for the week refrained from work and assembled each day to recite prayers, which mostly corresponded to the psalms being said at the Temple (Taan. 26a). If a Kohen were present, he would recite the Priestly Blessing (Pos. Comm. 26) at the end of these daily prayer meetings, which were timed to finish at the same time as those in Jerusalem. Eventually, these local gatherings attracted large crowds, who joined the *Anshei Ma'amad* in prayer. After the destruction of the Temple, some devout men would remain in the synagogue after daily services to read the same verses from Genesis that had formerly been recited by the *Anshei Ma'amad*. Some modern editions of the siddur (prayer book) still include a section (*Ma'amadot*) that contains these Scriptural passages from what may have been the origin of the synagogue service.[62]

The Rabbis ruled that prayer, especially the *Amidah*, substituted for the communal sacrifices mandated in the Torah (Ber. 26b). Thus *Shacharit* and *Minchah* (the morning and afternoon services) are based on the two required daily burnt offerings.

Meal offering of the Kohen Gadol (40)

"This is the offering of Aaron and his sons" (Lev. 6:13) commanded the *Kohen Gadol* to bring meal offerings in the morning and at dusk. The Talmud (Men. 76a) says that the meal offering was made of fine flour, baked into twelve unleavened loaves (corresponding to the twelve tribes of Israel), and completely burned on the Altar. According to Abravanel, the daily meal offering of the *Kohen Gadol* taught the poor not to be ashamed of their meal offering, which was the same size; it also taught the *Kohen Gadol* the virtue of humility.[63] The phrase "in the day when he

is anointed," which appears later in the verse, was interpreted by Ibn Ezra to mean that the *Kohen Gadol*, after his ordination, was to bring a daily *meal offering* at his own expense, not only on his behalf but for all the Kohanim as well.

Rashi noted that the *meal offering* referred to in this commandment was also brought by every Kohen when he was installed into the priestly service ("meal offering of initiation").[64]

Additional (*Musaf*) Offerings For Sabbath and Festivals (41-48, 50-51)

The Book of Numbers lists the offerings that were brought to the Temple in addition to the daily burnt offering (Pos. Comm. 39) for (41) the Sabbath (28:9-10) and various festivals. The special offerings for the festivals include those for (42) the New Moon (28:11-15), (43) Passover (28:16-25), (45) Shavuot (28:26-31), (47) New Year (29:1-6), (48) Day of Atonement (29:7-11), (50) Sukkot (29:12-34), and (51) Shemini Atzeret (29:35-38).

The offerings of Sukkot were unique in several respects. They were slightly different for each day of the festival and included sacrifices to beseech protection for the gentile nations.[65] There also was a special ceremony of "water-libation" celebrated at the end of the first day of Sukkot (but not on the Sabbath) at the Temple in Jerusalem. Known as *Simchat Beit ha-Sho'evah* (Rejoicing of the House of Water-Drawing), this ceremony was apparently based on the verse from Isaiah (12:3): "Therefore with joy shall you draw water out of the wells of salvation" — the text for the popular Israeli song and dance *Mayim* (water). The Rabbis observed that whoever had not seen the ceremony of the water-drawing had never witnessed real joy (Suk. 51b).

Today, a listing of the appropriate additional offerings constitutes the *maftir* portion of the Torah reading for each festival. In addition, during the *musaf* services on the Sabbath and festivals, a recitation of the required offerings for that specific day effectively serves as a replacement for the additional offerings that were brought to the Temple. Added to this in traditional synagogues are verses calling for the restoration of the sacrificial system. The Conservative prayer book calls for the return of the dispersed Jews to the land where their ancestors sacrificed the various offerings, but not for a resumption of the sacrifices themselves. The biblical verses detailing the specific sacrifice for the day are included in small print, with the instructions "some congregations add." The Reform prayer book makes no mention of the ancient sacrificial system.[66]

Two further offerings on festivals are listed among the positive commandments. These are (**44**) the meal offering of the new barley on the second day of Passover (Lev. 23:10), when the counting of the Omer begins (Pos. Comm. 161), and (**46**) the bringing of two loaves of bread from the new crop of wheat on Shavuot (Lev. 23:17-20). After these respective ceremonies, the new wheat crop could be used in the Sanctuary for the coming year, while the new barley crop became permissible for all non-Sanctuary purposes.

The two loaves of bread offered on Shavuot were the only meal offering baked with leaven (*chametz*). Menachen Leibtag suggests that whereas unleavened bread (matzah) symbolizes the initial stage of a process, the fully risen *chametz* symbolizes its completion. Thus bringing the leavened loaves on Shavuot may indicate that the giving of the Torah at Mount Sinai on that date should be understood as the culmination of the process of redemption from slavery that began on Passover, when only matzah could be consumed. Just as the two loaves marked the staple of our physical existence, so the historical process that began with the Exodus from Egypt and culminated with the giving of the Torah reflected the essence of our spiritual existence.

Service of the Day of Atonement (49)

This commandment (Lev. 16:1-34) mandated the various sacrifices and confessions that were required on Yom Kippur to atone for the sins of the Israelites. Because the Talmud states that if one service were performed out of order it would be as if it had not been done at all (Yoma 60a), Maimonides concluded that each of these specific rites should not be considered as an individual commandment.

Today, the *Avodah* (lit. "service") on Yom Kippur vividly describes the Temple ritual that took place on the Day of Atonement, based on the biblical account that was expanded in *Mishnah Yoma* (chapters 1-7) and the talmudic tractate of the same name. The *Avodah* service has preserved the quintessential rite of ancient Judaism, the most solemn moment of the Jewish year involving the holiest person (*Kohen Gadol*), the holiest time (Yom Kippur), and the holiest place (Temple in Jerusalem). Although not one of the pilgrimage festivals on which Jews were biblically required to appear at the Temple in Jerusalem (Deut. 16:16), on Yom Kippur huge throngs of worshipers came to see the awesome ritual and to hear the words of the *Kohen Gadol*.[67]

After the destruction of the Second Temple and the cessation of the sacrificial rites, how could the people achieve atonement? The Rabbis ruled that in this emergency situation, one could perform the Temple duties by reading about them, since the utterance of a person's lips is equivalent to the actual performance of the ritual. In addition, the Rabbis were convinced that a yearly recitation of the Yom Kippur ritual in the Temple would give Jews a sense of historic continuity and an intense longing for the restoration of their ancient homeland.[68]

Yom Kippur was the only time during the year when the *Kohen Gadol* entered the Holy of Holies in the Temple. Preparation for this event began a week prior to the Day of Atonement, when the *Kohen Gadol* went to a designated area of the

Temple court to study the sacrificial ritual for Yom Kippur. On the day before Yom Kippur, the *Kohen Gadol* emerged and was taken to another chamber in the Temple compound where he met with other priests and continued his study. On the Day of Atonement, the *Kohen Gadol*, dressed in gold-embroidered garments, conducted the daily cultic rituals. When performing the rituals exclusively associated with the sacrifices of atonement, the *Kohen Gadol* wore white linen vestments. During the course of the day, he immersed himself and changed his clothes five times and washed his hands and feet ten times.

The *Kohen Gadol* first offered a bull as his personal sin-offering. He confessed his sins and those of his family, then the sins of the tribe of Aaron (the Kohanim), and finally those of all Israel (Lev. 16:17). Every time the *Kohen Gadol* uttered the Holy Name of God (the Tetragrammaton), which was spoken only on Yom Kippur, the people prostrated themselves and responded: "Praised be His glorious sovereign Name, for ever and ever." It remains a custom in some communities for worshipers to completely bow down on the floor of the synagogue when this part of the *Avodah* service is read. A cloth or piece of paper must be placed between one's head and the floor (not between one's knees and the floor, as many erroneously do), because it is forbidden to bow down on a stone floor, except in the Temple.[69]

After drawing lots to determine which of the two male goats was sent off to the wilderness "for *Azazel*" and which would be sacrificed as "a sin-offering for the Lord," and a special incense-offering in the Holy of Holies, the *Kohen Gadol* recited a prayer that Israel be blessed with peace, prosperity, and fertility, and that no earthquake harm the inhabitants of the Sharon Plain ("their houses may not become their graves").

Some modern prayer books used in liberal congregations have minimized the references to sacrifice and either abridge the *Avodah* or make it optional.

General Laws of the Three
Pilgrimage Festivals (52-54, 59)

Celebration of the festivals (52)

"Three Pilgrimage Festivals shall you celebrate for Me during the year ... " (Exod. 23:14) is the basic biblical source for the celebration of Passover, Shavuot, and Sukkot. The Rabbis interpreted the phrase *"you shall not appear before Me empty-handed"* (Exod. 23:15) as requiring the bringing of offerings, not only a burnt offering and a special peace-offering for the specific holiday (*chagigah*), but also a second peace offering that could be shared by its owner, family, and guests in a festive meal.

Appearing before the Lord on the festivals (53)

"Three times a year ... all your males appear before the Lord your God" (Deut. 16:16) is the commandment requiring every Israelite to come up to Jerusalem on the three pilgrimage festivals, which respectively marked the spring (barley), summer (wheat), and autumn (fruit) harvests of the agricultural cycle. They are known as the *Shalosh Regalim* (lit., "three feet") because most people went up to Jerusalem on foot. According to Josephus, on one occasion more than 2.5 million pilgrims made their appearance in Jerusalem for Passover.[70]

All males were expected to fulfill the commandment of appearing before the Lord and bringing a burnt offering on the festivals. Exceptions were made for minors and those who were deaf, dumb, insane, blind, crippled, uncircumcised, aged, sick, or ritually impure.[71]

Rejoicing on the festivals (54)

The previous requirements of celebrating and appearing before the Lord on the festivals were only obligatory for men. However, the Talmud (Hag. 6b) declared that the third of this set of commandments—rejoicing on the festivals, based on the verse "*You shall rejoice on your festival*" (Deut.16:14)—was also binding on women.

Maimonides recounted the rabbinic statement that Jews must rejoice on their festivals in every way possible, including "by eating meat, drinking wine, putting on new garments, distributing fruits and sweetmeats to children and women, and making merry with musical instruments and dancing in the Sanctuary (though not elsewhere)." He added that "the most binding of these [modes of rejoicing] is the drinking of wine," since "Wine makes glad the heart of man" (Ps. 104:15).

The Torah obliged the Israelites to include in this rejoicing the poor, the needy, and the strangers, as well as the fatherless and the widow (Deut. 16:11). It was also important to invite the Levites to join in the festivity, for they did not receive any portion of the meat from the offerings brought to the Temple. Indeed, Maimonides[72] warned: "He who while eating and drinking in the company of his children and his wife bars the entries of his home, and fails to offer food and drink to the poor and the wretched, rejoices not in a manner suitable on the occasion of fulfilling a commandment, but merely to gratify his own belly."

Today, rejoicing on the festivals primarily takes the form of ceremonial meals. However, Jews must always remember the plight of those who are less fortunate, and it is traditional on the festivals to make donations to charity or to institutions of learning—the present-day equivalent of the festival sacrifices that were offered in Temple days.[73]

Blowing the trumpets in the Sanctuary on the festivals (59)

"*On a day of your gladness, and on your festivals, and on your new moons, you shall blow with the trumpets (over your burnt offerings and your peace offerings ...)*" (Num. 10:10) is the commandment for the Kohanim to sound silver trumpets in the Sanctuary in conjunction with the communal offerings for the festivals (and the Sabbath). This was in addition to the musical accompaniment that the Levites provided at various times during the sacrificial service.[74]

According to *Sefer ha-Chinuch*, the blare of the trumpets was like an alarm calling soldiers to prepare for battle, awakening the people to a critical moment in their spiritual lives and inspiring them to increase the intensity and fervency of their prayers to God.[75]

Passover Offering (55-58)

These commandments referred to (55) slaughtering the Paschal lamb and (56) eating of its roasted flesh on Passover (Exod. 12:6; 12:8), as well as to the (57) slaughtering and (58) eating of the second Passover offering (Num. 9:10-12). The second Passover offering was necessary for those individuals who were ritually unclean on the first Passover or were "far off" from Jerusalem and could not reach the city at the time when the offering was brought. Thus, they had to postpone their observance of these commandments for another month (Num. 9:11). If most of the community were unable to offer the Paschal lamb during the first Passover because of being ritually unclean due to defilement from corpses, they were obliged to proceed with the festivities and sacrifices even in their state of contamination (Pes. 79a). An individual Israelite was permitted to postpone the observance of the Passover for an entire month, but this was not an option for the entire people.[76]

The Talmud interprets the phrase "far off" to include a person who is spiritually distant from God and the Jewish people on the festival (JT Pes. 9:2). Such an individual should feel that this is only a temporary condition and, like the wicked child in the Haggadah, is always welcome to return to the community.[77]

These commandments became impossible to perform with the destruction of the Temple and the cessation of the sacrificial system. Negative commandments dealing with the Passover offering are 115-117, 119, 121-123, and 125-128.

Today, Jews place a roasted shankbone (*zero'a*) on the seder plate on Passover to commemorate the commandment to slaughter and eat the Paschal lamb. It also symbolizes the *zero'a netuyah* (outstretched arm), with which God brought the Israelites out of Egypt. Some vegetarians substitute a roasted beet for the shankbone.

Laws Related to Offerings (60-72)

The Israelites could bring five major types of offerings to God—burnt, meal, peace, sin, and guilt. The Torah provided precise regulations concerning how each of these sacrifices, and several variants, were to be offered, what part of them was to be burnt, and what portion was to be eaten.

Menachem Leibtag has developed the following superb approach to understanding the various offerings. He utilizes the order of the offerings as they are presented in Leviticus, which is different from Maimonides' list of the positive commandments (the numbers that appear in parentheses).

There were two basic classifications of offerings. The *voluntary* offerings (*nidava*) consisted of the burnt (*olah*), meal (*mincha*), and peace (*sh'lamim*) offerings that an individual *could* bring should he so desire. The *obligatory* offerings (*chovah*) consisted of the sin (*chatat*) and guilt (*asham*) offerings that an individual *must* bring if he had transgressed certain commandments.

The voluntary offerings reflected the individual's desire to *improve* his relationship with God, and the sections of the Torah describing them virtually always end with the phrase "an offering of fire, a pleasing odor to the Lord." These same words were used in connection with the burnt and peace offerings made when the children of Israel were standing at the foot of Mount Sinai, and thus the voluntary offerings reaffirmed the covenant made when the people declared "we will do and we will obey" (na'aseh v'nishma).

The obligatory offerings were designed to *amend* the relationship with God should it be tainted by sin, and the Torah sections describing them virtually always end with the phrase "the Kohen shall make expiation on his (the person offering the sacrifice) behalf ... and he shall be forgiven." These words are reminiscent of those used in seeking atonement for the sin of the Golden Calf. The obligatory offerings were considered "most holy" and, in so far as they were consumed, had to be eaten within the Sanctuary Court (Neg. Comm. 145). The voluntary offerings were deemed "less holy" and could be eaten anywhere in Jerusalem.

Voluntary Offerings

Burnt offering (Olah)

The *burnt offering* (63) was totally consumed on the Altar (Lev. 1:1-17), and it was forbidden for anyone to eat the meat from it (Neg. Comm 146). The Hebrew name *"olah,"* meaning "that which ascends," reflected its purpose to raise the owner from the status of sinner and bring him to a state of spiritual elevation. By bringing this sacrifice, a person expressed his desire and intention to devote himself entirely to God and to place his life totally in the Divine service.

The burnt offering could be brought by a person who (a) had failed to fulfill a positive commandment or who had intentionally committed a sin for which the Torah did not prescribe a specific punishment; (b) had been guilty of sinful thoughts that had not led to action; (c) came to Jerusalem for the three Pilgrimage Festivals; and (d) wished to feel closer to God.[78]

Before offering a burnt (or peace-thanksgiving) offering, the owner had to perform the act of *"semicha"*—resting all his weight on the animal—symbolically transferring his identity to the animal and offering it instead of himself. This was reminiscent of the Akedah, when Abraham sacrificed a ram as a burnt offering in place of his son, Isaac.

The person bringing a burnt offering could choose a bull, a sheep or goat, or a bird, depending on what he could afford. Regardless of the cost, as long as he was serving God to the best of his ability, his offering would be appreciated and rewarded.

Meal offering (Mincha)

The *meal offering* (67) consisted of finely ground wheat flour, oil, and frankincense (usually with water added), which could be merely a mixture of these ingredients or be cooked or baked in one of four different ways (Lev. 2:1-16). A meal offering was inexpensive and thus was most likely to be brought by a person too poor to afford anything more. Indeed, the word used in the Torah to refer to the person who brought a meal offering is *"nefesh"* (soul), which Rashi interpreted to mean that God would regard it as if the individual had offered his very soul. A portion of the meal offering was burnt on the fire of the Altar, but the rest was eaten by the Kohanim.

Communal meal offerings were brought on three occasions: Passover (the Omer, Pos. Comm. 161); Shavuot (the two loaves of bread, Pos. Comm 46); and the Sabbath (the twelve loaves of Show-bread, Pos. Comm. 27). Negative commandments relating to the meal offering are 102-105, 124, and 138.

Peace offering (Sh'lamim)

The *peace offering* (66) was brought by a person who was moved to express his love of God, his gratitude for Divine goodness (such as thanksgiving for deliverance from sickness or danger, or in fulfillment of a vow made in times of distress), and to enhance his closeness to God (Lev. 3:1-17). The word *"sh'lamim"* can also be translated as "whole" or "harmony," implying that it is motivated not by guilt or obligation, but rather by a feeling that the donor's life is "complete" in relation to family and God.[79]

The peace offering was the only one to which was attached the word *"zevach,"* which literally means "slaughter" but also can be translated as "feast." Unlike the *olah*, only a small part of the peace offering (cattle, sheep, or goat) was burnt on the Altar. All the rest, with the exception of portions reserved for the Kohanim, was eaten by the one who offered the sacrifice, along with his family and guests, at a festive meal where he would praise God and relate the divine blessings that had been bestowed on him.[80] None of the offering was permitted to remain until morning (Neg. Comm. 120).

Today, the obligation to thank God for being spared from a life-threatening situation is met by publicly reciting the thanksgiving blessing (*Birkat ha-Gomel*) in synagogue during the Torah reading (if possible, within three days of the event). Specific events that require one to recite the blessing are derived from Psalm 107 and include: (a) completion of a sea journey; (b) completion of a hazardous land journey; (c) recovery from a major illness; and (d) release from captivity.[81]

Obligatory Offerings

Sin Offering (Chatat)

The *sin offering* (64) was brought by one who sinned in error as a result of carelessness (*bishgagah*) (Lev. 4:1-5:13). The Hebrew term *"chatat,"* meaning "to miss the mark," implied that this was an inadvertent sin. No offering could atone for sins that were committed intentionally; only God can see into a man's heart and judge whether he has truly repented.

The purpose of the sin offering was not to bribe God to overlook the sin or to balance it with an act of generosity. Rather, its goal was to make the donor aware of his more generous side, so that he would not see himself as merely weak and rebellious.

It was an opportunity to clear one's conscience, not a penalty for having done wrong. The Hebrew word used in the verse for "person" is "*nefesh*," which is often interpreted as meaning "soul" in post-biblical literature. Thus, Nachmanides observed that, "It is in the soul that the impulse to do wrong begins … When a person sins, intelligence departs and for the moment one behaves like an animal." Consequently, *Sefer ha-Chinuch* maintains that, "It is an appropriate behavior to sacrifice an animal, which symbolizes the expulsion of one's animal nature."[82]

Why must one atone for inadvertent sins? Hirsch believed that this related to inexcusable carelessness in violating the Divine commandments. For *Sefer ha-Chinuch*, unintentional sins may reflect a lack of vigilance in guarding oneself against temptations. Furthermore, even an unintentional sin weighs on a person's conscience until the individual does something to atone for it. Because mere verbal regrets do not appear adequate, it is necessary to "sacrifice" something to demonstrate sincere remorse.[83]

A *variable* sin offering (72) was specifically required for (a) a witness who failed to give testimony by falsely claiming that he had no knowledge of the case and then admitted he lied (Lev. 5:1); (b) a person who contracted ritual impurity and unintentionally entered the Sanctuary, contaminating holy things (Lev. 5:2-3); and (c) one who violated a promise made under oath (Lev. 5:4). Termed an *"offering of higher or lower value"* by Maimonides, the type of offering depended entirely on the individual's financial status. A rich person brought a female sheep or goat, a member of the "middle class" brought two birds, while a poor person could bring a simple flour offering.

A *fixed sin offering* (69) was brought by an individual who had unintentionally committed a sin that would have incurred the penalty of *karet* (premature death at the hand of God) if he had done it intentionally (Lev. 4:27-35). The sin had to have been committed by performing an act and have violated a negative commandment.

Thus, this offering would not apply to the serious sin of blasphemy, since Jewish law does not consider speech as an "act."[84]

A special sin offering had to be brought by the members of the Great Sanhedrin that erred (68) by making a mistaken halachic ruling that resulted in the entire nation inadvertently sinning (derived from Lev. 4:13).

The specific animal brought for any sin offering depended entirely on the personal status of the violator. The *Kohen Gadol* or Sanhedrin brought a bull, the *nasi* (political leader) a male goat, and a commoner a female goat or sheep.

Guilt offering (Asham)

The *guilt offering* (65) was brought by a person who had committed one of the most serious types of sins (Lev. 5:14-26). The Hebrew word *"asham"* conveys the guilt and desolation of the perpetrator, who brought as sacrifice a ram, the most expensive type of offering.

A *suspensive guilt offering* (70) was brought by a person who was in doubt whether he had committed a major sin for which the penalty would have been *karet* if he had done it intentionally, but would have required only a fixed sin offering if he had committed it unintentionally (Lev. 5:17-19).

The *unconditional guilt offering* (71) was brought by a person who (a) unintentionally appropriated gifts to the Sanctuary or portions due to the Kohanim for his own personal use (Lev. 5:15-16) or (b) falsely denied under oath that he possessed property that his neighbor had deposited with him, robbed his neighbor, or oppressed his neighbor by withholding money due him (Lev. 5:21-27). In addition to the guilt offering, the individual had to make restitution of the item taken (or its value) and add a fifth to it. A guilt offering also was required for a person who had sexual intercourse with a non-Jewish female slave who was designated for another man (Lev. 19:20-21).

Other Commandments Related to Offerings

To be acceptable to God, all cattle and sheep offerings had to be unblemished animals (**61**) and the best that the owner possessed (Lev. 22:21). Just as Kohanim with bodily blemishes were not allowed to perform the Divine service, so blemished animals were unacceptable as offerings even if larger and more expensive than an unblemished one, since God does not assess perfection in monetary terms.[85]

Cattle used for an offering (**60**) had to be at least eight days old (Exod. 22:29, Lev. 22:27).

Salt had to be brought with every offering (**62**), whether animal, bird, or meal (Lev. 2:13). In his *Guide of the Perplexed*,[86] Maimonides wrote that the laws of sacrifices were ordained by the Torah as concessions to the universal ancient Near Eastern custom of bringing offerings to the various pagan deities. However, its specific requirements were diametrically opposite to those of heathen cults. Idolaters only offered leavened bread, seasoned their sacrifices with honey (a favorite food of their gods), and never used salt. Therefore, the Torah forbade the Israelites from offering leaven and honey and commanded them to bring salt with every offering. Interestingly, in his *Mishneh Torah*,[87] Maimonides rejected this rationalistic interpretation and stated that the commandments dealing with offerings were *chukim* (statutes), whose reasons must remain unfathomable to the human mind.[88]

Today, this commandment is recalled by sprinkling salt over the challah on the Sabbath eve. Because the dinner table is considered to be symbolic of the Altar in the Temple (Ber. 55a), where salt was brought with all offerings, the custom developed to commemorate the sacrificial system.[89]

When the Temple was destroyed, the Rabbis prescribed certain practices to take the place of the sacrifices. The most important of these were (a) prayer, based on the verse "So we will render for bullocks the offerings of our lips" (Hos. 14:3); (b) study of Torah, especially those portions concerned with sacrifices (Men. 110a); (c) fasting (Ber. 33a); and (d) charity (Ber. 10b).

Reasons for the Sacrificial System

The Hebrew word for offerings is *"korban,"* which derives from the root meaning "to draw near." Therefore, these rituals were designed to allow the Israelites to offer themselves, body and soul, to the will of God and draw nearer to Him.[90]

Maimonides maintained that the sacrificial system was necessary to counteract those of the pagans to their panoply of gods. Abravanel supported this thesis, noting that the Israelites at such an early stage in their historical development would not have comprehended any type of worship other than that practiced by the surrounding Canaanite cultures. For Nachmanides, animal sacrifices stressed that the sinner would have forfeited his own life had strict justice been applied. Only Divine grace permitted the sinner to substitute the life of an animal for his own. *Sefer ha-Chinuch* argued that sight of a living creature being completely consumed on the Altar was a vivid image of what would happen to the sinful soul, overwhelmed by selfish and animalistic desires, if it did not repent.[91]

Since the destruction of the Temple in Jerusalem, the elaborate system of sacrifices has been disbanded. Nevertheless, during the *musaf* (additional) services on the Sabbath and festivals, Orthodox congregations recite descriptions of the required offerings for that specific day, praying that God will return the Jewish people to the Land of Israel and permit them to rebuild the Temple in Jerusalem, where they will once again be able to perform the sacrificial rites. The Conservative prayer book also calls for the return of the dispersed Jews to the land where their ancestors sacrificed the various offerings, but not for a resumption of the sacrificial service. The biblical verses detailing the specific sacrifice for the day are included in small print, with the instructions "some congregations add." The Reform prayer book makes no mention of the ancient sacrificial system.

Making Confession (73)

"A man or woman who commits any trespass against the Lord... shall confess their sin that they have committed" (Num. 5:6-7) is the commandment requiring an oral confession as an essential part of the process of repentance. In context, the verse refers to a person who illegally retained the money of a fellow Jew (by failing to pay overdue wages or repay a loan, or by theft) and then exacerbated the transgression by falsely swearing that he owed nothing.[92] In Hebrew, the word for confess (*"hitvadu"*) is in the reflexive mode, suggesting that it is necessary to honestly admit to oneself that a sin has been committed. It is not sufficient to superficially perform an atonement ceremony while still privately believing that one has done nothing wrong.[93]

The Rabbis interpreted the phrase "their sin" as applying to violations of the negative commandments, while "that they have committed" referred to violations of the positive commandments. Bahya ibn Pakuda maintained that the phrase "any trespass" implied that any wrong that one person commits against another is at the same time an offense against God.

Although all agreed that it was essential for the penitent sinner to confess his or her sins, the talmudic Sages debated how this should be accomplished. R. Judah ben Bava required that the details of each sin be stated explicitly, considering a mere general confession to be insufficient. In contrast, according to R. Akiva a general confession of sins was enough. The Rabbis frowned on public displays of confession, unless the sins were committed in a public forum or, in the view of some, were offenses against other people (Yoma 86b). Convinced that confession without true repentance was a worthless endeavor, the Rabbis compared such behavior to the ancient parable of a man who immerses himself in the purifying waters of the *mikveh* (ritual bath) while still grasping in his hand a defiling reptile (Taan. 16a).

According to Maimonides,[94] the confession must include the two essential elements of repentance—regret over the sin committed and the resolve never to repeat the offense again. His formula was "I beseech you, O Lord, I have sinned, I have acted perversely, I have transgressed against You, and have done thus and thus (*specifying the sin*). I am sorry and ashamed for my deeds, and I will never do it again".[95] The fuller and more detailed the confession, the more praiseworthy. Those who were obliged to bring sin and guilt offerings or repay what they had taken from another were not forgiven until they confessed and remorsefully resolved never to commit the same offense again. As Maimonides noted, King David became worthy of eternal life when he confessed by simply and earnestly saying, "I have sinned."

Today, the personal and communal confession of sins that we have committed is a major aspect of the multiple services on Yom Kippur. *Al Chet* (For the sin [which we have committed before You]), the first Hebrew words of the formula for the major confession of sins recited on Yom Kippur, is a double alphabetical acrostic of 44 transgressions (two sins for each letter) that is divided into three parts (of 20, 12, and 12 verses, respectively), each of which is followed by the formula: "And for all these, O God of forgiveness, forgive us, pardon us, grant us atonement." This litany is followed by another nine lines enumerating sins according to their prescribed punishments in Temple times. (These are omitted from some modern *machzors* because the penalties are not operative in our day.) *Ashamnu* (We have trespassed) is the initial Hebrew word and name of the shorter confession of sins recited on Yom Kippur, which consists of 24 generic transgressions of a moral nature organized in alphabetic order in Hebrew, with the last letter used three times.

However, these confessions only secure atonement for trans-gressions between human beings and God (*bein adam la-Makom*). As the Talmud notes (Yoma 85b), for transgressions between one person and another (*bein adam la-chavero*), Yom Kippur does not secure atonement unless one has sought forgiveness from the other person and redressed any wrongs. This is the source of the custom in many communities, immediately preceding the recitation of *Kol Nidrei*, of worshipers walking around the synagogue and asking forgiveness from one another for offenses committed during the past year.

Offerings for Purification of Ritual Uncleanness (74-77, 100-106, 110-112)

The laws relating to ritual purity and impurity applied only in reference to the Sanctuary and the holy objects connected with it. They were of no significance in ordinary life and had no ap-plication to anyone who did not intend to enter the Sanctuary. Some have argued that these laws were "hygienic," designed to prevent the spread of infection among the community. They considered the prescribed purification (by water or fire) as a process of "disinfection." However, no prayer or formula was recited, and the sacrifice (which invariably took place *after* puri-fication) was only a formal indication sign that the person was eligible to return to the camp. Those who hold the other point of view maintain that the laws of purity and impurity were levitical (purely religious) and unrelated to sanitary concerns. They point to multiple biblical passages that stress that these laws were designed to direct the people to holiness, and to guard them against anything that was defiling or would prevent them from participating in activities related to the Sanctuary.[96]

Fluxes

A man (**104**) who had a chronic discharge from his sex organ (*zav*) and a woman (**106**) suffering from non-menstrual bleeding or a genital discharge (*zavah*) were said to suffer from a "flux" and were deemed ritually unclean (Lev. 15:2-18; 25-28). They were commanded (**74, 75**) to bring a bird offering when they were healed (Lev. 15:13-15; 29-30). A male who had an involuntary seminal emission could immerse himself immediately and become ritually pure the evening following the immersion. According to *Sefer ha-Chinuch*, an accidental ejaculation indicated that the man had impure thoughts, and his punishment was to be considered ritually impure for a whole day.[97] Ibn Ezra and Abravanel observed that the semen of a man within his body, or when transferred into the body of a woman during marital intercourse, is alive and has the potential for creating new life. Once ejaculated, however, it immediately begins to die. This contact with something that was alive and subsequently died rendered the man impure for that day.[98] Indeed, semen (**105**) itself was considered unclean and could make any garment or skin it touched ritually impure (Lev. 15:16-18).

Childbirth

Following childbirth (**100**), a woman was deemed ritually unclean (Lev. 12:2-8), presumably due to the physical secretions related to the birth process. Her period of impurity depended on the gender of her offspring. According to the Torah, a woman who gave birth to a son was ritually impure for seven days (like a menstruating woman; see Pos. Comm. 99); however, following the birth of a girl, the mother was a *niddah* for 14 days. The reason for doubling the impure period after the birth of a girl is unclear. One possibility is that the newborn daughter will one day herself be ritually unclean during menstruation and after giving birth. Another is that the normal period of ritual impurity following childbirth is two weeks, but is reduced after the birth of a son "to allow the mother to attend the *brit* [circumcision] in a state of ritual purity, or because the *brit milah* on the eighth day is a purifying rite."[99]

A woman who had delivered a child was required to wait for an additional 33-day period of purification before being permitted to bring a sacrifice to the Temple. On the 40th day after delivery, the mother was commanded **(76)** to bring both a burnt offering and a sin offering to finally become ritually clean (Lev. 12:6). This prolonged postpartum period of ritual impurity presumably related to the fact that bleeding often continues for four to six weeks after giving birth. The mother of a girl waited twice that time before bringing her purification offerings on the 80th day after delivery. In some Orthodox communities today, it is customary for the father of a newborn to be called to the Torah 40 days (for a boy) or 80 days (for a girl) after birth as a symbolic representation of the offerings that the mother would have brought to the Temple on that day.[100] Although in traditional communities women usually do not recite *Birkat ha-Gomel*, the thanksgiving blessing recited by a person who has been saved from a life-threatening situation, it is appropriate for them to do so after childbirth.

According to the Rabbis, the two offerings cited in the Torah were required because the mother was seeking atonement for two kinds of "sin." The burnt offering was to seek forgiveness for the bitter thoughts she may have had against God while she suffered labor pains; the sin offering atoned for the possibility that, in her travail, she may have "sworn impetuously that she would have no [further] intercourse with her husband" (Nid 31b).[101]

Tzara'at

A person afflicted with *"tzara'at"* (*metzora*) was deemed ritually unclean **(101)**. Although this term is often translated as

"leprosy," the signs described in the Torah and the revers-
ibility of this skin condition make it doubtful that it refers
to that incurable disease. To be made recognizable (112) so
that people could keep away from him, the *metzora* had to
rend his clothes, allow the hair of his head to go loose, cover
his upper lip, and cry "unclean, unclean" (Lev. 13:45). It was
forbidden for affected individuals to cut out or cauterize the
physical signs of *tzara'at* in order to change their appearance
(Neg. Comm. 307-308).

The Rabbis regarded *tzara'at* as a Divine punishment
for slander or tale-bearing (*lashon ha-ra*; lit. evil speech),
indicating that such a person is a "moral leper" who must
be excluded from the camp of Israel. The prime biblical
example is Miriam, who developed *tzara'at* after she "spoke
against Moses because of the Cushite woman whom he had
married" (Num. 12:1).

The cleansing of a person afflicted with *tzara'at* (110) initially
required the individual to bring two living birds, cedar wood,
crimson thread, and hyssop, and employing them in a prescribed fashion (Lev. 14:1-7). *Sefer ha-Chinuch* maintained that
the chirping birds were purification for the *lashon ha-ra* that
initially caused the condition. Rashi observed that wood from
the tall cedar tree symbolized the former haughtiness and arrogance of the *metzora*, whereas the crimson thread (dyed with
pigment from a type of insect or snail) and the lowly hyssop
bush symbolized that the penitent was now humbly begging
for Divine forgiveness.[102]

During the second stage of the cleansing process, the person
afflicted with *tzara'at* shaved his head (111) on the seventh day
(Lev. 14:9) and then washed his clothes and immersed himself
in a ritual bath. The Kohen shaved every hair on the outside of
the *metzora's* body, though the biblical verse only mentions his
head, beard, and eyebrows. According to Kli Yakar, these areas

symbolized his sin. The head represented the arrogant belief that he was superior to the object of his gossip or slander. The beard framed the mouth, which spoke the *lashon ha-ra*, while the eyebrows were a symbol of the underlying jealousy (*tzarut ayin*) that led him to defame another.[103]

The final stage in the process was to bring an offering (**77**) so as to become completely pure for ritual purposes (Lev. 14:10).

Tzara'at could also contaminate garments (**102**), through contact with an afflicted individual or his sores (Lev. 13:47-59). Some explain the spots on the garments as related to mildew or some parasitic infection.[104] In addition, *tzara'at* could affect a house (**103**), which might require partial or even complete demolition (Lev. 14:33-53). This condition was most likely due to a fungus similar to that which causes dry rot, though some have suggested that it represented parasitic insects or a collection of nitrous material that had formed in the walls.[105]

Tithe of Cattle (78)

"All the tithe of the herd or the flock, whatever passes under the rod, the tenth one shall be holy to the Lord" (Lev. 27:32) is the commandment to single out a tithe of the clean animals born every year. These animals were sacrificed, the fat and blood were offered on the Altar, and the flesh was consumed by the owner in Jerusalem. The tithe of cattle could not be redeemed (Neg. Comm. 109).

According to the Mishnah (Bech. 58b), the newborn animals were herded into a pen with a single narrow exit through which they could only pass in single file. As they came out, the owner marked the back of every tenth animal with a rod coated with red paint to indicate those selected for the tithe. In this way, he could not choose which animals would become part of the tithe. Indeed, an owner who tried to substitute another animal for one of those designated, whether of better or inferior quality, was compelled to forfeit both (Pos. Comm. 87).[106]

Sanctifying the Firstborn (79)

"Sanctify to Me every firstborn ... both man and beast" (Exod. 13:2) is the commandment to separate the firstborn for special treatment. All firstborn of clean animals (cattle and sheep) had to be presented to the Kohen and could not be redeemed (Neg. Comm. 108). If the animal was without blemish, the Kohen offered it as a sacrifice, burning its fat and blood on the Altar and then eating what was left of its meat. If the animal was not perfect, the Kohen could do as he pleased with it (selling it or using it for food). Jews who were not members of the priestly class were forbidden from obtaining any benefit from their firstborn animals (including shearing its fleece or using it for work).[107]

The regulations for the treatment of the firstborn human and the firstborn donkey (an unclean animal) are, respectively, Pos. Comm. 80 and 81-82.

Redeeming the Firstborn (80)

The verses *"the firstborn of your sons you shall give to Me"* (Exod. 22:28) and *"the firstborn of man you shall surely redeem"* (Num. 18:15) constitute the commandment requiring the redemption of the firstborn. This sanctification of every firstborn male (the rest of the verse also includes animals) was to be an eternal reminder of the miracle of the tenth plague, when God smote all the firstborn males in Egypt, both man and beast, but passed over those of the Israelites dwelling in Goshen.

The firstborn son, if the first child born to his mother, was to be dedicated to God and to perform religious services for the Kohanim in the Temple. However, on the 31st day after the child's birth (since Judaism considers a child viable only after thirty days), the father could pay a Kohen five shekels of silver to have the child released from this obligation. If the father failed to do so because of negligence or death, it became the duty of the son to redeem himself when he grew up. The rite is not performed if the father or the maternal grandfather is a Kohen or Levi, since the child would be obligated to serve in the Temple and could not be exempted. Because the firstborn must be the first to "open the womb" (*peter rechem*), it is not required if the firstborn son was delivered by Cesarean section, or if the mother had previously had an abortion or miscarried a fetus after 40days.[108] The first son of a Jewish mother must be redeemed, even if he has an older half-brother born to the father from a previous marriage. Conversely, it is not necessary to redeem a son who is the first-born of the father but not the mother. Thus, if a man marries a woman who already has a child from a previous marriage, any son issuing from their marriage need not be redeemed.

Today, the ceremony of the redemption of the firstborn son (*pidyon ha-ben*) is practiced by Orthodox and some Conservative Jews. However, it is not observed by Reform Jews, who do not recognize priestly status in modern times.

Redeeming/Breaking the Neck of the Firstborn Donkey (81-82)

As an unclean animal, the firstborn donkey could not be sacrificed in the same way as firstborn sheep or cattle (Pos. Comm 79). These two commandments effectively presented a choice to the owner of a firstborn donkey.

"The firstling of a donkey you shall redeem with a lamb" (Exod. 13:13) was one option (**81**). The Kohen received the lamb, and the owner could retain the firstborn donkey for his own use. The donkey was the only non-kosher animal that had firstborn status, meaning that it was declared sacred unless redeemed.

According to Sforno, this recalled the Exodus, when the Egyptians forced the Israel's to leave so quickly that they could not find sufficient wagons to haul their substantial possessions. Consequently, everything had to be loaded onto donkeys, which normally could never have carried such heavy weight. Because the donkeys miraculously were up to the task, they were accorded special firstborn status.[109]

The alternate option (**82**) was *"If you do not redeem it, then you shall break its neck"* (Exod. 13:13). According to rabbinic tradition, the donkey was killed by a hatchet blow from behind. This unusual technique was employed lest anyone misinterpret it as the ritual slaughter of an unclean animal.[110] In practice, this option ensured the scrupulous execution of the law of redemption, since every person would prefer parting with a lamb to losing a donkey.

Bringing Offerings to the Sanctuary (83-85)

"But only in the place that the Lord shall choose ..., there you shall bring up your burnt offerings, and there you shall do all that I command you" (Deut. 12:14) commanded the Israelites to offer all sacrifices only in one central Sanctuary (**84**). This was to develop national unity by gathering the twelve separate tribes together at a single site. Although Jerusalem was the place that was ultimately chosen, it is not explicitly indicated in the Torah. Indeed, at various times the Israelites were commanded to build an altar and offer sacrifices at such places as Mount Ebal (Deut. 27:5-7), Shiloh (Jer. 7:12), and on the threshing floor of Araunah in Jerusalem (2 Sam. 24:18). The essential point was that sacrifices could not be performed anywhere the worshiper chose, but only at the place selected by God.[111] Maimonides[112] regarded this commandment as a critical protection against idolatry and the pagan practice of sacrificing to the forces of nature in open fields.[113]

Any obligatory offerings (sin, burnt, guilt, peace), even if the obligation had been incurred outside the Land of Israel, had to be brought to the Sanctuary (85). This was in accordance with the verse, *"Only the holy things which you have, and your vows offerings, you shall bring to the place that the Lord shall choose"* (Deut. 12:26). Nachmanides considered this obligation as part of the preceding commandment, since the effect of both was that all offerings must be brought to the Sanctuary.[114]

"There you shall come, and there you shall bring your burnt offerings and feast offerings" (Deut. 12:5-6) was interpreted as requiring that a person bring every offering he owed when he came to the Sanctuary on each of the three Pilgrimage Festivals (83). According to Maimonides, these include all "offerings of one kind or another, or money, or valuations [Pos. Comm.114-117], or things devoted (to the Lord) [Pos. Comm.145], or things dedicated to the Sanctuary, or gleanings, forgotten sheaves and the unharvested corner of the field [Pos. Comm.120-122]." Nachmanides maintained that the purpose of this commandment was to enhance the joy of the festivals for the Kohanim and Levites ministering in the Temple, as well as for all those dependent on charity.[115]

Substitution of Offerings (86-87)

The commandment to redeem any offering that has developed a blemish (86), so that it could be available for ordinary use as well as slaughtered and eaten, is derived from the verse *"But whenever you desire, you may slaughter and eat meat in any of your settlements"* (Deut. 12:15). The redemption money was then used to buy another offering to substitute for the blemished animal that had been redeemed.

"If a person substitutes one animal for another, then both it and that for which it is changed shall be holy" (Lev. 27:10) means that both became the property of the Sanctuary and all profane use of it was prohibited (87). This rule applied regardless of whether the substituted animal was inferior or superior to

the original one. Maimonides[116] delved into the psychological reasons that would lead a person to make such a substitution. After having sanctified an animal, a person may regret having parted with such a valuable asset. To prevent him for retrieving it by substituting an inferior animal, the Torah penalizes him by decreeing that both animals are sacred. Conversely, the owner might want to substitute a superior animal, but the same penalty applies lest at another time the owner might think it acceptable either to substitute an inferior animal or to claim that an inferior animal was actually a superior one. To further discourage a person from attempting to regain something he has sanctified, the Torah requires one who redeems an object to add a surcharge of one fifth.[117]

Eating by the Kohanim (88-89)

The Kohanim were specifically required to eat two offerings— the meal offering and the meat of the "consecrated offerings."

"Aaron and his sons shall eat what is left of it" (Lev. 6:9) is the commandment (**88**) that the Kohanim eat the residue of the meal offerings and not dispose of them in any other way.

"They shall eat those things whereby atonement was made" (Exod. 29:33) is the commandment (**89**) that the Kohanim eat the meat of the consecrated offerings, namely the sin and guilt offerings, which were termed "most holy." As the *Sifra* (Lev. 10:7) states, "the Kohanim eat, and Israel gets atonement."

The sacrifices offered in the Temple may be classified under two main categories. The "most holy" included the guilt offerings (Pos. Comm. 63) and sin offerings (Pos. Comm. 64). A person bringing these animals to the Temple gave them to the Kohen on duty, who was required to perform the sacrifice and eat its flesh within a prescribed time and within the confines of the Temple Courtyard (Neg. Comm. 145). *Sefer ha-Chinuch* stressed that these offerings must be handled with extreme care, because they were brought by a person who had sinned and was asking for Divine forgiveness. Before consuming the meat, the Kohen was required to sprinkle the blood of the animal upon the Altar (Neg. Comm. 147) as an indication that the needs of the soul take precedence over those of the body. The Kohen was forbidden to give any of the meat to his servants or animals, or to negligently allow it to putrefy (Pos. Comm. 91). Assured that the Kohen would pay rigorous attention to every detail, the person could return home confident that he would be forgiven for the sin that had prompted his bringing the offering to the Temple.[118]

The sacrifices of "lesser holiness" included the offerings of thanksgiving, the peace offering (Pos. Comm. 66), the firstborn animals (Pos. Comm. 80), the tithe of cattle (Pos. Comm. 78), and the Paschal lamb (Pos. Comm. 55). These sacrifices also had to be offered at a specified place (the Altar) and eaten within a certain time. However, unlike the "most holy" offerings, the meat from a sacrifice of "lesser holiness" could be eaten by the Kohen anywhere within the walls of Jerusalem and shared by members of his household.[119]

Consecrated Offerings (90-91)

"The flesh that touches any unclean thing may not be eaten; if shall be burned in fire" (Lev. 7:19) is the commandment (**90**) to burn "consecrated offerings" that have become unclean.

The meat from consecrated offerings had to be eaten by the priests (Pos. Comm. 89). However, any remnant of the consecrated offering had to be burned (**91**), as indicated in the verse *"But that which remains of the flesh of the sacrifice on the third day shall be burnt in fire"* (Lev. 7:17). This law applied when an offering had been properly sacrificed, but some of its meat had not been eaten within the time permitted for its consumption (Neg. Comm. 91).[120]

Sefer ha-Chinuch maintained that food once considered sacred, but subsequently made ritually impure, could not be eaten

by humans or animals and had to be totally destroyed by fire
(Neg. Comm. 90). The rapid spoilage of meat mandated it be
burned promptly, lest the sacrificial service be tainted with the
stench of rotting flesh.[121]

The Nazirite (92-93)

The Nazirite, meaning either one who was "separated" (from the
temptations of the environment) or "consecrated" (to God), was a
person who voluntarily assumed austere modes of self-dedication
beyond the obligatory commandments. He or she vowed to (1)
allow the hair to remain uncut during the period of the vow; (2)
abstain from grapes or grape products such as wine (other alcoholic beverages were permitted); and (3) avoid any contact with
a human corpse (Neg. Comm. 202-209). The Nazirite vow was
often taken purely for personal reasons, such as thanksgiving for
recovery from illness or for the birth of a child. The minimum
period of the vow was thirty days, but some persisted for years.[122]

   "(He shall be holy;) he shall let the locks of the hair of his head grow
uncut" (Num. 6:5) commanded the Nazirite to let his hair grow
(**92**). This same verse contains the negative commandment (209),
"no razor shall come upon his head." Just as hair protects the
skin from the elements, it metaphorically created a barrier against
the outside world. By letting the hair grow, the Nazirite could be
shielded from all external influences and devote every thought and
action toward God (Hirsch).[123] In addition, because the hair was a
symbol of a person's natural power (as in the case of Samson, the
most famous Nazirite), allowing the hair to grow freely indicated
that the Nazirite was dedicating all of his or her strength to serving God. Indeed, the hair of the Nazirite was compared to the
crown of the king and the miter of the Kohen Gadol.[124]

   At the completion of the vow (**93**), the Nazirite was required to
bring four offerings (burnt, sin, peace, and meal) to the Sanctuary,
where his hair was cut off (Num. 6:13-21). From this moment on,

the Nazirite was permitted to drink wine and to contract ritual uncleanness by coming in contact with the dead (Naz. 45 a-b).

The commentators debated why the Nazirite was required to bring a sin offering after a period dedicated to the Divine service. Nachmanides maintained that it atones for the Nazirite's decision to return to mundane activities rather than indefinitely extending the vow to abstain from worldly pleasure.[125] According to this view, a community is blessed by having in its midst a handful of individuals who commit themselves to a more strenuous religious regimen.

Conversely, Simon the Just (a *Kohen Gadol* in the days of the Second Temple) refused to eat of the offerings brought by a Nazirite. He believed that the vows of the Nazirite often did not reflect a sincere commitment, but rather were made rashly at a time of extreme guilt or uncontrollable fervor (Num. R. 10:7). Maimonides, who advocated moderation in all activities, viewed the vows of the Nazirite as excessive and quoted the rabbinic statement, "Is it not sufficient for you to abstain from what the Torah has forbidden, that you seek to forbid yourself other things as well?" This concept was echoed by Rav, who observed that, "In the World to Come people will have to account for all the good food God put in the world which they refused to eat" (JT Kid. 4:12). Thus, the offering of the Nazirite can be interpreted as atoning for the sin of rejecting the delights of the world that God had created for human beings, instead misconstruing them as sources of temptation and evil.[126]

The Nazirite brought a peace offering, the symbol of satisfaction and delight, to celebrate the fulfillment of his vow (Ibn Ezra).[127]

All Oral Commitments to be Fulfilled (94)

"You shall observe and carry out what emerges from your lips" (Deut. 23:24) is the commandment to faithfully fulfill every oral

obligation to God (oath, vow, offering). This commandment is also found in the verse *"He must fulfill whatever comes out of his mouth"* (Num. 30:3).

The Rabbis took vows to God extremely seriously, explicitly stating that it is better to take no vows at all rather than to fail to fulfill them (Hul. 2a). Nevertheless, they understood the natural inclination of human beings to make rash vows in times of sickness and danger, only to forget them once they becomes healthy and secure. Just as oral commitments to God must be fulfilled, this commandment can be extended to the obligation that a person fulfill all commitments made to other individuals.

Concern about unfulfilled vows was likely an important factor in the emergence of *Kol Nidrei* as a significant ritual on Yom Kippur. *Kol Nidrei* states that all vows that one makes unwittingly, rashly, and unknowingly should be null and void. It initially encountered intense rabbinic opposition as an invalid practice that made light of vows, primarily because the first accepted version invoked Divine pardon, forgiveness, and atonement for those sins "from the *previous* Yom Kippur until *this* Yom Kippur" (i.e., the *past* year). The Tosafists of 12th-century France and Germany (especially Rabbenu Tam) reworded this phrase to read "from *this* Yom Kippur until the *next* Yom Kippur" (i.e., the *coming* year). Ashkenazim have adopted this formulation of Rabbenu Tam, while Sephardim generally accept the earlier version. The early Reform movement recommended eliminating *Kol Nidrei* from the Yom Kippur service; later it offered several alternative versions. However, current editions of the Reform prayer book retain the traditional Aramaic text.

Kol Nidrei assumed special significance during the time of the Spanish Inquisition, when Jews at pain of death were forced to give up their faith and assume the rituals of the Roman Catholic Church. For the many Jews who continued to practice their religion in secret, *Kol Nidrei* provided a welcome opportunity for solemnly renouncing the vows that they had made only under duress.[128] The melody used today for *Kol Nidrei*, which originated in southern Germany during the 16th century, exquisitely voices sorrow and suffering before rising triumphantly in hope and faith.[129]

Anti-Semites often pointed to *Kol Nidrei* as proof that Jews could not be trusted and that their oaths were meaningless. To combat this, the rabbis took great pains to stress that the *Kol Nidrei* formulation relates *only* to vows and promises to God and was never meant to apply to oaths taken before secular courts of law.

Revocation of Vows (95)

This commandment requires the application of the biblical rules regarding the revocation of vows (Num. 30:1-17). In this section, the Torah emphasizes the solemnity and binding character of religious vows (*nedarim*), as well as those circumstances in which the vows of women could be annulled by their fathers or husbands.

The general rule (see previous section) is that whatever a person has promised to God must be carried out, as indicated by the verse *"He shall not break his word; he must fulfill all that comes out of his mouth"* (Num. 30:3). However, there were three situations in which the vow of a woman "under authority" could be annulled. A father could annul the vow of a young unmarried woman while she was under his guardianship. Halachically, this was restricted to the six-month period following her puberty. After that time, she was considered sufficiently mature to be responsible for her own vows. The father had to annul the vow on the day he heard of it; if he remained silent, it was inferred that the vow met with his approval.[130] When a woman had completed the first step in marriage (*kiddushin*) but not the second phase (*nesuin*) that permitted the couple to live together (Pos. Comm. 213), both her father and her prospective husband shared authority over her vows. The assent of either was sufficient to block the other's revocation.[131] Following the completion of the marriage ceremony, a husband was empowered to annul a vow of his wife when he first learned about it. However, his authority was restricted to vows that "cause personal affliction" (Num. 30:15), which Rashi understood as impairing her personal comfort and Nachmanides considered as adversely affecting the relationship with her husband.[132] The vow of a widow or divorcée could not be annulled by anyone.

According to Nachmanides, the law of the revocation of vows is not a separate commandment, but rather one aspect of the law that all oral commitments must be fulfilled (Pos. Comm. 94).[133]

Ritual Defilement (96-98, 107)

A person who touched any type of ritual uncleanness (or in certain circumstances, was only near it) was himself rendered ritually impure and subject to all the obligations relating to unclean persons. For example, he could not come into the Sanctuary (Neg. Comm. 75-78), touch any holy thing, or eat any hallowed food. However, Maimonides stressed that those who did not intend to perform such actions were "not guilty of any sin if they remain unclean as long as they like, and eat, according to their pleasure, ordinary food that has been in contact with unclean things." [134]

Among those things that could cause ritual impurity were (96) the carcasses of animals (Lev. 11:24); (97) the carcasses of certain creeping creatures (weasel, mouse, great lizard, gecko, land-crocodile, lizard, sand-lizard, chameleon), which also were prohibited as food (Lev. 11:29-30); and (98) food and drink in an earthen vessel into which one of these dead creatures or their droppings had fallen (Lev. 11:34).

The most potent source of ritual impurity (107) was a dead

human body (Num. 19:11). It conveyed ritual uncleanness to anyone or any thing that entered or remained within the same tent or under the same roof as a corpse (including household utensils and wearing apparel), even if the person had no direct contact with it (Kel.1:4). A person who had contact with an individual who had become ritually unclean became himself ritually impure and could even transmit this state to food and drink.

Another important source of ritual uncleanness was contact with a menstruating woman (Pos. Comm. 99). During her period of separation, anyone who touched her, her bedding, or anywhere she sat would become ritually impure.

The Menstruant (99)

This commandment (Lev. 15:19-24) contains the regulations concerning the ritual uncleanness of the menstruating woman (in Hebrew, "niddah," one who is "separated"). Because the normal menstrual period was regarded as lasting seven days, the Bible deemed a woman ritually impure for one week from the time blood first appeared. After this time, she bathed herself, washed her clothes, and regained her ritual purity. The Talmud subjected the niddah to more stringent regulations. Her period of impurity was extended from the biblical maximum of seven days to up to fourteen days—as many as seven days of menstrual flow followed by a mandatory period of seven "white days" (free of bleeding). Therefore, during the period of her menstrual bleeding and for a full week thereafter, a woman was prohibited from having sexual relations with her husband (Neg. Comm. 346).

The laws of sexual separation are known as taharat ha-mishpachah (purity of the family). Although the Bible only forbids intercourse during a woman's menstrual period, subsequent rabbinic rulings have also precluded any physical contact that could conceivably be sexually stimulating. This includes kissing, hugging, or otherwise touching one's spouse during the forbidden days, during which husband and wife sleep in separate beds. Rather than handing something directly to their wife, some Orthodox men place the object on a table for her to pick up.[135] The rule forbidding touching a *niddah* has led many Orthodox men to protect the privacy and modesty of their wives by never touching them in public, so that no one knows whether or not they are in a state of *niddah* at the time. Similarly, they do not shake hands with any woman, not knowing whether or not she is a *niddah*. For the same reason, Orthodox men and women generally do not dance together in public; when doing so, they grasp a handkerchief between them rather than holding hands.[136]

On the evening of the completion of the twelfth day—assuming there has been no bleeding during any of the seven days following the five days of menstrual flow, which would require the count of seven days to begin again from that time—the woman must immerse herself in the *mikveh* as an act of symbolic ritual purification before marital relations can be resumed (Pos. Comm. 109). After undressing, she immerses herself fully in the water and then recites the appropriate blessing. According to *halachah*, the purification attained by immersion in a *mikveh* is not in itself a mitzvah, but is only required when the resumption of sexual relations depends on it. Unmarried women (except a bride just before her wedding) do not go to the *mikveh*, lest this be seen as encouraging premarital sex.[137]

R. Meir considered the period of separation to be of great benefit to the conjugal relations between man and wife. "Being in constant contact with his wife, [a husband might] develop a loathing towards her. The Torah, therefore, ordained that she be unclean for seven days in order that she shall be beloved by her husband as at the time of her first entry into the bridal chamber" (Nid. 31b). Indeed, many couples renew their sexual relationship each month with an eagerness and passion that is reminiscent of their honeymoon. In addition, the resumption of sexual relations between husband and wife generally occurs near the time when she is most fertile, thus increasing the chance of pregnancy and assuring the continuity of the Jewish people.

Ashes of the Red Heifer/ Water of Sprinkling (108, 113)

The mysterious rite of the red heifer (*parah adumah*) led to the paradoxical situation in which its ashes purified people who had become ritually unclean through contact with a human corpse, yet made those who engaged in its preparation ritually impure (Num. 19:1-22). It is the quintessential example of a *chok*, a statute that defies rational explanation, the observance of which represents unconditional obedience to a Divine decree.[138]

The Midrash (Num. R. 19:3) describes King Solomon, the wisest man in the Bible, as exclaiming that he had understood all the words of God except for the ritual of the red heifer. Nevertheless, many commentators have sought to discover the hidden meaning behind this perplexing ritual. Some have suggested that it was designed to cleanse the Israelites from moral as well as physical impurity, especially the sin of idolatry manifest during the episode of the Golden Calf. As the Midrash notes, "Let the mother come [red heifer] repair the damage the offspring [Golden Calf] has caused" (Num. R. 19:8). Noting that this section comes immediately after the completion of the Tabernacle and the rebellion of Korach against the leadership of Moses and Aaron, Israel of Ruzhin believed that the red heifer was a symbol that God would purify those Israelites who humbly approached the Tabernacle with full awareness of their own failings, but would condemn those who came arrogantly with a false sense of their own perfection.[139]

The preparation of the ashes of the red heifer (**113**) required an animal that was completely red (no more than one hair of a different color), free from blemish (fit for sacrifice), and not yet broken to the yoke (never used for secular purposes). Rashi maintains that during the wandering in the wilderness, the red heifer was slain outside the Israelite camp; according to Sifre, in the Land of Israel it was killed on the Mount of Olives, outside the walls of Jerusalem.[140] The animal was then burned on a pyre, to which was added cedar wood, hyssop, and crimson thread (which had the same symbolic significance as the additions to the bird offering of the person afflicted with *tzara'at*; Pos. Comm 110). The ashes were gathered up and stored outside the camp. When needed, the ashes were dissolved in fresh water that was sprinkled (**108**) on those who had become contaminated through contact with a dead body, rendering them ritually purified.

According to the Mishnah, the ceremonial burning of a red heifer was performed only seven times—once by Moses, once by Ezra, and five times after Ezra. With the destruction of the Temple, this practice was no longer relevant and thus was discontinued.[141] Because there is no longer any way to purify those who are ritually contaminated, some halachic authorities have forbidden all Jews from entering the Temple Mount in Jerusalem.[142]

Today, the section of the Torah dealing with the red heifer is read as the *maftir* portion for *Shabbat Parah*, one of the four special readings before Passover. Originally a call for all those planning to participate in the Passover pilgrimage to Jerusalem to ritually cleanse themselves in time, today *Shabbat Parah* reminds Jews to begin the extensive cleansing of *chametz* from their homes, which must be accomplished before the celebration of Passover.

Immersing in a Ritual Bath (109)

"He shall bathe his whole body in water" (Lev. 15:16) is the commandment to immerse oneself in the waters of a ritual bath (*mikveh*) to become cleansed of any impurity that would prevent the in-

dividual from bringing sacrifices to the Sanctuary. The conditions producing ritual impurity all related to some type of *loss*—of bodily fluid, potential life, or life itself—and included the person with the skin disease *tzara'at* or a bodily discharge (considered signs of some "spiritual defect"); a man with a seminal discharge or a menstruating woman (loss of the potential to create life); a woman following childbirth (who is unable to conceive for some time thereafter); and a person who came in contact with a corpse. Ritual immersion also was performed by the Kohanim during their consecration ceremony (Exod. 29:4; Lev. 8:6) and by the *Kohen Gadol* prior to the Yom Kippur rituals (Lev. 16:4).

Initially, ritual immersion took place in a natural, flowing body of water (*mayim chaim*; lit. "living water")—a river, stream, or ocean. However, these venues were not available for Jews living in areas where such sources of water cannot be found or in climates where bodies of water freeze for part of the year. This led to the development of an alternative place to perform ritual immersion—the *mikveh*.[143]

A *mikveh* (lit. "a collection [of water]") is a pool or bath that must contain forty *se'ah* (about 200 gallons) of clear water and be deep enough to cover the entire body of the person undergoing immersion. The water must be taken directly either from a river or a spring, or from rain water that is led into the bath. No water stored in a vessel or receptacle may be used. Prior to entering the *mikveh*, it is essential to wash thoroughly. This indicates, both literally and symbolically, that the purpose of immersion is ritual purity rather than physical cleanliness. No object can be interposed between the body and the water of the ritual bath. Therefore, before entering the *mikveh* it is necessary to remove all jewelry, makeup, and even nail polish.[144]

Today, the *mikveh* is most frequently used by a woman prior to resuming sexual relations with her husband after the completion of the period of separation related to her menstrual cycle (Pos. Comm. 99). A bride typically goes to the *mikveh* just before her wedding. The *mikveh* is also indispensable in the conversion of non-Jews to Judaism. The only ritual act required of female converts is immersion in a *mikveh*, while men who convert are required to immerse themselves and undergo circumcision (for those already circumcised, a symbolic drop of blood is taken from the male sex organ). Some Orthodox Jewish men immerse themselves in the *mikveh* on Fridays and/or before Jewish holidays.[145] Scribes (*soferim*) immerse themselves in the *mikveh* before embarking on the sacred task of writing a Torah scroll, and there is an ancient custom of immersing all new cooking pots and dishes purchased from non-Jews in a *mikveh*.

Valuations (114-117)

Voluntary contributions for the upkeep of the Sanctuary were considered a true expression of devotion to the House of God. In general, there were two kinds of sanctified property—monetary and physical. *Monetary* property was animals or objects that belonged to the Sanctuary. Although not intrinsically holy, they could not be used for any secular purpose. In contrast, *physical* sanctification referred to animals that were deemed intrinsically holy and were to be sacrificed as offerings on the Altar.[146]

In addition to vowing to donate a specific amount of money to the Sanctuary, Israelites also could obligate themselves to contribute their own "value" (or that of another person or thing) to the Temple treasury for maintenance or any other necessary expenditures. Rather than predicated on the commercial value of the individual person (relating to his or her health, strength, and earning capacity if sold as a slave), the biblical approach to the "valuation" of a person (**114**) was based solely on age and sex.[147]

The valuations for persons were based on four age categories: 1 month–5 years; 5-20 years, 20-60 years, and over age 60 (Lev. 27:2-8). The precise amounts (in silver shekels) for men and women in these categories were, respectively: 5 and 3 (male/

female); 20 and 10; 50 and 30; 15 and 10. If the person making the vow did not have sufficient funds to pay the full valuation, a designated Kohen would evaluate the available assets and determine what he or she could afford to pay (Ar. 17a, 23b).[148]

The Rabbis developed ingenious rationales for these valuations. Abravanel maintained that a person who vowed the value of an infant less than 30 days old paid nothing, because it was still not clear whether he or she would be viable. For a child age one month to five years, he paid five shekels for a boy because he had only attained one-tenth of his potential (the maximum vow was fifty shekels), and three shekels for a girl since she had lived 60 months (three shekels equaled 60 *gerah*). From ages 5-20, the worth of a female was exactly half that of the male. Women from ages 20-60 women had added value during their childbearing years, while those over 60 were "more useful around the house" than men of the same age.[149]

Alshekh observed that for a child between age 30 days and 5 years, the father paid five shekels for a male because during that period he had derived the five benefits of (a) witnessing his son emerging from initial 30-day period before viability could be established; (b) performing the ritual of circumcision; (c) performing the ceremony of the redemption of the firstborn; (d) partially fulfilling his duty of procreation; and (e) fulfilling the mitzvah of kindness by supporting the child. Because females were not subject to the mitzvot of circumcision or redemption of the first born, the father paid only three shekels. Between ages 5 and 20, boys were valued higher than girls because during this period they began Torah studies and became responsible for fulfilling their own mitzvot (Bar Mitzvah). From age 20-60, men were valued higher because they were subject to many mitzvot from which females were exempt. After age 60, the percentage difference between the valuations of men and women decreased because the man had lost a far higher percentage of his strength.[150]

The valuation of animals **(115)** referred to the situation in which an animal dedicated to the Temple as an offering was found to be unsuitable (such as because it was blemished). The owner could redeem the animal, with the money going to the Sanctuary for a replacement offering. The Kohen would determine the actual monetary value of the animal, and the owner would be required to pay that amount plus an additional fifth to have the animal returned to him (Lev. 27:9-13).

The valuation of houses **(116)** was similar, with the owner required to pay the monetary value (determined by the Kohen) plus an extra fifth in order to redeem a house that had been dedicated to the Temple (Lev. 29:14-15).

The valuation of fields **(117)** was not determined according to their actual value and quality, but rather on the basis of their size and the number of crops remaining until the Jubilee Year (Lev. 26:16-25). The measurement of area was calculated by the quantity of seed required to sow it.

The rabbis discussed the reasoning behind the requirement of adding a fifth (see Pos. Comm. 194) of the value for redeeming an animal, house, or field dedicated to the Temple. *Sefer ha-Chinuch* noted that this would discourage people from redeeming objects previously designated as holy. Maimonides and Abravanel took a more cynical view. Because a person usually valued possessions that were his inheritance, planning to redeem them later, he might conspire with the Kohen to set a low price for its redemption. The added fifth was designed to thwart the efforts of those attempting such a dishonest practice.[151]

Restitution for a Sacrilege (118)

A person who unintentionally used Temple property or ate some holy thing (termed "sacrilege") was required to make restitution for what he had used or eaten, with the addition of a penalty of one fifth of its estimated value (Lev. 5:16, 22:14) (see Pos. Comm. 194). Once remitted, it all became the property of the Kohen.

To guard against even the slightest suspicion of impropriety, the attendants who dealt with the baskets full of half shekels (Pos. Comm. 171) were not permitted "to wear a sleeved cloak or shoes or sandals or tefillin or an amulet," lest if they became rich it would be charged that their wealth was the result of embezzling from the Temple treasury (Shek. 3:2).

Fruits of Fourth-Year Plantings (119)

"(In the fourth year) all its fruit shall be sanctified [set aside] for praising the Lord" (Lev. 19:24) is the commandment to bring the fruits of a four-year-old tree to Jerusalem and eat them there (with no portion given to the Kohanim). The fruit had to be brought in its natural state except for grapes and olives, which could be in the form of wine or olive oil.[152] As with the second tithe (Pos. Comm. 128), if it was too difficult for the owner to bring the fruits to Jerusalem, he could redeem them for money, add a fifth to their value (Pos. Comm. 194), and spend all the proceeds in Jerusalem for food and drink that he and his guests would eat there. However, this option only applied to the fruits of fourth-year plantings more than a day's journey from Jerusalem, for the Rabbis wanted to have the "market places of Jerusalem adorned with fruit" (Maas. Sh. 5:2).[153]

The Torah forbids a person from eating the fruit of a tree during its first three years (Neg. Comm. 192). Nachmanides explained that these fruits were not mature enough to be used for the sacred purpose of praising and thanking God. Because they were unfit as first-fruit offerings to God, they also were forbidden for human consumption.[154]

Produce Left for the Poor (120-124)

These five commandments deal with produce of the fields and vineyards that had to be left for the poor. This obligation to leave part of the crop for the poor was a reminder that the land and its produce were given by God in trust for all the people and not for the owner's use alone.

When reaping the harvest, the farmer was commanded (**120**) to leave a corner (*pe'ah*) of the field for the poor (Lev. 19:9). Although the precise size of this section was not pre-scribed in the Torah, the Rabbis (Pe'ah 1:2) declared that it should be not less than one-sixtieth part of the harvest, and always proportional to the number of the poor and the yield of the crops.

Similarly, the farmer was commanded (**121**) to leave the "glean-ings" of the harvest (Lev. 19:9). This referred to the single ears of corn that fell to the ground at the time of reaping. The Rabbis decreed that if two ears dropped they belonged to the poor; but if three or more ears fell together they could be retrieved by the farmer (Pe'ah 4:10). This same rule applied to (**122**) the forgotten sheaf of grain in the fields (Deut. 24:19) and to (**124**) single grapes that fell to the ground in the vineyard (Lev. 19:10). The Rabbis took these laws seriously: "He who places a basket under the vine when he is gathering the grapes [so that no single grapes fall to the ground] is robbing the poor" (Pe'ah 7:3). In contrast, Rashi said: "He who leaves the gleanings, the forgotten sheaf, and the *pe'ah* for the poor in due is considered as if he had built the Temple and offered his sacrifices there."

Defective grape clusters (**123**) found during the harvest also had to be left for the poor (Lev. 19:10). This referred to undeveloped twigs in which single grapes had not formed clusters.

The corresponding negative commandments are 210-214.

Bringing First Fruits to the
Sanctuary (125, 132)

"The choicest first fruits of your land you shall bring to the house of the Lord your God" (Exod. 23:19) is the commandment (**125**) to set aside the first fruits (*bikurim*) and bring them to the Sanctuary for the Kohanim, who were required to eat them in Jerusalem (Neg. Comm. 148). This only applied to the seven kinds of produce for which the Land of Israel was famed—wheat, barley, grapes, figs, pomegranates, olives (oil), and (honey from) dates (Deut. 8:8).

Each year, when the Jew went out to his fields and saw that these crops were beginning to ripen, he would mark his "first fruits" by tying straw around them (Bik. 3:1). When they had ripened completely, he would bring them to the Temple in Jerusalem, at any time between Shavuot (also known as *Chag ha-Bikurim*) and Sukkot.[155] "Those who lived near [to Jerusalem] brought fresh figs and grapes, but those from a distance brought dried figs and raisins [since fresh fruit would rot on the way]" (Bik. 3:3). Because the *bikurim* symbolized the readiness of the Jew to devote the first fruits of his labors on earth to the service of God, the trip to Jerusalem was celebrated in every town and city along the way with music and parades.[156] "An ox with horns bedecked with gold and with an olive-crown on its head led the way, and a flute was played before them" (ibid.). "The rich brought their *bikurim* in baskets overlaid with silver or gold, while the poor used wicker-baskets of peeled willow branches" (Bik. 3:8). When they reached the Temple Mount, those bringing their first fruits were greeted by Levites raising their voices in song.

After presenting his basket of first fruits to the Kohen, the farmer was commanded (**132**) to recite a brief synopsis of Jewish history—humbly thanking God for treating Jacob mercifully in his hour of need, delivering the Israelites from slavery in Egypt, and bringing the Jewish people to their Promised Land flowing with milk and honey (Deut. 26:1-11). Beginning with words that can be translated either "A wandering Aramean (Jacob) was my father" or "An Aramean (the deceitful Laban) tried to destroy my forefather (Jacob)," these verses became an important part of the Passover *Haggadah*.

The thanksgiving offering of first fruits was visible proof of the fulfillment of the Divine promise to the patriarchs—that their descendants would become a great nation dwelling in comfort in a rich and fertile land. The recitation had to be in Hebrew, and those that could not speak the language were required to repeat the words after the Kohen. When farmers not conversant in Hebrew began to refrain from bringing their first fruits out of shame, it was decided that everyone must repeat the words after the Kohen (Bik. 3:7).

According to Maimonides,[157] this ceremony taught that when serving God in days of comfort, it was essential "to remember the times of trouble and the history of past distress."[158]

Tithes (126-131)

The Torah commanded a variety of tithes and heave offerings that were obligatory only with respect to produce from the Land of Israel. Eventually, these regulations were extended to produce from Babylon, Egypt, and Syria. It was forbidden to alter the prescribed order of harvest tithing specified below (Neg. Comm. 154).

The Israelites were commanded to set aside what Maimonides termed the *great heave offering* (**126**) for the Kohanim (Deut. 18:4). Known as *terumah*, no precise amount was prescribed, though the Rabbis observed that "a generous man gives one-fortieth; ... an average man one-fiftieth, and a miserly one one-sixtieth" (Ter. 4:3).

A *first tithe* (**127**) of one-tenth of the crops was given to the Levites as a reward for their dedication to the service of God. From this tithe, the Levites had to set aside a heave offering of one-tenth (**129**) to give to the Kohanim (Num. 18:26-29). The Torah (Num. 18: 21, 24) states twice that the Levites receive tithes because there were two aspects to the gift. First, they received produce to make up for the portion of the Land that they were required to forego. Second, they received the tithes only after all the labors in the field had been done by others, in return for the labor that they devoted to their sacred service.[159] The nine-tenths of the tithe to the Levites that remained (after their own tithe to the Kohanim) had no sanctity and could be eaten by Israelites and in a state of ritual impurity.[160] In contrast, the heave offerings (*terumah*) were accorded extreme sanctity and could only be eaten by ritually pure Kohanim. A non-Kohen who intentionally consumed any of it merited the punishment of *karet* (premature death by the hand of Heaven); if eaten without willful intent, the person was required to add a penalty of one fifth of its value when making restitution.[161]

After the Kohen's portion and the Levite's first tithe had been removed from a harvested crop, the owner was required to separate a *second tithe* (**128**). During the first, second, fourth, and fifth years of the seven-year Sabbatical Year cycle, this second tithe had to be brought to Jerusalem, where it was to be eaten by the owner and members of his family (Deut. 14:22). If this were impossible due to the distance or the weight of the produce, the owner was to redeem the tithe and bring its monetary value (plus one fifth extra) to the Temple, where he was required to spend it exclusively on food and drink (Neg. Comm. 141-143, 152).

The commentators provided several reasons for the commandment to eat the second tithe in Jerusalem. As the seat of the Sanhedrin, Jerusalem was filled with wise men and Torah scholars, from whom Jews consuming their tithes and offerings could learn. According to Rashbam, those coming on a pilgrimage to Jerusalem would be privileged to see the Temple (where the Divine Presence dwelled), the Kohanim performing the sacrificial rites, and the Levites offering their musical accompaniment—experiences that would engender feelings of awe and reverence for God.[162] Maimonides[163] noted that the

requirement that the owner consume this large amount of produce in Jerusalem meant that he would have to give some of
it away as charity. Assembling such large numbers of people
eating and drinking in one place "strengthened the bond of
love and brotherhood among the children of men."

The *poor man's tithe* (**130**) was due in the third and sixth
years of every Sabbatical cycle (Deut. 14:28). In these years, what
would have been the second tithe (to be eaten in Jerusalem)
was kept at home for the poor to eat.[164]

The avowal of the tithe (**131**) was the command to make a verbal
declaration that one had set aside all the obligatory tithes and heave
offerings and delivered them to their proper destinations (Deut.
26:13-15). This avowal was recited at the time of the afternoon offering on the last day of Passover, in the fourth and seventh years
of the Sabbatical Year cycle, preferably in the Temple.[165]

Dough Offering (*Challah*) (133)

"Of the first of your dough you shall set aside a loaf for a gift" (Num.
15:20) is the commandment to separate the *challah* offering for the
Kohen. It applied to five kinds of cereal grains—wheat, barley,
spelt, oats, and rye (Hal 1:1). The amount prescribed was 1/24 of
the dough for a private person and 1/48 of the dough for a baker.[166]

Sefer ha-Chinuch observed that since bread is a staple food
("staff of life"), this commandment enabled a person to easily
perform a mitzvah each day, sustaining the body and soul at
the same time. Moreover, this commandment made life easier
for the Kohanim, who spent most of their days performing
the Temple service. Rather than requiring the Kohen to carry
out all steps in the process of preparing bread (sifting grain,
grinding it into flour, and kneading the dough), all that he
needed to do was to take the gift of dough and bake it in
an oven.[167]

According to the Torah, the *challah* offering was only obligatory in the Land of Israel. After the destruction of the Temple, the Rabbis declared that this practice would remain in force everywhere (Bech. 27a). It is still observed in observant Jewish households, and kosher bakeries, where bread is baked. Because Kohanim can no longer observe the laws of priestly purity and thus are prohibited from eating anything related to a holy sacrifice, the *challah* is thrown into the fire and burned rather than given to a Kohen.[168]

Today, the term "challah" is also applied to the special braided breads used for the Sabbath and festivals. The two challot may represent the double portion of manna that the Israelites received on the sixth day (so as not to have to gather it on the seventh day and violate the prohibition of working on the Sabbath; Pos. Comm. 320) or the two rows (twelve loaves) of the Show-bread (Pos. Comm. 27), which was continually placed before God on the Table in the Sanctuary and then eaten on the Sabbath by the Kohanim.

Sabbatical Year (134-135, 141)

"[Even] at plowing time and harvest time you shall rest [cease from labor]" (Exod. 34:21), *"But the seventh year shall be a complete rest for the land, a Sabbath for the Lord"* (Lev. 25:4), and *"Then shall the land observe a Sabbath rest for the Lord"* (Lev. 25:2) are three of the verses commanding the Israelites to cease from working the land during the seventh year **(135)**. Observance of the Sabbatical Year (*Shemittah*) reminds Jews that they are merely tenants with temporary rights to farm Divinely owned property, as in the verse from Psalms (24:1): "The earth is the Lord's, and all the fullness thereof." Indeed, Rashi claimed that the exile of the people from the Land of Israel was due to their neglect of the Sabbatical Years,[169] while Jeremiah predicted 70 years of exile in Babylonia to make up for the 70 Sabbatical Years the people neglected during the approximately 500 years they lived in the Land of Israel (2 Chron. 36:21).

"But in the seventh year you shall leave it (the land) untended

and unharvested, (that the poor of your people may eat ...so shall you deal with your vineyard and with your olive grove)" (Exod. 23:11) is the commandment (**134**) to renounce as ownerless the produce of the land during the Sabbatical Year, so that everything growing in the fields was available to all. In an ordinary year, the gleanings of the harvest and the corners of the fields were left for the poor (Pos. Comm.120-122, 124). In contrast, during the Sabbatical Year there was no harvesting. Owner, servants, the poor, the stranger, and even wild and domesticated animals had equal rights to the produce (Lev. 25:6-7).

"Every creditor shall remit the due of that which he has lent to his neighbor" (Deut. 15:2) is the commandment (**141**) to cancel all debts that were outstanding at the end of the sixth year of the seven-year cycle. This rule applied only to fellow Jews and not to gentiles living in the Land. While the law of release of the Sabbatical Year canceled the right of a creditor to claim his debt, the debtor nevertheless remained morally obligated to pay it.[170]

The Torah warned against letting the approach of the Sabbatical Year of release prevent one from helping a needy fellow Jew (Deut. 15:7-11). Nevertheless, as the Israelites moved from an economy based on agriculture to one founded on business and commerce, the release of debts contracted in trading became onerous, and people refrained from making loans to one another as the Sabbatical Year approached. Consequently, in the first century C.E., Hillel enacted the *prosbul* (Shev. 10:4), in which a creditor declared before a court of law (attested by witnesses) that all debts due to him were given over to the court for collection. Since remission of loans during the seventh year applied only to individuals but not to public loans, the effect was to render the individual's loan public and thus not nullified and collectable after the Sabbatical Year.

Jubilee Year (136-140)

"You shall count off seven cycles of Sabbatical Years" (Lev. 25:8) is the commandment (**140**) for the Great Sanhedrin to count the years from the time the Israelites conquered the land.

"You shall sanctify the fiftieth year...and it shall a Jubilee for you" (Lev. 25:10) is the commandment (**136**) for the Israelites to observe the Jubilee Year. During this year, all Jewish slaves (with their families) had to be freed, even if they either had not worked the usual minimum of six years or had elected to remain with their masters after that amount of time (see Exod. 21:5-6). Some have suggested that the Jubilee Year not only brought freedom to slaves, but also freed their owners from the moral and ethical dilemmas inherent in exercising such power over fellow human beings.[171]

"In the Jubilee Year, each of you shall return to your ancestral heritage" (Lev. 25:13) is the commandment (**138**) that every 50 years all landed property was to revert to its original owner, who may have been forced by poverty to sell it at some time since the last Jubilee. Exceptions were the houses and the land on which they stood in a city that had a wall around it from the time of Joshua (**139**), based on the verse *"If a man sells a dwelling house in a walled city ... it shall not be released in the Jubilee Year"* (Lev. 25:29-30). According to Rashi, the Jubilee Year was observed only as long as all Israelites were in the Holy Land, and therefore ceased as soon as some of the tribes across the Jordan went into exile.

The unique biblical idea of returning land to its original owner at the end of a 50-year cycle prevented the development of the dramatic differences in financial resources between the richest and poorest segments that plague many societies today. Rav Kook viewed the Jubilee Year in spiritual rather than economic terms. In addition to allowing the impoverished the opportunity to restore their self respect and erase their sense of failure, the Jubilee Year served to unify the nation and recreate the single-mindedness of purpose that once characterized Israel.[172]

The Jubilee Year was ushered in with *"a broken blast [ter-uah] of the shofar on the tenth day of the seventh month, the Day of Atonement"* (Lev. 25:9). Indeed, the Hebrew word for the Jubilee Year (*yovel*) means ram, alluding to the blowing of the ram's horn that consecrated it and the shofar ceremony was identical to that of Rosh Hashanah.[173] This commandment (**137**) is recalled today by sounding a final long blast of the shofar at the end of the concluding *Ne'ilah* service on Yom Kippur. The shofar blast was designed to "proclaim liberty throughout the land and to all the inhabitants thereof" (Lev. 25:10)—words selected by the American patriots to be inscribed on the Liberty Bell, which announced the signing of the Declaration of Independence and the birth of their new free land.

Exacting Debts From Idolaters (142)

"Of a foreigner you may exact it" (Deut. 15:3) is the commandment (or the permission, according to Nachmanides and the literal meaning of the text) to exact debts from a non-Jew and press him for payment. In biblical days, this referred to a trader who was visiting Canaan only temporarily and was not subject to the law freeing the Israelite from debts every seventh (Sabbatical) year.[174]

This commandment is diametrically opposite to the requirement to be merciful to a fellow Jew and the prohibition against demanding payment from one whom you know to be poor (Neg. Comm. 234).

Gifts to the Kohen (143-145)

"This shall be the due of the Kohanim from the people ..." (Deut. 18:3-4) is the source of the commandments for the Israelites

to set aside and give to the Kohen: (144) the first of the fleece and (143) the right foreleg, cheeks, and maw (stomach) of every clean domesticated animal slaughtered for common food rather than as a consecrated offering for the Temple. Ibn Ezra maintained that these parts of the animal symbolized the various roles of the Kohanim in the Temple service—right foreleg for the right arm used to slaughter offerings; cheeks, including the tongue, for blessing the people; and maw for checking the internal organs of the animal for possible disqualification.[175]

Abravanel viewed these parts of the bodies as representing the three types of transgressions for which a person must seek Divine forgiveness. These include sins committed by word of mouth (cheeks), deed (foreleg), and thought (innards). According to Bahya ben Asher, the Kohanim were granted these gifts because of the zeal of the Kohen Pinchas in slaying the Israelite Zimri and the Midianite princess Cozbi who were brazenly fornicating in public view before Moses and the elders at the entrance to the Tent of Meeting. Pinchas grabbed a spear (foreleg), prayed for Divine help and guidance (cheeks), and then thrust the weapon through the stomachs (innards) of the sinning couple.[176]

The Tosefta enumerated 24 classes of gifts given to the Kohanim. Ten were designated for those in the Temple, four to those in the city of Jerusalem, and the remaining ten to Kohanim anywhere within the borders of the Land of Israel. Positive commandments relating to these various gifts include numbers 27, 44, 46, 79, 80, 81, 88, 89, 117, 125, 126, 129, 133, 143, 144, and 145.[177]

All "devoted property" that was not specifically earmarked for the Temple treasury for the upkeep of the Sanctuary (i.e., indicated by explicitly stating that it was "to God") was given to the Kohanim (145), as derived from the verse "... *its pos-*

session shall be the Kohen's" (Lev. 27:21). The Hebrew word used for "devoted property" is *cherem*, which is customarily used to denote utter destruction or an object that is banned from human use (as well as meaning excommunication in later rabbinic literature). In the context of this section of the Torah, the word refers to an object that was consecrated and therefore forbidden for personal use.[178] Any item devoted to the Kohanim could not be redeemed and became their personal property. This is contrary to items devoted to the Sanctuary, which could be redeemed for their full monetary value and then used for any secular purpose.[179]

Shechitah (Kosher Slaughtering) (146-7, 149-152)

The law of ritual slaughtering (**146**) is derived from the verse *"then you may slaughter any of your cattle or sheep... as I have commanded you"* (Deut. 12:21). The Rabbis connected the words "as I have commanded you" with the phrase "then you shall kill," implying that Moses had previously taught the people a method for slaughtering animals. However, since the precise details are not mentioned in the Torah, it follows that the Jewish method of ritual slaughter must have been communicated as part of the Oral Law. [180] Today, the complex and minute regulations dealing with ritual slaughtering must be carried out by a licensed *shochet*, who in addition to being a skilled professional must be a pious individual who is well trained in Jewish law.

Jewish ritual slaughtering strives to prevent unnecessary suffering to the animal. It requires one continuous deep horizontal cut with a perfectly sharp blade that has no nicks or unevenness. This severs the windpipe and all of the great blood vessels of the neck so that the animal instantly loses all sensation. Because an animal may not be eaten unless it has been properly slaughtered, the technical requirements must be strictly observed.

Jewish ritual slaughtering also requires that the blood of any species of kosher bird or non-domesticated animal be covered up after it has been killed. This commandment (147) is derived from the verse *"he shall pour out its blood and cover it with dust"* (Lev. 17:13). As the symbol of life, blood must be treated in a reverent manner and, like a human corpse, not left exposed. The covering with dust was thus the symbolic equivalent of the burial of a dead body.[181] This commandment did not apply to those species used for sacrificial offerings – cattle, sheep, or goats – because sacrificial blood was never covered.[182]

Maimonides included as four other positive commandments the need to "search for prescribed tokens" in the animals that Jews eat. Based on the overriding principle "these are the living things that you may eat" (Lev. 11:2), he argued that one is obliged to search for specific indications of suitability in each animal, whether tame or wild; only if these prescribed tokens are found, can the animal be consumed. Thus one must look for (149) the *"cloven hoof and chewing of the cud"* in quadrupeds (Lev. 11:3); (150) *"clean birds"* that are neither predators nor carrion eaters (Deut. 14:11); (151) locusts or grasshoppers that have *"jointed legs above their legs"* (joints higher than the body at rest) (Lev. 11:21); and (152) fish that have *"fins and scales"* (Lev. 11:9).

Nachmanides disagreed with Maimonides, stating that the search for prescribed tokens was merely incidental to the negative commandments (172-179) that prohibit the eating of various unclean things. Because close examination of the physical features of each mammal, bird, grasshopper, and fish was necessary to determine whether one must abstain from eating it, Nachmanides argued that these should not be deemed independent positive commandments.[183]

Sending Away the Mother Bird
When Taking Its Young (148)

The commandment relating to the humane treatment of a mother and her young derives from the verse, "*If along the road you chance upon a bird's nest ... and the mother bird is sitting over her young or on her eggs ... you shall surely send away the mother bird but may take the young for yourself*" (Deut. 22:6-7).

Maimonides[184] explained that one may not kill an animal and its young on the same day so that "people should be restrained and prevented from killing the two together in such a manner that the young is slain in the sight of the mother; for the pain of the animals in such circumstances is very great. There is no difference in this case between the pain of man and the pain of other living beings, since the love and the tenderness of the mother for her young ones is not produced by reasoning but by feeling, and this faculty exists not only in man but in most living things." He added: "If the Law provides that such grief should not be caused to cattle and birds, how much more careful must we be that we should not cause grief to our fellow man." According to Nachmanides, the purpose of this commandment was directed not toward the animal but toward humans, to purge them of callousness, cruelty, and savagery. For Abravanel, allowing the mother bird to live would encourage her to lay more eggs and thus preserve bird species for the long-term benefit of humanity.[185]

The reward for sparing the mother bird is "so that it will be good for you and prolong your days" (Deut. 22:7). This is strikingly similar to the effect of observing the Fifth Commandment honoring parents—"that your days may be long upon the land that the Lord your God is giving you" (Exod. 20:12)—implying that God will treat human beings in accordance with how well they care for animals. Commenting on the Talmud (Hul. 142a),

Rashi noted that if God gives long life and material success for fulfilling the simple mitzvah of sparing the mother bird, which requires neither intense physical effort nor financial loss, how much more is the Divine reward for discharging commandments that are difficult to perform.[186]

Determining the New Moon (153)

"This month [i.e., Nisan] *shall be for you the beginning of the months, the first of the months of the year"* (Exod. 12:2). The rabbis interpreted the words "to you" as meaning that the exact fixation of the timing of the months and the festivals was in the hands of the Israelites themselves.

The Jewish calendar is based on twelve lunar months, whose names are of Babylonian origin and came into use among Jews only after the destruction of the First Temple. The time span between one New Moon and the next is 29 days, 12 hours, 44 minutes, and 3 1/3 seconds. Since a month must be composed of complete days, in the Jewish calendar they vary between 29 and 30 days. Five months (Nisan, Sivan, Av, Tishrei, and Shevat) have 30 days; five (Iyar, Tammuz, Elul, Tevet, and Adar) have 29 days; and two (Cheshvan and Kislev) have either 29 or 30 days. The day following the evening on which the new moon first appears is called Rosh Hodesh (New Moon) and is a minor festival. In a 29-day month, Rosh Hodesh is observed for only one day; in a 30-day month, it is observed for two days (the last day of the outgoing month and the first day of the new month).[187]

In biblical and early talmudic times, the Sanhedrin in Jerusalem determined whether a particular month had twenty-nine or thirty days, based on the visual observation of witnesses. The members of the Sanhedrin gathered on the 30th of each month and awaited testimony. If witnesses appeared, Rosh Hodesh was celebrated, and that day was counted as the first day of the next month. If no witnesses appeared, the next day was celebrated as Rosh Hodesh. To spread word that the new month had begun, fires were lit on the Mount of Olives and then successively throughout Israel. Jews living far from Jerusalem always celebrated Rosh Hodesh on the 30th day of the month. When informed that it had been postponed to the next day, they also celebrated that day.

The twelve lunar months add up to approximately 11 days less than the solar year (365 days, 48 minutes, and 46 seconds). Without any adjustments, the festivals would "wander" and be shifted from their appointed seasons of the year. For example, Passover could fall in the fall, winter, or summer, whereas according to the Torah it must be observed in the spring (Deut. 16:1). (Of course, this applies only to countries on the same side of the equator as the Land of Israel.) Therefore, an additional month is added 7 times in every 19 years.[188] This added month, which is called Adar Sheni (Second Adar), is inserted immediately preceding the month of Nisan (the first month in the Jewish year). During Second Temple times, the Sanhedrin was responsible for keeping track of discrepancies in length between the solar and lunar years, intercalating the extra month when needed according to agricultural conditions.

After the destruction of the Temple, the power to declare the day of the New Moon passed to the head of the court at Yavneh. During the fourth century, however, the Christian authorities in the Land of Israel prohibited the dissemination of information regarding the New Moon. Consequently, in about 360, Hillel II published a fixed calendar based on astronomical calculations, thus freeing Jewish communities from having to rely on the declaration by the high court in the Land of Israel.[189]

The current practice is to publicly announce in the synagogue the name of the new month and the day(s) on which Rosh Hodesh will be celebrated. This ceremony is part of *Birkat ha-Hodesh*, a blessing recited before the open ark following the reading of the haftarah on the Sabbath before the New Moon, in which Jews pray that the upcoming month will be a good and blessed month for all Israel.

Work is permitted on Rosh Hodesh. Since earliest times, however, it was customary for women to abstain from work as a reward for not having surrendered their jewelry for the fashioning of the Golden Calf. In certain communities, no work was done; in others only heavy work was forbidden. In recent years, women have formed Rosh Hodesh groups to study and celebrate together.[190]

Resting on the Sabbath (154)

"Six days shall you labor, but on the seventh day you shall rest" (Exod. 34:21) is the commandment to rest on the Sabbath. According to Maimonides,[1] the abstention from work on the Sabbath (Neg. Comm. 320) is designed to remind us of the role of God as the Creator of the universe and the Deliverer of Israel from Egypt.[191]

This second half of the verse—"(even) at plowing time and harvest time shall you rest [cease from labor]"—implies that the Israelite must rest and not violate the Sabbath even during these critical periods of the year when he might believe that his very livelihood depends on laboring in the fields.[192]

In observing the Sabbath rest, Jews traditionally "extend" the day by beginning it with the lighting of candles 18 minutes before sunset on Friday and delaying its departure until three stars appear in the night sky (about 42 minutes after sunset) on Saturday evening. Nachmanides deemed this practice to be required by the Torah, while Maimonides said no such obligation existed.[193]

Proclaiming the Sanctity of the Sabbath (155)

The Sabbath is the focus of the fourth of the Ten Commandments. The Exodus version (20:8) is *"Remember the Sabbath day and keep it holy [sanctify it],"* while the parallel commandment in Deuteronomy (5:12) is *"Observe the Sabbath day and keep it holy [sanctify it]."* According to the Talmud (Shev. 20b), the two words "remember" and "observe" were miraculously "pronounced in a single utterance" by God.

In addition to the prohibitions concerning work, travel, and punishing on the Sabbath (Neg. Comm. 320-322), the Rabbis instituted specific actions to "sanctify it on its coming in and sanctify it on its going out" (Pes. 106a)—the blessings over wine on the Sabbath eve (*kiddush*) and after nightfall on Saturday (*Havdalah*).

The Rabbis ruled that the Sabbath should be made the specific object of honor (*kavod*) and delight (*oneg*), based on the verse in Isaiah (58:13): "and you shall call the Sabbath a delight, and the Lord's holy day honorable." Traditionally, "honor" implied the duties of bathing immediately before the Sabbath, wearing special Sabbath clothes, and receiving the Sabbath with joy. "Delight" meant lighting candles on Friday night (primarily the prerogative of the mother of the household), enjoying special delicacies, a minimum of three Sabbath meals, cohabitation with one's spouse, and general repose and added sleep.[194]

Maimonides[195] considered the proper observance of the Sabbath as equal to all of the other commandments in the Torah. In the 20th century, Abraham Joshua Heschel described the Sabbath as "a sanctuary in time."[196] For Ahad Ha-Am, the father of cultural Zionism, the Sabbath was the key to the centuries of Jewish national survival in the Diaspora. "More than

Israel has kept the Sabbath, the Sabbath has kept Israel."[197] A similar sentiment was expressed by the national poet of Israel, Chaim Nachman Bialik, who wrote: "Without Shabbat, there is no people of Israel, no Land of Israel, no culture of Israel. Shabbat is the culture."

Removal of Leaven (156)

"On the previous day you shall remove all leaven from your houses" (Exod. 12:15) is the commandment to remove all *chametz* (including leavened bread made from any of the five species of grain indigenous to the Land of Israel—wheat, spelt, barley, rye, and oats) from one's dwelling before the beginning of Passover, the feast of unleavened bread.

According to Maimonides,[198] it is sufficient to mentally disown all the leaven in one's possession. However, the Rabbis made it obligatory to rid the home of *chametz*. After a thorough housecleaning, a formal search for leaven (*bedikat chametz*) is conducted on the night before Passover to symbolize the final removal of *chametz* from the home. Before the search, it is customary to deposit small pieces of bread (ten pieces, according to kabbalistic lore) in rooms throughout the house where *chametz* may have been used during the year. The search is traditionally carried out by candlelight, with a feather and a wooden spoon to collect the *chametz*. The use of a candle ("lamp") is required (Pes. 1:1) to enable an extremely rigorous and thorough source, though some now use a flashlight for safety's sake.[199] After the search, one recites an Aramaic statement: "All *chametz* in my possession which I have not seen or removed, or of which I am unaware, is hereby nullified and ownerless as the dust of the earth." In the morning, after the last meal of *chametz*, any leftovers are added to the crumbs gathered the previous night, and all are burned or thrown out. Finally, the declaration of annulment of *chametz* said on the previous night is repeated to conclude the ritual of banishing *chametz* from our dwellings.[200]

In the late Middle Ages, Ashkenazic Jews in Poland were often tavern owners, and destroying their *chametz*-containing wares before Passover would have caused serious economic harm. Consequently, Moses Isserles promulgated the "legal fiction" of permitting a Jew to sell his leavened products to a trusted gentile neighbor, who would then sell them back to him after Passover. This custom of sealing up *chametz* that is too valuable to be destroyed and selling it to a non-Jew for the duration of Passover has persisted to this day. Because a formal legal document is required, the sale usually is done through a rabbi, who is empowered to act as the agent in the transaction. After Passover, the agent buys back the *chametz* and restores it to the original owner.[201]

Recounting the Departure from Egypt (157)

"And you shall tell your son on that day ..." (Exod. 13:8) is the commandment for Jews to recite the story of the Exodus from Egypt on Passover (the 15th of Nissan in Israel; also the next day in the Diaspora). The Hebrew verb meaning "tell" is *higad'ta*, from which is derived *Haggadah*, the book that contains the prayers and blessings, legends and commentaries, psalms and songs that are traditionally recited at the Passover seder.

In addition to specifying the foods and rituals required for the seder, the Mishnah (Pes. 10:4) set out four questions that children should ask their parents about this ceremony. In turn, parents are advised to answer their children according to their level of understanding. Over the years, these answers became an anthology of biblical, talmudic, and midrashic sources, which were added to the prescribed order of blessings and rituals and codified into a precise order during the Middle Ages. In addition, the *Haggadah* includes various psalms, table hymns, and popular folksongs calculated to appeal to children.

The redemption of the Exodus is not a mere historical event of the remote past, but rather a symbolic representation of Israel's history to the present day. As the Mishnah teaches (Pes. 116b), "In every generation, a man is bound to regard himself as though he personally had gone forth from Egypt." Extensive discussions on the story are encouraged, for as it is written in the *Haggadah*: "And the more one elaborates on the story of the departure from Egypt, the more he is praiseworthy."

Eating Unleavened Bread on the Evening of Nisan 15 (158)

"In the first month, on the 14th day of the month in the evening, you shall eat unleavened bread" (Exod. 12:18) is the commandment to eat matzah on Passover. Unlike the prohibition against eating *chametz* or even having it in one's possession, which is in force throughout Passover (Neg. Comm. 197-201), the positive duty to eat matzah applies only to the first night (first two nights in the Diaspora). Eating matzah is optional thereafter (Pes. 120a).

The *Haggadah* explains that Jews eat unleavened bread because the dough of their ancestors did not have time to become leavened, since "they were driven out of Egypt and could not delay, nor had they made any provisions for themselves" (Exod. 12:39).

Although a symbol of the newfound freedom of the Israelites, the Bible also describes matzah as *lechem oni* (bread of affliction; Deut. 16:3), the minimal food provided for the Jewish slaves while toiling in bondage under Pharaoh.[202]

Resting on the Festivals (159-160; 162-163; 165-167)

The commandments to resting on the first (**159**) and seventh (**160**) days of Passover, Shavuot (**162**), Rosh Hashanah (**163**), Yom Kippur (**165**), the first day of Sukkot (**166**), and Shemini Atzeret (**167**) are derived from the phrase that introduces each festival, "You shall have a holy convocation [*mikrah kodesh*]" (cited, respectively, in Lev. 23:7; 23:8; 23:21; 23:24; 26:31; 23:35, and 23:36).

By rabbinic ordinance, all the festivals specifically listed above are observed in the Diaspora for two days instead of only one, with the sole exception of Yom Kippur (since fasting for two consecutive days was thought to be too difficult). In the Land of Israel, all these festivals are observed for only one day, with the exception of Rosh Hashanah, which is observed even there for two days.[203]

Passover is celebrated for eight days in the Diaspora, but for only seven days in the Land of Israel. After the first day of Passover (or the second day in the Diaspora), there are a varying number of intermediate days (*hol ha-mo'ed*; "non-sacred" days). In the Land of Israel, five days of *hol ha-mo'ed* are observed before the seventh day of the festival; in the Diaspora, there are four days of *hol ha-mo'ed* before the final two festival days.

Shavuot is observed for one day in the Land of Israel and two in the Diaspora, despite the fact that its precise date could never have been in doubt, even in ancient times—because it always falls on the 50th day from the beginning of the counting of the Omer on the second day of Passover. Originally a spring harvest festival celebrating the ripening of the first wheat in Israel, according to rabbinic tradition Shavuot commemorates the Revelation at Mount Sinai, when God gave the Torah to the Israelites.

On Sukkot (also called Tabernacles), six intermediate days are observed in the Land of Israel and five in the Diaspora. The single day of Shemini Atzeret (Eighth Day of Assembly) was added to the festival of Sukkot. Because *atzeret* comes from a root meaning "to hold back," the Rabbis deemed that God instituted this holiday so that all those who made the pilgrimage to Jerusalem for Sukkot would remain with Him in the city for one additional day (or as Rashi wrote, like a "small banquet made by the King for His beloved"). Maimonides explained that this eighth day was added so that Jews "complete our rejoicings, which cannot be perfect in booths [sukkot], but in well-built houses."[204] In post-talmudic times, a ninth festival day (Simchat Torah, or Rejoicing in the Law) was added after Shemini Atzeret. This has become a joyous celebration on which the annual reading of the Torah is completed and then immediately restarted.

In Babylonia, the talmudic Sages contemplated eliminating the second day of festivals as soon as a permanent calendar was fixed. In our day, the Reform movement has dropped the second day of festivals and there has been some debate in the Conservative movement about following suit, primarily based on the realization that the overwhelming majority of its members do not observe both days.

According to Maimonides, [205] work is permissible on *hol ha-mo'ed*. Those rabbis who disagreed were lenient when financial loss could be caused by delays, though they discouraged heavy labor and work deliberately deferred to the intermediate days. The days of *hol ha-mo'ed* are still festive days, marked by liturgical changes and rejoicing, and it is customary to greet people by saying *mo'adim l'simcha* ("joyous times").

Maimonides considered the injunctions to rest (abstain from work) on festivals as positive commandments, while actually performing work on festivals is a violation of Negative Commandments 323-329.

Counting the Omer (161)

"You shall count from the day of rest on which you bring the sheaf of wave offering (omer), seven complete weeks until ... the fiftieth day" (Lev. 23:15-16). The *omer* (lit., a sheaf) was the measure of the new barley crop that the Israelites were commanded to bring to the Temple as a harvest offering on the 16th of Nisan, the eve of the second day of Passover (Pos. Comm. 44). Until this time, the Israelites could not eat bread, roasted grain, or fresh ears of the new barley crop (Neg. Comm. 189-191). Each Israelite was responsible for counting the 49 days of the Omer, which repre-

sent the seven weeks between the anniversary of the departure from Egypt and the receiving of the Torah at Mount Sinai. Maimonides[206] stressed that the giving of the Law was the ultimate aim of the Exodus, not merely the deliverance from bondage in Egypt. "To emphasize the importance of this day [Shavuot], we count the days that pass from the preceding festival [Passover], just as one who expects his most intimate friend on a certain day begins to count the days and even the hours."

The season between Passover and Shavuot is known as the *Sefirah* (time of counting). The Omer period is observed as a period of semi-mourning. Traditional Jews do not get haircuts, celebrate weddings, or play musical instruments during this time (except for the 33rd day; see below). Initially, these restrictions may have been related to the intense anxiety felt by the Israelites during the vulnerable weeks leading up to the harvest.[207] Ultimately, however, the mourning was connected to a "plague" that killed 24,000 disciples of R. Akiva's students during that time (Yev. 62b). This may refer to the overwhelming defeat suffered by the forces of Bar Kochba, whom Akiva strongly supported in the unsuccessful rebellion against the Romans. Tradition maintains that the plague ceased on Lag ba-Omer (the 33rd day), possibly an allusion to the brief recapture of Jerusalem that is said to have occurred on this date.

A popular custom during the Omer period is the study of the mishnaic tractate *Pirkei Avot* (Ethics of the Fathers). Beginning after Passover, one of its six chapters is studied each Sabbath following the afternoon service. In this way, the final chapter dealing with the Torah is read just before Shavuot, the festival commemorating the Revelation at Mount Sinai. Most Ashkenazic congregations repeat the entire treatise three times until the Sabbath before Rosh Hashanah.

Fasting on Yom Kippur (164)

The rabbis interpreted the Torah commandment that on Yom Kippur *"You shall afflict your souls"* (Lev. 16:29) to refer to those activities on which life depends— abstinence from eating and drinking (Neg. Comm. 196). According to Maimonides, the tradition also forbids washing, anointing oneself, wearing shoes, and marital intercourse (Yoma 73b), based on the repetition of the phrase "You shall afflict your souls" in conjunction with "It is a Sabbath of solemn rest to you" (Lev. 16:31), which also implies the requirement to abstain from work of all kinds including care of the body.

Those who are seriously ill and would endanger their lives by fasting are exempted from this commandment and obligated to eat, according the principle of *pikuach nefesh* (saving of life). Even a healthy person seized by a fit of "ravenous hunger" that causes faintness must be fed on Yom Kippur with whatever food is available until he recovers. According to tradition, children under the age of nine and women in childbirth (from the time labor begins until three days after birth) are forbidden to fast even if they want to.[208]

As a general rule, the decision whether to fast on Yom Kippur depends on the subjective opinion of the patient who claims the need to eat, even if contradicted by 100 doctors. Conversely, a patient must eat if a doctor declares that it is essential for health, even if he or she thinks it is not necessary.[209]

Because the gratification of bodily appetites is the major cause of sin, the 25-hour fast of Yom Kippur is evidence that human beings can conquer their physical cravings – that the spirit can master the body.[210] However, fasting is not sufficient in itself to secure atonement. To gain Divine forgiveness, there must be sincere repentance combining contrite confession and a solemn resolve to abandon the ways of evil. Even this repentance only secures atonement for transgressions between human beings and God. As the Talmud notes (Yoma 85b), for transgressions between human beings, Yom Kippur does not effect atonement unless one has sought forgiveness from the other person and redressed the wrongs done to him.

Dwelling in a Booth During Sukkot (168)

"You shall dwell in booths (sukkot) for seven days" (Lev. 23:42) is the source of the name for the fall holiday of Sukkot. The Hebrew word "sukkot" (singular, sukkah) refers to the hastily constructed, unsubstantial structures that the Israelites set up during their wanderings in the wilderness after the Exodus from Egypt and before their entry into the Promised Land.

The Talmud (Suk. 11b) records a dispute as to whether the sukkot mentioned in the Torah were actual or metaphysical booths, the latter referring to the protective "clouds of glory" that accompanied and sheltered the Israelites during their 49-year journey.[211] Some believe that they originated from the temporary shelters in which workers lived in the fields and vineyards during the harvest season.

The sukkah must be a temporary structure, only strong enough to withstand normal gusts of wind. It must have a minimum of three walls (31 inches or higher), at least two of which must be complete (Suk. 6b). The sukkah may be constructed of any material, though it is usually of wood or canvas suspended on a metal frame. It must be built under the open sky, not under a tree or inside a house. The roof of the sukkah is covered with *s'chach*—plants that cannot be used for food; are in their natural state (i.e., not wooden boards); and are detached from the ground (Suk. 1:4). Therefore, a grape arbor or any growing vine cannot be used. Typically consisting of cut branches or bamboo sticks, the *s'chach* must be arranged so that there is more shade (covered space) than sunshine inside the sukkah during the day (Suk. 9b-10a). However, it should not be so dense that the stars cannot be seen through it at night. It is customary to decorate the sukkah with colorful fruit, which must remain in place and not be eaten during the festival (Suk. 10a), and with signs quoting verses from the Bible or depicting beautiful scenes from Israel.

The command to dwell in the sukkah during Sukkot has been interpreted by the Rabbis to mean that one must eat, drink, and sleep in it. However, modern rabbinical authorities, recognizing the cold and rainy climates to which Jews have wandered during their long exile, have permitted sleeping and eating inside the house when the weather is bad.[212] Not only is a person not obliged to sleep or eat in the sukkah when rain penetrates the roof, but one is forbidden to do so, for it is improper to insist on carrying out a religious duty from which there is exemption.

The sukkah has become a general symbol of Divine protection, as in the evening prayer that asks God to "spread over us the 'sukkah' of Your peace" (*sukkat sh'lomecha*). The Midrash (Gen. R. 48:10) states that God protected the Israelites in sukkot during their journey in the wilderness because of the shelter that their father Abraham had provided to the three strangers beneath a tree on his land (Gen. 18:2-5). Maimonides declared that a person should remember his bad times in his days of prosperity, so as to be induced to lead a modest and humble life. Therefore, on Sukkot Jews leave their comfortable homes and dwell in simple booths exposed to the elements to remind them that this once was their condition in the desert.[213] Similarly, the festival stresses that material wealth is transitory; the only possessions that a person can amass for all eternity are the future spiritual rewards for living righteously and performing mitzvot during one's relatively short physical life.[214]

Four Species (Taking the Lulav) on Sukkot (169)

"On the first day, you shall take the fruit of goodly trees, branches of palm trees, boughs of thick trees, and willows of the brook, and you shall rejoice before the Lord your God seven days" (Lev. 23:40). According to tradition, the four species specified in this commandment refer to the etrog (citron), the lulav (palm tree), and sprigs of myrtle and willow trees. The lulav, myrtle, and willow are bound together and held in the right hand, while the etrog is taken in the left (Suk. 37b). Holding all together, the person says the appropriate blessing and then waves the four species in all four directions (east, south, west, north), as well as upward and downward, indicating that the presence of God is everywhere and acknowledging the Divine rule over nature (ibid.). As the appropriate blessing is for *"netilat lulav,"* Maimonides termed this positive commandment "taking the lulav."

In the Temple, Kohanim carrying the four species circled in a procession around the Altar once each day during the first six days of Sukkot, and seven times on the seventh day, Hoshana Rabbah. Today, similar processions are made around the synagogue, except on the Sabbath.

The rabbis viewed the four species in symbolic terms. The *etrog* is shaped like the heart, which the ancients believed was the seat of a person's intelligence; the *lulav* is like a person's spine, reminding us of the rabbinic ideal that the normal posture at prayer is to stand erect before God; the *myrtle* is shaped like an eye, implying that one should never go straying after temptations that one sees on the day of his heart's rejoicing; and the *willow* is like the lips, which a person should hold in restraint (lest it lead to idle talk and falsehoods) while focusing solely on being in awe of God.

The *etrog*, which has both a taste and a pleasant aroma, symbolizes one who possesses both scholarship and good deeds; the *lulav*, a branch of the date palm whose fruit has a taste but no aroma, symbolizes a scholar who is deficient in good deeds; the *myrtle*, which has no taste but does have an aroma, symbolizes a person who is deficient in Torah; and the *willow*, which lacks both taste and aroma, symbolizes a person who has neither scholarship nor good deeds (Lev. R. 30:12). The four species are held together while making the blessing because all sorts of people must be united in the community of Israel, and the failings of one are compensated for by the virtues of the others.

The four species remind us of the four great kingdoms that conquered the Jews and afflicted them greatly—Babylon, Persia, Greece, and Rome. Just as the Jews endured these powerful oppressors, so shall they survive others with the help of God.[215]

Finally, each of the four species represents one of the ancestors of the Jewish people. The etrog, a beautiful fruit, is compared to Abraham, who had a beautiful and fruitful old age. The lulav, whose Hebrew name stems from a root meaning "to bind," is compared to Isaac, who was bound and willing to be offered as a sacrifice. The myrtle, thick with leaves, is compared to Jacob, who was blessed with many offspring. The willow dries up quickly and is compared to Joseph, who perished before all his brothers. The four species are held together so that Jews gain Divine blessings because of the merits of their ancestors—Abraham, Isaac, Jacob, and Joseph.[216]

Hearing the Shofar on Rosh Hashanah (170)

"In the seventh month, on the first day of the month ...it shall be a day of blowing the horn for you" (Num. 29:1) is the commandment to hear the sounding of the shofar on Rosh Hashanah. Traditionally, the shofar recalls the ram that Abraham sacrificed in place of his son Isaac, and the Akedah, or Binding of Isaac (Gen. 22), is the Torah portion read for the second day. Blowing the ram's horn is to remind God of the merits earned by our

ancestors Abraham and Isaac—who were willing to unquestion-
ably obey the Divine command—with the hope that this will
tip the scales of judgment in our favor.

Maimonides[217] stressed that the sound of the shofar is a call
for the people to awaken from their sleep, to search their deeds,
and ultimately to repent for the sins that they have committed.

In the tenth century, Saadia Gaon offered ten reasons for
sounding the shofar. In addition to the ones already mentioned,
he suggested that it was (a) to proclaim the sovereignty of God
on Rosh Hashanah, the anniversary of Creation; (b) to remind
us of the Revelation at Mount Sinai, where the ram's horn was
sounded; (c) to announce the beginning of the period of repentance, to warn people against transgressing; (d) as a reminder
of the warnings of the prophets, who raised their voices like the
shofar to touch our consciences; (e) to remind us of the alarms
of battle that accompanied the destruction of the Temple; (f) to
cause us to be in awe of Heaven and obey the will of God, for
as Amos (3:6) asked, "Shall the horn be blown in a city, and
the people not tremble?"; (g) to remind us of the great Day of
Judgment, when the horn will be sounded as a summons to
the Heavenly Court (Zeph. 1:14, 16); (h) as a reminder that the
shofar will herald the ingathering of Israel's scattered remnants
to return to the Holy Land in the Messianic Age (Isa. 27:13);
and (i) to remind us of the revival of the dead.[218]

According to the Talmud (RH 27a), the ritual commandment to hear the sound of the shofar on Rosh Hashanah can
be fulfilled using a shofar made from an antelope, gazelle,
goat, mountain goat, or ram. All of these are kosher animals
that have horns with removable cartilage. This second feature
is important because a shofar must be hollow, since it is derived from the word *shefoferet* meaning "tube." The Talmud
explicitly forbids using a cow's horn because it is known as
a "keren," not a "shofar," adding that it is forbidden because

our advocate on Rosh Hashanah should not be a reminder of the Golden Calf, our great sin and accuser. We do not want our past transgressions to prejudice God against forgiving our current sins ("the accuser may not act as defender;" RH 26a).

The Rabbis originally decreed that the shofar be blown during the main service of Rosh Hashanah, which in their day was the morning service. Later, this practice was changed, so that the sounding of the shofar and the reading of the biblical verses connected to it were postponed until much later in the day during the *Musaf* (additional) service. An explanation for this delay is that on one occasion the Romans, assuming that the early morning shofar blast was a signal for an uprising against them, attacked the Jews and killed them. Consequently, the decision was made to sound the shofar later in the day to prevent any misunderstanding, for at that time it could only be construed as part of a religious ritual. However, delaying the shofar service meant that the main commandment of the day was not performed until a relatively late hour. To solve this problem, the rabbis added an additional blowing of the shofar at the conclusion of the Torah service—the custom that is still practiced today.

There are three distinct sounds of the shofar—*tekiah* (a single long blast); *teru'ah* (a wailing sound of three broken notes); and *shevarim*, a series of nine short staccato notes. Traditionally, 100 shofar blasts are blown each day of Rosh Hashanah. According to legend, this is equal to the number of sobs of Sisera's mother as recounted in the Song of Deborah (Judg. 5:28) and designed to show that, just as Jews were sensitive to the tears of the mother of an arch enemy, so we hope God will be sensitive to our tears and judge us mercifully on the High Holy Days.

The shofar is not blown on the Sabbath. Rather than a manifestation of the prohibition against playing musical instruments on that day, the shofar is not sounded because of the danger that an inexperienced blower might seek help from a more experienced one, thus violating the law of carrying on the Sabbath.

The shofar is also blown at the conclusion of the daily morning service (but not on the Sabbath) during the month of Elul, which precedes Rosh Hashanah. According to tradition, the first of Elul was the day when Moses ascended Mount Sinai in preparation for receiving the second tablets 40 days later on Yom Kippur. Because the second tablets represented the reconciliation between God and Israel after the sin of the Golden Calf, sounding the shofar is a reminder that the month of Elul is also a time of favor in our day.[219]

Giving a Half-Shekel Annually (171)

When Moses took a census of the Israelite males 20 years and older who were eligible to fight in the army, it was commanded that *"This they shall give, every one that passes among those that are numbered, half a shekel"* (Exod. 30:13). The shekel was a specific weight of silver that Moses instituted as the standard coinage.

The threefold use of the word *terumah* (portion) in this passage led the Rabbis to deduce that there were three separate gifts of silver (Shek. 1:1; Meg. 29b). Two required gifts of a half shekel each included an annual contribution to the cost of purchasing the animals that were offered twice daily by the Kohanim on behalf of the Jewish people, and a one-time donation of silver needed to construct the sockets on which the walls of the Tabernacle rested (Exod. 26:19). The third gift was a voluntary contribution for the construction of the Tabernacle and its utensils.[220]

Once the Israelites had entered the Land of Israel, biblical law mandated that each man pay an annual levy of a half shekel for the maintenance of the Sanctuary. The qualification that "the rich shall not pay more and the poor shall not pay less" indicated that the Tabernacle belonged to the entire community, without regard to wealth or social status, since all were equal in the eyes of God. The half-shekel tax also taught the moral lesson that one Jew alone is only half a Jew; one must join with another Jew to becomes a complete individual.[221] The Mishnah reported that the Jew of the Second Temple period, whether he lived in the Land of Israel or in the remotest corner of the Diaspora, cherished this commandment as a sacred privilege and as a means of participating in the public offerings brought daily in the house of God in Jerusalem.[222]

In ancient days, the annual half-shekel contributions were collected during the month of Adar. This is commemorated in synagogues today by reading the relevant Torah portion on the Sabbath that falls on or immediately precedes the first of Adar (*Shabbat Shekalim*). Just before reading the *Megillah* on the eve of Purim (which occurs in Adar), it is customary to donate three half-dollars to charity.

Heeding the Prophets (172)

"A prophet ... unto him shall you hearken" (Deut. 18:15) is the commandment to listen to every prophet and do whatever he bids. The phrase "from your midst, among your own people" in the middle of the verse was interpreted to mean that prophecy would be limited to the Land of Israel and to members of the Children of Israel.[223]

The competence of a prophet was not unlimited. He was bound by the laws of the Torah, to which he could neither add nor subtract except as a temporary measure of extreme urgency.[224] Maimonides[225] noted that any attempt to make such a change permanent would label him a false prophet and liable to death by strangulation. With respect to commandments relating to idolatry, any attempt to suspend them even temporarily would brand him as a false prophet to be punished by death (Neg. Comm. 26-29).[226]

A supposed prophet who predicted a certain event that did not occur was deemed a false prophet, despite any other miracles he may have performed or previous prophecies that had occurred.[227]

Appointing a King (173)

"You shall surely set a king over yourself"(Deut. 17:15) is the commandment to appoint a king who would unify and lead the nation. It was explicitly stated that the king would be a person "whom God shall choose" and not a foreigner. Along with building the Temple (Pos. Comm. 20) and eliminating the offspring of Amalek (Pos. Comm. 189-190), appointing a king was one of the three commandments of the nation of Israel once it was established in the Promised Land.

Almost all commentators have viewed the idea of a monarchy as contrary to the essential nature of Judaism. However, they concluded that the Torah included a series of rules related to a future king because God foresaw that the Israelites would eventually demand a king so that they could "be like all the other nations."[228] The king was required to write a copy of the Torah (Pos. Comm.17), had to be a native Israelite (Neg. Comm. 362), and was limited in the number of horses he could own, wives he could marry, and personal wealth he could amass (Neg. Comm. 363-365).

Obeying the Great Court (174)

"You shall act according to the teaching that they will teach you and according to the judgment that they will say to you" (Deut. 17:11) is the injunction to follow the rulings of the judges of the High Court at the Central Sanctuary concerning whether things are forbidden or permissible. This court dealt with those cases that were too difficult for the local courts (Deut. 17:8).

In talmudic times, the Great Sanhedrin was composed of 71 judges who sat in the Temple in Jerusalem. This corresponded to the 70 elders and officers who assisted Moses in dispensing justice during the biblical period (Num. 11:16–17). Headed by the *nasi* (president), the Great Sanhedrin exercised sweeping judicial, legislative, and executive powers.

According to Maimonides, this commandment laid down the basis for the authority in Judaism of the Oral Law, which has come down to us from the Great Sanhedrin throughout all succeeding generations and was finally preserved in the Talmud.[229]

Each person was enjoined to strictly obey the decisions of the Court, even if convinced that they were in error (Neg. Comm. 312). This is implied from the verse "You shall not deviate from the word that they will tell you, right or left" (Deut. 17:11), which numerous commentators interpreted as meaning that the rulings of the Court must be followed even if it appears that they were declaring that right is left and left is right.[230]

Abiding by a Majority Decision (175)

"(You are) to follow after a multitude" (Exod. 23:2) is Maimonides' rather free interpretation of the verse that he cites as the source of the commandment to follow the majority if there is a difference of opinion among the rabbis regarding any of the laws of the Torah. Similarly, if there is a difference of opinion in a private lawsuit, the litigants must accept the majority opinion.

The actual verse reads *"You shall not follow a multitude to do evil; neither shall you bear false witness in a dispute to pervert justice in favor of a multitude."* Maimonides apparently interpreted the verse as implying that if one *should not* follow the majority to do "evil," then one *should* follow the majority when it is a matter of doing "not evil" (i.e., the good).

The first part of the verse means that if the majority of judges or witnesses are agreed on an opinion that another judge knows is unjust, he should not abandon his own view in order to fall in line with others. Even if the other judges are more learned, he should not alter his thinking to coincide with theirs, for his own analysis of the case may be superior their theirs.[231] *Sefer ha-Chinuch* adds that automatically accepting the reasoning of another judge, however brilliant, without arriving at the same conclusion through independent thinking, would establish the dangerous situation in which the opinion of a single judge dictates the decisions of an entire court.[232] A single person who has honestly and accurately analyzed the case and arrived at the correct opinion, in combination with God, represents the true majority.

An extension of the principle embodied in this commandment is that a majority decision is binding not only in a court, but also in all aspects of public life.[233]

Appointing Judges and
Officers of the Court (176)

"Judges and officers you shall appoint in all of your gates ... and they shall judge the people with righteous judgment" (Deut. 16:18) is the commandment to establish courts throughout the Land of Israel. The rabbis considered the establishment of courts of law one of the seven Noahide laws, which were essential to the existence of any civilized human society (Gen. 9:7). The other six Noahide laws were the prohibition of blasphemy, idolatry, incest, bloodshed, robbery, and the eating of flesh cut from a living animal. Although an Israelite was bound to carry out all the precepts of the Torah, in ancient times obedience to the Noahide laws alone was sufficient for non-Jews who lived among the Israelites or attached themselves to the Jewish community.

The highest court in Israel was the Great Sanhedrin, which was composed of 71 judges. The head of this body was called the *nasi* (president). Communities with fewer than 120 people had a Lesser Sanhedrin composed of 23 judges. If the community was too small to merit even a Lesser Sanhedrin, three judges were appointed to decide minor cases (monetary disputes) and to remit the important ones to the superior court.

According to Maimonides,[234] "judges must be wise and understanding, learned in the law, and versed in many other branches of learning ... such as medicine, mathematics, astronomy and astrology; and the ways of sorcerers and magicians and the superstitious practices of idolaters [so as to be competent to judge them]; ...[a judge must be] neither a very aged man nor a eunuch ... or childless; ... just as he must be free from all suspicion with respect to conduct, so must he be free from all physical defects, ... a man of mature age, imposing statute, and good appearance, and able to express his views in clear and well-chosen words and be conversant with most of the spoken languages ... [so there is no need] of the services of an interpreter." The seven fundamental qualities of a judge are "wisdom, humility, fear of God, disdain of gain [money], love of truth, love of people, and a good reputation." A judge must have "a good eye, a lowly [humble] spirit, must be friendly in intercourse [pleasant in company], and gentleness in speech and dealings with others; he must be very strict with himself and control his passions; he must have a courageous heart to rescue the oppressed from the hand of the oppressor, cruelty, and persecution, and eschew wrong and injustice." According to the Talmud (Sanh. 3:3), those who "are ineligible [to be witnesses or judges include] a gambler with dice [i.e., any type of gambler], a userer [one who loans money at interest], a pigeon-trainer [who races birds], and traders [in the produce] of the Sabbatical Year."

As Maimonides wrote, "judges are to enforce the observance of the Commandments of the Torah; to compel [those] who have strayed from the path of truth to return to it; to command the performance of what is good and the avoidance of that which is evil; and to inflict the penalties on the transgressors, so that the commandments and prohibitions of the Torah shall not be dependent on the will of the individual."[235]

Officers of the court were appointed to execute the decisions of the judges. According to various commentators, they would patrol the streets and markets to ensure honest behavior. Those who violated the law would be brought before the court for a judicial decision.[236]

Treating Litigants Equally Before the Law (177)

"...you shall judge your neighbor fairly [lit., in righteousness]" (Lev. 19:15) is the source of the commandment for judges to treat all litigants fairly and equally and to allow each one to have his say, whether he speaks at length or briefly. During a trial, it is forbidden to allow one party to say all he wishes and then order the other to be brief. One litigant must not be allowed to be seated in court while the other is kept standing. Both parties should appear in similar clothing, lest the judge be favorably disposed to the one wearing more costly garments.[237] The judge must evaluate the case of each person strictly on the basis of merit and refuse to condemn by appearances.

The Mishnah (Avot 1:6) requires each Jew to "judge all men in the scale of merit," which Maimonides interpreted as meaning that "a person is obliged to judge his neighbor [in matters of general conduct] with an inclination in his favor, and always put a good and charitable interpretation on his deeds and words." At first glance, there appears to be a contradiction between the requirement that a judge must be strictly objective while the general populace should make every effort to give other people the benefit of the doubt. Hirsch maintained that a judge in court may not consider factors that may explain the reason for a person's actions but are not sufficient to exonerate him from guilt. However, members of the general public must take into consideration all extenuating circumstances, for one who is liable for damages may not be deserving of condemnation by his peers.[238]

Limitations on judges are described in Neg. Comm. 273, 281, 283, and 286-287.

Testifying in Court (178)

"... *if he does not testify, he is subject to punishment [lit., he shall bear his iniquity]*" (Lev. 5:1) is the commandment requiring a person to provide evidence in court whether it "will ruin the person on trial or save his life or his money." When called by one of the disputing parties as a witness, Jews are "obliged to testify on every point, and to tell the judges what we have seen or heard" concerning the case.

An "adjuration" was a statement addressed to a person allegedly in possession of relevant evidence to come forward and testify. It was accompanied by the pronouncement of a curse upon the person should he remain silent. In context, the biblical verse refers to a person who falsely swore that he had no knowledge of the case and then later admitted he had lied. Interfering with the execution of justice by suppressing evidence was considered a grievous transgression that required expiation through a sin offering.

Maimonides[239] observed that one who caused loss to a litigant by the suppression of testimony would not be prosecuted in an earthly court of law, but was strictly accountable to the higher "law of Heaven." According to *Sefer ha-Chinuch*, "he who suppresses testimony is like one who stands idly by the blood of his neighbor" (Lev 19:16; Neg. Comm. 297).[240]

Inquiring into the Testimony of Witnesses (179)

"*You shall seek out and investigate, and ask diligently; if it is true, the fact is established*" (Deut. 13:15) commands the judge to inquire into the testimony of witnesses and interrogate them rigorously in the greatest possible detail before giving a verdict or inflicting punishment. Meticulous care is required lest the judge render an "ill-considered and hasty decision and so harm an innocent person."

According to the Rabbis (Sanh. 40a), there were seven inquiries by which witnesses were tested: "In what sabbatical cycle [did the matter under consideration take place] ? In what year? In what month? On which day of the month? On what day? At what hour? In what place?" Failure to provide a reasonable response led to his evidence being inadmissible. In cross-examination, however, the witness could be asked a limitless number of questions. Indeed, the Talmud states that "the more exhaustive the cross-examination, the more praiseworthy the judge."[241]

Condemning Witnesses Who Testify Falsely (180)

"You shall do to him as he schemed to do to his fellow; (so shall you destroy the evil from your midst)" (Deut. 19:19) is the commandment to punish witnesses who testify falsely (Neg. Comm. 285) by making them suffer what they sought to inflict on others by means of their testimony. As Maimonides noted, if the testimony was calculated to produce a monetary loss or whipping, the court should inflict on the witness a loss of equal value or the identical number of lashes, respectively. If the false testimony was designed to lead to the death of the accused, the guilty party would suffer the same kind of death – stoning, burning, beheading, or strangling, the four methods of death that could be the sentence of a Jewish court of law (Pos. Comm. 226-229).

Ironically, in capital cases this law was applicable only when the person falsely accused had *not* been put to death. Once the person falsely accused had been executed, witnesses who were proved to have testified falsely were no longer liable under this law. Instead, their punishment was left to Heaven.

The Axed Heifer (181)

"If someone slain is found lying in the field..." (Deut. 21:1) is the

opening line of the commandment relating to the situation in which the victim of an unwitnessed murder was found lying in the open. The Torah required that the elders of the nearest town slay a young heifer in an uncultivated valley with a stream (Deut. 21:4). In conjunction with this public ritual, the elders would testify that they were neither directly nor indirectly culpable for the person's death—"Our hands have not spilled this blood, and our eyes did not see" (Deut. 21:7). Had they only known of his existence, they would have provided the traveler with food and accompanied him on his way. Moreover, they would never have allowed a known murderer to wander in their land. However, Ibn Ezra maintained that the elders bore some responsibility for the murder, since it would never have occurred unless there was some corruption in their town. The elders then prayed for Divine forgiveness for the Jewish people, since murder was also considered a sin against God.[242, 243]

Maimonides suggested that the shocking nature of the crime and the extensive publicity accompanying the ritual might lead to the uncovering of information leading to the identification and capture of the murderer.[244]

The valley where the heifer was slain could never be tilled or sown again (Neg. Comm. 309). As the Rabbis observed (Sot. 46a), "Let the heifer that has never produced fruit have its neck broken in a spot which has never produced fruit, to atone for one [the death of a man] who was not allowed to produce fruit [i.e., have future children]."[245]

Establishing Six Cities of Refuge/ Law of Manslaughter (182, 225)

"You shall separate three cities for yourselves … (and) prepare the way for yourself, and divide the borders of your land" (Deut. 19:2-3) commanded the Israelites to establish six cities of refuge (three on each side of the Jordan) to which a person could flee if he unintentionally

killed another individual (182). This injunction also required the building of wide, level roads with appropriate directional signs to these cities, and the removal of anything obstacles that might hinder the fugitive in his flight (see Num. 35:9-34).

According to the Talmud (Mak. 9b), every person who killed another, "whether he had slain unintentionally or with intent," would immediately flee to a city of refuge to escape the "avenger of the blood," a close relative of the victim who had the right to kill the perpetrator. From the city of refuge, the individual would be sent to the court for trial. If the killing had been completely accidental, the perpetrator would be absolved of any responsibility and set free (and the blood avenger had no right to harm him). If the killing had been intentional, the murderer properly warned in advance, and his act witnessed, the court would order his execution by beheading. If the act was unintentional but associated with some culpable carelessness (i.e., involuntary manslaughter), the perpetrator would be exiled to a city of refuge (225), and the court would be responsible for providing safe passage so that the blood avenger could not kill him on the way.

A perpetrator who had been exiled to a city of refuge by the court was required to remain there until the death of the High Priest (Num. 35:25). According to the Talmud (Mak. 11b), the High Priest bore some responsibility for the death, because his prayers should have been powerful enough to avert such a tragedy as murder occurring in Israel. Maimonides noted that the death of the High Priest was so moving an event that no thoughts of vengeance could arise in the blood avenger.[246]

Assigning Cities to the Levites (183)

"You shall assign to the Levites 48 cities" (Num. 35:7) commanded

the Israelites to provide the Levites with 42 cities, in addition to the six cities of refuge (Pos. Comm.182), in which they could reside. Because members of the tribe of Levi were to devote themselves to the service of God, they received no portion when the Israelites entered the Land. By scattering the levitical cities throughout the land, all parts of the nation were exposed to those responsible for teaching the Divine statutes to the people.

The 48 cities assigned to the Levites did not form a continuous territory, and each remained in the possession of the tribe in whose territory it was situated. Surrounding each levitical city was open space in which it was forbidden to build or cultivate crops (Neg. Comm. 228).

Removing Sources of Danger from our Habitations (184)

"(When you build a new house), you shall make a parapet for your roof, (so that you do not bring blood on your house if anyone should fall from it)" (Deut. 22:8) is the source of the commandment "to remove all obstacles and sources of danger from the places in which we live" (Neg. Comm. 298). Homes in the ancient Middle East had flat roofs, which were used for sleeping, walking, and other household duties. Thus, to prevent one from accidentally falling off the roof it was necessary to erect a barrier, two cubits (three feet) high.[247]

Maimonides noted that this commandment also required the building of "walls or parapets [restraining devices] around cisterns, trenches, and the like, so that no one should fall into them or fall from them." In modern terms, this would require protective barriers around a swimming pool, a tall stairway, or a construction site. Similarly, dangerous structures must be rebuilt or repaired so as to remove all danger. He added that this commandment requires that all people must safeguard their own lives and not place themselves in dangerous situations.[248]

The Rabbis extended this prohibition to such activities as drinking from a polluted stream and putting coins in one's mouth (since germs are usually found on them).[249] According to Maimonides,[250] "one may not put his mouth to a flowing pipe of water and drink from it, or drink at night from rivers or ponds, lest he swallow a leech while unable to see. Nor may one drink water that has been left uncovered, lest he drink from it after a snake or other poisonous reptile has drunk from it, and die." Today, some rabbis have also applied this prohibition to the dangerous practice of smoking cigarettes

The word "blood" in the verse meant that any failure to protect human life exposed the builder, owner, or resident of the house to "blood-guilt" in the eyes of God. The Rabbis extended this to apply to all negligent actions endangering life, such as keeping a dangerous dog or placing a broken ladder against a wall.[251]

Destroying Idolatry (185-187)

Maimonides declared the abolition of idolatry to be "the principal and first object of the whole Law."[252] Indeed, the first 59 of the negative commandments (as listed by Maimonides) are related to banning all vestiges of idolatry and idolatrous practices.

The Israelites were commanded (185) to totally destroy all idol worship and heathen temples in the Land by whatever means necessary, including shattering, burning, and cutting them to pieces (Exod. 34:13; Deut. 7:5, 12:2). The people were even forbidden to befriend idolaters or allow them to dwell in the Land (Neg. Comm. 50-52), lest they seduce Jewish children into following their pagan practice.[253]

The apostate (wayward) city was one that was so spiritually corrupt that all or most of its citizens worshipped idols. The Israelites were commanded (186) to slay all the guilty inhabitants of the city and burn all its property (even that of the non-sinners), leaving it a desolate heap never to be rebuilt (Deut. 13:17). According to Maimonides,[254] this law was virtually impossible to invoke because of the strict conditions limiting its application. For example, when they received a report of idolatry in any city in Israel, the Great Sanhedrin in Jerusalem was obliged to send two sages to warn the population to repent. If those who continued their idolatrous practices constituted less than a majority, the entire city would not be destroyed and only the individual idolaters would be subjected to the penalty of death by stoning.[255]

The Israelites were commanded (187) to "utterly destroy" the Seven Nations that inhabited the Land of Canaan (Deut. 20:17). This edict of extermination referred to the Hittites, Girgashites, Amorites, Canaanites, Perizzites, Hivites, and Jebusites, who were the original idolatrous inhabitants of the Land of Israel (Neg. Comm. 48-49). Nachmanides maintained that the initial purpose behind this draconian law was to prevent any heathen practices from infiltrating into the Jewish community, lest the Israelites be tempted to actually worship idols. However, the Israelites failed to heed this command and permitted many Canaanites to remain in the Land, which led to idolatry becoming widespread among the Jews.[256] Indeed, tradition attributes the destruction of the First Temple to rampant idol worship among the Israelites.

The Extinction of Amalek and Remembering His Evil Deeds (188-189)

"You shall blot out the memory of Amalek (from under the heaven — do not forget!)" (Deut. 25:19) is the commandment (188) to utterly exterminate the seed of Amalek, male and female, young and old. This obligatory war was against the predatory tribe who had perpetrated a cowardly and unprovoked attack on the faint and weary stragglers at the rear of the column of

Israelites, who were exhausted from the march out of Egypt (Exod. 17:8-16).

God instructed the Israelites to destroy the Amalekites whenever the opportunity arose. Hundreds of years later, the prophet Samuel gave this precise order to Saul, the first king of Israel. Saul defeated the Amalekites in battle, but he did not execute their monarch, Agag. For this act of disobedience, God withdrew the kingship from Saul and replaced him with David.[257]

The biblical command to "blot out the name of Amalek" is the source of the popular custom to noisily drown out the name of Haman—the murderous enemy of the Jews and by tradition a descendant of Amalek (Meg. 13a)—each of the 54 times that it occurs during the reading of the *Megillah* on Purim. While any kind of noisemaking device is acceptable, including booing and stamping one's feet on the floor, it is traditional to use a *grager* (rattle) for this purpose. Some even write the name Haman on the soles of their shoes, so as to literally blot out the name as they stomp their feet.

Jews are also commanded (**189**) to *"Remember what Amalek did to you"* (Deut. 25:17). According to Maimonides, this includes frequently speaking of his crimes to provoke the people to wage war on him and to ensure that the bitter hatred of Amalek does not dissipate over time. Today, this commandment is fulfilled by the annual reading of the Torah portion dealing with Amalek on *Shabbat Zachor* (Sabbath of Remembrance), which immediately precedes the feast of Purim when the Book of Esther is read.

The attacks by Amalek against the Israelites appear in the text immediately after a discussion of the need for just weights and measures (Neg. Comm. 272). Commentators have explained that dishonest business practices decrease mutual trust and national unity, so that Jews become vulnerable to the predations of the Amalek of their time.[258]

Laws Related to War (190-193)

In wars against cities other than those belonging to the Seven Nations against whom they were required to make war (Pos. Comm.187), the Israelites were commanded (**190**) to give their enemy an opportunity to make peace (Deut. 20:10). If these peace overtures were accepted, no person or property would be harmed, and the city would become a tributary (paying a fixed yearly sum in taxes, performing national service, and obeying the order of the Israelite king "in fear and humility, as befitted subjects"). Most traditional commentators (excluding Rashi) agreed that these offers of peace had to be made to all enemy cities, even those of the Canaanites. If the inhabitants of the enemy city refused the offer and it was one of the Canaanite nations, everyone had to be destroyed—men, women, and children (Neg. Comm. 49). If it was another nation, the Israelites were commanded to slay all the male population (young and old) and take everything that belonged to them (including the women).

When Israel was preparing to fight a non-obligatory war, the people were commanded (**191**) to appoint a Kohen to rouse the troops and remind them that God would fight for them and save them from their enemies (Deut. 20:2-9). At his urging, the officers would announce that all soldiers who were excessively fearful should not go into combat (lest they adversely affect the morale of their comrades in arms), though they were required to help supply food and water to the troops.[259] Three groups of men were required to be excused from battle: (a) a person who had built a house and not dwelled in it; (b) one who had planted a vineyard and not eaten its fruit; and (c) an individual who had betrothed a woman but not yet married her, or a newlywed during his first year of marriage (Pos. Comm. 214). These people were not only freed from actual military service but were allowed to return home.

The encampment of an Israelite army was to be completely

different from that of any other nation. Because Israel's success was in the hands of God, the camp must be a place of purity, free from dirt and waste, as befitting the Divine Presence.[260] One mechanism for ensuring the cleanliness and sanctity of the camp was the command (192) to reserve a place outside the camp where the troops could go to relieve themselves so that God would not *"see an unseemly thing among you and turn away from you"* (Deut. 23:13). Each soldier was commanded (193) to provide himself with a shovel or paddle in addition to his weapons, so that he could dig up the earth and cover his excrement (Deut. 23:15). Maimonides counted these as two distinct commandments, since the former was the responsibility of the general military unit while the latter was the duty of the individual soldier.[261]

A Robber to Restore the Stolen Article (194)

"He shall restore that which he took by robbery...he shall repay the principal amount and add a fifth to it" (Lev. 5:23-24) is the commandment that a thief "return the actual article which he took by robbery if it is still available, with the addition of a fifth of its value." According to the literal meaning of the text, a thief who stole a wooden plank and incorporated it into his house would be required to return that identical plank, even if its removal would destroy the house. The Rabbis rejected this harsh interpretation and, in an attempt to encourage robbers to repent for their crimes, ruled that it was sufficient to pay full monetary value of the plank. This resulted in the general rule that if the stolen object has undergone a permanent alteration (such as wool that has been woven into a garment), the robber is to pay its equivalent value in money.[262]

The Biblical term "add a fifth" was calculated in a unique way, not the 20% that it would imply today. For example, if the stolen object was worth four shekels, the robber would have to pay a total of five shekels. Thus, the additional amount would be a fifth of the *total* payment.[263]

This same method of calculation also applied to the redeeming of animals, houses, and fields consecrated to the Temple (Pos. Comm. 115-117) and restitution for sacrilege (Pos. Comm. 118).

The punishments for stealing a sheep or an ox are given in Pos. Comm. 239. The prohibition against stealing is Neg. Comm. 245.

Charity (195)

The verse *"For the poor shall never cease out of the land"* (Deut. 15:11) is the biblical recognition of the inevitability of poverty in the real world. Thus there is the commandment to give charity, support the needy, and ease their distress, which is found in multiple verses such as *"You shall surely open your hand to your brother, to your poor, and to the destitute in your Land"* (Deut. 15:11) and *"If your brother becomes impoverished ... you shall uphold [strengthen] him"* (Lev. 25:35).

The Hebrew word for charity (*tzedakah*) literally means "righteousness" and is closely related to the concept of "justice" (as in the famous phrase *tzedek tzedek tirdof*— "justice, justice shall you pursue;" Deut. 16:20). For the Rabbis, charity is not merely a generous or magnanimous act. Rather, it is the performance of a religiously mandated duty to provide something to which the needy have a right. By providing the chance to carry out an important mitzvah, "The poor man does more for the householder [in accepting alms] than the householder does for the poor man [by giving him the charity]" (Lev. R. 34:8). Both wealth and poverty are determined by God, who is the ultimate owner of all human possessions—"Give unto God of what is His, seeing that you and what you have are God's"

(Avot 3:8)—and therefore a person should be willing to give whatever he or she has to fulfill the Divine will.

The general rabbinic principle is that one is required to give a tenth of one's annual income to charity. Although generosity is commendable, they warned against giving away more than one-fifth of one's possessions, lest the person himself risk becoming dependent on charity (Ket. 50a). Even a poor man who lives on charity is obligated to observe the commandment and give charity, however little, to one who is as poor or even poorer than he.

Maimonides[264] offered a list of eight degrees of charity. The highest is giving money to prevent another person from ever becoming poor, such as by offering him a loan or employment or investing in his business. It is much harder for someone to emerge from bankruptcy than for him to be helped before his business fails. Rashi noted that when a donkey's load begins to slip from his back, a single man is capable of adjusting it and keeping the donkey from falling. Once the animal has fallen, however, even five people cannot get it back on its feet.[265]

The second highest level of charity is to give to the poor in such a way that neither the donor nor the recipient knows the identity of the other. In descending order, the next levels of charity are: (3) the donor knows the recipient, but the recipient does not know the donor; (4) the recipient knows the donor, but the donor does not know the recipient; (5) giving directly to a poor person without being asked; (6) giving only after being asked; (7) giving cheerfully but less than one should; and (8) giving grudgingly.

Charity is not only required of the individual Jew, but also is an obligation of the entire community. Indeed, Maimonides[266] observed that: "In every town where there are Jews they must appoint 'charity wardens' (*gabba'ei tzedakah*), men who are well-known and honest, who should collect money from the people before every Sabbath and distribute it to the poor... We have never seen or heard of a Jewish community which does not have a charity fund."

Laws Concerning Hebrew
Bondmen/Bondwomen (196, 232-234)

"If you buy a Hebrew servant" (Exod. 21:2) is the commandment (**232**) to adhere to the regulations concerning Hebrew bondmen. There were two ways in which a Jew could be sold into slavery. A free man could choose to sell himself to escape from extreme poverty (Lev. 25:39), becoming a member of the household of another and earning his food and shelter through his labor; or a thief might be sold by the court to raise funds to pay his victims (Exod. 21:2).

Until a girl reached puberty, an impoverished father had the right to "sell" her to a wealthy family as a bondwoman. However, this practice was designed to be for *her* benefit, because the Torah commanded (**233**) that the purchaser or his son was to marry her (Exod. 21:7-11) or be guilty of a "betrayal." The girl went free (without any redemption payment) in one of three ways: (a) after six years; (b) with the arrival of the Jubilee Year; or (c) when her puberty began.[267]

The duty of redeeming a Hebrew bondmaid fell upon her father (**234**). If neither the master nor his son married her, the father was compelled (despite his poverty) to seek ways and means to redeem her "lest it be a reflection on his family."[268] To facilitate this, the master was required to set an unusually low figure for the value of her remaining years of servitude, thus "assisting in her redemption" (Exod. 21:8).[269]

The master was commanded (**196**) to give generous gifts to Hebrew bondmen and bondwomen when they gained their freedom (Deut. 15:13-14) and not let them leave empty-handed (Neg. Comm. 233). This would help the former servants to make a fresh start in life. This commandment applied only to those forced into slavery by judicial decision, since the phrase *"will be sold to you"* in the opening verse of this section implies that someone else (i.e., the court) did the selling.[270] *Sefer ha-Chinuch* noted that, although this commandment is no longer binding, one should still present gifts to servants when their services are no longer needed.[271]

The negative commandments relating to Hebrew bondmen and bondwomen are 257-262.

Lending Money to the Poor (197)

"When you lend money to any of My people, to the poor person who is with you" (Exod. 22:24) is the commandment to lend money to the poor. Although the Hebrew word *"im"* that begins this verse usually means "if" (which would imply an option), the Torah later makes it unequivocally clear that lending money to the poor is an obligation when it says, "You shall surely lend him whatever he needs" (Deut. 15:8).

According to Kli Yakar, the words "My people" and "who is with you" reflect major reasons why the wealthy should want to lend money to those in need. Because the borrowers are "My people" (God's nation), anyone who assists the poor is effectively contributing to the Divine responsibility of maintaining them and thus is assured that God will repay him. The phrase "with you" means that just as the rich person aids the one who is poor, so that poor person provides a superb opportunity for the rich person to receive a Divine reward for performing the important mitzvah of charity.[272]

This intense feeling toward alleviating the distress of the poor has led to the institution of a Free Loan Society in every well-organized Jewish community.

(The prohibition against charging interest on a loan to a fellow Jew is found in Neg. Comm. 235.)

Interest (198)

"To a foreigner you may lend at interest" (Deut. 23:21) is interpreted by Maimonides as a *command* to exact interest from

non-Jews to whom one lends money. Virtually all other commentators prefer the literal translation, arguing that a Jew is
permitted (but not required) to charge interest to a non-Jew
for a loan.[273] The permission to exact interest from a non-Jew
applied only to money borrowed for commercial purposes.
If a non-Jew needed money for his subsistence, no interest
could be charged.[274]

The Rabbis prohibited courts from admitting the testimony
of usurers, classifying them in the same disreputable category
as thieves and professional gamblers. Ironically, Jews in the
Middle Ages were effectively forced to become usurers, since
they were barred from most other means of earning a living.[275]

A Jew was strictly forbidden to charge or pay interest on
loans to a fellow Jew (Neg. Comm. 235, 236).

Restoring a Pledge to a Needy Owner (199)

"You shall surely restore his pledge to him when the sun sets" (Deut.
24:13; see also Exod. 22:25) is the commandment "to restore a
pledge [security for a loan] to its Israelite owner whenever he
was in need of it." (See Neg. Comm. 240)

Paying Wages on Time (200)

"You must give him his wages on the same day, before the sun sets"
(Deut. 24:15) is the commandment that the wages of a day laborer
must be promptly paid on the day he earns it and not delayed for
another day (Neg. Comm. 238). Similar sentiments are expressed
in the verse "You shall not withhold a worker's wage with you
all night until the morning" (Lev. 19:13). The reason offered is
that the laborer is poor, living from hand to mouth, and needs
to buy food for his family in the evening.[276] Maimonides[277] extended this commandment to require that workmen should be
treated mercifully and not denied any of their rights.[278]

Allowing an Employee to Eat of the Produce Among Which He is Working (201)

"When you enter another man's vineyard, you may eat as many grapes as you want, until you are full, (but you must not put any in your vessel.) When you enter another man's field of standing grain, then you may pluck ears with your hand, (but you must not put a sickle to your neighbor's grain)" (Deut. 23:25-26) is interpreted as the commandment that a laborer must be allowed to eat of the produce among which he is working, provided that it is plucked from a growing plant that is still attached to the soil. Although the biblical verse refers to any passerby, the Rabbis limited this permission to the laborer engaged in harvesting crops, who could eat from them while working but was forbidden from either taking any produce home or giving it to others who were not entitled to take it.[279]

Although the Rabbis permitted a laborer to eat more than the value of his wages, they warned against this practice by noting that "a man should not be so greedy as to shut the door in his face [i.e., make him unable to obtain other employment]" (BM 92a).

Unloading a Tired Animal/Assisting the Owner in Lifting Up His Burden (202-203)

"If you see the donkey of one who hates you lying under its burden ... you shall surely help him" (Exod. 23:5) is the commandment that a person must help unload a beast that has fallen under its burden in the field, even if it belongs to his enemy (Neg. Comm. 270). Indeed, if two individuals who hate each other work together and demonstrate their compassion for the animal, they might even overcome their mutual animosity and become friends. This injunction (202) combines a humanitarian action on behalf of the animal (*tza'ar ba'al chaim*; prevention of pain to living things)[280] and a charitable gesture toward the enemy.[281] According to Maimonides,[282] the prohibition against

causing undue pain to an animal (thus not forming the habit of cruelty) decreases the likelihood of inflicting pain on others and teaches Jews "to show pity and mercy to all living creatures." He noted that unloading the burden from a laboring animal is even permitted on the Sabbath.

If the owner is absent or physically unable to be of assistance, the passerby is responsible for doing it himself. However, if the owner "went, sat down [refused to help] and said since the obligation rests on you to unload, unload [you do it yourself, since it is a commandment], he [the passerby] is exempt" (BM 32b). This is based on the qualifying phrase in the Torah indicating, in the original Hebrew, that the commandment must be performed "*with him*" (i.e., the animal's owner). Kli Yakar extended this principle to apply to any person who is in difficulty, who initially should attempt to help himself and, if unsuccessful, should then seek assistance from others. He condemned those poor people who prefer resorting to charity rather than seeking work that would enable them to support their families and preserve their sense of self-respect.[283]

Just as Jews are commanded to assist in unloading the burden from a tired donkey, they also are enjoined to help a person "to load a burden on his beast or on himself, if he is alone, after it has been unloaded by us or by another." This injunction (**203**) comes from the verse "*You shall surely help him to raise it*" (Deut. 22:4).

The Torah does not permit the acceptance of remuneration for relieving a beast of its burden whenever the animal is experiencing unnecessary suffering. However, payment may be accepted when one assists the owner in lifting up his burden (BM 32b).

Maimonides[284] noted that the commandment to assist in unloading comes in the Torah before that of loading, since the former action aids the animal (removing its burden) as well as the owner. He added that if both a friend and an enemy need assistance at the same time, the enemy takes precedence, even when the latter is unloading and the former is only loading. In this way, a person "should learn to conquer his selfish instincts."[285]

Other commandments that express the concern of Judaism for the welfare of animals include Pos. Comm. 148 and Neg. Comm. 218, 219.

Returning Lost Property to its Owner (204)

The commandment to return lost property to its owner is derived from the verses "*If you encounter an ox of your enemy or his donkey wandering, you shall surely bring it back to him*" (Exod. 23:4) and "*... you shall surely bring them back to your brother*" (Deut. 22:1). The finder is required to care for the lost article he has found until it is claimed by its owner (BM 29b) and is not permitted to "shut his eyes" to lost property (Neg. Comm. 269). Talmudic examples include unrolling and reading a scroll and shaking a garment every 30 days. Indeed, this commandment was interpreted as also requiring each person to care for the possessions of others.

The Talmud brands as a thief any person who finds a lost object or animal and does not attempt to return it to its rightful owner. The finder must make a public announcement and return the item to a person who can describe its identifying signs or provide evidence of ownership. If the lost property lacks identifying marks and is found in a public place or appears abandoned (e.g., spilled fruit along a road), it is deemed ownerless and can be taken by the finder (BM 25b, 28a-b).[286]

This commandment applies to the property of both a friend and an enemy. Bahya ibn Pakuda viewed it as fulfilling the biblical injunction to "love you neighbor as yourself" (Lev. 19:18); because property is an extension of the human being, loving your neighbor means safeguarding all that is of importance to him.

Rebuking a Sinner (205)

"You shall surely admonish your neighbor, and not incur any guilt [lit., bear a sin] because of him" (Lev. 19:17) is the commandment to criticize "one who is sinning or is disposed to sin, to forbid him to act so and to reprove him." This commandment is binding on everyone, "so that an inferior ... must rebuke a man of high rank, even if he is met with curses and insults." Of course, a reproof must be kindly administered with delicacy and tact. Whenever possible it should be done in private, for shaming a person in public is a mortal sin, and the verse states that "you shall not bear sin because of him" (Neg. Comm. 303).

Criticism should never be offered haughtily or lightly, but always with the deepest regard for the feelings of others and a sincere desire to help, support, and benefit the recipient. Indeed, to refrain from admonition may indicate a lack of caring or involvement. If one sees a person traveling down a self-destructive or harmful path, be it physical or spiritual, love for that individual requires action. True caring does not always afford the taking of a "live and let live" approach (Pinchas Lipner). As noted in Proverbs (24:25), "To them who admonish shall come delight, and a good blessing shall come to them."

The goal of this commandment is either to prevent the person from sinning or, if he has already committed a transgression, to inspire him to repent for his actions. Maimonides[287] wrote that, just as "all the prophets admonished Israel for their sins until they were brought to repentance," so each community should appoint a great scholar, whom the people love and respect, "to admonish them and lead them to repentance."

Love Your Neighbor (206)

"You shall love your neighbor as yourself" (Lev. 19:18) is the commandment to let the honor, property, and desires of other hu-

man beings be as dear to you as your own. R. Akiva declared this commandment "a fundamental principle of the Torah." His contemporary, Ben Azzai, stressed that it should be read in conjunction with the verse describing human beings as being created in the image of God, so as to emphasize the essential brotherhood of man. As the Talmud (JT Hag. 2:1) states, "He who elevates himself at the expense of his neighbor has no portion in the World to Come."

The negative form of this commandment is presented in the well-known story of the heathen scoffer who asked Hillel to condense the entire Law in the shortest form possible (while standing on one foot). Hillel replied, "What is hateful to you do not do to your neighbor," followed by "this is the whole Torah, the rest is commentary; now go and learn!" (Shab. 31a).

The commandment to love your neighbor is the basis for numerous important rabbinic ordinances relating to social obligations. Maimonides[288] observed that it was the foundation of such activities as visiting the sick, consoling the mourners, attending to the dead, escorting guests, dowering the bride, cheering the bride and groom, and providing for newlyweds. This principle also is the basis for requiring that criminals subjected to execution suffer the least painful death (Ket. 37b; Sanh. 45a) and the prohibition of a husband putting his wife into a situation in which she might seem disgusting to him (forbidding "performing his marital duties in the day time" because "he might observe something repulsive in her and she would thereby become loathsome to him"; Nid. 17a).[289]

Nachmanides wrote that it is impossible to truly love others as much as oneself. Therefore, the commandment must merely mean that one wish that others receive the same blessings and good fortune that one desires for himself (since envy and jealousy breed hatred), and that a person treat others with respect and consideration.[290]

It must be remembered, however, that the commandment is to love your neighbor "as" and not "more than" yourself. Thus, regard for self has a legitimate place. Hillel stated, "If I am not for myself, who will be for me?" just before saying "And if I am only for myself, what am I?" One classic rabbinic story (BM 62a) describes two men in the desert, with a small amount of water in the possession of one of them. If he drinks it, he will reach civilization; but if the two of them share it, both will die. Ben Petura said that both should drink, but R. Akiva disagreed, arguing that your own life takes precedence over the life of your fellow man. He could not justify having two die when only one death was necessary, observing that if the Torah had meant that a man was required to love his neighbor to the extent of sacrificing his life for him in all circumstances, the commandment would have been phrased to love your neighbor "more than" yourself.

Loving the Stranger (207)

"You shall love the stranger [ger], for you were strangers in the land of Egypt" (Deut. 10:19) is one of the many citations in the Torah that commands us to protect the alien—one who was born elsewhere but is residing in Israel. The explicit reason for this commandment is that the Jews knew from bitter experience the lowly position and frequent oppression of the stranger and could sympathize with his often-desperate plight in contemporaneous cultures. Samson Raphael Hirsch noted that the way a society treats the stranger is a test of its moral and ethical values. In view of their long history of persecution and desire to remain a holy people, Jews should be especially sensitive to the suffering of aliens and are obliged to love them simply because they are fellow human beings and creations of God.

In later Hebrew, the word *"ger"* (stranger) came to mean a person who had voluntarily adopted the Jewish religion and had become part of the Jewish people. It is forbidden to taunt converts by reminding them of their non-Jewish past and suggesting that this makes them unfit to study God's Torah (Neg. Comm. 252-253). Indeed, according to Resh Lachish, "the stranger who accepts the Torah from inner conviction is to be rated higher than the hosts of Israelites who stood at Mount Sinai and accepted the Torah when they heard the thunder and saw the lightning" (Midrash Tanhuma). At the time of the Rabbis, more stress was laid on learning and piety of the individual that on his birth and ancestry. For example, the great sages R. Akiva and R. Meir were both descendants of converts (Yoma 71b; Git 56a).

The Law of Weights and Balances (208)

"Yo shall have just balances, honest weights, a true ephah, and an accurate hin" (Lev. 19:36) is the commandment to have honest weights, scales, and measures and to regulate them with extreme precision. An "ephah" was the standard dry measure (somewhat larger than a bushel), and the "hin" was a measure for liquids (one sixth of an *ephah*, or about 1.25-1.5 gallons).[291] A grain merchant was required to wipe his measuring vessel clean at least once every 30 days, so that he always sold the exact amount and not less (BB 88a).

The rationale for this injunction is given at the end of the verse—"I am the Lord your God who brought you out of Egypt." God had delivered the Israelites from a land where they suffered from injustice; thus they should not deal unjustly with others. Baal ha-Turim labeled those who violate this law as rebels against God and all the commandments, because no person should pretend to serve God while at the same time misleading other people.[292] According to Judaism, dishonesty in business is not merely a legal crime but also a religious transgression against the will of God. The Babylonian teacher

Rava said that on Judgment Day the first question God asks is: "Were you reliable in your business dealings?"

In Babylonia, R. Papa argued that the rule no longer applied, since the secular governing authorities controlled the weights and measures, and those utensils without the appropriate seals and marks could never be used. However, the Talmud (BM 89b) disagreed, on the grounds that a customer calling at twilight when people are in a hurry might accidentally accept a faulty measure. Therefore, the Jewish communities in both Babylonia and the Land of Israel appointed special market commissioners to control weights and measures.

The Rabbis insisted that the sin of falsifying weights (Neg. Comm. 271-272) was more serious than incest. Incest is also a sin against God, so repentance is possible; however, when one cheats people through the use of false weights, the sin is primarily against his fellows. Because of the impossibility of making restitution to countless unknown victims, his repentance is doomed to remain imperfect (BB 82b). The Rabbis compared the person who falsifies weights to a judge who perverts justice (Lev. 19:35) and thus brings about the same five catastrophic results – defiles the land, profanes the Name, causes the Divine Presence to depart, and causes Israel to fall by the sword and to be exiled from their Land (*Sifra* Lev. 19:35).

Honoring Scholars and the Aged (209)

"You shall rise before the aged and honor the presence of a sage" (Lev. 19:32) is the commandment to show respect for sages and the elderly, who in ancient times were honored for their wisdom and life experiences. The rabbinic attitude to the elderly is well expressed in *Pirkei Avot* (4:26), which states: "A person who learns from the young is compared to one who eats unripe grapes and drinks wine from a vat, whereas a person who learns from the old is compared to one who eats ripe grapes

and drinks wine that is aged." The Midrash (Lev. R. 25) relates the tale of a king who, when standing up to honor an elderly commoner, would say: "God has chosen to reward him [with long life]; how can I not do the same?"[293]

Rashi maintained that the commandment is to rise and honor a sage who is *both* elderly and righteous. However, the *halachah* disagrees, considering each half of this verse to be a separate commandment. According to this view, it is necessary to rise for and honor any person over the age of 70, even if not learned; and to rise for and honor a sage, even if young. All agree that this requirement does not apply when seeing a wicked person.[294]

According to Maimonides, this commandment was especially obligatory for a disciple, who owed the ultimate respect to his teacher and had the duty of both honoring and respecting him. Although the Torah explicitly commands one to honor and respect one's father (Pos. Comm. 210, 211), "the duty to one's teacher is greater." When a teacher dies, his disciple must rend his garments in mourning, as for a close relative. The Mishnah (BM 33a) notes that if a person's father and teacher are in captivity (or other serious condition), he must help his teacher first, "for his father [only] brought him into this world, whereas his teacher who taught him wisdom brings him into the World to Come." However, a father who is learned in Torah has precedence over a teacher.

The Rabbis taught that the obligation to respect the aged transcends race or religion (Kid. 33a). However, one must not always defer to the views of the elderly. When considering a halachic issue, the most important factor was the strength of a person's proof and analysis, because "a decision of law depends not on the teacher's age but on his reasoning"(BB 142b).

Honoring and Respecting Parents (210-211)

"Honor your father and your mother, (so that your days may be long upon the land that God is giving you) " (Exod. 20:12) and *"You shall*

revere [fear] your mother and your father" (Lev. 19:3) are, respectively, the commandments to honor (**210**) and respect (**211**) parents. Honoring parents is the fifth of the Ten Commandments, and one of only two for which a reward (i.e., length of days) is promised to one who observes it. Saadia Gaon observed that honoring parents and taking care of them in their old age will inspire one's own children to do the same. Thus the person can look forward to enjoying a long life and a comfortable old age, surrounded by the loving care of his or her own sons and daughters.[295]

According to the Rabbis, *honoring* one's parents means serving them, providing them with food and drink, clothing, and shelter, and assisting them when they are too old and infirm to walk. Respect for one's parents forbids any act that might offend them or reduce the esteem in which they are held. Thus a child may not sit in their regular places, interrupt them, insolently challenge their statements, or call them by their first names. These filial responsibilities extend beyond the grave, for the child is obligated to say *Kaddish* in memory of a departed parent for eleven months and on the annual anniversary of his or her death. *Respecting* parents means to treat them as if they were rulers with the power to punish those who treat them disrespectfully.

In the version of the Decalogue in Exodus, the father is mentioned before the mother and "honor" is the word used. In contrast, in Deuteronomy the word used is often translated as "fear" and the mother is listed first. This reflects the difference in the relationships between the child and each parent. The father is generally the disciplinarian, while the mother is typically the parent who is more associated with kindness and affection. Consequently, it would be natural for the child to "love" the mother but "stand in awe" before the father. Therefore, the Torah insists that the child show love (honor) and reverence (fear) to both.[296]

The Hebrew words used for "honor/love" and "respect/fear"

in these verses are the same as those used in describing attitudes that human beings are required to display toward God. For the child, mother and father are more than ordinary mortals. Thus this commandment serves as the connecting link between the first four (duties toward God) and the final five (duties to other human beings). According to the sages, God says that honoring, fearing, or cursing one's parents is equal to honoring, fearing, or cursing Him.

The commandment to honor parents is placed just after the injunction to remember the Sabbath and keep it holy. Just as a person is required to honor the Sabbath to praise God for His works of Creation, so honoring one's parents is a reminder of God's partnership in creating a child.

It was strictly forbidden to curse or strike a parent (Neg. Comm. 318-319).

Be Fruitful and Multiply (212)

"Be fruitful and multiply, (fill the earth and subdue it)" (Gen. 1:28), is the first commandment in the Torah. It obligates a man to marry, build a home, and raise a family. Maimonides states that the purpose of this injunction is to perpetuate the species, while *Sefer ha-Chinuch* says the requirement to bear children reflects God's desire to have the world inhabited with people who can fulfill His commandments. According to the Mishnah (Yev. 6:6), each married couple must have at least one son and one daughter to fulfill this commandment. However, both law and historical practice urge Jews to have as many children as possible (Yev. 62b), Of course, couples who cannot have children naturally are exempt from the commandment; they may pursue fertility treatments, but are not obligated to do so.[297]

The commandment to procreate applies only to men. Therefore, if a husband and wife both deliberately refrain from having children, it is only the man who is culpable. Similarly, only a man is obligated to marry. Whereas a woman is permitted to marry a eunuch, a man must marry a woman capable of being a mother.[298]

According to the Rabbis, even if a man has reached the age when he can no longer father children, he has a duty to marry so that he will not devote time to sexual diversion. Although Jewish law does not require a woman to marry, she should do so even after her child-bearing days are over so that she not be suspected of participating in immoral activities.[299]

Traditionally (Yev. 6:6), if a couple was married for 10 years without children, a man was permitted to divorce her and marry a second wife to be able to fulfill the commandment to procreate.

The Law of Marriage (213)

"When a man takes a wife, and marries her" (Deut. 24:1) is considered the commandment regarding the marriage ceremony. Initially interpreted as indicating that a woman could be "acquired" by intercourse (i.e., physically taken), the Rabbis (Kid. 12a) explicitly prohibited this practice as a breach of decency and "in order to curb licentiousness."

There were two other biblical ways to contract a binding marriage. The next verse in this chapter "and she leaves his house and went and marries another man " (Deut. 24:2) teaches that just as her "going out" (divorce) is accomplished by her husband handing her a writ (get), so a woman can become a man's wife by a formal document ratifying the marriage. Finally, a man can marry a woman by making her a gift of definite monetary value. This is derived from the verse "(Then she shall go out free), without payment" (Exod. 21:11) in connection with a Hebrew bondmaid. This was interpreted to mean that, although her master received no money when she left his authority, her father did receive money. In practice, a father received the "bride-money" when giving his minor daughter in marriage to a man; but if she were older than 12 years and six months, the money was given to her (Kid. 4a).

Today, betrothal is by an unadorned ring, which the man places on the forefinger of the right hand of the woman, while addressing her with the words *Harei at mekudeshet li be-tabba'at zo ke-dat Moshe ve-Yisrael* (Behold, you are consecrated to me with this ring, according to the law of Moses and Israel) (Kid. 2a, 5b).

For a discussion of betrothal (*kiddushin* or *erusin*) and the marriage ceremony (*nesuin*) see Pos. Comm. 219.

The Jewish tradition views marriage as the ultimate human condition and basic to a healthy life. As the Talmud observes, "One who does not have a wife lives without joy, without blessing, and without goodness" (Yev. 62b) as well as without Torah, protection, and peace. Marriage is believed to have been established by God at the time of Creation both to provide humans with warm companionship and to allow them to fulfill the Divine plan for procreation. It is considered a holy covenant between a man and woman, with God as the intermediary.

According to Jewish law, when a man marries a woman, he obligates himself to her for ten things. Of these, three are biblical in origin—food, clothing, and conjugal rights (Exod. 21:10). The other seven obligations are rabbinic: "to treat her if she falls ill, to ransom her if she is captured, to bury her if she dies, to provide for her maintenance out of his estate after his death, to let her dwell in his house after his death for the duration of her widowhood, to let the daughters sired by him receive their maintenance out of his estate until they become espoused, to let her male children sired by him inherit her *ketubah*, in addition to their share with their half-brothers in his estate." [300]

Bridegroom Devoting Himself to His Wife for One Year (214)

"When a man takes a new wife, ... he shall be exempt one year for the sake of his household, to bring joy to the woman he has married" (Deut. 24:5) is the commandment that a bridegroom devote himself to his new wife and rejoice with her for a full year from their marriage day. The end of the verse stresses that the new husband is not merely to celebrate his own marriage, but also to bring happiness to his wife.[301]

During this time, the newly married man was forbidden to go on a journey, go to war (Pos. Comm. 191), or be encumbered with any public duties and responsibilities (Neg. Comm. 311). This limitation on a bridegroom's activities applied to all marriages except remarrying one's divorced wife, so as to prevent a man from gaining deferrals from his military and civic duties by divorcing and then remarrying his wife.

Law of Circumcision (215)

"Every male among you shall be circumcised" (Gen. 17:10) is the commandment obligating a father to circumcise his son. Circumcision (*brit milah*, popularly pronounced in its Yiddish form, *bris*) must be performed on the eighth day after birth, even if it falls on the Sabbath or Yom Kippur. If the child is physically unfit to undergo the procedure on that day, the ceremony may be postponed for health reasons. However, if the circumcision is not done on the eighth day, when finally performed it may not be done on a Sabbath or holiday.

According to *halachah*, circumcision ideally should be performed by a *mohel* who is specially trained in the medical procedure and is familiar with the Jewish ritual. In the traditional community, a *mohel* must be ritually observant in all respects;

among more liberal Jews and in remote communities where *mohalim* are not readily available, a physician may be called upon to perform the circumcision while a rabbi conducts the ritual. However, circumcision may be performed by any Jew, or even by a Jewess, if no male is available.

Circumcision is the physical sign of the everlasting covenant between God and Abraham (and his descendants). Among the many rationales later given for the practice of circumcision are: to safeguard cleanliness and health (Philo); to weaken the sex drive of a man and counteract excessive lust (Maimonides); and as a sacrifice to God, somewhat like having the blood of an animal atone for one's sins (Nachmanides).

If the father has failed to carry out the commandment to circumcise his son, it becomes the duty of the son to have this procedure performed when he reaches the age of Bar Mitzvah. Nevertheless, circumcision is not technically a requirement for membership in the Jewish people—any male child born of a Jewish mother is a Jew, whether circumcised or not.

Male converts to Judaism must become circumcised. One who has already been circumcised is required to undergo a symbolic circumcision by having a single drop of blood drawn from the site of the previously removed foreskin (*hatafat dam brit*).

Levirate Marriage and *Chalitzah* (216-217)

"If brothers dwell together and one of them dies childless ... her husband's brother shall take her as a wife" (Deut. 25:5) is the commandment **(216)** of levirate marriage (*yibbum*). Coming from the Latin word for brother-in-law (*levir*), this is the technical name for the obligation of a surviving brother to marry the widow of his brother who died without having sired children. The corollary is that the widow must marry him rather than anyone outside of the family (Neg. Comm. 357). The oldest of

the surviving brothers had the first obligation to perform this commandment. The next verse "shall succeed to the name of his dead brother" (Deut. 25:6) was interpreted to mean that the brother who entered into a levirate marriage would inherit all his dead brother's property.[302]

The explicit purpose of this commandment was to have the surviving brother produce an heir in order to perpetuate the name of his dead brother, so that it would not "be blotted out of Israel" (Deut. 25:6). The literal meaning implies that the firstborn child of a levirate marriage would be named after the dead brother, to carry on his memory, but this is true only in the spiritual sense.

The most famous levirate marriage in the Bible is the story of Tamar (Gen. 38), who became the ancestress of King David. After the death of his older two sons (who had both married her), Judah refused to allow his third son to perform this obligation with the childless Tamar. Eventually, Judah himself unknowingly fulfilled the commandment when he had relations with Tamar, and she subsequently gave birth to a child.

After the Biblical period, it became customary for the surviving brother to perform *chalitzah* (**217**) instead of levirate marriage. This term (meaning "taking off the shoe") is derived from the verse "*(Then shall his brother's wife draw near to him) ... and remove his shoe from his foot (and spit before him)*" (Deut. 25:9). If the brother-in-law refused to marry the childless widow, she would (in the presence of the elders) take off his shoe (a symbol of mourning, because his failure to perform levirate marriage meant that his brother was now irrevocably dead) and spit on the ground in front of him (a symbol of contempt), declaring that "thus shall it be done to the man who will not build up his brother's house" (Deut 25:10). From then on, the widow was free to marry anyone.

The Rabbis of the Talmud (Bek. 13a) preferred *chalitzah* because they believed that the brother should marry his sister-in-law only out of a sincere desire to perform the commandment, not for monetary or sensual motives. They realized that such lofty thoughts are most difficult except for the "most elevated people."[303]

The two greatest medieval scholars took opposite points of view on this issue, with Maimonides favoring levirate marriage and Rashi preferring *chalitzah*. This led to a split in the *halachah* between the two traditions, with Sephardim following Maimonides and his preference for levirate marriage and Ashkenazim upholding Rashi's view that *chalitzah* supersedes it. This dichotomy was not permitted in the State of Israel, where the Rabbinate ruled in favor of *chalitzah* and effectively outlawed levirate marriage. Similarly only *chalitzah* is permitted in the United States.

Maimonides[304] noted that the commandments of levirate marriage and *chalitzah* are obligatory only on one who was alive at the time of the death of his childless brother and had the same father. If either of these conditions was not fulfilled, the childless widow was immediately free to marry anyone she chose.

Law of the Violator and the Seducer (218, 220)

"Then the man who lay with her ... she shall become his wife because he has violated her; (he may never divorce her)" (Deut. 22:29) is the commandment (**218**) that a man who rapes an unbetrothed virgin *must* marry her and can never divorce her (Neg. Comm. 358). He also is required to pay a fine to her father.

The Mishnah (Ket. 39a) describes the effect of this commandment as, "The violator must drink out of his pot [an earthen vessel used as a receptacle for refuse]," meaning that he must marry her "even is she is lame, blind, or afflicted with boils." Nevertheless, the violator does not have to marry her unless she and her father give their consent.

"If a man seduce a virgin ..." (Exod. 22:15-16) is the commandment (**220**) that the seducer of an unbetrothed virgin *should* marry the girl, though he is not required to do so. Both the girl and her father have the right to refuse the marriage (Ket. 39b). If all agree, the seducer must provide her with the same marriage contract that every husband gives his wife. If any of the three parties disagrees, the seducer must pay a fine to the girl's father (or directly to her, if she has no father). He also must pay a statutory fine and monetary damage for "indignity and blemish" (i.e., the humiliation he caused her).[305]

Law of the Defamer of a Bride (219)

"She shall remain his wife; (he may never divorce her)" (Deut. 22:19) is the commandment concerning a husband who defamed his wife by falsely accusing her of adultery.

Jewish marriage consists of two stages – *kiddushin* and *nesuin*. Although they now take place sequentially under the wedding canopy (*huppah*), in the past they were separated by substantial time. In the talmudic era, a man and woman formally signified their intention to marry a full year before the wedding ceremony (*kiddushin*). At this time, the man gave his future bride a ring or something else of value. Although generally translated as "betrothal," this ceremony actually was much more than a simple engagement. *Kiddushin* created a special legal and personal relationship between a man and woman that can be dissolved only by divorce or the death of either party. For all practical purposes, the *arusah* (affianced bride) is regarded as a married woman (*eshet ish*) and thus is prohibited to any other man (any such relationship would be considered adultery). During the next twelve months, the woman was expected to assemble her trousseau and prepare for marriage, while the man readied himself financially.[306] Only after the *nesuin* (marriage ceremony) were the couple permitted to live together.

This commandment refers to the situation in which a husband accused his new wife of not being a virgin. If this were true, she would not be able to collect the divorce settlement stipulated in her marriage contract (*ketubah*), because she had falsely represented herself as a virgin. Rashi notes that the wife's parents were responsible for defending her, because if the charge proved to be true it would reflect badly on how they raised her.[307] If the husband was shown to have defamed his wife falsely, (a) the elders of the city would beat him; (b) he would be forced to pay a fine to her father; and (c) he would never be able to divorce her (Neg. Comm. 359).

Law of the Captive Woman (221)

"And you see among the captives a beautiful woman [lit., of goodly form]..." (Deut. 21:11) is the introduction to the commandment concerning the law of the captive woman. Recognizing that an Israelite soldier in battle might not be able to restrain his passion when coming across a beautiful woman among the enemy captives, the Torah ordered him to bring the woman into his home and begin a complicated process before he was permitted to have relations with her (though most commentators agree that he was allowed to cohabit with her one time).[308] She was required to "shave her head and let her nails grow" and "weep for her father and mother for a full month" (Deut. 21:12-13) before being permitted to become his wife.

The underlying purpose of these regulations was the hope that the time delay, coupled with her mourning and generally disheveled state, would make the captive woman so unattractive that the desire of the Israelite would disappear and he would no longer want to marry her. Otherwise, according to Rashi, this unacceptable passion for a captive woman would only lead to a series of family tragedies.[309]

If the Jewish captor eventually decided not to marry the captive woman, he was required to set her free. He was forbidden to sell her for money or enslave her (Neg. Comm. 263-264). The rationale given is that he had "afflicted her," either by forcing her to have sexual relations with him when she was first captured or by requiring that she stay in his home for a prolonged time.[310]

Law of Divorce (222)

"When a man takes a wife and marries her, and it happens that she fails to please him [lit., finds no favor in his eyes] because he has found something obnoxious about her, then he shall write her a bill of divorcement and hand it to her" (Deut. 24:1) is the commandment requiring this written document for a man divorce his wife. The term used for divorce in the text is *"keritut"* (cutting off), implying that a divorce must unconditionally sever all legal bonds between the husband and the woman with whom he had previously lived "as one flesh" (Gen. 2:24). The later talmudic name for this written document is a *"get,"* which is required for every Jewish divorce. According to this commandment, divorce was no longer to be at the arbitrary whim of the husband and by mere word of mouth. Instead, there had to be a reason given and a formal document that demanded the intervention of a public authority.[311]

An entire volume of the Talmud (*Gittin*, or divorces) elaborates the specific details instituted by the Rabbis concerning the divorce procedure. The precise meaning of the term *"ervat davar"* ("something obnoxious" or "a matter of indecency" in the biblical verse engendered much controversy among Beit Hillel, Beit Shammai, and R. Akiva (Git 90a–b). Beit Shammai argued that it meant adultery, so that the only proper grounds for divorce was sexual impropriety. Beit Hillel disagreed, maintaining that "something obnoxious" might refer to any act that made the husband unhappy, even something as minor as his wife's cooking.[312] Although Beit Hillel prevailed in the law of divorce, the concept of Beit Shammai still has effect. Whereas in the case of "something obnoxious" the husband has the *right* to divorce his wife, in the case of sexual transgression he has an *obligation* to do so, even if he would prefer to forgive her (Sot 27b).[312] R. Akiva took a different approach, interpreting the biblical verse as including two separate statements regarding the grounds for divorce. For him, the exact nature of *ervat davar* is immaterial, for the first part of the clause "she fails to please him" stands as an independent justification. Thus a man was permitted to divorce his wife "if he finds another woman more beautiful than she is" (Git. 90a).

In addition to being unable to initiate a divorce action, for centuries a woman could be compelled to accept a divorce against her will. This practice ended around 1000 C.E., when Rabbenu Gershom of Mainz issued an edict declaring that a man may not divorce his wife except with her consent. Unlike many other legal systems, in Jewish law the mutual consent of the parties is sufficient for dissolution of the marriage and delivery of the *get*. There is no requirement for a court to become involved in the process.

Today, a *get* follows a standard format and is handwritten by a trained scribe. It must be handed to the wife by the husband or his agent before witnesses. After this ceremony, the rabbi informs the woman that she cannot remarry for a minimum of 90 days, lest she become pregnant immediately and questions arise as to the paternity of the child.[314]

Without a *get*, a divorced woman cannot be remarried according to *halachah*. A woman who does so is regarded as an adulteress, and any children of her second union are considered "*mamzerim*," who are only permitted to marry others with this same status or one who has converted to Judaism (Neg. Comm.

354). This is the sole instance in which the Torah punishes an innocent party (the *mamzer*) for the sin of another (his or her parents).[315]

All too frequently, religious men have taken advantage of their estranged wives' need for a *get* and have refused to grant it. Although this can be the act of a vindictive husband, refusal to issue a *get* more commonly is a form of blackmail to secure a more favorable financial settlement or even an actual cash payment if the wife comes from a wealthy family.[316]

A woman who has been refused a *get* is known as an "*agunah*" (chained woman), a term that well describes the feelings of a deeply religious woman who legally remains married (bound to a husband who no longer lives with her) and thus is unable to marry anyone else. This has become a highly controversial issue, as some rabbis have devised ingenious halachic reasoning to free these women from their fate. One increasingly popular way to prevent this problem is the use of a prenuptial agreement, which requires that the husband consent to issue a *get* in the event of a civil divorce. However, some observant Jews question whether such a *get* issued under duress is binding.[317]

The Reform movement does not require couples to obtain a *get* and considers a civil divorce agreement as sufficient.[318]

Law of a Suspected Adulteress (223)

"If a man's wife has gone astray and broken faith with him ... then he shall bring her to the Kohen" (Num. 5:12-15) introduces the commandment concerning the law of the suspected adulteress (*sotah*). The suspicions of a jealous husband were proved or disproved by the complicated ordeal of drinking the "water of bitterness." The wife could not be forced to undergo this test; however, if she refused, she had to be divorced from her husband and did not receive the financial settlement stipulated in the *ketubah*.

In the scenario described in the Torah, a man and a married woman had been alone for enough time that they could have engaged in sexual relations. To be eligible for undergoing the ordeal, the wife must have had ignored the warning given by her jealous husband who, based on previous suspicious activity, had admonished her not to be alone with the man. Two witnesses had to testify that the pair had the opportunity to commit adultery, though they could not attest to what actually took place. It was essential that the wife not have been coerced against her will into any illicit activity, for if she had been physically forced by the other man she would be innocent of all charges.[319]

The woman would be taken to the Sanctuary in Jerusalem, where the Kohen would mix "sacred water" with earth (from the sandy floor of the Tabernacle or soil under a marble stone lifted from the floor of the Temple for this purpose) in an earthenware vessel. Into this was dipped a parchment scroll containing a curse, the letters of which were dissolved in the water. Before drinking the mixture, the woman was forced to take an oath that she was not guilty of any improper acts. If she were indeed innocent of the charge, no injuries would result. Ibn Ezra and Rashbam said that she would bear a child to compensate for her ordeal.[320] If she were guilty, however, the combination of the ordeal and the accompanying oath would produce terrible physical effects. According to the Rabbis (Sot. 28a), the ordeal was not effective if the husband himself was guilty of immorality.

The ordeal of jealousy (the only trial by ordeal mentioned in the Bible) was intended to remove the very suspicion of marital unfaithfulness from the midst of the Israelite community. As such a crime is destructive of the foundations of social order, it was necessary to be certain in cases of doubt. At the same time, this procedure provided protection to the innocent wife against the unreasonable jealousy of her husband.[321]

This law of the suspected adulteress was only binding during Temple times, and it was abolished soon after the Temple was destroyed. From then on, divorce was the only remedy for well-proven unfaithfulness.[322]

Whipping Transgressors of Certain Commandments (224)

"If the guilty [lit., wicked] one is to be flogged, the judge shall have him lit down and be given lashes [in his presence]" (Deut. 25:2) is the injunction to "whip with a strap the violators of certain commandments." The maximum number of lashes according to the text was 40 (Deut. 25:3), but the Rabbis reduced this to 39 so that in the event of an error of one, the person would not be flogged more than his due. Before administering this punishment, an expert was called in to establish the sinner's physical condition (Mak. 22a-b). If he could not safely tolerate the requisite number of lashes, he received only as many as he could bear (Neg. Comm. 300). The number had to be divisible by three, so that if the expert recommended 25, only 24 were actually given.[323] The minimum number of lashes administered was three.

Violations that incurred lashes had to be transgressions of negative commandments, involve a physical act, and be sins that could not be rectified by a payment or by performing a subsequent positive commandment.[324]

Capital Punishment (226-230)

"He who strikes a person so that he dies shall surely be put to death" (Exod. 21:12) is one of several Biblical verses prescribing capital punishment for a variety of offenses. The Rabbis interpreted other verses as indicating the different forms of capital punishment that were meted out to violators of specific positive and

negative commandments. (The legal limitations that precluded the infliction of capital punishment are Neg. Comm. 282, 290, 291).

Beheading (226) was derived from *"He shall surely be punished"* (Exod. 21:20), which specifically referred to the case of a person killing his "bondman" (heathen slave). Strangling (227) was predicated on the verse *"They shall surely be put to death"* (Lev. 20:10), which was the fate of an adulterer and adulteress. Burning (228) was the punishment decreed for all parties when a man was married to a woman and her mother, as was explicitly stated in the verse, *"Both he and they shall be burnt with fire,"* (Lev. 20:14). Stoning (229) was based on *"You shall stone them to death"* (Deut. 22:24), referring to the situation in which a man had relations with a consenting betrothed woman. According to Maimonides, these were four separate positive commandments. Nachmanides disagreed, arguing that they should be counted as merely diverse modes of implementing a single commandment based on the verse, "So shall you put away the evil from your midst" (Deut. 17:7).

Those executed for certain transgressions were subsequently hanged after death (230), based on the verse, *"You hang him on a tree"* (Deut. 21:22). According to the Talmud, this hanging could apply only to a man (Sanh. 45b), was to last for only for a few moments (Sanh. 46a), and the body could not remain hanging overnight (Neg. Comm. 66). Maimonides[325] observed that all devices used to carry out the death penalty by any of the four techniques (including the tree on which the corpse was hung after death) were then buried, so that they would not be a persistent stain on the memory of the condemned or the lives of his surviving relatives.

Instead of being buried in the communal burial ground, individuals who were executed initially were interred in two separate cemeteries (one for those who had been stoned or burned; the other for those who had been killed by the sword or by strangulation). Eventually, their remains could go into the communal burial ground.

In the Torah, the death penalty was prescribed for a multitude of offenses, including murder, adultery, blasphemy, profaning the Sabbath, idolatry, incest, striking one's parents, false prophecy, witchcraft, and giving false testimony in capital cases. However, capital punishment was actually imposed only when the Temple still existed.

The Rabbis were generally opposed to capital punishment. They ruled that the death penalty could not be carried out unless the guilty party had been forewarned of the seriousness of his proposed action. In addition, the law of evidence and the proof of premeditation in capital cases were made so severe that a death verdict was almost impossible. The Talmud states that, "a Sanhedrin [Great Court] that executes one man to death is seven years is branded a 'destructive' tribunal. R. Eleazar ben Azariah says 'one in seventy years'. R. Tarfon and R. Akiva say 'Were we members of a Sanhedrin, no person would ever be put to death'" (Mak. 7a). However, Rabban Shimon ben Gamaliel retorted: "[Yes] and they would also multiply shedders of blood in Israel!" All members of a court that pronounced a capital sentence were obliged to abstain from eating on the day of execution (Sanh. 63a).

The modern State of Israel has no capital punishment except for participation in genocidal activities and under certain conditions of warfare. The only person ever put to death in Israel was Adolph Eichmann in 1962, for his crimes against humanity and the Jewish people during the Holocaust.

Law of Burial (231)

"You shall surely bury him the same day" (Deut. 21:23) is the commandment to bury all Jews who have died. Although in its original context the verse applied specifically to those executed

by order of the Court, it was extended to apply to all other dead. Every Jew must be buried in the earth; cremation is not permitted, based on the statement "for dust you are and to dust you shall return" (Gen. 3:19). Burial must take place as soon as possible following death – preferably on the first day but no later than the third day (Neg. Comm. 66).

The community as a whole is obligated to attend to the burial and other duties related to the death of any Jew. To avoid disrupting communal life, special societies (*Chevra Kadisha*, lit., "Holy Society") were developed to act on behalf of the entire community and voluntarily assume the sacred duty of preparing the body for interment and ritually cleaning the corpse (*tahara*). Nevertheless, everyone in the community has the duty of paying their last respects to the dead by attending the burial procession.[326]

An example of the seriousness of this obligation to respectfully care for the dead is the requirement that a Kohen (even the *Kohen Gadol*), who in all other circumstances is forbidden to suffer defilement by coming into contact with the dead (including his own relatives) (Neg. Comm. 167), is required to attend to the last rites of a person whose relatives are unknown (*met mitzvah*).

Law of a Canaanite Bondman (235)

"They shall remain yours as an ancestral heritage" (Lev. 25:46) is the commandment that a Canaanite bondman is to remain the property of his owner forever. In order to deter the owners of non-Jewish slaves from mistreating them, the Torah stipulated that a slave could go free if such ill treatment resulted in the permanent loss of an organ of the body that cannot grow again (lit., "an eye or a tooth") (Exod. 21:26-27).

According to Maimonides,[327] a Canaanite bondman could be employed in the most onerous tasks, but the Jewish master should be merciful and just with him, not making his labor unduly heavy or afflicting him, and allowing him to share in whatever the master ate and drank. The master was forbidden to abuse him physically or verbally; instead, he was to speak to him softly and listen to his complaints. The Hebrew master had to circumcise his Canaanite bondman, who, after immersion in a ritual bath, became bound by all the negative commandments and those positive commandments that did not have to be performed at specific times. [328]

A Canaanite bondman became fully a Jew when he was freed, whether by redemption through the payment of money, by a "Writ of Liberation" (Kid. 14b), or as compensation for the loss of an eye or limb. He also could be freed if needed to complete a minyan for a prayer service or whenever a minimum number of people was required to fulfill a commandment (Git. 38b).[329]

Nachmanides maintained that this commandment should be divided into two separate ones: retain the Canaanite bondman for the duration of his life; and free him if his master caused him severe injury. He argued that this was analogous to marrying and divorcing a woman, which are considered the subjects of two distinct commandments.[330]

Penalty for Inflicting Injury (236)

"If men quarrel and one strikes the other with a stone or with his fist and he does not die ... he shall pay him for the loss of his time and shall cause him to be thoroughly healed" (Exod. 21:18-19) is the commandment regarding the imposition of a financial penalty on the person who has caused a non-fatal injury. *"As he has done, so shall it be done to him"* (Lev. 24:19), the verse preceding the famous "an eye for an eye," has been interpreted to mean that an individual who injured another must pay the monetary equivalent to the person he has harmed. Although the Torah speaks only of compensation based on time lost from work and the cost of medical treatment, the Rabbis (BK 83b) expanded the

compensation to include payment for physical disability, pain, and the "indignity inflicted" (humiliation and mental anguish).

The Mishnah (BK 92a) stresses that the payment of full compensation is not sufficient. To be completely forgiven, it is necessary that the person who inflicted the injury seek a pardon from his victim (who is required to be merciful and forgive him).

Laws of Negligence (237-238, 240-241)

The commandments that describe the essence of the biblical approach to damages caused by negligence can be derived from several examples found in the text (Exod. 21:28-36; 22:4-6). Maimonides[331] stressed that each person is responsible for all damage caused by his property or his actions if he fails to take appropriate care to prevent them from becoming dangerous. This is an excellent description of the modern concept of negligence as a failure to meet the duty of "reasonable care."

If an ox gored a person or the animal of another (237), the degree of punishment depended on whether the owner of the ox was aware of any dangerous tendencies of the animal. If the animal was known to be savage and had caused damage in the past, the owner was considered negligent and held responsible for all damages. However, if the animal had not been in the habit of causing damage, the owner need only pay half.

Similarly, if a person willfully or negligently allowed his cattle to graze in the field or vineyard of another (240), the owner of the animal was responsible for making restitution for any damage it caused by eating or trampling his neighbor's crops or grapes. However, if the animal merely wandered there without any culpable negligence on the owner's part, or if the animal caused damage in a public thoroughfare (because those who set their things in such a place are themselves guilty of contributory negligence), the owner of the animal was not liable.[332]

The liability of a person who opened a pit in a public

thoroughfare, or left any other source of potential danger in such a place, depended on whether he had taken adequate precautions to protect it from passersby (238). If he covered it adequately, he was free from liability; if he negligently failed to cover it properly, he was liable for any damages that resulted. The Mechilta (Exod. 21:33) offers several additional scenarios. If a person covered the pit and someone else uncovered it, the one who uncovered it was liable. If two partners owning a pit covered it and then one of them uncovered it, only the one who uncovered it was liable. If, after these same partners covered the pit, someone else uncovered it and only one of the partners became aware of it and did nothing to correct the situation, the one who knew about it was liable and the other was free from guilt.[333]

If a person kindled a fire in his own field and the wind carried sparks that set fire to a neighboring field (241), he was liable for negligence and must make full restitution for any damage caused.

Law of Theft (239)

This commandment is the overall basis for the restitution required for various types of theft. The general rule was that if witnesses testified that a man committed a theft, the thief "shall pay double" (Exod. 22:3, 8), meaning that he would be fined an amount equal to the value of the stolen property. From the use of the word "alive" to refer to a stolen animal (Exod. 23:3), the Rabbis (BK 64b) deduced that the thief also was responsible for returning to the victim the full value of the stolen item when it was taken. If a stolen animal died or suffered some injury, the thief would retain it (since it was no longer the "same animal") and be forced to pay its owner the original value of the animal plus the fine (i.e., double the value of the property he had stolen).[334] A thief who had a change of heart and freely admitted the theft to the court was required only to repay the basic value of the stolen item, without having to make double restitution.[335]

Special rules pertained to the theft of a sheep or an ox (Exod. 21:37). A thief who sold or slaughtered the animal was required to make fourfold restitution for a sheep and fivefold restitution for an ox. This meant that in addition to the value of the stolen animal, the thief must pay a fine of three times the value of a sheep and four times that of an ox.[336]

Maimonides maintained that the restitution for stolen property related to the risk of the thief in committing the crime – the less the risk, the greater the punishment. A person who stole in a place where there was a large crowd ran a high risk, and thus he must only restore twice the value of the stolen property. Stealing a sheep in an open field involved less risk, since it was impossible for any shepherd to watch his entire flock at the same time. Therefore, the apprehended thief was liable for fourfold restitution. If a person stole an ox that often wandered away from the rest of the herd, there was even less risk and the restitution was fivefold.

R. Meir viewed this rule as indicating the "the importance attached to labor." Therefore, the damage to the owner of the ox was more serious because that animal usually plows in the field (while the sheep performs no work) and the owner was deprived of its productive efforts. R. Yochanan ben Zakkai ascribed the difference in penalties to "the importance attached to the dignity of man." "An ox walks away on its own feet ... while a sheep was usually carried on the thief's shoulder [i.e., and the embarrassment suffered warranted less of a fine]" (BK 79b).

In a burglary, a homeowner was permitted to kill a thief to save his own life, but not if only his property was at risk. This was derived from the verses "If the thief is discovered while tunneling in, and is beaten to death, there is no blood-guilt on his account. If the sun shone upon him, there is blood-guilt on his account" (Exod. 22:1-2). The first verse applied to a thief who entered a house in the dead of night and presumably would not hesitate to kill the owner. A homeowner who killed this apparent "pursuer" (Pos. Comm. 247) would not be guilty of murder but rather be deemed to have acted in self-defense. Conversely, the second verse applied to breaking into a home in broad daylight. In this scenario, the Rabbis assumed that the intruder was not planning to physically harm the householder, because he would surely be apprehended. Because only his property was at risk and it was not necessary to take a life to protect himself, the homeowner was forbidden to kill the thief.[337]

A thief who was unable to pay restitution could be sold as a bondman to raise the funds to pay his victim (Exod. 22:2) (Pos. Comm. 232).

Law of Guardians of Property (242-244)

These commandments address the law regarding people who were entrusted to safeguard someone else's property (Exod. 22:6-14). If that property was lost, stolen, or damaged, the liability of the custodian varied according to whether the guardian was compensated for the task and whether what occurred was reasonably foreseeable.

According to the Talmud (Shev. 49a), "there are four types of guardians [custodians of the property of another]"—unpaid custodian, paid custodian, hirer, and borrower. In his *Guide of the Perplexed* (3:42), Maimonides described the responsibilities of each.

An unpaid custodian (242), who kept the property of his neighbor without deriving any benefit from it, was only responsible for damages if he was negligent. To be free from liability, the unpaid custodian was required to take an oath that any loss or damage to the goods entrusted to his care was not caused by his neglect (BM 93a).

A paid custodian (243), or one who paid for using the

property (hirer), was expected to be more vigilant and thus had more liability because he, as well as the owner, was profiting from it. The paid custodian or hirer was generally responsible for loss or theft, because he should have protected the property more diligently. However, if the occurrence was an accident that the paid custodian could not have prevented, the owner bore the risk of loss or theft. Similarly, the owner was financially responsible if the loss or theft was due to unforeseen circumstances, such as an animal stolen in an armed robbery. Of course, both unpaid and paid custodians were forbidden to make unauthorized personal use of the property in their charge. In such situations, they would be considered thieves and liable in all cases, even accidental ones.[338]

A borrower (**244**), who was keeping the property solely for his own advantage, was responsible for every type of loss, unless it occurred in the course of its normal use. Thus, a borrower would not be liable for the head of a hammer that broke off when inserting a nail or an ox that died while performing routine labor in the field. According to Nachmanides, the fault in these cases lay squarely on the shoulders of the owner, who should never have offered the item or animal to the borrower if it could not stand up to the demands of ordinary use.[339]

Law of Burying and Selling (245)

"When you sell anything to your neighbor, or make a purchase from the hand of your fellow, (you shall not wrong one another)" (Lev. 25:14) is the commandment to establish a uniform set of procedures for the buying and selling of goods.

The Talmud (BM 44a) developed precise rules to determine how a sale was effected. For example, a buyer who had taken possession of goods, but had not yet paid money to the seller, could not cancel the transaction. Conversely, a buyer who had paid for his purchase, but not yet received the goods from the seller, could escape from the deal and get his money back. Nevertheless, the Rabbis appear not to have endorsed these practices, because they warned: "He who punished the generation of the Flood and the generation of the Dispersion will take vengeance on a person who does not stand by his [spoken] word."

Although the simple meaning of the verse is that it is forbidden to cheat anyone in business, Rashi took the word "fellow" to imply that one should give preference in commercial affairs to a fellow Jew. Because the highest form of charity is to prevent another person from ever becoming poor, such as by giving him employment or investing in his business (Pos. Comm. 195), the ideal way to assist a Jew in need is to do business with him.[340]

Law of Litigants (246)

"(For every item of liability …or lost thing), where one says 'This is it!' — the claims of both parties shall come before the judge" (Exod. 22:8) is the commandment that led to the extensive talmudic discussion on the law of plaintiffs and defendants. The verse refers to the situation in which an unpaid custodian of property (Pos. Comm. 242) swore that the item placed in his possession had been lost or stolen, so he had no liability. However, witnesses came and contradicted his oath by identifying the precise item in his possession, exclaiming: "This is it!." The court would be required to question all parties and weigh the evidence. According to Rashi, if the custodian lied, he would be labeled a common thief and required to return the item plus a fine equal to its value (Pos. Comm. 239). If the witnesses conspired to testify falsely (Pos. Comm. 180), they would be required to make the double payment to the custodian for having attempted to convict him.[341]

This commandment was later expanded to encompass the entire range of talmudic rulings on the law of litigants.[342]

Saving the Life of the Pursued (247)

*"(If two men struggle together, and the wife of one draws near
to save her husband from the one who is hitting him, and she
stretches out her hand and grasps his genitals); then you shall cut
off her hand, (your eye shall have no pity)"* (Deut. 25:11-12) is the
commandment to do whatever is necessary to save the life of
one who is being pursued. Although in this case preserving
the life of the pursued only required cutting off the pursuer's
hand, the Rabbis extended this principle to include even taking the life of the pursuer (*rodef*) on the basis of the words
"your eye shall have no pity" (Neg. Comm. 293). However, if
he can save the one being pursued by merely wounding the
pursuer, the rescuer must not take his life lest he be considered guilty of murder.[343]

According to Maimonides,[344] the duty to kill a pursuer only
applies when a person runs after another to commit murder or
fornication, since these two crimes, "once committed, cannot
be remedied." All other transgressions that warrant the death
penalty according to the Torah (such as idolatry and desecration
of the Sabbath) do not harm another person. In such cases,
"no person may be killed for the mere intention [to sin], if he
has not [yet] carried it out."

Saving the life of the pursued is the basis on which abortion
is required if the life of the mother is in danger. In this situation, it is obligatory to save the life of the pregnant woman
(the pursued) by destroying the fetus (the pursuer). However,
if the child's head has emerged from the womb, it is regarded
as alive and may not be harmed, for it is forbidden to destroy
one independent life to save another.[345]

Law of Inheritance (248)

"If a man dies without leaving a son, (his inheritance shall pass to

his daughters) ..." (Num. 27:8-11) is the commandment on which is based the distribution of property of a person who died intestate (without a will). This verse begins the ruling in the case of the five daughters of Zelophehad. After hearing that only men were counted in preparation for the distribution of the Land, the daughters complained that, because they had no brothers, their family would be without a share. The passage begins by asserting that the daughters were correct, and that they should receive their late father's share in the Land. It then goes on to establish their legal right by setting forth the laws of inheritance.

As developed by later Jewish law, the order of inheritance is as follows: (1) sons and their descendants; (2) daughters and their descendants; (3) the father; (4) brothers and their descendants; (5) sisters and their descendants; (6) the father's father (grandfather); (7) the father's brothers (uncles) and their descendants; (8) the father's sisters (aunts) and their descendants; (9) the great-grandfather and his collateral descendants, and so on.[346]

Each son of the deceased receives an equal share of the estate of his father or mother, with the exception of the firstborn of the father who receives a double share. (Nachmanides considered this latter provision to be a separate positive commandment.) If a son dies during his father's life, his children inherit his portion of the estate. [347]

Daughters were denied a share in the inheritance as long as there were sons. However, as long as they were unmarried, the cost of supporting daughters was the first duty of the estate of the deceased: "If the property is small, the daughters are maintained [from it] and the sons shall go begging" (BB 139b).

A husband is heir to his wife's property. The converse, however, is not true—a wife does not inherit her husband's estate, though she receives her dowry. The Talmud (BB 126b) rules that a will that "makes a stipulation contrary to what is written in the Torah" is "disregarded" (null and void). As

examples, it offers such phrases as "my firstborn shall not receive a double portion" and "my son shall not be heir with his
brothers." However, oral or written "gifts" to the same effect
are valid, since a person is entitled to dispose of his property
as gifts in any way he desires, as long as they do not include
the words "as an inheritance."

NEGATIVE
COMMANDMENTS

Belief in a Deity Other Than the One God (1)

"You shall have no other gods beside Me" (Exod. 20:3) is the second of the Ten Commandments. It unequivocally forbids a Jew from believing in any deity other than the One God (Pos. Comm. 1), who is described in the First Commandment as having taken the Children of Israel out of slavery in Egypt (and bringing them to the foot of Mount Sinai where the Decalogue was pronounced). This sweeping commandment prohibits belief in saints and evils spirits and can be extended to witchcraft and a host of superstitious practices.[1]

Maimonides[2] divided those violating this commandment into five classes of heretics: (a) "One who says that there is no God, and that the world has no Sovereign Ruler; (b) one who says that there is a Sovereign Power, but that power is vested in two or more beings; (c) one who says that there is one Sovereign Ruler, but that He is a body and has form; (d) one who denies that He alone is the First Cause and Rock of the Universe; and (e) one who worships any power besides Him, to serve as a mediator between himself and the Sovereign of the Universe."

Making Idols for Worship (2-3)

"You shall not make a sculptured [graven] image nor any likeness" (Exod. 20:4) is the commandment (2) forbidding a Jew from making an idol "for purposes of worship." This prohibition also extended to acquiring or even merely possessing an idol. According to Hirsch, a "sculptured image" refers to a precise depiction in three dimensions, whereas the term "likeness" means a symbolic image, whether drawn, sculpted, or fashioned in any manner.[3] It was also forbidden (3) to make an idol for others to worship, even if they requested it (Lev. 19:4). Because the incorporeality of God is a fundamental concept in Judaism,

worshiping an image of God produced by human hands is an unpardonable transgression.

According to Maimonides and Nachmanides, the practice of idolatry began once human beings realized the existence of a Creator. Initially this was manifest by honoring the servants of the Creator who controlled aspects of their universe (such as heavenly bodies and the four elements), but soon people started worshiping them as separate entities with independent powers. These were joined by a variety of benevolent heavenly beings (such as angels) as well as by temporal rulers (such as kings, Pharaohs) who exerted absolute power over their lives. Eventually, even demons became popular objects of worship in the hope that this would prevent them from exercising their evil powers. Therefore, the Torah contains these commandments to unequivocally prohibit Jews from making idols of any kind that could possibly be worshiped.[4]

Throughout the centuries, Jews have willingly suffered martyrdom rather than make and worship idols. Josephus wrote that on one occasion all the Israelites refused to obey a direct order to erect a statue of the Roman emperor Caius in the Sanctuary at Jerusalem. They reportedly told the Roman commander "that if he would place the images among them, he must first sacrifice the whole Jewish nation; and that they were ready to expose themselves, together with their children and wives, to be slain."[5]

Making Figures of Human Beings (4)

"With Me, you shall not make for yourselves any gods of silver or gods of gold" (Exod. 20:20) is the commandment prohibiting Jews from making three-dimensional figures, such as sculptures and statues, "of human beings out of metal, stone, wood, and the like, even if they are not made for purposes of worship." However, two-dimensional images of human figures (paintings, tapestries, stained-glass windows) were permitted.[6] Indeed,

archeological excavations of many synagogues from the talmudic period have revealed floors with elaborate mosaics depicting human figures.

The ban on making three-dimensional sculptures of human beings was primarily to prevent the temptation to idol worship. *Sefer ha-Chinuch* maintained that just as Jews are forbidden to portray God in a human form, so they are not permitted to depict human beings who were created in the image of God (Gen. 1:27).[7] According to Maimonides, "the purpose of this [commandment] is to deter us [Jews] from making images altogether, so that we should not think, as the masses do, that they possess supernatural powers."[8]

Contrary to popular belief, this commandment forbidding the making of statues for ornamental purposes did not preclude Jewish artistic creativity. Maimonides[9] noted that this prohibition did not apply to painting, and that it was permissible to make figures of various living things (cattle, trees, plants). He added that, "Just as the body becomes exhausted from hard labor, and then by rest and refreshment recovers, so it is necessary for the mind to have relaxation by gazing upon pictures and other beautiful objects, that its weariness be dispelled. From this point of view, therefore, the use of pictures and embroideries for beautifying the house, the furniture, and the clothes is not to be considered immoral or unnecessary"[10]

Bowing Down to/Worshiping Idols (5-6)

"You shall not bow down to them or worship [serve] them" (Exod. 20:5) is the verse from which are derived the commandments forbidding (5) bowing down to and (6) worshiping idols. Jews were prohibited from paying homage to an idol by any of the forms of Divine service—(a) bowing down, (b) sacrificing, (c) bringing offerings or pouring libations of wine or other liquids upon an altar, and (d) burning incense. They

also were forbidden to perform any rite generally associated with a pagan god.

By rabbinic law, a person is forbidden to bend down before an idol either to remove a thorn lodged in his foot or pick up coins that have fallen in front of it, or to bend down and drink from a spring flowing in front of an idol, if it would look as though he were bowing down to it. Similarly, "one should not place one's mouth on the mouth of human figures that act as water fountains in the cities, for the purpose of drinking, because he may seem as kissing the idolatrous figure" (Av. Zar. 12a).

The Torah provides a reason for these prohibitions in the next phrase of the verse, "for I, the Lord your God, am a jealous God." The term "jealous" is used only with reference to idolatry and to the claim of a suspicious husband that his wife was unfaithful (Pos. Comm. 223). Idolatry is the most heinous sin, and the Mechilta quotes God as saying, "For idolatry, I zealously exact punishment, but in other matters I am gracious and merciful."[11]

According to Nachmanides, the prohibitions against making, bowing down to, and worshiping idols (respectively, Neg. Comm. 2, 5, 6) should not be considered distinct negative commandments, but rather as merely explanations of how to abstain from having "other gods" before the Lord (Neg. Comm.1).[12]

Handing Over Some of Your Offspring to Molech (7)

"You shall not allow any of your children to be given [offered up] to Molech" (Lev. 18:21) is the commandment prohibiting the handing over of one's child to this Canaanite god. Maimonides maintained that this type of idolatry "consisted of kindling a fire and fanning its flame, whereupon [the father] would take some of his offspring and hand them over to a priest engaged in the service of that idol, and then cause them to pass through the fire from one side to the other." Although this indicates that

the child was not burned, some commentators disagree, arguing that the ritual of Molech called for the child to be consumed by the flames as a human sacrifice to the idol.[13]

This commandment is found in a chapter that is otherwise totally devoted to a listing of sexual perversions (Neg. Com. 330-352). One explanation is that Molech worship, like sexual immorality, "contaminated the Land," which then "disgorged its inhabitants" (the future expulsion of the Canaanites by the Israelites). According to Sforno, Molech is the most despicable type of idol worship. Although the Israelite who served Molech might still dutifully bring his animal offerings to God at the Temple, he clearly showed the true object of his devotion by taking his (more precious) children to this Canaanite god.[14]

Practicing the Sorcery of the *Ob* and *Yid'oni* (8-9)

"Do not turn to the sorcery of the ob and the yid'oni" (Lev. 19:31) is the verse from which are derived the commandments forbidding these types of idolatry, magical practices that purported to foretell the future by communicating with the spirits of the dead ("ghosts and familiar spirits"). According to Maimonides,[15] the *ob* (8) was a person who, after burning incense and performing a specific ritual that included the use of a skull, answered questions by pretending that he heard an exceedingly deep voice coming from under his armpit. The *yid'oni* put the bone of a bird in his mouth, burned incense, recited certain prayers, and performed a specific ritual until he fell into a trance and predicted the future.[16]

Rashi noted that this verse concludes, "I am the Lord, your God"—a stern warning to anyone tempted to follow this type of idolatry that he was effectively rejecting God when seeking knowledge of the future through the false prophets of the *ob* and *yid'oni* (Neg. Comm. 36-37).[17]

Studying Idolatrous Practices (10)

"Do not turn to idols" (Lev. 19:4) is the commandment prohibiting one from even studying or discussing the rites and philosophy of idolatry. Merely thinking about idols and learning about the ritualistic practices associated with them may eventually result in one frequenting idols and worshiping them. Ibn Ezra maintained that instead of regarding idols as the legitimate gods of the pagans, the Jew should view them as totally insignificant and not warranting any attention.[18]

This prohibition extends even to someone who seeks to learn about idols and idolatrous practices only to ridicule those who believe in them. Throughout history, it has been amply shown that people convinced of their ability to remain steadfast to their traditions have been seduced into becoming adherents of the belief system they had sought to attack.[19] *Sefer ha-Chinuch* condemned even an academic study of false gods as the sinful waste of time that could be better utilized studying Torah.[20]

Erecting a Pillar Which People Will Assemble to Honor (11)

"You shall not erect a pillar, which the Lord your God hates" (Deut. 16:22) is the commandment forbidding the erecting of a column for any sort of worship, even that of the One True God. The purpose of this prohibition was that Jews "should not imitate idolaters, whose custom it was to erect pillars," single large stones on which to place their idols. Consequently, the Torah had previously specified that God required only an Altar made of earth or stones that have not been not cut with iron tools, a symbol of war (Exod. 20:21-22).

Making Figured Stones Upon Which to Prostrate Ourselves (12)

"You shall not place a figured stone upon which to prostrate your-selves" (Lev. 26:1) is the commandment forbidding the making of a stone floor patterned with designs and figures upon which to lay face down, even if in the service of God. The purpose of this prohibition was to "not imitate the idolaters, whose custom it was to set up a beautifully sculpted stone before an idol and prostrate themselves upon it in worship." According to Maimonides,[21] this commandment was not violated "unless one spreads out his hands and feet on the stone so that he lies completely stretched out across it." By rabbinic law, however, any kind of prostration was forbidden, except on the stone floor of the Sanctuary.

This commandment has led to the development of the custom of covering the stone floor of a synagogue with mats or other material, such as a cloth or piece of paper, so that the heads and faces of the worshipers do not come in contact with the stone when they prostrate themselves before God on Rosh Hashanah and Yom Kippur (Pos. Comm. 49).

Planting Trees Within the Sanctuary (13)

"You shall not plant an idolatrous tree of any kind near the Altar of the Lord your God" (Deut. 16:21) is the commandment forbidding the planting of trees within the Courtyard of the Sanctuary, where the Altar stood, "for purposes of adornment and beautification, even for the worship of the Lord." The term used in the text is *Asherah*, a sacred symbol of Astarte, the Canaanite goddess of fertility.[22] The purpose of this prohibition was to not imitate "the custom of the idolaters to plant beautiful, shapely trees in honor of the idols in their houses of worship."

Alshekh maintained that planting a tree (or erecting a pillar;

Neg. Comm 11) was forbidden because it could eventually lead to pagan worship. Even such a seemingly insignificant act can propel an unsuspecting person along the slippery slope from full Jewish observance to complete apostasy.[23]

According to Maimonides,[24] to preclude even the slightest hint of violating this commandment, "all of the colonnades and cornices projecting from the Temple walls were of stone and not of wood [even though they were built structures and not planted trees]."

Swearing by an Idol (14)

"You shall not mention the name of other gods" (Exod. 23:13) is the commandment prohibiting one from swearing by an idol, "even in dealings with idolaters."

Idol worship is so dangerous that a Jew is forbidden even to speak of idols or be the cause of others mentioning them. According to the Talmud (Sanh. 63b), one may not even say to a friend: "Wait for me at the side of that idol." In addition, "One [a Jew] may not enter into a business partnership with a heathen [non-Jew], lest the latter be obliged to take an oath [in case of a dispute], and he swear by his idol."

Misleading Others into Idolatry (15-21)

Leading the community, or an individual Israelite, into idolatry was regarded as among the most horrible crimes. Consequently, the perpetrator was treated harshly, "since to be cruel to those who lead people astray after foolishness is to be merciful to mankind."[25] For those who enticed others toward idolatry, God "does not give an opportunity to repent because of the enormity of their sins."[26]

It was forbidden (16) to seek to persuade an individual Israelite to worship idols (Deut.13:12). Unlike all other Jews, it was forbidden (17) to love or even listen to the person attempting to mislead you into idolatry, as well as (18) to relax one's aversion to the misleader (Deut. 13:9). It was forbidden (19) to save the life of a misleader if one discovered that he was in a dangerous predicament (Deut. 13:9).

So great was the sin of enticing people to worship idols, that even his closest relatives were obligated to report his nefarious actions to the court. During the trial, it was forbidden (20) to plead for the misleader, even if one knew an argument in his favor, or (21) to suppress evidence that was unfavorable to the misleader (Deut. 13:9). Thus the responsibility of preparing a defense fell entirely on the accused misleader. For almost all crimes, witnesses were required to have forewarned the criminal of the potential consequences of his action. However, they could remain hidden while the misleader beguiled his victim and go directly to the court to charge him with the crime. Normally, the court was obligated to search for any extenuating circumstances that would spare the convicted sinner from execution, but this did not apply in the case of the misleader.[27]

Similarly, it was forbidden (15) to mislead the community by urging the people to worship idols (Exod. 23:13; Deut. 13:12), "even if the enticer does not worship them himself and does nothing whatever except summon others to do so."

Because of the seriousness of the offense, the punishment of the misleader was carried out in full public view to deter others from emulating his crime. Rather than the normal practice of executing a criminal immediately, R. Akiva maintained that the misleader was taken to Jerusalem and killed during the next Pilgrimage Festival, presumably to dramatically emphasize the gravity of the crime of misleading toward idolatry to the large number of Jews who flocked to the capital at that time. R. Yehudah disagreed, saying that the death sentence was carried out immediately but that messengers were sent throughout the country to proclaim the name and the fate of the person who had been convicted as a misleader.[28]

Deriving Benefits From Idols (22, 25)

"You shall not covet the silver or the gold that is on them and take it for yourself" (Deut. 7:25) is the commandment (22) prohibiting one from benefiting "from the ornaments with which an idol has been bedecked" or the precious metals plated over a wooden image. According to Maimonides,[29] "Objects in the making of which human hands have had no part, such as mountains, cattle, and trees, though they are worshiped, may nevertheless be used. The coverings of any such objects, however, may not be used."

"You must not bring an abomination into your home" (Deut. 7:26) is the commandment (25) prohibiting a person from increasing his wealth from anything connected with idolatry. Instead, one must avoid all idols, their temples and anything associated with them. Maimonides[30] observed that if a person profited in a business in which he had invested money received from some activity related to idolatry, he might be misled into thinking that the idol was the underlying cause for his success.

Sefer ha-Chinuch extended these prohibitions to all activities in which money or tangible goods are acquired in violation of Torah law, because these rewards were achieved by yielding to the same sinful desires that lead people to worship idols.[31]

Rebuilding/Deriving Benefit from the Property of an Apostate City (23-24)

The apostate (wayward) city was one that was so spiritually corrupt that all or most of its citizens worshiped idols. The Israelites were commanded to slay all the guilty inhabitants of the city and burn it to the ground (Pos. Comm. 186).

It was forbidden **(23)** to rebuild an apostate city (Deut. 13:17). Nevertheless, Maimonides[32] maintained that it was permitted to convert the site into "gardens and orchards [parks]" (Sanh. 111b).

It was forbidden **(24)** to use or derive benefit from the property of an apostate city that had been destroyed (Deut. 13:18). Even the belongings of those righteous individuals who were not led astray with the majority, and therefore were not liable for the death penalty, had to be brought along with the remainder of the goods into the public square and burned with the rest of the city (Sanh. 111b).[33]

The reason for both of these commandments is "so God will turn back from His burning wrath and show you mercy" (Deut. 13:18), because "as long as the wicked [idolatry] exists in the world there is [God's] fierce anger in the world; [only] when [all of] the wicked perish from the world [will the Divine] fierce anger disappear from the world" (Sanh. 111b).

False Prophets (26-29)

The prophet was the spiritual channel through which the Divine word was transmitted to Israel (Pos. Comm. 172). Therefore, the Israelites did not have to resort to pagan augury and sorcery to know the future or to discern the will of God.[34]

It was forbidden **(27)** to prophesize falsely (Deut. 18:20) — "to utter in the name of the Lord... a prophecy that God had not spoken" or to proclaim as one's own a prophecy that the Lord had spoken to another. According to Maimonides,[35] if a prophet predicted a calamity, such as war, famine, or the death of a specific individual, that was not fulfilled, this "does not disprove his prophetic standing ... for God is long-suffering and abounding in kindness, and repents of the evil [He has threatened]." Those who were warned of impending doom may have repented and been forgiven, such as the people of Nineveh after the prophesy of Jonah, or "the execution of the sentence [may have been] deferred, as in the case of Hezekiah." However, failure of a prophesy of good fortune to occur is an unequivocal sign of a false prophet, "for no blessing decreed by the Almighty, even if promised conditionally, is ever revoked."

The false prophet was to be strangled. It was forbidden (**29**) to have pity upon him or to avoid executing him, either because of his high standing or because he prophesied in the name of God (Deut. 18:22).

It was forbidden (**26**) to prophesy in the name of an idol, saying that one was worshiping the idol at the command of God or the idol itself, and that he was promised a reward for doing so and threatened with punishment if he did not (Deut. 18:20). The prohibition against prophesying in the name of an idol applied even if the prophet invoked his god to declare that Jews should obey a commandment of the Torah (Sanh. 89a).[36]

It was even forbidden (**28**) to listen to one who prophesied in the name of an idol (Deut. 13:4). Rather than asking him questions or debating the issue with him, the Jew must warn a person prophesying in the name of an idol to desist immediately, lest he receive the biblically mandated punishment, regardless of his alleged miracles or proofs. [37]

Adopting the Habits and Customs of Unbelievers (30)

"Do not follow their traditions [practices]" (Lev. 18:3) is the commandment prohibiting the Israelites from adopting the customs of the people of Egypt (where they had dwelt for 210 years) or those of Canaan (where they were going). This included their dress, social gatherings, promiscuous practices, and places of

entertainment ("theaters, circuses, and arenas... where they would gather for purposes of idol worship").

Throughout the ages, the Rabbis railed against the practice of *hukkat ha-goyim*, imitating the gentiles. However, as Hirsch clarified: "You may imitate the nations among whom you live in everything that has been adopted by them on rational grounds, and not on grounds that belong to their religion or are immoral; but do not imitate anything that is irrational or has been adopted on grounds derived from their religion, or for forbidden or immoral purposes. You may not, therefore, join in celebrating their holy days, or observe customs that have their basis in their religious views. You must not, however, do anything that disturbs their holy days or mars their festival spirit; and do not parade your non-participation in their holy days in a manner that might arouse animosity."[38]

Nevertheless, based on the principle of *dina d'malchuta dina"* — the law of the [gentile] government is binding" (Git. 10b) — the Rabbis clearly stated that Jews must obey the *civil* laws of the lands in which they live. However, they were to scrupulously avoid the *religious* customs of their non-Jewish neighbors.[39]

Practicing Esoteric Arts to Predict the Future (31-38)

"There shall not be found among you one who practices divinations, an astrologer, one who reads omens, a sorcerer, one who casts spells, one who inquires of the ob or yid'oni, or one who consults the dead" (Deut. 18:10) is the source of the commandments prohibiting various pagan practices for predicting the future and determining what action to take or avoid.

It was forbidden (31) to practice divination, any of the "various means of stimulating the faculty of conjecture." According to Maimonides, some people have a highly developed faculty of conjecture that enables them to foretell the future with reasonable accuracy. However, they require some stimulus to "rouse them to activity." "One of them will knock on the ground several times with his staff, utter strange cries, and concentrate his thoughts for a long time, until he falls into a kind of trance and commences predicting the future ... Another will throw pebbles into a piece of skin ... [or] throw a long leather belt on the ground, observe [the shape in which it falls] and prophesy." He stressed that these actions are performed only to rouse the diviner's innate abilities and do not "produce any effect or give him any information."[40]

It was forbidden (32) to regulate one's conduct by using the stars to decide whether the time was auspicious for a particular action on the basis of an astrological forecast of good luck or success. Maimonides attacked "the absurd ideas of astrologers, who falsely assert that the constellation at the time of one's birth determines whether one is to be virtuous or vicious, the individual being thus necessarily compelled to follow a certain line of conduct." On the contrary, "man's conduct is entirely in his own hands, no compulsion is exerted, and no external influence is brought to bear upon him that constrains him to be either virtuous or vicious."[41] Therefore, the object of this commandment was to safeguard the critical doctrine of free will, "the pillar of the Torah and the Commandments," and the essential foundation of the concept of reward and punishment, the eleventh of his Thirteen Principles of Faith.[42]

It was forbidden (33) to practice the arts of the soothsayer by discovering omens in ordinary occurrences. Among the many examples listed by the Sifre are deciding where to go and whether or not to do something based on such accidental events as: "the bread fell from my mouth," "the stick fell from my hand," "a snake passed me on the right," and "a fox passed me on the left." Other examples included making predictions from "[the cry of] a weasel, or [the twittering of] birds, or [the position of the] stars."[43]

According to Maimonides,[44] it was permitted to say, "This dwelling I built turned out lucky for me; this woman I married was a blessing to me; from the moment I bought this beast, I became rich ..." His rationale was that, "the person concerned does not regulate his conduct by them, or refrain from any action because of them, but merely regards them as signs relating to what has already happened."

It was forbidden (34) to practice sorcery, which was defined by one commentator as the use of drugs or herbs to magically cure or inflict diseases.[45]

It was forbidden (35) to practice the art of the charmer, which the *Sifre* described as one who recited charms over snakes or scorpions either to prevent them from biting him or, if already bitten, to decrease the pain. Ironically, Maimonides[46] appreciated the placebo effect of this practice: "If one has been stung by a scorpion or a snake, it is permitted (even on the Sabbath) to whisper a spell over the affected part, so as to soothe the patient and give him reassurance. Although the procedure is absolutely useless, it is permitted because of the patient's dangerous condition, so that he may not lose his mental balance. One who whispers a spell over a wound, and at the same time recites a verse from the Torah, or one who recites a verse over a child to dispel its fears, or one who places a scroll or phylacteries on an infant to induce it to sleep — these are not in the category of sorcerers and soothsayers, but they are included among those who repudiate the Torah; for they use its words to cure the body, whereas they are only medicine for the soul... On the other hand, any one in the enjoyment of good health is permitted to recite verses from the Scriptures or a psalm, in order that he may be shielded by the merit of the recital and saved from trouble and hurt."

It was forbidden to consult (36) a necromancer who used the *ob* (Neg. Comm. 9) and (37) a sorcerer who used the *yid'oni*

(Neg. Comm. 8). According to Maimonides,[47] "the word of diviners are like chaff with which a little wheat has become mixed,
but the word of God is like pure wheat, wholly free from chaff
... the prophet [of God] will give you true knowledge on all
those matters on which soothsayers and diviners, who profess
to instruct nations, tell falsehoods."

It was forbidden (**38**) to seek information from the dead,
thinking that the performance of specific acts or the wearing of
certain clothes would induce the dead to appear while he was
asleep and provide information about the future. Another approach was to starve oneself and spend the night in a cemetery
in the hope of attracting a demon to consult.

Jews are forbidden from practicing all of these esoteric
arts, which collectively are disparaged as "abomination to the
Lord." Bahya ben Asher argued that seances, tea-leaf readings,
and horoscopes appealed only to those who are so insecure or
mentally disturbed that they fall victim to practitioners of "black
magic," who take advantage of their weaknesses and cause them
to unwittingly violate Torah commands.[48] Instead, the Jew is
required to "be wholehearted with the Lord your God" (Deut.
18:13)—believing with such complete faith and assurance of
Divine protection that he has no need of foreknowledge of
what will happen.[49]

Wearing Clothes/Adornments of the Opposite Sex (39-40)

*"A woman shall not wear the garments of a man, nor shall a man
wear the garments of a woman (for anyone who does so is abhorrent
to the Lord your God)"* (Deut. 22:5) is the source of these commandments forbidding men and women to adopt the attire (or
other practices) of the opposite sex. Underlying this prohibition
was the desire to avoid the promiscuity that might result from
men and women mixing too freely together.

A man was forbidden to be overly concerned with certain aspects of personal grooming, such as not shaving his face to appear feminine or adorning himself with jewelry. Conversely, a woman was not to appear masculine, such as being clad in military armor. According to the Rabbis, other violations of this commandment included a man dying his hair or pulling out gray hairs from his head to retain a youthful appearance.[50]

For Maimonides,[51] wearing the clothes and adornments of the opposite sex was related to idol worship and designed to arouse sexual desire. He referred to a book urging "a male should wear the colored dress of a woman when he stands before Venus, and a female should wear a buckler and other armor when she stands before Mars" as a clear indication that "the interchange of dress begets lust and leads to immorality."

Tallit and tefillin have traditionally been considered male attire, though there are recorded instances of them being worn by women. Judah the Prince is described as having personally attached fringes (tzitzit) to his wife's apron (Men. 43a), and the daughters of Rashi wore tefillin. According to a *baraita* (Er. 96a), Michal, the daughter of Saul and wife of King David, "wore tefillin and the Sages did not protest." Maimonides[52] maintained that a woman may wear tzitzit, but should not recite the blessing. In Conservative and Reform synagogues today, some women have begun wearing *tallitot* and tefillin for worship, either at their Bat Mitzvah or later as adults. The more traditional still do not wear them.[53, 54]

Imprinting any Tattoos Upon Our Bodies (41)

"You shall not...place a tattoo on yourself" (Lev. 19:28) is the commandment prohibiting making incisions into the skin and inserting colors of indelible dyes or inks to create a tattoo on one's body. Both the person who wore the tattoo and the one who

produced it were guilty of violating this commandment According to Maimonides,[56] this heathen custom indicated "that the tattooed person was a slave sold to the idol and marked for its service."

Wearing a Garment of Wool and Linen (*Sha'atnez*) (42)

"You shall not wear combined fibers [sha'atnez], wool and linen together" (Deut. 22:11; also Lev. 19:19) is the commandment prohibiting wearing a garment made from wool and linen fibers that are pressed or woven together.

The Rabbis (Kil. 8:1) ruled that the law of *sha'atnez* refers only to the weaving together of these two specific animal and vegetable fibers in the same garment. Thus, a linen tie worn with a wool suit is permitted, but a wool suit with linen-threaded buttons is prohibited. The combination of wool and linen may be mixed with cotton, silk, and other fibers in the manufacture of products other than clothing.[57] Based on the general principle that a positive commandment overrides a negative one, it is permitted to attach woolen tzizit (fringes) to a linen garment (Men. 40a).

Although Rashi observed that the law of *sha'atnez* defies logic and must be obeyed without question like a royal command, many commentators have offered explanations. Maimonides[58] maintained that wearing such a combination of fibers was the custom of the idolatrous priests at the time the Torah was given, but this rationale is somewhat puzzling since the Kohanim wore various garments of interwoven linen and colored wool when they served in the Sanctuary (Kil. 9:1). For Nachmanides, a person mixing diverse kinds of materials was guilty of defiantly attempting to improve upon the species created by God. Recanati related the prohibition against wearing garments from a mixture of wool and linen to the offerings brought by Cain and Abel. The plant-based linen represents Cain's "fruit of the ground," whereas the wool, derived from sheep, symbolized the Abel's "firstlings of the flock." God's acceptance of Abel's gift and rejection of Cain's led to the first murder in the history of the human race, suggesting that linen and wool denote two conflicting materials.[59]

Despite these various rationales, the prohibition of *sha'atnez* remains one of the quintessential *chukim* — commandments for which there is no convincing explanation, but which loyal Jews simply obey to demonstrate their obedience to the Divine will.[60]

Shaving the Temples of our Heads (43)

"You shall not round off the corners [side-growths] of your heads" (Lev. 19:27) is a prohibition designed to distinguish Israelite practice from that of certain pagan priests. A person was forbidden from making a straight line from the hairline behind the ear to the hairline at the front of the head, which would make it appear that the hair at the top of the head was rounded off.

According to the Rabbis (Mak. 20b), the temples (sideburns area) must not be rendered as smooth as the forehead. The required length of the sidelocks (*payot* in Hebrew or *payes* in Yiddish) is not specified, but it was understood to be that of a line drawn from the top of the forehead to the base of the earlobe and long enough to be grasped by two fingers. The custom arose, first in Hungary and Galicia, of allowing the sidelocks to grow completely uncut. Yemenite Jews follow a similar custom, but this originated in a decree forbidding Jews to cut their sideburns in order to distinguish them from Moslems.[61]

A mystical reason for this commandment was provided by the Lurianic kabbalists, who noted that the numerical equivalent of the Hebrew word *"pe'ah"* (a single sidelock) is 86, the same as *"Elohim"* (a major Name of God).[62]

Shaving the Beard (44)

"You shall not mar the corners [destroy the side-growths] of your beard" (Lev. 19:27) is the commandment prohibiting a man from imitating the idolaters' practice of shaving the beard. Although it was forbidden to shave any of the five corners of the beard (both upper jaws, both lower jaws, and the peak of the beard), since these precise areas were not sharply defined it became the general practice not to shave the entire beard.[63] Nevertheless, shaving the beard is halachically permitted if one uses scissors, a chemical depilatory, or an electric shaver with two cutting edges. Only instruments with a single cutting edge are forbidden.

The Talmud (BM 84a) termed the beard "the glory of the face" (Shab. 152a), a sign of maturity and piety. Young priests in the Temple had to wait until their beards were "fully grown" to "act as the representative of the community and to descend before the ark [lead the congregation in prayer] and to pronounce the priestly benediction" (Hul. 24b).

Some European rulers, including Nicholas I of Russia, demanded that Jews to shave off their beards and sidelocks, while Maria Theresa of Austria required that Jews keep their beards to be easily differentiated from Christians. Today, some strictly observant Jews do not shave their beards as a sign of their devotion to tradition. Many more Jews do not shave during the *Sefirah* period of counting the Omer and for the three weeks preceding Tisha b'Av, but do trim their beards and have their hair cut before Sabbaths and the festivals.

The reason for this ban was presumably to distinguish the Israelites from the priests of pagan cults, who ritually shaved certain areas of their faces to designate their sacred status. Another interpretation is that leaving the corner of the head uncut serves as a visual reminder of the commandment to also leave unharvested the corner of the field (*pe'ah*) that was designated for the poor (Pos. Comm. 120), thus emphasizing the ethical requirement to provide for the needy.[64] Bahya ben Asher observed that men were forbidden to shave the corners of their beards because facial hair was a natural feature that distinguished men from women (see Neg. Comm. 39-40).

Making Cuttings in our Flesh (45)

"You shall not make gashes in your flesh for the dead" (Lev. 19:28) is the commandment prohibiting Jews from following the ancient pagan custom of cutting their flesh in mourning for the dead. A subsequent sentiment using a different verb (Deut. 14:1) was interpreted as meaning that cutting is forbidden whether it is done by hand or with an implement (Mak. 21a). The Israelites were not to gash or mutilate themselves in their grief, because any deliberate disfigurement of the body was forbidden. As Sforno observed, the only "cutting" of the body permitted by biblical law was "the sign of the covenant" (circumcision).[65] Moreover, Jews were to regard bereavement as a Divine decree and accept it with resignation. Indeed, those present at the time of death recite the blessing describing God as *Dayan ha-Emet* (the True Judge).

Keriah, the tearing of a garment as a sign of grief, is a traditional Jewish mourning custom that probably developed as a symbolic substitute for the pagan practice of mutilating one's flesh upon learning of the death of a loved one. Before the funeral of one of the seven relatives for whom mourning is decreed—father, mother, children (at least 30 days old), brother, sister, husband, wife—a rent of at least four inches long is made in the lapel of an outer garment. Among non-Orthodox Jews, it is common to cut and tear a black ribbon, which is pinned to a garment of the mourner as a substitute for destroying the garment itself.

Settling in the Land of Egypt (46)

"You shall never return on this road again" (Deut. 17:16) is the
commandment forbidding the Israelites from ever settling in
the land of Egypt, lest they "learn the heresy of the Egyptians
or follow their customs, which are repugnant to the Torah."
According to the Talmud (JT Sanh. 10:8), it was permissible to
return to Egypt for commercial purposes or to pass through it
en route to another country.

Ironically, Maimonides himself lived in Egypt during much
of his life, and numerous attempts have been made to explain
how this was permitted. One view maintains that the phrase
"on this road" applies only to returning to Egypt "by way of
Palestine," whereas Maimonides was born in Spain and arrived
in Egypt after years of wandering. Another idea is that this
commandment only applies when all Jews live in their own
land, not when large numbers remain in the Diaspora. Some
argue that the prohibition relates only to those who intend to
settle permanently in Egypt. Like all other traditional Jews in
Egypt, Maimonides fervently believed that all Israel would be
gathered together from the four corners of the earth at the time
of the messianic redemption. A final justification is based on the
fundamental principle of *pekuach nefesh* (the saving of human
life), because Maimonides lived at a time when the Crusaders
had conquered most of the Middle East and threatened the
Jews residing within their midst.[66]

Accepting Opinions Contrary to Those Taught in the Torah (47)

*"You shall not follow after your own heart and your own eyes, after
which you stray"* (Num. 15:39) is considered by Maimonides as the
source of the commandment prohibiting "one to exercise freedom
of thought so far as to accept opinions contrary to those taught

us by the Torah." Instead, he urged Jews to limit their thoughts by a fence consisting of the Divine commandments. This verse is part of the commandment regarding the fringes (tzitzit) (Pos. Comm. 14), whose explicit purpose is "that you may see them and recall all the commandments of the Lord and obey them, so that you do not go astray after your own heart and eyes."

Maimonides[67] argued that Jews must avoid any thought that could entice them to reject a fundamental tenet of the Torah. Because of the limits of human intelligence, following random thoughts can destroy one's world. For example, a person lacking knowledge and judgment who ponders such issues as the existence of God, the truth of the prophecies, and whether the Torah is of Divine origin may be led into heretical beliefs.[68]

Relationships with the Seven Nations of Canaan/Heretics (48-52)

"You shall make no covenant with them, nor shall you show mercy to them. You shall not intermarry with them " (Deut. 7:2-3) is the source of the commandments prohibiting the Israelites from forging relationships with the Seven Nations of the Canaanites – the Hittites, Girgashites, Amorites, Canaanites, Perizzites, Hivites, and Jebusites. This was extended to severely limit any relationships with heretics and idol worshipers, especially any intermarriage that would lead the Israelites to worship pagan gods.

It was forbidden (**49**) for the Israelites to spare the life of any member of the seven Canaanite nations, which they were commanded to utterly destroy (Pos. Comm. 187). In this way, these people would be powerless to corrupt the Israelites and seduce them into idol worship (Deut. 20:16).

It was forbidden (**48**) to make a covenant that would permit the Canaanites to remain in the Land of Israel and continue to worship idols. However, Israel was allowed to make peace with the Canaanites if they agreed to reject idolatry and accept the seven Noahide laws.

It was forbidden (50) "to show mercy to idolaters or praise anything belonging to them." According to Maimonides, this prohibition did not apply to those gentiles who accepted the Noahide laws.

It was forbidden (51) to permit idolaters to dwell in the Land, lest the Israelites be influenced by their heresy. However, one who swore to give up his idolatrous practices was permitted to remain as a *ger toshav* (resident alien). Maimonides disagreed,[69] arguing that an idolater could not stay in the Land of Israel even as a temporary resident or as a traveling merchant until he had renounced idolatry. The Rabad adopted a different view, maintaining that this commandment applied only to those members of the Seven Nations thinking of taking up permanent residence.[70]

It was forbidden (52) to intermarry with heretics and, by extension, to any non-Jew because all intermarriages carried the danger of apostasy. The reference to "marriage" is not meant literally, since any marriage-like relationship between a Jew and a gentile has no halachic validity, regardless of whether it is recognized by secular authorities.

According to Jewish law, the status of children from a mixed relationship is determined exclusively by the faith of the mother. If the mother is Jewish and the father non-Jewish, the children are considered Jewish in every respect; if the father is Jewish but the mother is not, the children are not considered Jews. In 1983, the Reform movement broke with this tradition and formally adopted the principle of patrilineal descent. They view this as a way to compensate for demographic decline by broadening the definition of a Jew and extending a welcome and a sense of legitimacy to people who otherwise would most likely be lost to the Jewish community. However, by defining Jews differently from traditional Jewish law, this practice has effectively established a new category of people who are deemed Jewish by the standards of some Jews but not by the standards of the majority.

Maimonides[71] offered a lengthy discussion of the practical relationships between Jews and idolaters in his own day. "In the interests of peace, the Sages decreed that even idolaters who conform to none of the laws known to civilized humanity are to be treated in all respects with kindness and consideration: we are to visit their sick, bury their dead as we bury the dead of Israel, and support their poor as we support the poor of Israel."

Jews are required to have full secular relations with Muslims and Christians, assisting them when needed and praying on their behalf, since these religions derive from the Torah and their adherents believe in Creation, Divine Revelation, and the sacredness of the Bible.[72]

Intermarrying with a Male
Ammonite or Moabite (53)

"No Ammonite or Moabite shall be admitted into the congregation of the Lord" (Deut. 23:4) is the commandment prohibiting a female Israelite from marrying a male Ammonite or Moabite, even after they have converted to Judaism.

These Transjordan neighbors of Israel were descended from Lot, who was redeemed from captivity by his uncle Abraham (Gen. 14:16). However, instead of showing hospitality to the Israelites during their wandering through the wilderness after the Exodus from Egypt, Ammon "did not greet you with bread and water" and Balak (king of Moab) hired Balaam to curse them (Num. 22:5-6).[73] As *Sefer ha-Chinuch* observed, "The Torah here teaches us the great virtue of *gemilut chasadim* (acts of lovingkindness) and the great wickedness of meanness."[74]

The Rabbis (Yev. 76b) declared that this prohibition applied only to Ammonite and Moabite men and not to the women, based on the use of the masculine gender in the biblical text—implying that only the males customarily went out into the desert to offer provisions to travelers and would have been sent to employ Balaam. Thus, it was possible for Ruth, the righteous Moabite princess, to marry Boaz and become the great-grandmother of King David.[75]

The Assyrian conquest led to many of the inhabitants of the Middle East being driven from their homes and an intermingling of tribes and races.[76] Therefore, this and the following three commandments no longer apply "since we do not know the identity of these ancient nations; consequently, a male or female proselyte of any nation is permitted immediately to enter into the Assembly of the Lord."[77]

Excluding Descendants of Esau/Egyptians (54-55)

"You shall not reject an Edomite, for he is your kinsman; you shall not reject an Egyptian, for you were a sojourner in his land" (Deut. 23:8) is the source of the commandments forbidding the exclusion of (54) the descendants of Esau and (55) Egyptians from the community after they have become proselytes, as well as prohibiting Israelites from intermarrying with them after the second generation.

Although both Edom (the descendants of Esau) and Egypt (the slave masters of Israel) had caused serious harm, Israel was prohibited from treating them in kind. As the blood brother of Jacob (Israel), Esau could not be placed under a ban of exclusion. Egypt initially showed kindness by providing Israel with food and lodging during the severe famine at the time of Joseph, for which Israel was to be always grateful.[78]

The commentators sought additional explanations for why the Ammonites and Moabites were eternally excluded from intermarrying with the Israelites, while Edomites and Egyptians were allowed to marry into the Jewish community in the third generation. According to Rashi, inducing another to sin is a greater transgression than murder, because the sinner not only loses his life in this world but also forfeits his share in the World to Come. Although Edom attacked Israel (Num. 20:20) and Egypt murdered Israelite babies by casting them into the Nile, the deeds of Ammon and Moab were especially heinous because they enticed the Israelite men into sexual depravity and debauchery (Num. 25:1-8).[79] *Sefer ha-Chinuch* observed that although Egypt enslaved the Israelites for many years, Ammon and Moab demonstrated single instances of great wickedness (Neg. Comm. 53). This teaches that the commission of several relatively small sins is less serious that a single severe transgression, "for by acting once in a shameful and degrading manner he demonstrates his absolute moral worthlessness, and shows himself unfit ever to be received into the assembly of the Lord."[80]

Offering Peace to Ammon or Moab (56)

"You shall not seek their peace or welfare, (all your days, forever)" (Deut. 23:7) is the commandment prohibiting the Israelites from the general obligation to offer proposals of peace if war ever broke out with these nations. Another interpretation of this verse is that the Israelites should do nothing for the benefit of Ammon or Moab.[81]

Previously, however, the Torah had prohibited the Israelites from conquering and possessing the ancestral homeland of these two descendants of Lot (Deut. 2:9, 29). Because Lot refused to divulge the truth when he traveled with his uncle Abraham to Egypt and the latter introduced his wife Sarah as his "sister," Lot's descendants were rewarded with a share of the land that had been destined for Israel.[82]

According to Maimonides,[83] this commandment prohibited

Israel only from *offering* proposals of peace to Ammon or Moab, but not from *accepting* peace proposals made by them.

Destroying Fruit Trees During a Siege (57)

"(When you besiege a city) ... do not destroy its trees ...and you must not cut them down" (Deut. 20:19) is the commandment prohibiting the Israelites from using this method of warfare "to cause distress and suffering to the inhabitants of a besieged city." Even during times of war, Jews must avoid unnecessary destruction and remain conscious of the need to maintain concern for the general welfare, even of their enemies.

Because fruit trees are vital to man, the Rabbis deduced that this commandment prohibits the wanton destruction of anything valuable to human existence, including vessels, clothing, buildings, springs, and food.[84]

Fearing the Heretics in Time of War (58)

"Do not fear them (for it is the Lord your God who will battle for you)" (Deut. 3:22) and *"Do not be frightened of them, for the Lord your God is among you, a great and awesome God"* (Deut. 7:21) are the sources of the commandment prohibiting the Israelites from fearing or retreating before the heretics in time of war. Instead, each Israelite was to have complete faith in God, which would enable him to be brave and summon his strength so that he would stand his ground during battle. Recognizing that the "great and awesome God" was in their midst, the Israelites could banish any fear of the Canaanite nations.

According to the Mishnah (Sot. 44a-b), "They stationed guards [warriors] in front of them [the soldiers] and others at the rear [behind them], with iron axes in their hands, and should anyone wish to flee, they have permission to smite his thighs [strike him down]," because flight is the initial step toward defeat. Maimonides observed that any Israelite who cowardly retreated from the front line was responsible for any loss of life that resulted from his deplorable conduct.[85]

Forgetting What Amalek Did to Us (59)

"*Do not forget*" (Deut. 25:19) is the commandment prohibiting Jews from forgetting the unprovoked attack of Amalek on the weak and defenseless stragglers of the Israelites during their arduous journey out of Egypt (see Pos. Comm. 188-189).

Blaspheming the Great Name (60)

The commandment forbidding blaspheming the great Name of the Lord (the four-letter name YHVH, which is never pronounced but read as "*Adonai*") is implied by the verse (Lev. 24:16) that "expressly prescribes stoning as the punishment" for its will-ful violation. Uttering a curse against God in the absence of witnesses or warning was not punishable by an earthly court, but resulted in *karet* (spiritual extinction or premature death at the hand of God).

According to Maimonides,[86] a person "who asserts that idolatry is true, even if he does not worship an idol, reviles and blasphemes the Honored and Revered Name of the Lord." Both idol worshipers and blasphemers were hanged – the blas-phemer after being first stoned to death – because they "deny the fundamental principles of our religion." He added:[87] "Of all those who are condemned to death by a court of law, the blasphemer is the only one in whose case all the witnesses and judges are required to place their hands, one after the other, upon the head of the culprit and say to him, 'Your blood be upon your head, for you have brought it on yourself.'"

Violating a *Shevuat Bittui* (61)

"You shall not swear falsely by My Name (thereby desecrating the Name of your God)" (Lev. 19:12) is the commandment prohibiting the uttering of an oath by which one swears "to do or not do something which religion neither enjoins nor forbids [*shevuat bittui*]." Thus, it is forbidden to take an oath declaring that one will eat or not eat a specific food, or go or not go to a given place.

This commandment is different from the prohibition against bearing false witness (perjury) in a court of law (Neg. Comm. 285).

Swearing a *Shevuat Shav* (62)

"You shall not take the Name of the Lord your God in vain (for the Lord will not absolve anyone who takes His Name in vain)" (Exod. 20:7) is the third of the Ten Commandments. The repetition of the word "vain" in this biblical verse was interpreted to mean that this commandment prohibits the use of the Name of God to validate either of two varieties of vain oaths (*shevuat shav*): (a) swearing to an obvious, self-evident fact, such as that a stone object is stone; and (b) swearing that an existing object is what it obviously is not, such as that "a pillar of stone is of gold" or "a man is a woman" (Shev. 29a). Other examples include swearing that something impossible exists, such as a camel that flies, and swearing to violate any of the commandments of the Torah, such as not to read the *Shema*, build a sukkah, or wear tefillin.

In view of the serious consequences that result from breaching any of the various commandments regarding taking oaths, pious Jews generally qualify their resolution to do something with the words *"b'li neder"* (without vowing or swearing).[88]

Profaning the Name of God (63)

"*You shall not profane My holy Name*" (Lev. 22:32) is the negative correlate of the positive commandment (9) to sanctify the Name of God (*Kiddush ha-Shem*). Each Jew must scrupulously avoid any misdeed toward a non-Jew, lest his actions negate the lofty moral standards of Judaism. The offense of a single Jew can bring shame on the entire House of Israel, as well as reflecting adversely on the Name of God, their Father and King.[89]

The rabbis considered desecration of the Divine Name (*Chillul ha-Shem*) to be one of the most serious of all transgressions. In describing various aspects of repentance, the Talmud (Yoma 86a) notes: "But if he has been guilty of profaning the Divine Name, then penitence has no power to suspend punishment, nor Yom Kippur to procure atonement, nor suffering to finish it, but all of them together suspend the punishment and only death finishes it." One who violated this commandment was obliged to attempt to sanctify the Name of God in a similar way. As R. Bahya suggested, the slanderer should study Torah and speak the sacred words; a person who gazed at something forbidden should let tears of repentance flow from his eyes; and one who committed "bunches of sins" should atone for them by performing "bunches of mitzvot."[90]

Testing God's Promises and Warnings (64)

"*Do not test the Lord your God (as you tested Him at Massah)*" (Deut. 6:16) is the commandment prohibiting one from testing God's promises and threats. At *Massah u-Meribah* (lit., "Test and Strife"), the people of Israel effectively challenged God by saying that they would follow Him only if He gave them water, retaining the option of leaving God if He did not accede to their demand). Because God proved His unlimited power and unquenchable love for Israel then and on numerous subsequent occasions, the people are no longer entitled to question God's ability to provide for their needs.[91]

Nachmanides extended this commandment to include a prohibition against Jews doubting the reality of the "promises and threats" found in the Torah or the Divinely inspired words of the prophets. Moreover, the Jew must not serve God only if promised a reward.[92] Similarly, one is forbidden from obeying any of the mitzvot "on trial" to see whether he will be rewarded for fulfilling it.[93] Finally, Kimhi interpreted this commandment as prohibiting a person from exposing himself to mortal danger and relying on God to perform a miracle to save him.[94]

Breaking Down Houses of Worship (65)

"You shall not do so to the Lord your God" (Deut. 12:4), which directly follows the verse requiring the Israelites to destroy the idols, temples, and altars of the heathens, is literally the commandment prohibiting Jews from demolishing houses of worship of the Lord. Because there obviously was no need for Moses to warn the people against destroying their own Temples and synagogues, the Rabbis inferred that this commandment was designed to forbid Jews from obliterating the Name of God written in a scroll or book.[95]

Maimonides[96] noted that the law against destroying sacred writing "applies only to Scriptures written by an Israelite, conscious of their sacred character. But if an Israelite who is an infidel writes a Scroll of the Torah, it is to be burnt with all the Names of God contained therein. The reason is that he does not believe in the sanctity of the Divine Name, and did not write the Scroll as a religious duty, but regarded it as being like any other writing. This being his view, the Divine Name which he wrote never became holy. It is therefore a religious duty to burn the Scroll, so as to leave no record of infidels or their works."

In many synagogues, a special storeroom (*genizah*) was set aside for the disposition of torn prayer books, Bibles, and other holy texts that have deteriorated and can no longer be used, so as to show respect for the Name of God contained within them. The contents of the *genizah* are removed periodically and reverently buried in the cemetery.[97] Another tradition is to bury such items rather than destroying something containing a Divine Name.[98]

Leaving the Body of a Criminal Hanging Overnight after Execution (66)

"You shall not leave his body overnight on the gallows... (for a hanging person is an affront to God)" (Deut. 21:23) is the commandment forbidding the body of an executed criminal to be left hanging overnight on the tree, lest the sight of it "give rise to sacrilegious thoughts." This was the exact opposite of the Egyptian practice (Gen. 40:19), in which the impaled body of the offender was left unburied and its flesh was eaten by birds.[99] According to the Torah, the body of a person executed by stoning for idolatry or blasphemy must be hung, but the corpse had to be taken down and buried before nightfall (Pos. Comm. 230). Because Judaism teaches that death atones for his sin, the body of an executed criminal should be treated reverently like any other deceased person. Therefore, hanging was typically performed near sunset, so that the body might be taken down for burial without delay.[100]

The last half of the verse indicates that, because human beings are created in the image of God, the dignity of humanity must be respected even in a criminal. Rashi uses the analogy of a king whose twin brother was a bandit and hanged for his crimes. If the body remains hanging, people who viewed it body might mistakenly think it was the king.[101]

The prohibition against allowing the body of a criminal to

remain unburied overnight was extended to also apply to a person who died naturally. Ideally, every Jew should be buried on the day of his death (Pos. Comm. 231), unless a delay is required to provide a coffin or shroud, to await the arrival of close relatives, or to bring honor to the deceased. In such cases, burial must be performed no later than the third day.

Interrupting the Watch Over the Sanctuary (67)

"You shall safeguard the holy things (of the Sanctuary)" (Num. 18:5) is the commandment forbidding any break in the guarding of the Sanctuary, which had to be protected continually throughout the night (Pos. Comm. 22).

Kohen Gadol Entering the Sanctuary at Any But the Prescribed Time (68)

"(Speak to Aaron, your brother,) that he shall not come at all times into the Sanctuary (within the Curtain, in front of the Cover that is upon the Ark, lest he die)" (Lev. 16:2) is the commandment forbidding the *Kohen Gadol* from entering the Holy of Holies except at the prescribed times. Throughout the year, no one was permitted to enter this most sacred space, the inner sanctum of the Sanctuary. Even on Yom Kippur, when the *Kohen Gadol* was commanded to enter the Holy of Holies and observe the prescribed rites, he could not do so "at all times" of the day, but only on the four occasions when he was engaged in carrying out the sacrificial service. Similarly, all Kohanim were forbidden from entering any portion of the Sanctuary except during their time of service.

According to Maimonides,[102] the purpose of this commandment was to "raise the estimation of the Sanctuary in the eyes of the people," so as to enhance the awe one should have of the Divine Presence.

Limitations on Kohanim with Blemishes (69-71)

A physical defect disqualified a Kohen from ministering in the Sanctuary. Thus, a Kohen with a permanent blemish (**70**), or even a temporary one as long as it persisted (**71**), was forbidden to officiate in the performance of the service (Lev. 21:17-20). However, Kohanim with physical defects were only deprived of their right to officiate in the sacrificial system. They were still entitled to receive their various gifts, because their actions were not responsible for the defects they suffered.[103]

In his *Mishneh Torah*, Maimonides enumerated 140 types of blemishes that would disqualify a Kohen from performing the service in the Sanctuary.[104] These included Kohanim who were blind or lame, or who had a moist or dry skin eruption, crushed testicles, abnormally long eyebrows, or one limb longer than the other. "Priests with a physical defect used to pick out the wood which had worms, [because] every piece with a worm in it was unfit for use on the Altar" (Mid. 2:5). The Mishnah (Mid. 5:4) indicates that one of the functions of the Great Sanhedrin was to pass judgment on the lineage, qualifications, and physical fitness of the Kohanim who were to minister in the Sanctuary.[105] "A priest in whom was found a disqualification [i.e., that his mother had been a divorced woman], used to put on black undergarments and wrap himself in black and depart; one in whom no disqualification was found used to put on white undergarments and wrap himself in white and go in and minister along with [his] brother priests. They used to make a feast because no blemish had been found in the seed of Aaron the Priest."

A Kohen who had a physical defect was thought to also have a spiritual defect and thus should not serve in the Temple, which represented spiritual perfection. According to *Sefer ha-Chinuch*, because ordinary people tend to lack confidence in a leader who is physically disabled and requires assistance, the presence of a handicapped Kohen would destroy the idea of perfection in the Temple.[106]

Maimonides maintained that a Kohen with a blemish was not even permitted to enter any part of the Sanctuary (**69**), based on a literal translation of the verse, *"he shall not approach the Altar"* (Lev. 21:23). Nachmanides disagreed with this interpretation, arguing that there were only two negative commandments dealing with blemished Kohanim.[107]

Levites and Kohanim Performing Each Other's Allotted Services (72)

"Every man to his work and his burden" (Num. 4:19) is the general commandment forbidding the Levites and Kohanim from performing those services assigned to the other. Maimonides maintained that the phrase *"They shall not approach the holy vessels and the Altar, lest they die"* (Num. 18:3) was addressed to the Levites, forbidding them to perform the priestly service. The subsequent words, *"neither they, nor you,"* were meant for the Kohanim, indicating that they similarly were prohibited from engaging in levitical duties.

Maimonides[108] observed that, "Those who ministered in the Temple were strictly forbidden to interfere with each other's work; for if, in public duties and offices, each one had not his particular task assigned to him, general carelessness and neglect would soon be noticed."

Entering the Sanctuary or Giving a Decision on Any Law of the Torah While Intoxicated (73)

"(God spoke to Aaron saying:) Do not drink wine nor strong drink ... when you enter the Tent of Meeting ... (and when) you teach the children of Israel" (Lev. 10:8-11) is the commandment prohibiting the Kohanim from entering the Sanctuary or rendering a decision on any law of the Torah while intoxicated.

For the servants of God, Torah and the performance of the commandments provided every enjoyment and delight and there was no need for external stimuli such as alcohol.[109] Some of the Rabbis connected this injunction against intoxicating wine and liquor to the immediately preceding incident involving Nadab and Abihu, two sons of Aaron who died immediately after bringing "alien fire" before the Lord. They reasoned that the sin of Aaron's sons, which is not clearly explained in the text, must have been entering the Sanctuary in an intoxicated state. Nevertheless, as long as enjoyed in moderation, wine is a gift of God that "gladdens the heart of man" (Ps. 104:15), and "there can be no true rejoicing without wine" (Pes. 109a). The drinking of wine has long been an essential element of Jewish ceremonial celebrations, including circumcisions and weddings. The Sabbath and festivals are greeted and conclude with blessings over a cup of wine (*Kiddush*; *Havdalah*), and four cups of wine are drunk at the seders on Passover and Tu b'Shevat.

Kohanim need not abstain from drinking wine, except when performing their sacred roles as priests and teachers. "The lips of the Kohen should keep knowledge, and they should seek the law at his mouth; for he is the messenger of the Lord of Hosts" (Mal 2:7). The Kohanim also must be sober when deciding halachic issues affecting the daily life of the people.[110]

Limitations on the *Zar* (74, 149)

Maimonides translated the term "*zar*" as a "common man," meaning one who is not a Kohen. Others have considered the word to mean an "alien" (stranger).

"*A* zar *shall not draw near to you*" (Num. 18:4) is the commandment (74) forbidding this type of person from ministering in the Sanctuary. Regardless of its precise meaning, according to Maimonides[111] a *zar* was permitted to perform the follow-

ing services—slaughtering, flaying, and dismembering of both
public and private sacrifices; carrying of wood to the Altar; and
kindling of the lamps of the Menorah, in case the Menorah
was removed by a Kohen from the Sanctuary and taken to the
Court of the Israelites.

"*A zar shall not eat of them, for they are holy*" (Exod. 29:33) is the
commandment (**149**) forbidding those who were not Kohanim
from eating the "most holy offerings" (sin- and guilt-offerings).

Unclean Kohanim (75-76)

"*That they separate themselves from the holy things of the children of
Israel ... and that they do not profane My holy Name*" (Lev. 22:2) is
the commandment (**75**) prohibiting a Kohen who was ritually
unclean from participating in the Sanctuary service. The term
"holy things" is a comprehensive expression for all the offerings presented at the Altar. The sacred foods brought by the
Israelites could only be eaten by Kohanim (and the members
of their family) if they were ritually clean.[112] Even the offerings
that the Kohanim themselves brought to the Altar on their own
behalf could not be sacrificed or eaten by them when they were
ritually unclean.

"*Tevul yom*" is the term for a person who had contracted
any of the many types of impurities for which it was ordained
that "he shall be unclean until evening." Even after immersing himself in a ritual bath, the *tevul yom* had to wait until
sunset before he could be completely clean in ritual terms.[113]
Although citing no biblical verse explicitly referring to a Kohen
in this condition, Maimonides considered the prohibition of a
tevul yom from ministering in the Sanctuary until sunset (even
though he had already cleansed himself) as a separate negative
commandment (**76**).

Any Unclean Person Entering Any
Part of the Sanctuary (77)

"That they not contaminate the camp of those in whose midst I dwell)" (Num. 5:3) is the commandment prohibiting a ritually unclean person from entering any part of the Sanctuary. Rashi maintained that this injunction was transmitted to the nation on the day the Tabernacle was sanctified, indicating the importance of freeing the camp of ritual contamination to make it a worthy home for the Divine Presence.[114]

Maimonides[115] noted that, "Among other things that tend to display the greatness and the glory of the Temple and to inspire us with awe, is the rule that none shall approach it in a state of drunkenness or uncleanness, or in a disorderly condition [i.e., the hair undressed and the garments rent]."

Any Unclean Person Entering the
Camp of the Levites (78)

"Any among you who is impure (because of a nocturnal emission, he must go outside the camp;) and he must not reenter the midst of the camp" (Deut. 23:11) is the commandment forbidding every unclean person from entering the middle of the three zones into which the sacred city of Jerusalem was divided. It extended from the entrance to the Temple Mount to the Gate of Nicanor (entrance to the Temple Courtyard). The outer zone (camp of the Israelites) was the area between the walls of the city and the Temple Mount, while the inner zone (camp of the Divine Presence) was the area that stretched from the Temple Courtyard to (and including) the Holy of Holies, where the Ark rested.

According to Maimonides, the site of the destroyed Temple still maintains its holiness today because it once housed the Divine Presence (*Shechinah*). Because the rabbis have ruled that all Jews have been defiled by contact with dead bodies, they are ritually unclean and not privileged to stand on the Temple grounds. Consequently, many observant Jews refrain from visiting the Temple Mount in Jerusalem, lest they inadvertently walk in an area where ritual purity was required. The Western Wall is a suitable site for all Jews to congregate in prayer, since it is a part of the outer enclosure (Herodian retaining wall) that circled the entire Temple Mount.[116]

Limitations Regarding the Altar (79-81)

The Altar located in the courtyard of the Tabernacle was the focal point of the sacrificial service. It was also known as the Altar of the Burnt or Elevation Offering (because the sacrificial parts were burned on it), the Copper Altar (because it was coated with copper), and the Outer Altar (because it was situated outside the confines of the Tabernacle proper). The Altar played a major role in the life of the Israelites as the site where Divine atonement was secured in the Tabernacle and later in the Temple.

"It shall not go out" (Lev. 6:6) is the commandment (81) forbidding the extinguishing of the Altar fire, which was to be kept burning continually day and night (Pos. Comm. 29). The perpetual fire expressed the devotion of the Israelites to God, demonstrating that they were always serving Him in the Sanctuary. [117]

"And when you make for Me an Altar of stones, do not build it of hewn stones (for if you lift up your tool [lit., sword] upon it, you will have profaned it)" (Exod. 20:22) is the commandment (79) prohibiting the use of stones that have been touched by iron in building the Altar. This referred to the future Temple in Jerusalem, where a stone Altar would be built to replace the wooden one filled with earth in the Tabernacle. As the raw material for swords and other implements of war that shorten life, iron tools were forbidden in constructing the Altar, which prolonged life

by giving the Israelites the opportunity to repent and secure atonement (Rashi).[118] The sword symbolized conflict, whereas the Altar was the symbol of peace among human beings and between God and man.[119] For Nachmanides, the similarity of the Hebrew words for sword (*cherev*) and destruction (*churban*) indicated that because swords bring destruction to the world, tools of iron (the material from which a sword is fashioned) should not be used in making the Altar.[120]

"Do not ascend My Altar on steps, (so that your nakedness will not be uncovered upon it)" (Exod. 20:23) is the commandment (80) forbidding the construction of steps going up to the Altar. Instead, the approach to the Altar was in the form of an inclined plane, so that the Kohanim would not have to take large strides when ascending to it, but could walk up on a ramp with one foot closely following the other. If there were steps, the Kohanim would have been forced to expose their genitalia to those very steps, which would be inconsistent with the Torah's stress on modesty.[121]

According to Rashi, these last two commandments teach Jews the importance of sensitivity to all around them. If the Torah cautions against "shaming" the Altar and the steps leading to it—inanimate objects that would be unaware that iron tools were used in construction and could not perceive the uncovered anatomy of the Kohanim—how much more should one avoid embarrassing or humiliating a living human being.[122]

Offering any Sacrifice on the Golden Altar (82)

"You shall not offer any strange incense on it, or a burnt offering or meal offering, nor may you pour a libation on it" (Exod. 30:9) is the commandment prohibiting the offering of any sacrifice on the Golden Altar. The Golden Altar was to be used exclusively for the burning of incense every morning and evening (Pos. Comm.

28). The only exception related to the ritual for the Day of Atonement, when the *Kohen Gadol* took blood from the special sacrifices and sprinkled it on the Golden Altar (Lev. 16:18-19).

Menachem Mendel Schneerson, the Chabad Rebbe, provided a mystical interpretation for this commandment. Situated within the Sanctuary, the Golden Altar was closer to the Divine Presence in the Holy of Holies than the Outer Altar, which was made of stone and stood in the Sanctuary Court. Therefore, the Golden Altar represented a "closer approach to truth" and could only be the site of acts performed "in quietness," such as the burning of incense. This teaches that quiet meditation is a powerful way to draw nearer to the Creator.[123]

The Golden Altar is the last portion of the Tabernacle described in the Torah. Sforno suggested that this Incense Altar differed from the other parts of the complex. The construction of the Tabernacle allowed God to dwell among the people (Exod. 25:8-9), and the sacrificial rituals provided a "Tent of Meeting" between God and the Children of Israel (Exod. 29:43). Once everything else was in place for the Divine Presence, incense could be offered on the Golden Altar as the final step to welcome and honor the King.[124]

Making Oil Like the Oil of Anointment (83)

"You shall not make any like it in the same proportions" (Exod. 30:32) is the commandment prohibiting anyone from preparing oil having the exact formulation of the Oil of Anointment (Pos. Comm. 35), especially with the intent of using it himself. As Maimonides observed,[125] "If everyone were allowed to prepare the Oil of Anointment, people might anoint themselves with it and imagine themselves distinguished; much disorder and dissension would then follow."

Anointing Anyone Except the *Kohen Gadol* and Kings with the Oil of Anointment (84)

"On the flesh of [any] man it shall not be poured" (Exod. 30:32) is the commandment forbidding the anointing of any persons other than the *Kohen Gadol* and kings with the Oil of Anointment that Moses prepared (Pos. Comm. 35). Thus, this holy oil was not to be used for secular purposes.[126] However, Rashi notes that a non-Kohen was permitted to use oil made from the same spices as Moses employed, as long as they were in different proportions.[127]

In ancient civilizations, the use of rich and fragrant oils was reserved exclusively for kings and priests. *Sefer ha-Chinuch* maintained that the ritual of anointing the descendants of Aaron indicated that the Kohanim in Israel were to be considered as royalty among the people.[128]

According to Maimonides, the term "kings" referred only to those of the House of David. The rulers of any other Jewish royal house, such as the those of Jeroboam or Ahab, were not anointed with the oil that Moses had made, but rather with oil of a different composition prepared by the prophets of the time.[129]

Making Incense Like That Used in the Sanctuary (85)

"(When you make this incense), you shall not make any in the same proportions for yourselves" (Exod. 30:37) is the commandment prohibiting making incense using the identical ingredients in the same relative weights as that used in the Sanctuary. This activity was forbidden regardless of whether one intended to burn it or smell it for private or non-sacred use (Exod. 30:38).

The art of making the incense was the special skill of members of the house of Abtinas in Jerusalem, who refused to divulge its secret. Knowing "that this House [the Temple] is going to be destroyed," they feared that "an unworthy person will learn [the secret of its preparation]" and use the incense to "serve an idol with it" (Yoma 38a).

Removing the Staves From Their Rings in the Ark (86)

"The staves shall remain in the rings on the side of the Ark; they may not be removed from it" (Exod. 25:15) is the commandment forbidding the removal of the poles that were inserted into the four rings (two on each side) of the Ark. These permitted the Ark to be carried during the wanderings of the Israelites in the Wilderness (Pos. Comm. 34). Although the bearers holding the staves on their shoulders appeared to be carrying the Ark when the Israelites under Joshua crossed the Jordan River into the Promised Land, the Talmud (Sot. 35a) states that "the Ark carried its bearers" (based on Josh. 4:11), just as the Torah eternally sustains the Jewish people. This commandment also indicates that the Torah accompanies the people wherever they may choose or be forced to go, for the staves carrying its transport (the Ark) always remain attached to it. [130]

Sefer ha-Chinuch explained that the Ark contained the Torah, which the Israelites were required to honor as the core of their existence. The prohibition against removing the staves was to prevent the disastrous situation in which, when forced to suddenly depart from one place to another, the Israelites might fail to check the staves "to see whether they are strong" and the Ark might fall down. Such a horrible accident would be impossible if the staves always remained in the rings of the Ark and were never removed, thus precluding even the remotest risk of disrespect to the Torah kept within it.[131]

Removing the Breastplate from the Ephod (87)

"That the Breastplate not come loose from the Ephod" (Exod. 28:28) is the commandment prohibiting the separation of these two items of clothing of the *Kohen Gadol*. The Breastplate (Pos. Comm. 35) contained the names of the twelve sons of Jacob. Whenever the *Kohen Gadol*, as the representative of the Israelites, entered the Sanctuary with the Breastplate in place, God would remember the merits of their ancestors and grant the Jewish people peace" (Sforno).[132]

The Breastplate was secured by two pairs of gold rings. Those on the top attached to shoulder straps of the Ephod, where they were sewn onto the belt. Below, the gold rings attached to its lower, inner side. A "turquoise woolen cord" tied together the two sets of rings on each side to keep the Breastplate safely in place.[133]

According to the Talmud (Zev. 88b), the juxtaposition of the sections of the Torah describing the sacrifices and the priestly garments teach that both make atonement for specific sins:

Coat—bloodshed ("They killed a goat, and dipped the coat in the blood;" Gen. 37:31).

Breeches—lewdness ("You shall make for them linen breeches to cover their nakedness;" Exod. 28:42).

Mitre—arrogance ("Let an article placed high up [on the head] come and atone for the offence of excessive pride").

Girdle—impure meditations of the heart (it was placed at the level of the heart).

Breastplate—neglect of civil laws ("You shall make a breastplate of judgment;" Exod. 28:15).

Ephod—idolatry ("Without Ephod there are *teraphim* [idols];" Hos. 3:4)

Robe—slander ("Let an article of sound [fringed with bells] atone for an offence of sound").

Headplate—brazenness (of the headplate it is written, "It shall be upon Aaron's forehead" [Exod. 28:38]; of brazenness it is written, "Yet you had a harlot's forehead" [Jer. 3:3].

Therefore, the wearing of the garments precisely as described in the laws of the Torah was an essential part of the worship of God.

Tearing the Edge of the Robe of the *Kohen Gadol* (88)

"(It shall have a binding of woven work around its opening), like the opening of a coat of mail, so that it does not tear" (Exod. 28:32) is the commandment requiring that the hem of the robe of the *Kohen Gadol* be whole and unbroken. The hem of the Robe (Pos. Comm. 35) was adorned with 72 pomegranate-shaped tassels of richly colored material. Interspersed among these pomegranates, there was the same number of golden bells (each with a ringer). According to Baal ha-Turim, these corresponded to the 72 possible shades of white of *tzara'at*, the skin disease that afflicted those guilty of *lashon ha-ra* (Pos. Comm. 101). Since the Robe atoned for the sin of evil speech, it was fitting that it reminded the Israelites of the penalty for such gossip.[134]

Nachmanides maintained that the bells were to announce the arrival of the *Kohen Gadol* on Yom Kippur, when not even the angels were permitted to be present during the awesome rites when he prayed for Divine forgiveness for Israel.[135]

This negative commandment also includes the prohibition against destructively tearing any of the other priestly garments (Yoma 72a).

Slaughtering or Offering any Sacrifice Outside the Sanctuary Court (89-90)

"Take care that you do not bring up your burnt offerings in any place you like; (rather, only in the place that the Lord will choose...)" (Deut. 12:13-14) is the commandment (**89**) forbidding all sacri-

fices outside the Court of the Sanctuary. Maimonides inferred that there also was a second negative commandment (90) prohibiting the slaughtering of any holy offering outside the Sanctuary Court (though no biblical verse explicitly states this). The importance of a single central Sanctuary to which offerings could be brought is stressed in Pos. Comm. 83-85.

According to Hizzekuni, these prohibitions against offering sacrifices outside the Temple stress the difference between pagan sacrifices, which could be performed anywhere, and those made to the One True God. Because the Divine Presence dwelled in the Temple, sacrificing anywhere else would damage the deep spiritual relationship between God and the Jew and would be an act that was the symbolic equivalent of bloodshed.[136]

Jacob ibn Chabib viewed these commandments as proof that prayer is greater than sacrifice; the former may be offered anywhere, while the latter was limited to the Temple in Jerusalem.[137]

Blemished Sacrifices (91-97)

Only unblemished animals could be offered as sacrifices to God (Pos. Comm. 61). In his *Mishneh Torah*,[138] Maimonides enumerated 73 blemishes that could cause the disqualification of an animal as an offering. Some of these, such as blindness, lameness, skin eruptions, and castration, are similar to the physical defects (Lev. 21:18-20) that rendered a Kohen unfit for service (Neg. Comm. 69-71). To emphasize this concept, Maimonides included seven negative commandments related to blemished animals.

The Israelites were forbidden to (91) dedicate blemished animals to be offered on the Altar; (92) slaughter them for sacrifices; (93) dash their blood on the Altar; or (94) burn the sacrificial portions of their bodies on the Altar (Lev. 22:22-24). Even an animal with a temporary blemish could not be sacrificed (95). Although blemished animals could not be sacrificed, their monetary value could be contributed to the Temple (Rashi),[139] or they could be donated for the purpose of performing work.[140]

A non-Jew was permitted to bring animals to be offered in the Temple, but it was forbidden (96) to offer blemished sacrifices of a gentile (Lev. 22:25). Maimonides stressed that although burnt offerings were allowed from gentiles, sacrifices were not accepted from Israelites who had worshiped idols or publicly desecrated the Sabbath.[141] Similarly, a Kohen who had worshipped idols, either intentionally or accidentally, was forever prohibited from serving in the Sanctuary, even if he had repented.[142]

Finally, the verse *"There shall not be any blemish in it"* (Lev. 22:21) was interpreted as a negative commandment (97) prohibiting the infliction of a blemish on an animal that had been sanctified for an offering.

The Rabbis extended the scope of these laws by requiring that the oil, wine, flour, and incense offered and used in the Temple must be of the highest quality. Even the wood burnt on the Altar was subjected to vigilant inspection to make certain that it was free of worm-eaten pieces.[143] Maimonides maintained that these commandments also applied to charitable activities. A hungry person should be given the best food. When clothing the naked, a person should use the finest garments in his wardrobe. A house of worship should be at least as beautiful and spacious as one's own home.[144]

Offering Leaven or Honey Upon the Altar (98)

"No leaven or honey may be turned into smoke as a gift to the Lord" (Lev. 2:11), is the commandment prohibiting the offering of leaven or honey upon the Altar. The Rabbis adduced multiple moral lessons from this injunction. As leaven was

regarded as a symbol of physical fermentation and corruption, the tendency to sin was viewed as a process of moral fermentation.[145] Leaven was forbidden because it causes the dough to rise, and no one who comes to the Altar should allow himself to be "puffed up" by any excessive sense of his own importance. Instead he should keep his eyes firmly fixed on the greatness of God, for all created beings are ultimately weak even if they are prosperous (Philo).[146] Unlike the slow process of leavening, man should not be sluggish in performing services to God; nor should anyone be consumed with the pursuit of pleasures, as symbolized by the sweetness of honey (*Sefer ha-Chinuch*).[147] Honey was deemed to be a favorite food of heathen gods, and its prohibition was intended to free the mind of the Israelite from any degrading notion that sacrifices might be the food of the One incorporeal God (Maimonides).[148]

Offering a Sacrifice without Salt (99)

"*You shall not omit the salt of your covenant with God (from your meal offerings)*" (Lev. 2:13) is the commandment forbidding the offering of a sacrifice without salt (Pos. Comm. 62). According to Maimonides, this emphasized the difference of the Israelites from their heathen neighbors, who deliberately refrained from salting the meat of their animal sacrifices because salt absorbs the blood relished by their pagan deities.[149]

Salt can be caustic (corroding most substances and preventing the growth of plants) or a valuable preservative to prevent decay. Thus the use of salt in the sacrificial service preserves Israel, while neglect of the appropriate rituals leads to destruction and exile (Nachmanides). As a substance that never spoils and is indestructible, salt also symbolizes God's everlasting covenant with the Jewish people (Hirsch).[150]

Offering on the Altar the Hire of a Harlot
or the Price of a Dog (100)

"You shall not bring a harlot's fee or the price of a dog into the House of the Lord (for fulfilling any vow, for both of them are an abomination)" (Deut. 23:19) is the commandment forbidding bringing the profits (either in money or kind) earned in an immoral way to the Sanctuary in fulfillment of a vow or for any other religious purpose.[151]

The first portion of the verse alludes to Canaanite cults, in which both men and women committed acts of immorality as part of their idolatrous worship.[152] This commandment underscores that such activities were unequivocally prohibited in Israelite practice.

"Dog" was a Semitic term for a male who practiced immoral conduct as a religious rite. The Rabbis took the phrase literally to mean that anything obtained in exchange for a dog could not be used for an offering on the Altar, because it would be degrading to God (Ibn Ezra).[153] Though valuable for herding, dogs were regarded with disgust. They were only semi-domesticated, scavengers and predators, and often trained to be vicious (thus becoming a menace to the public).[154]

Although some people attempt to legitimatize the profits of their illicit activities by contributing to charitable causes, this commandment emphasizes that such ill-gotten gains cannot be laundered by using them for sacred purposes (Nachmanides).[155] The prohibition against gifts of funds achieved by immoral means also applies today to synagogues, houses of study, and other charitable Jewish institutions.[156]

Slaughtering the Mother and Her Young on the Same Day (101)

"*(But an ox or a sheep or a goat), you may not slaughter it and its offspring on the same day*" (Lev. 22:28) is the commandment forbidding the slaughtering of a mother and her young on the same day, "whether for a sacrifice or for ordinary food."

Maimonides[157] wrote: "It is prohibited to kill an animal and its young on the same day, in order that people should be restrained and prevented from killing the two together in such a manner that the young is slain in the sight of the mother; for the pain of the animals in such circumstances is very great. There is no difference in this case between the pain of man and the pain of other living beings, since the love and the tenderness of the mother for her young ones is not produced by reasoning but by feeling, and this faculty exists not only in man but in most living things..."

Nachmanides disagreed on the grounds that, had God wanted to pity the lower animals, He would not have allowed man to slaughter them for food. In his view, the purpose of this commandment was directed not toward the animal but toward humans, to purge them of cruelty and insensitivity.[158]

There is a similar prohibition against taking a mother bird with her young (Pos. Comm. 148).

Putting Olive Oil On/Bringing Frankincense with the Meal Offering of a Sinner (102-103)

"*He shall not add oil to it or lay frankincense on it (for it is a sin offering)*" (Lev. 5:11) is the basis for the commandments prohibiting putting olive oil on the meal offering of a sinner (102) or bringing it with frankincense (103). According to Rashi, these substances were not used because it would be inappropriate to embellish in any way an offering brought to atone for sin.[159]

Sefer ha-Chinuch added that oil rises to the top of an offering and symbolizes greatness, which is why it is used to anoint kings and priests (Pos. Comm. 35). However, a person seeking atonement should not present himself regally, but rather as lowly and contrite. It also may be that the Torah has pity on the poorest people (who would bring a meal offering, rather than a mammal or bird, to atone for sin; Pos. Comm. 72), and seeks to spare them the expense of oil and frankincense. This teaches that God is not interested in placing burdens upon human beings, but merely wants them to repent for their transgressions, choose the righteous path, and return to Him.[160]

Mingling Olive Oil With/Putting Frankincense on the Meal Offering of a Suspected Adulteress (104-105)

"He shall not pour oil over it, nor shall he put frankincense upon it (for it is a meal offering of jealousies ...)" (Num. 5:15) is the basis for the commandments forbidding mingling olive oil with the *meal offering* of a suspected adulteress (**104**) or putting frankincense on it (**105**).

Prior to beginning the complicated ordeal of the drinking of the "water of bitterness" for a suspected adulteress (Pos. Comm. 223), the aggrieved husband was required to bring a meal offering on behalf of his wife. It was composed of coarse barley flour, rather than fine wheat, to indicate the abased condition of the suspected woman.[161] In addition, because barley was generally used as animal feed, the composition of the offering reflected that she had allegedly degraded herself by behaving like an animal. It was not beautified with frankincense and oil (like the *meal offerings* for other occasions), which respectively recalled the fragrance of the Matriarchs and symbolized light, because the suspected adulteress failed to follow their example and instead was forced to hide in the dark shadows to conceal her sin.[162] In addition, frankincense and oil were symbols of joy, inappropriate for the gravity of the occasion (Philo).[163]

The word "jealousies" is in the plural to indicate that the suspected adulteress had betrayed both her husband and her Creator (Rashi).[164]

Changing an Animal that has Been Consecrated as an Offering (106)

"He shall not alter it nor change it" (Lev. 27:10) is the commandment forbidding the substitution of an animal that has been consecrated as an offering for one that has not. *Alter* means to replace one species for another, such as a sheep for a bull; *change* refers to different members of the same species.[165] Any attempt to substitute one animal for another, even one of higher value, resulted in both animals becoming the property of the Sanctuary and being prohibited from all non-sacred use (Pos. Comm. 87).

Menachem Hababli connected this commandment with the irrevocable character of God's covenant with Israel. Just as God has not substituted another people for Israel, His "hallowed portion" (Jer. 2:3), so Jews are forbidden from substituting an unconsecrated animal for one that has been consecrated as a holy offering.[166]

Changing One Holy Offering for Another (107)

"No man shall sanctify it" (Lev. 27:26) is the commandment prohibiting one from changing one kind of holy offering for another (such as a guilt offering into a sin offering or a peace offering into a guilt offering). In context, this phrase refers to a firstborn male animal from the cattle or the flock, which was sacred from birth as an offering (Pos. Comm. 79). Because it was not really his property, the owner was not permitted to

consecrate it as another kind of offering to the Sanctuary (Rashi). Nachmanides interpreted this verse differently, saying that an animal that was holy from birth did not need to be formally sanctified.[167]

Redeeming the Firstling of a Clean Animal (108)

"But the firstborn of cattle, sheep, or goats may not be redeemed; they are consecrated [lit., holy]" (Num. 18:17) is the commandment prohibiting the redemption of the firstborn of a clean animal (see Pos. Comm. 79). Because they were available for sacrifice on the Altar, these firstborn animals could not be redeemed unless blemished.[168]

Sefer ha-Chinuch related this to the positive commandment (Pos. Comm. 181) permitting one to redeem the firstling of a donkey, an unclean animal. Lest one think that it also was allowed to redeem the firstborn of a clean animal, this negative commandment expressly forbids it.[169]

Selling the Tithe of Cattle (109)

"(Any tithe of cattle)… it may not be redeemed" (Lev. 27:33) is the commandment prohibiting the selling of the tithe of cattle (Pos. Comm. 78). This rule applied whether the cattle were alive or already slaughtered, whether perfect or blemished.

Limitations on Devoted Property (110-111, 113-114)

"No devoted thing … may be sold" (Lev. 27:28) is the commandment (**110**) prohibiting the selling to another person of property that had been devoted to the Sanctuary (Pos. Comm. 145).

The Hebrew word translated as "devoted thing" is *"cherem,"* which customarily is used to denote property that is to be destroyed or forbidden for personal use. There were two general types of "devoted things." One was designated for the Temple treasury, to be used exclusively for maintenance and other Temple needs. Any "devoted thing" that was not specifically allocated to the Temple treasury was considered a gift to the Kohanim and became their private property.[170]

This same verse is also the source of the commandment (111) forbidding the redemption of devoted land fitting into the second category of *cherem* (i.e., not specifically designated for the Temple treasury and thus considered as a gift to the Kohanim). A person could dedicate inherited property to the Sanctuary but not a purchased field, since the latter only belonged to the owner temporarily and passed out of his possession in the Jubilee Year (Pos. Comm. 138). Unless the owner or his son had redeemed it, the devoted field would be divided among the Kohanim or family group who were on duty in the Temple on Yom Kippur when the Jubilee Year took effect. The Kohanim were required to pay the Temple treasury for the field, because sanctified property could not leave the ownership of the Sanctuary unless it had been redeemed.

From these commandments, the Rabbis derived the general rule that things devoted to the Sanctuary were redeemable and then available for common use, with the redemption money belonging to the Temple treasury. However, things specifically devoted to the Kohanim, or items devoted without any statement of purpose, could not be sold or redeemed before they came into the actual possession of a Kohen, at which time they were no longer considered holy, so that the Kohen could do with them as he wished.[171]

"You shall do no work with your firstborn ox, nor shall you shear your firstborn sheep" (Deut. 15:19) is the source of the commandments forbidding (113) doing any work with or (114) shearing an animal that had been dedicated as a sacrifice. The rabbis

extended these rules to apply to all animals belonging to the Temple treasury.[172]

Severing the Head of the Bird of a Sin Offering During *Melikah* (112)

"He shall pinch off (nip) its head close by its neck without severing it" (Lev. 5:8) is the commandment prohibiting the severing of the head of the bird of a sin offering during *melikah*. If the Kohen severed or divided it, the offering became invalid. According to Rashi, the *melikah* procedure must not be done with an instrument, but by the Kohen himself. It entailed nipping with his fingernail close by the nape, cutting through the neck bone including the major organs (windpipe and gullet).[173]

This prohibition prevented the offering of a poor person from being diminished, which is how it would appear if the head of the bird were severed. In addition, the *melikah* procedure reminded the sinner that his stiff-neckedness must be destroyed before his sin could be forgiven (*Sefer ha-Chinuch*).[174]

Limitations on the Passover Offering (115-119, 121-123, 125-128)

The Passover offering commemorated God's mercy toward the Jewish people on the night when God "passed over" the homes of the Israelites while taking the lives of the firstborn of Egypt in the tenth plague. Four positive commandments (55-58) deal with the slaughtering of the Paschal lamb and the eating of its roasted flesh.

It was forbidden (115) to slaughter the Passover offering while any leavened bread remained in one's possession (Exod. 23:18). Thus, the sacrifice was not performed until the afternoon of Nisan 14, when all *chametz* had been destroyed (Pes. 5a). Although the sacrificial service had to be done during the day, the burning of the sacrificial parts (the fats) on the Altar could take place at any time during the night. However, it was forbidden (**116**) to allow the fat to remain unburned on the pavement of the Sanctuary Court after dawn (Exod. 23:18), because from that time on, it was rendered unfit for the Altar.[175]

According to the Torah, it was forbidden (**117**) to allow any of the meat of the Passover offering to remain until the morning of Nisan 15 (Exod. 12:10). To prevent the possibility of a transgression of the law, the Rabbis decreed that everything had to be eaten by midnight, thus making a "fence around the Torah."[176] Anything that remained had to be burned; it could not be used for an ordinary meal or thrown away disrespectfully.[177] Similarly, it was forbidden (**119**) to allow any of the meat of the second Passover offering to remain until the morning (Num. 9:12).

Passover was a Pilgrimage Festival, and those who came to Jerusalem for the holiday typically brought a festival offering (*chagigah*). It was forbidden (**118**) to allow any of the meat of this festival offering brought on Nisan 14 to remain until the third day (Deut. 16:4). As a type of voluntary peace offering, the festival offering could be eaten during two successive days and the intervening night. However, the Rabbis decreed that if any of its meat was placed on the same table as that of the Passover offering, it could be eaten only until midnight of Nisan 14 (like the Passover offering itself). The festival offering was only offered in addition to the first Passover offering (not to the second).[178]

It was forbidden to break any of the bones of (**121**) the Passover offering (Exod. 12:46) or (**122**) the second Passover offering (Num. 9:12). As Maimonides explained,[179] just as the Israelites were commanded to eat unleavened bread, which could be prepared in haste, so they were required to roast the lamb because there was not enough time to boil it. Even the delay that would be needed to break the bones and extract the marrow was prohibited. These temporary commandments eventually were made permanent to remind the Israelites of the laws pertaining to the generation of the Exodus.[180]

The Passover offering was to be eaten "in one house" (Exod. 12:46), and it was forbidden (123) to remove any of the meat from the place where the company assembled to eat it. According to *Sefer ha-Chinuch*, the removal of meat from one place to another would be an indication of poverty, a condition inconsistent with the general purpose of the Passover offering as a reminder that the Israelites had become a free people blessed with material wealth.[181]

The Passover offering must be roasted whole, and it was forbidden (125) to eat it boiled or raw (Exod. 12:9). Eating raw sacrificial meat was the custom of many heathen peoples. Boiling would make dismemberment of the lamb indispensable, an action that was prohibited. The whole animal represented the perfect unity of Israel as a nation – one meal, at one table, eaten whole and in its entirety, with nothing left over until the morning.[182]

It was forbidden for the Passover offering to be eaten by (126) a *ger toshav* (Exod. 12:45), (127) an uncircumcised person (Exod. 12:48), or (128) an apostate Israelite (Exod. 12:43). A *ger toshav* was a gentile living in the Land of Israel who had renounced idolatry and agreed to observe the seven Noahide laws, but had not converted to Judaism. An apostate Jew was one who worshiped idols, desecrated the Sabbath, or denied the Divine authority of any of the commandments in the Torah.[183]

Allowing any of the Meat of a Thanksgiving Offering to Remain until Morning (120)

"You shall leave none of it until the morning" (Lev. 7:15, 22:30) is the commandment prohibiting any of the meat of a thanksgiving offering to remain until the next morning. It must be eaten on the day of the offering, and anything that remains must be burned with fire. Maimonides extended this prohibition to

apply to all offerings remaining after the time appointed for their consumption (*nothar*; Neg. Comm. 131), which also had to be burned (Pos. Comm. 91).

Baking the Residue of a Meal Offering with Leaven (124)

"It shall not be baked with leaven; I have given it as their share from My fire offerings" (Lev. 6:10) is the commandment prohibiting the Kohanim from letting their own share of the *meal offering* become leavened. Just as leaven was prohibited in that part of the *meal offering* burnt on the Altar (Neg. Comm. 98), it may not be part of the offering consumed by the Kohanim.[184]

Unclean Persons and Offerings (129-130)

Both the meat of offerings and those eating it must be in a state of spiritual purity (*taharah*).[185]

"She may not touch any sacred thing (nor enter the Sanctuary)" (Lev. 12:4) is the commandment (**129**) forbidding a ritually unclean person from eating sacrificial meat. Although the Torah relates this specifically to a woman after childbirth, this injunction was extended to include all people who were ritually unclean.

"The flesh that touches any unclean thing shall not be eaten" (Lev. 7:19) is the commandment (**130**) prohibiting the eating of meat of consecrated offerings that have become ritually unclean, requiring instead that they be burned.

Eating *Nothar* (131)

The Israelites were forbidden to eat *nothar*, "the meat of offerings that was left beyond the time assigned for its consumption" (loosely derived from Lev. 19:6-8). Whenever it was written in the Bible that an offering must be consumed during the day of slaughtering and the following night (such as the sin-offering, guilt-offering, thanksgiving-offering, and Passover-offering), the duty could be performed until dawn the next morning. However, "in order to keep a man far from transgression," the Rabbis ordained that the time should extend only until midnight (Ber. 1a). Thus eating the last piece of matzah (*afikoman*) at the seder, which commemorates the Passover offering, must take place before midnight.[186]

Eating *Piggul* (132)

The Israelites were forbidden to eat *piggul*, the term used (Lev. 7:18) to refer to a sacrifice that was rendered unfit due to the Kohen performing the sacrificial service while having an improper thought in mind. This could occur if the Kohen intended that either the burning of the appropriate parts on the Altar or the consumption of the meat of the offering would take place after its allotted time.

The law of *piggul* demonstrates that the sacrificial ritual in the Sanctuary required that the Kohen have the proper inner feeling and intent and was not merely a matter of outward performance. After the destruction of the Temple, sacrifice was replaced by prayer, which also requires the correct motivation and degree of concentration (*kavanah*).[187] According to the *Shulchan Aruch*: "Let him not intermingle other thoughts with it [prayer], for like consecrated offerings, it will become inefficacious. He should recite his prayers standing, just as the service [of the Kohanim] was performed standing. In the House of Prayer [where he worships], he should have a set place, just as the offerings had their appointed places in the Sanctuary Court and on the Altar ... It is proper that one should have seemly clothes especially designed for prayer, as were the garments of the Kohanim. And if one cannot afford to spend money for this purpose, he should at least be careful that his clothes are clean."[188]

Limitations on Eating *Terumah* (133-137)

Terumah (heave offering) was the generic term for offerings given to the Kohanim. The word comes from a Hebrew root signifying "to be high" and meaning "that which is lifted up." In addition to the great heave offering (Pos. Comm. 126), they also included the heave offering of the tithe (Pos. Comm. 129), the first fruits (Pos. Comm. 125), and the dough offering (*challah*; Pos. Comm. 133).

The *terumah* could be eaten only by a Kohen and members of his household, including his Israelite wife and his gentile slaves. However, it was forbidden (**133**) for a *zar* (common man, but in this context, anyone not descended from Aaron) to eat it (Lev. 22:10). Ironically, a Canaanite slave purchased by a Kohen, who was completely subject to his master, became part of the family and was allowed the share in the *terumah*, whereas the most righteous Israelite who did not descend from Aaron could not.[189]

The daughter of a Kohen could share in the *terumah* as long as she remained in her father's house. However, it was forbidden (**137**) for her to continue eating any of it if she married a *zar* (Lev. 22:12) and thus became a *chalalah* (a woman of "impaired priestly stock") (Yev. 68a).

It was forbidden (**134**) for the hired servant or the Hebrew tenant of a Kohen to eat *terumah* (Lev. 22:10). The former was a Hebrew servant who had been acquired for only a limited number of years and went free at the end of six years (Exod. 21:2). The latter referred to a Hebrew servant who spurned his freedom in the seventh year and elected to remain his master's possession forever (i.e., until the Jubilee Year), and whose ear had been pierced (Exod. 21:6). These Israelites were considered *b'nai chorin* (free persons), except for the master having certain rights to their services, unlike slaves who were the absolute property of their masters (and thus could eat of the *terumah*).[190]

It was forbidden **(136)** for a ritually unclean Kohen to eat *terumah* (Lev. 22:4). Maimonides noted that since some Kohanim were ignorant of Torah requirements and thus failed to eat their food in the prescribed condition of ritual purity, the heave offering had to be given only to a Kohen knowledgeable in religious law.

Maimonides also included the prohibition **(135)** against an uncircumcised Kohen eating *terumah* among the negative commandments, though it is not explicitly cited in any biblical text.

Eating the Meal Offering of a Kohen (138)

"Every meal offering of a Kohen is to be made to go up in smoke in its entirety; it shall not be eaten" (Lev. 6:16) is the commandment prohibiting a Kohen from eating of his own *meal offering*. Instead, it had to be completely burned on the Altar. As Maimonides observed,[191] "if he were to offer it, and at the same time eat it, it would appear as if he had not performed any service." This applied to all meal offerings brought by the Kohanim, whether voluntary or required to atone for sins (Rashi).[192]

Eating Meat of Sin Offerings Whose Blood has Been Brought Within the Sanctuary (139)

"No sin offering from which some blood has been brought to the Tent of Meeting to make atonement in the holy place shall be eaten; it shall be burned in fire" (Lev. 6:23) is the commandment forbidding the Kohanim from eating portions of the sin offerings that had been offered in the Sanctuary. This rule refers to the general expiatory sacrifices (Lev. 4:1-12), the rites for the investiture of the Kohanim (Lev. 8:17), and the Yom Kippur ritual (Lev. 16).[193] With few exceptions, the blood service was performed only on the Altar in the Courtyard. Nachmanides interpreted this verse as meaning that if a Kohen mistakenly took the blood into the

Sanctuary, intending to secure atonement there, the entire offering became invalid and had to be burned.[194]

Eating Invalidated Consecrated Offerings (140)

"You shall not eat any abominable thing" (Deut. 14:3) is the commandment prohibiting the eating of consecrated offerings that have become invalid through a blemish caused either *deliberately* or after slaughter. This prevented a person from being tempted to retain a firstborn animal by producing a blemish that would disqualify it from being used as an offering, for it still could not be eaten by the owner (Rashi).[195] From this scenario, the Rabbis developed the rule against deriving any benefit from something that had been rendered "permissible" through a sinful act (Hul. 114b). A consecrated offering could also be invalidated after slaughter, such as when the sacrificial portions of the offering were allowed to remain overnight outside the Altar.

Any consecrated offering in which a blemish appeared *naturally* had to be redeemed (Pos. Comm. 86). This allowed the animal to be free for common use and permitted the owner to slaughter and eat it.

Eating Certain Sacred Foods Outside of Jerusalem (141-145, 148, 150, 152-154)

"(In your settlements,) you may not eat the tithe of your new grain or wine or oil; or of the firstborn of your cattle and your flocks; ... and what you raise up with your hands [terumah] ... Rather, you must eat them before the Lord, in the place that He shall choose" (Deut. 12:17-18) is the source for several commandments prohibiting the eating of specific foods outside of Jerusalem.

The Torah established a set order of tithing. First, the

great heave offering (*terumah*), which usually amounted to a fiftieth of the produce, was set aside for the Kohen (Pos. Comm. 126). From the remainder, a first tithe was given to the Levite (Pos. Comm. 127), who then gave a tenth of what he had received to the Kohen (Pos. Comm. 129). This made the rest of the Levite's portion permitted food that could be eaten everywhere, even by those in a state of ritual impurity. In the first, second, fourth, and fifth years of the Sabbatical cycle, the layman set aside a second tithe (Pos. Comm. 128). This had to be taken up to the city of Jerusalem and eaten there in a state of ritual purity. Alternatively, the layman (i.e., an Israelite who was neither a Kohen nor a Levite) could redeem the second tithe and take its monetary value (plus a fifth) to Jerusalem. Therefore, it was forbidden to consume an unredeemed second tithe of grain (**141**), wine (**142**), or oil (**143**) outside of Jerusalem. However, if the second tithe became unclean, it was forbidden (**150**) to eat it even in Jerusalem. If the owner had elected to redeem the second tithe, it was forbidden (**152**) to spend the redemption money in Jerusalem on anything other than food and drink. In the third and sixth years of the Sabbatical cycle, the second tithe was not set aside. Instead, a tithe was required for the poor (Pos. Comm. 130), who could eat it anywhere and even in a state of ritual impurity.[196]

It was forbidden (**153**) to eat produce from which the heave-offering and the tithes had not been taken (*tevel*). In addition, it was forbidden (**154**) to alter the prescribed order of harvest tithing specified above. According to Menachem Hababli, this reflected a hierarchy of holiness in Israel. Setting aside the sacred gifts in their proper order reminded the owner of the superior spiritual status of the Kohanim (heave offering and first fruits), then the position of the Levites (first tithe), and finally the holiness of Israel as a people (second tithe). Any alteration in the prescribed order of the gifts might eventually undermine respect for the traditional regulations and authority concerning sacred things.[197]

The male firstborn of cows, sheep, and goats were holy from birth (Pos. Comm. 79). It was forbidden (144) to eat an unblemished firstborn outside Jerusalem. A blemished firstborn was considered a gift to the Kohen and could be slaughtered and eaten anywhere (Deut. 15:21-22).

It was forbidden (145) to eat the sin offering and the guilt offering outside the Sanctuary Court, or even to consume any meat of these offerings that had been removed from this site and later returned. The eating by the Kohanim of the meat of these offerings was the final step in securing atonement of the sinner (Pos. Comm. 89). To always be aware of the underlying importance and purpose of these offerings, it was essential that they be eaten only within the Sanctuary Court (Menachem Hababli).[198]

The phrase "what you raise with your hands" was interpreted to mean the first fruits. Therefore, it was forbidden (148) for the Kohanim to eat the first fruits outside Jerusalem.

Eating the Meat of a Burnt Offering (146)

"In your settlements, you may not eat ... all your vow offerings that you vowed" (Deut.12:17) is the commandment prohibiting the eating of the meat of a burnt offering. Failure to observe this prohibition would be "sacrilege," the inappropriate deriving of benefit from any holy thing (Pos. Comm. 118). As atonement for "evil thoughts," the entire burnt offering had to be consumed by fire on the Altar, just as a person's evil thoughts must be totally eradicated and not permitted to adversely influence his or her conduct (Menachem Hababli).[199]

Eating a Lesser Holy Offering Before Dashing Their Blood on the Altar (147)

"In your settlements, you may not eat ... your free-will offerings"
(Deut. 12:17) is the commandment prohibiting the eating of the
lesser holy offerings before sprinkling their blood on the Altar.
This referred to the peace offering, the thanksgiving offering, the
firstborn animals, the tithe of cattle, and the Passover offering.[200]

After dashing its blood on the Altar, the peace-offering
could be eaten anywhere in Jerusalem, by anyone, during two
days and a night. The thanksgiving offering could be eaten by
anyone at any place in Jerusalem on the day it was sacrificed
until midnight that evening. The firstborn animal (eaten only
by the Kohanim) and the tithe of cattle (eaten by anyone) could
be consumed anywhere in Jerusalem during two days and a
night. The Passover offering, which had to be roasted, could
be eaten only until midnight; it was limited to the number
of people assigned to it (i.e., who had previously registered
themselves for that particular animal) (Zev. 55a, 56b).

Menachem Hababli observed that because the dashing of
blood upon the Altar (atoning for the soul) precedes the eating
of the meat (atoning for the body), this commandment teaches
that the needs and desires of the body must not be given priority over those of the soul.[201]

Eating the Second Tithe During Mourning (151)

"I have not eaten of it in my intense mourning" (Deut. 26:14) is
the commandment prohibiting eating the second tithe when
in mourning on the day of a close relative's death. Similarly,
a mourner was forbidden to eat of the consecrated offerings
(Lev. 10:19). The second tithe (Pos. Comm. 128), like all sacrificial meats, had to be eaten in a spirit of joy.[202] *Sefer ha-Chinuch*

explained that one's thoughts when eating holy food must be directed towards heaven. Because a person in mourning cannot completely banish depressing thoughts, mourners are forbidden to eat of the second tithe or any consecrated offering.[203]

Delaying Payment of Vows (155)

"When you make a vow to the Lord your God, you shall not be late in fulfilling it" (Deut. 23:22) is the commandment prohibiting one from delaying "payment of vows, free-will offerings, and other offerings for which we are liable." Although a vow is a purely voluntary act, once made it must be fulfilled. As written in Ecclesiastes (5:4), "It is better that you should not vow, than that you vow and not pay."[204]

According to the Talmud (RH 6a), vows must be paid before the passage of the next three Pilgrimage Festivals (i.e., Passover, Shavuot, Sukkot). If a person failed to do so, the verse later states, "God will demand it of you," meaning that one who reneges on a vow will only lose any money he was attempting to save.[205]

A person who vowed a specific amount of money to relieve the suffering of the poor must pay at once, because there are always poor people around who will accept the gift. Even if no one required assistance at the time, the money should be set aside so that is immediately available when necessary.[206]

Sefer ha-Chinuch observed that everyone acts promptly when civil authorities request payment for debts. Why should people not be at least as quick to respond when God demands the fulfillment of vows made to Him?[207]

Appearing on a Festival without a Sacrifice (156)

"You shall not appear before the Lord empty-handed" (Exod. 23:15; Deut. 16:16) is the commandment forbidding anyone from going

up to the Sanctuary for one of the three Pilgrimage Festivals without a sacrifice to be offered there. These included the festive peace offerings and burnt offerings, for which each person should give whatever he can, "according to the blessing that the Lord your God gives you." As the Mechilta observed, "It is not right that your own table be full while your Master's table is empty."[208]

Infringing any Oral Obligation, Even if Undertaken without an Oath (157)

"He shall not break his word" (Num. 30:3) is the commandment prohibiting people from failing to faithfully fulfill any obligations to which they have bound themselves orally, even without a formal oath. A Jew's word is sacred (Pos. Comm. 94), and thus to violate it is sacrilegious. According to Hirsch, a vow is "self-imposed legislation," an obligation as binding as God's commandments in the Torah.[209]

Limitations on Whom a Kohen May Marry (158-162)

As representatives of the people in the Divine service, the Kohanim assumed a particular responsibility to maintain the highest standards of holy behavior and purity.

"They shall not marry a woman who is a zonah or a chalalah, and they shall not marry a woman who has been divorced by her husband (for each one [Kohen] is holy to God)" (Lev. 21:7) is the verse underlying the negative commandments limiting those women whom a Kohen could marry. A Kohen who married a woman who was forbidden to him was disqualified from ministering in the Sanctuary. However, after giving a solemn promise to divorce her, the Kohen was allowed to resume his priestly functions.[210]

A Kohen was forbidden (158) to marry a *zonah*. Although usually translated as "harlot," this term applied specifically to a woman who had intercourse with any man who was not permitted to her as a husband because of a negative commandment. Rashi noted that such forbidden relationships included not only those punishable by death or *karet* (spiritual extinction), but also living with a *mamzer* or a non-Israelite woman.[211]

A Kohen was forbidden (**159**) to marry a *chalalah*. Generally translated as "desecrated" or "profaned," Rashi maintained that this term referred to a woman who was forbidden to marry a Kohen but had previously married one anyway (such as a divorcée who had married a Kohen or a widow who had married a *Kohen Gadol*), or to any daughters born of such relationships.[212] If a Kohen married one of these women, however, the marriage was binding and a legal divorce was required if the Kohen later wanted to be separated from his wife.[213]

A Kohen was forbidden (**160**) to marry a divorced woman.

In addition to the limitations placed on regular Kohanim, the *Kohen Gadol* was forbidden (**161**) to marry a widow (Lev. 21:14). Indeed, he was required to marry a virgin (Pos. Comm. 38). As Maimonides observed,[214] "the High Priest, the noblest of the priests, may not marry even a widow, or a woman who has had sexual intercourse of any kind."

The *Kohen Gadol* was forbidden (**162**) to have intercourse with a widow (even without marriage), based on the verse, "*He shall not desecrate his offspring among the people*" (Lev. 21:15). Some have translated this as "profane his seed," meaning that such an action would impair the pure descent of the family of Aaron by an improper relationship.[215] Rashi explains that if the *Kohen Gadol* and the widow had a male child, the son could not perform the service in the Temple or eat *terumah*; unlike other sons of Kohanim, he would be permitted to come in contact with a dead body. If the *Kohen Gadol* and the widow had a daughter, she would not be permitted to marry a Kohen. Similar restrictions applied to the children of an ordinary Kohen with a woman whom he was forbidden to marry because of his priestly status (see above).[216]

Kohanim and the Sanctuary (163-165)

"Do not leave your heads unshorn nor rend your garments..." (Lev. 10:6) is the source for the commandments prohibiting a Kohen from entering the Sanctuary with (163) long disheveled hair or (164) torn garments. These words were spoken by Moses to his brother Aaron immediately after the tragic death of the latter's two sons Nadab and Abihu, who performed some unauthorized service and lost their lives (Lev. 10:1-2). In order to not interfere with the joy of the inauguration of the priestly service in the Tabernacle, Aaron and his surviving sons were forbidden these usual expressions of grief (leaving hair uncut and tearing garments). The Rabbis extend these prohibitions to all Kohanim when ministering in the Sanctuary.

The *Kohen Gadol* had his hair trimmed every Friday, just before the arrival of new divisions of Kohanim on the Sabbath (Pos. Comm. 36); an ordinary Kohen did this once a month (Taan. 17a). Just as he would trim his hair to prepare for any joyous occasion in his life, how much more should a Kohen do so before entering the Sanctuary, since the privilege of participating in the Divine service should be a moment of incomparable happiness (Menachem Hababli). A Kohen wearing torn garments was considered to be like a mere layman, who was forbidden to participate in the Sanctuary service. [217]

The next verse, *"Do not go outside the entrance of the Tent of Meeting lest you die, for the Lord's anointing oil is upon you"* (Lev. 10:7) is the commandment (165) forbidding a ministering Kohen from abandoning the Sanctuary. According to Maimonides,[218] a common Kohen who learned of the death of a close relative was required to interrupt his ministering in the Divine service and arrange for an alternate Kohen to continue to ritual. However, he was forbidden to leave the confines of the Sanctuary until the service had been completed by the substitute Kohen (lest his premature departure be considered disrespectful to the service).

Kohanim and the Dead (166-168)

"None of you shall contaminate yourself for a dead person among his people" (Lev. 21:1) is the commandment (**166**) prohibiting an ordinary priest from defiling himself for any dead person other than those relatives specified in the Torah. These included his mother, father, son, daughter, and a brother or sister by the same father (Pos. Comm. 37). The phrase "among his people" may also be interpreted to mean that a Kohen is forbidden to participate in caring for the dead in any situation in which there are other Jews available to take care of the burial.[219] However, Maimonides[220] noted that the burial of the corpse of a person whose relatives are unknown (*met mitzvah*) is obligatory on everybody, and even the *Kohel Gadol* was required to interrupt his ministrations in the Sanctuary to attend to the burial rites of a destitute person.

"He shall not come near any dead person; he shall not contaminate himself [even] for his father or his mother" (Lev. 21:11) are the commandments (**167**) forbidding the *Kohen Gadol* from being under the same roof as a dead body, even that of one of the close relatives described above, and (**168**) defiling himself for any dead person, whether by contact or by carrying. These special regulations were necessary because the *Kohen Gadol* was required to be in the Sanctuary at all times and thus could not become ritually unclean through contact with the dead. According to Maimonides,[221] although the *Kohen Gadol* was forbidden to rend his garments or let his hair grow long, or even to follow the funeral procession of one of his relatives, he was still obliged to observe the laws of mourning. He was, however, granted certain marks

of distinction in view of his position. "When they prepare for him the first meal after the burial of a relative, all the people sit on the ground, and he sits on a bench. When comforting him, they say 'may we be your expiation,' and he replies 'be you blessed of Heaven'."[222]

Levites and the Land (169-170)

"The Kohanim and the Levites, the entire tribe of Levi, shall have no portion nor inheritance with Israel" (Deut. 18:1) is the command-ment **(169)** prohibiting the whole tribe of Levi from taking a portion of the territory of the land of Israel. Instead, they received various gifts of the produce of the Land, so that they could devote their efforts to religious duties without the need to produce their own food and other necessities.[223] The levitical cities (Pos. Comm. 183) were not considered an "inheritance" because they merely represented a place to live and a small amount of surrounding land, rather than a discrete territorial region like that allotted to the other tribes.[224]

This verse also is the basis for the commandment **(170)** for-bidding the whole tribe of Levi from sharing in the spoils taken during the conquest of the Land of Israel. As \ explained, "It is not fitting for servants of the Lord to make use of things that have which been taken by force. Only things that have been peacefully, fairly, and honestly acquired can enter the House of God, not those acquired by means which have brought sorrow to the heart of any man or woman."[225]

Tearing Out Hair for the Dead (171)

"You shall not make a bald spot between your eyes for the dead" (Deut. 14:1) is the commandment forbidding the Israelites from expressing their mourning by self-mutilation. Although the verse only speaks of tearing out the hair at the hairline above the

area between the eyes, Rashi noted that elsewhere the Torah prohibited tearing out the hair anywhere (Lev. 21:5). He added that the specificity of the verse may reflect that this was the prevailing custom among the pagan Amorites.

The beginning of the verse, "You are children of the Lord your God," implies that this and subsequent laws reflected that special status and the unshakable belief of the Israelites that after death their souls would ascend to the Divine realm to be reunited with God. Convinced that they will enjoy eternal peace in the World to Come, the Israelites should not be so terrified of death that they tear their hair, cut themselves, or otherwise mutilate their bodies like those who consider death to be absolutely final (Nachmanides, Sforno).[226]

Weeping for the dead is a normal and proper human reaction, as in Abraham's response to the death of his beloved wife, Sarah (Gen. 23:2). All Israel mourned the deaths of Aaron (Num. 20:29) and Moses (Deut. 34:8). However, mourning is permissible only in the forms prescribed by the law. Mutilating the body in any way as a form of mourning is an act of rebellion against the Divine judgment that has been visited on the family (*Sefer ha-Chinuch*).[227]

Jewish Dietary Laws (*Kashrut*) (172-179)

"Sanctify yourself and be holy, for I am holy" (Lev. 11:44) is the underlying rationale for the laws of *kashrut*. This demand has two aspects: (a) the positive aspect of imitating God by manifesting such Divine traits as being merciful, loving, and long-suffering; and (b) the negative aspect of withdrawing from things that are impure and abominable. Thus, the Jews were required to avoid anything that could pollute them, either physically or spiritually.[228] Maimonides noted that "the dietary laws train us in the mastery over our appetites; they accustom us to restrain both the growth of desire and the disposition to consider the pleasure of eating and drinking as the end of

man's existence."[229] This concept is illustrated in the *Sifra* (11:22): "Let not a man say, 'I do not like the flesh of swine.' On the contrary, he should say, 'I like it but must abstain seeing that the Torah has forbidden it'."

For Ezekiel (33:25), the eating of blood was equivalent to the sins of idolatry and murder. Conversely, abstaining from this practice decreases the innate human instinct for violence. The Zohar extended this to all forbidden food, noting that the consuming of blood and the worshiping of idols are both referred to as "abominations." The prohibition of birds of prey, which survive by their ability to kill other creatures, is a moral injunction against taking advantage of one another, for such predatory behavior is out of character with the Jewish attitudes of compassion and mercy.[230] For Ibn Ezra, the prohibition against aesthetically repulsive animals (such as eels, roaches, and ants) was simply that it would be impossible for one to have a pure, clean conscience with the knowledge that his own flesh is the product of a diet of insects, snakes, and other vermin.[231] In his allegorical Torah commentary *Akedat Yitzhak*, the 15th-century Isaac ben Moses Arama wrote: "The reason behind all the dietary prohibitions is not that any harm may be caused to the body, but that these foods defile and pollute the soul and blunt the intellectual powers, thus leading to confused opinions and a lust for perverse and brutish appetites that lead men to destruction, thus defeating the purpose of creation."

As a physician, Maimonides[232] observed that, "all food which is forbidden by the Law is unwholesome." *Sefer ha-Chinuch* noted, "the injurious effect of some forbidden foods in not known to us, or even to physicians. The True Faithful Doctor who has commanded us in all these things is infinitely wiser than we. How petty and foolish is the man who thinks that only those things which his understanding grasps are true, and everything else, everything unknown to him, is not true."[233]

"These shall you not eat among those that only chew the cud or only have a cloven hoof: the camel, the hare, and the hyrax ... and the pig" (Deut. 14:7-8) is the commandment (**172**) forbidding the eating of unclean domestic or wild quadrupeds. A kosher mammal must be a ruminant (cud-chewing) with a completely divided (cloven) hoof (Pos. Comm. 149). The camel, hare, and hyrax chew their cud but have incompletely split hooves; the pig has a completely cloven hoof but does not chew its cud.

Maimonides[234] observed that pork "contains more moisture than is necessary (for human food) and too much superfluous matter. The principal reason why the Law forbids swine's flesh is that the habits and food of the swine are very dirty and loathsome ... A saying of the Sages declares: 'The mouth of a swine is as dirty as dung itself' (Ber. 25a)."

"They shall be an abomination to you; you shall not eat of their flesh..." (Lev. 11:11) is the commandment (**173**) forbidding the eating of unclean fish. A kosher fish must have both fins and scales (Pos. Comm. 152). The scales must be capable of being scraped off easily with a knife, which excludes creatures whose scales are not clearly defined such as shellfish, shark, catfish, and amphibians.[235] Nachmanides explained that fish with fins and scales can swim close to the surface and, on occasion, come up for air. This warms their blood so that they are able to remove excess fluids and other impurities from their bodies. In contrast, those lacking fins and scales swim close to the sea bottom, cannot purify their bodies, and thus are be harmful to humans if eaten.[236] Jews are also forbidden to eat *"from all that teems in the water, and from all living creatures in the water"* (Lev. 11:10), which, respectively, prohibits small aquatic creatures and large water animals that are not fish (such as seals, dolphins, sharks, and whales).[237]

"These are abominations among the birds, they may not be eaten" (Lev. 11:13) is the commandment (**174**) forbidding the eating of

unclean birds (Pos. Comm. 150). Although kosher quadrupeds and fish are mentioned by characteristics so that their identities are clear, the Torah specifically names 20 non-kosher species of birds, thus implying that all others are kosher. The forbidden birds include the osprey, kite, vulture, raven, falcon, and hawk. Unfortunately, over time the precise identities of these non-kosher birds became unclear. Consequently, the *Shulchan Aruch* (YD 82:2) ruled that it is forbidden to eat any species of bird (or its eggs) unless there is a well-established tradition that it is kosher.[238]

"All winged swarming creatures that walk on all fours are unclean to you; they shall not be eaten" (Deut. 14:20) is the commandment (**175**) forbidding the eating of any winged swarming thing, such as flies, bees, hornets, and similar insects. An exception is the product of an insect that is not part of its body, such as honey from bees (Bek. 7b). The Torah mentions a few species of insects that can be eaten (Pos. Comm. 151), all of which have two jumping legs whose joints are higher than the insect's body when it is at rest (like locusts). However, because none of the four types of permitted insects can be unequivocally identified, later rabbis declared all species of locusts to be forbidden.

"Every swarming creature that swarms on the earth is an abomination; it shall not be eaten" (Lev. 11:41) is the commandment (**176**) forbidding the eating of worms, beetles, snakes, scorpions, and lizards, which Rashi defined as being low, having short legs, and appearing to creep along the ground.[239]

Based on verses in Leviticus (11:42-44), Maimonides cited as negative commandments three other prohibitions concerning eating various types of creatures. These include (**177**) any creeping thing that breeds in decayed matter, (**178**) living creatures that breed in seeds or fruit, and (**179**) any swarming creature (whether it swarms in the air, in water, or on land).

Eating *Nevelah* (180)

"You shall not eat of any animal that has died" (Deut. 14:21) is the commandment prohibiting the eating of the flesh of any kosher animal that has died without kosher slaughter (*nevelah*). This includes not only an animal that died a natural death, but also one that has been killed by shooting or incorrectly slaughtered. Unlike the non-kosher creatures that the Torah terms "abomination," *nevelah* may be consumed by gentiles residing in the Land but is forbidden to the Israelites only because it is not appropriate food for a holy people (Sforno).[240] Maimonides[241] considered both blood and *nevelah* indigestible and harmful as food. Abravanel deemed *nevelah* to be reprehensible to God because it was a pagan custom to eat this particular kind of meat.[242] However, R. Meir (Pes. 21b) stated that the owner of the carcass had the right to benefit from it by selling it to a gentile, even though it could not be eaten by a Jew.

Eating *Terefah* (181)

"You shall not eat any flesh of an animal that was torn in the field" (Exod. 22:30) is the commandment that originally prohibited the eating of "*terefah*," the flesh of an animal torn by a wild beast or a wild bird. Later the term was applied to the flesh of any injured or diseased animal that, although ritually slaughtered, would not have lived more than a year.[243] In his *Mishneh Torah*,[244] Maimonides lists 70 diseases and injuries that render an animal *terefah*. The word *terefah* is now used to refer to any meat that is not ritually fit for Jewish consumption.

The concluding portion of this verse indicates that the flesh of a *terefah* should be thrown to the dogs. According to Rashi, tossing forbidden meat to them was a reward for their actions during the Exodus, when the dogs did not bark or attack the

Israelites escaping from Egypt (Exod. 11:7). Ibn Ezra noted that dogs act as the guardians of flocks of sheep and herds of cattle. Should one of the flock or herd, nevertheless, fall prey to a wild beast, the dogs should be given the meat of the dead animal in gratitude for their efforts in protecting them.[245]

Eating a Limb of a Living Creature (182)

"You shall not eat the life with the flesh" (Deut. 12:23) is the commandment prohibiting the eating of a limb cut off from a living creature. The forbidding of this barbarous practice, which Maimonides wrote was associated with the idolatrous worship of heathen kings and would "produce and develop cruelty,"[246] was one of the seven Noahide laws that constituted the fundamental requirements of any civilized society.

Eating *Gid ha-Nasheh* (Sinew of the Thigh Vein) (183)

"Therefore, the children of Israel do not eat the sinew of the thigh vein" (Gen. 32:33) is the commandment forbidding the eating of the sciatic nerve, which extends from the rear of the spinal column and runs down the inner side of the leg. This nerve and its surrounding fat (as well as, according to rabbinic law, the common peroneal nerve along the outside of the leg and several other nerves and blood vessels) must be removed before the hindquarters of an animal can be ritually prepared for Jewish consumption.

This prohibition is an eternal reminder of the wrestling contest between Jacob and the mysterious "man," which took place as the Patriarch was returning to the Land of Israel after dwelling 20 years with his father-in-law, Laban (Gen. 32:25-32). During this titanic struggle—which resulted in Jacob's name being changed to Israel because "you have struggled with the

Divine and with man and have overcome" — the attacker injured Jacob's thigh, resulting in a residual limp.

Sefer ha-Chinuch maintained that this commandment is a symbol of Israel's survival. Just as Jacob faced a daunting task yet emerged victorious, so Jews throughout the ages should have confidence in God's assistance in helping them overcome the fiercest attacks of their enemies. Sforno viewed the commandment as symbolically teaching Jews that physical handicaps should not discourage their fight for survival.[247]

Eating Blood (184)

"You shall eat no blood" (Lev. 3:17; 7:26; 17:14; Deut. 12:23) is the commandment forbidding eating any blood. The reason given in the Torah for this prohibition is "for the soul of the flesh is in the blood... to make atonement for your souls" (Lev .17:11). All life depends on the blood, and thus God decreed that blood be sprinkled on the Altar to secure atonement, effectively allowing one life to be offered to atone for another. In view of its sacred symbolic purpose, blood should not to be eaten by Jews (Rashi). Sforno stressed that God, unlike pagan deities, has no desire for blood as such, but only for the dedication of human beings to the Divine service that the blood represents.[248]

According to Maimonides, the Torah forbade the use of blood except for rituals, sacrifices, and purification to emphasize the distinction between Judaism and idol worship. Nachmanides feared that the intermingling of the blood of an animal with that of a human being who ate it would inevitably lead to the latter acting like the former.[249]

The blood of sacrificial offerings had to be treated with respect and covered with dust, equivalent to the reverent burial of a dead body (Pos. Comm. 147). In addition, all meat must be soaked and salted (or broiled) until all traces of blood are removed. Liver contains so much blood that soaking and salting are not sufficient to remove it, and thus it must be broiled over an open flame.[250]

Throughout the centuries, Jews were victims of blood libel, the accusation that they murdered non-Jews in a religious ritual and either drank their blood or used it to bake matzah for Passover. Ironically, these ridiculous claims were made against the first nation in history to outlaw human sacrifice and the only people in the ancient Near East to prohibit the consumption of any blood.

Eating the Fat of a Clean Animal (185)

"You shall eat no fat of ox, sheep, or goat" (Lev. 7:23) is the commandment prohibiting eating the fat of a clean animal, whether consecrated or not. Although the word *"chelev"* is commonly translated as "fat," it actually referred only to the fatty tissue attached to the stomach and extending over the kidneys, liver, and intestines of a sacrificial offering that was placed on the Altar.[251, 252] Therefore, it was permitted to eat the ordinary fat (*shemen*) that adheres to the flesh of the deer and other kosher wild animals that could not be used for sacrificial offerings.

The major commentators considered the eating of *chelev* to be prohibited because it was harmful to human health (Maimonides, *Sefer ha-Chinuch*) or could make a person fat and decrease physical or mental function (Abravanel). Because it was part of animal sacrifices, the *chelev* was considered sacred and forbidden as food (Renacati).[253]

Cooking Meat in Milk/Eating Meat Cooked in Milk (186-187)

"You shall not boil a kid in its mother's milk" (Exod. 23:19, 34:26; Deut 14:21) is the source of the commandments pro-

hibiting (186) cooking meat in milk and (187) eating meat cooked in milk. These commandments are the source of the separation of meat and milk, and the requirement of separate sets of dishes and utensils, that is at the heart of the Jewish dietary laws. The prohibition referred to all sheep and cattle, not only to the milk of its own mother, and was later extended by the Rabbis to apply to all other kosher meat and fowl. The Rabbis (Hul. 115b) interpreted the threefold repetition of this verse (Exod. 23:19; 34:26; Deut. 14:21) as defining three separate prohibitions—cooking meat and milk together; eating such a mixture; and deriving any benefit from it, such as savoring the aroma or feeding it to a pet. The term "milk" was interpreted to mean all dairy products, such as butter, cheese, and fresh and sour cream. Because many commonly eaten processed foods contain unsuspected dairy ingredients—such as bread, cakes, and cookies (which can also contain lard or beef tallow) made with buttermilk, nonfat dry milk, whey, or dairy-derived additives—kashrut-observers always read the labels carefully and only buy such products with a *hechsher* (kosher certification). Those Jews who are strictest about their observance of kashrut have special requirements for the dairy products they eat, only consuming those labeled *chalav Yisrael* (milk of the Jewish people). In addition to making certain of the standard requirement that all milk and dairy products never come into contact with any meat products, *chalav Yisrael* requires that cows be closely watched to ensure that they never eat any non-kosher food or have their milk mixed with any that is not kosher. The production of cheese is also tightly regulated. Hard cheeses often use rennet, an enzyme derived from the inner lining of the stomach of a calf. To be strictly kosher, the rennet must come from a kosher animal that was slaughtered in a ritually correct manner and whose stomach was correctly prepared and thoroughly dried. Today, many cheeses are made using vegetable enzymes.²⁵⁴

Because meat takes a long time to digest (or due to residual meat particles caught in the teeth or its taste remaining on the palate), Jewish law rules that one must wait a designated period after eating a meat meal before ingesting milk products. Customs range from an hour for Jews of Dutch ancestry to three hours for German Jews and six hours for those from other European countries. The waiting time between milk and meat is much shorter. One is generally permitted to eat meat almost immediately after a milk meal, after thoroughly rinsing the mouth and eating a piece of bread or some other "neutral" solid.²⁵⁵ After consuming hard cheese, however, it is customary to wait a longer period (up to six hours in some traditions) before eating meat. Today, there is wide availability of imitation "milk" derived from soybeans, coconuts, almonds, rice, and oats that may be used with meat. Fruit, vegetables, grains, and eggs are all considered neutral (*pareve*) and may be eaten together with milk or meat dishes. Fish is also a neutral food, but the Rabbis prohibited cooking or eating fish and meat together because they were convinced that this mixture was dangerous for one's health.

In order to create a "fence around the Torah," the Rabbis decreed that the separation of meat from milk must be as complete as possible. Thus, it is necessary to use separate pots and utensils for dairy foods and meat, respectively known in Yiddish as *milchig* and *fleishig*. This entails storing them in separate areas, washing them in separate bowls or sinks, and drying them with different dishcloths that are ideally of distinct colors to prevent any mistake.

Maimonides²⁵⁶ saw this prohibition as an attack on idolatry and superstition, labeling the mixing of meat and milk a pagan custom and thus not appropriate for Jews. For Abravanel and

Luzzatto, eating meat and milk was banned because it produced a callous, heartless attitude inconsistent with the care and compassion expected of a Jew.[257]

Eating the Flesh of a Stoned Ox (188)

"(If an ox gores a man or a woman to death, the ox shall surely be stoned) and its flesh shall not be eaten" (Exod. 21:28) is the commandment prohibiting the eating of the flesh of an ox killed in this manner in accordance with a court-imposed death penalty (Pos. Comm. 237). The carcass must be buried, and the owner was forbidden to sell it to non-Jews, feed it to the dogs, or benefit from it in any other way.[258]

According to Maimonides,[259] "the killing of an animal that has killed a human being is not punishment to the animal ... but is a fine imposed on the owner." Similarly, the prohibition against eating the meat of the animal was to ensure that the owner would use the utmost care in guarding it, realizing that if the ox killed a human being he would forfeit at least the animal (plus a fine if he had received prior warning as to the animal's dangerous tendencies).[260]

Eating Bread/Roasted Ears/Fresh Ears of Grain of the New Crop (189-191)

"You shall eat no bread or parched grain or fresh ears (until that very day)" (Lev. 23:14) is the source of the commandments prohibiting the eating of (**189**) bread, (**190**) roasted grain, and (**191**) fresh ears of grain before the *"omer,"* the offering of the new barley crop on Nisan 16 (Pos. Comm. 161). Before eating any of the grain he has reaped, the Jew must first bring some as a thanksgiving offering to God (*Sefer ha-Chinuch*).[261]

Eating *Orlah* (192)

"For three years they shall be forbidden to you, not to be eaten" (Lev. 19:23) is the commandment forbidding the eating of *orlah*, the fruit of a tree during its first three years. All such fruit had to be burned; if in liquid form, it must be buried.

Maimonides[262] maintained that idolaters offered part of the first fruits of every tree as a thanksgiving sacrifice and consumed the rest in the idol's temple, lest the tree dry up. In opposition to this principle, the Torah commanded the Jews to burn the produce of fruit trees for the first three years. Ibn Ezra and Nachmanides believed that fruit from such young trees was harmful to health.

Eating *Kelai ha-Kerem* (193)

"(You shall not sow your field with a mixture,) lest the growth of seed that you plant and the produce of the vineyard be forfeited" (Deut. 22:9) is the commandment prohibiting the eating of *"kelai ha-kerem."* The Hebrew word *"kelayim"* implies mutually exclusive kinds, such as the produce of a vineyard sown with different kinds of seeds (grape with grain or vegetables).[263]

Maimonides[264] noted that this commandment was in opposition to the heathen custom of sowing barley and grape seeds together in the belief that this was the only way that the vineyard would thrive. If a Jew followed this procedure, both the barley and the produce of the vineyard would be burned. The rationale was the need to prohibit any practices that pagans deemed magical, even if they did not contain any blatantly idolatrous element.

Drinking *Yain Nesech* (194)

"Who ate the fat of their offerings, and drank the wine of their libations" (Deut. 32:38) is cited by Maimonides as the source

of the commandment forbidding the drinking of *yain nesech* — "libation-wine that has been used in connection with idol worship." Nachmanides and *Sefer ha-Chinuch* disagreed, arguing that this prohibition derived from the verse "Lest you make a covenant with the inhabitants of the land, and stray after their gods... and he invite you and you eat from the sacrifice to his gods" (Exod. 34:15).[265]

Eating and Drinking to Excess (195)

"You shall not eat anything with its blood" (Lev. 19:26) is cited by Maimonides as the source of the commandment prohibiting eating and drinking to excess. In context, this phrase refers to the forbidden practice of sorcerers who would collect blood in a dish, cast a spell or invoke their pagan gods, and predict the future.[266] However, Maimonides understood the words as meaning that one should not eat in such a debased way as to merit the Divine punishment of premature death.

For Maimonides,[267] "intemperance in eating, drinking, and sexual intercourse ... counteract the ultimate perfection of man ... and generally disturb the social order of the country and the economy of the family." He noted that the Torah has "commanded us to slay a person from whose conduct it is evident that he will go too far in seeking the enjoyment of eating and drinking." This refers to the "rebellious and stubborn son," who is described in the Bible as "a glutton and drunkard" (Deut. 21:20) and whose punishment is to be stoned and removed from society, "lest he grow up in this character, and kill many, and injure the condition of good men by his great lust." Rashi echoes these sentiments, observing that in view of the high cost of meat and alcoholic drinks, the boy must have stolen money from his parents to pay for them. This indicates that he likely will grow up to become a vicious robber to finance his voracious appetite.[268]

Eating on Yom Kippur (196)

"Any person who does not afflict his soul [practice self-denial] throughout that day will be cut off from his people" (Lev. 23:29) is the commandment providing the punishment of *karet* (spiritual extinction) for violating the prohibition against eating on the fast day of Yom Kippur (Pos. Comm. 164).

Yom Kippur is characterized by a 25-hour fast—unlike most fast days, other than Tisha b'Av, which last only from dawn to dusk. However, a sick person whose health would be jeopardized by fasting is obligated to eat, according to the principle of *pikuach nefesh* (saving of life). Even a healthy person seized by a fit of "ravenous hunger" that causes faintness must be fed on Yom Kippur with whatever food is available until he recovers. According to tradition, children under the age of nine are not allowed to fast; over that age, they should fast for a longer period each year. A woman is not allowed to fast within three days of giving birth; from four to seven days after delivery, she should follow her doctor's advice.[269] As a general rule, the decision whether to fast on Yom Kippur depends on the subjective opinion of the patient who claims the need to eat, even if contradicted by 100 doctors. Conversely, a patient must eat if a doctor declares that it is essential for health, even if he or she thinks it is not necessary.[270]

Forbidden *Chametz* on Passover (197-201)

These commandments deal with the prohibition of eating or possessing leavened bread or any product made from the five kinds of grain or flour (wheat, barley, spelt, oats, and rye) that is prepared in water and leavened (*chametz*) during Passover.

"Chametz *may not be eaten*" (Exod. 13:3) is the command-ment (197) that explicitly forbids the eating of leavened prod-ucts during Passover. The willful violation of this injunction was punished by *karet* (spiritual extinction), based on the verse "that soul shall be cut off from Israel" (Exod. 12:15). Pots in which *chametz* has been cooked absorb and retain some of it—"imparting a flavor" into any other food cooked in them—so those that have been used during the year are forbidden for use during Passover unless they have been rigorously cleansed in accordance with halachic requirements (Sh. Ar., OH 451). For the same reason, separate dishes must be used for Passover; however, this is not required for non-permeable glass, which only needs to be soaked and washed to be permissible for Passover use.

Foods containing any amount of *chametz* (not just bread) are prohibited on Passover (198), based on the verse "*You shall eat nothing leavened*" (Exod. 12:20). Ashkenazic authorities forbid the use of rice and millet on Passover, and included a group of foods known as *kitniyot* in the prohibition as well. *Kitniyot*, generally translated as "legumes," are foods such as beans, peas, corn, lentils, buckwheat, and, according to some authori-ties, peanuts. One reason for this ruling is to prevent possible confusion if flour made from these substances were stored near *chametz* flour. Otherwise, one might inadvertently bake matzah using rice or a legume flour, which was not permissible since matzah theoretically may only be made with one of the five grains that are capable of becoming leavened (but in practice, only with wheat).

Chametz may not be eaten after noon on Nisan 14, the day before Passover (199), based on the verse "*You shall not eat any-thing leavened with it*" (Deut. 16:3), which referred to the Paschal lamb that was required to be sacrificed later in the afternoon on that day (Exod. 12:6). Nachmanides maintained that this was already the subject of the positive commandment (156) to destroy all leaven in our possession (which would obviously includes a ban on eating *chametz*), and thus he did not consider this as a separate negative commandment.[271]

Chametz may not even be seen in the habitation of a Jew during Passover (**200**), based on the verse *"No chametz may be seen in your possession, nor any leaven found in all your territory"* (Exod. 13:7). As the Mechilta observed, this does not apply to *chametz* actually owned by a Jew, but subject to the control of a non-Jew; even if the Jew could destroy it, he does not have the right to do so. *Chametz* actually owned by a non-Jew, but under the control of a Jew, is also excluded (he has no right to destroy it), as is *chametz* buried under debris (he cannot physically destroy it).[272]

The possession of *chametz* during Passover is also forbidden (**201**), based on the verse *"For seven days, no leaven may be found in your houses"* (Exod. 12:19). In contrast to the previous commandment, which applies only to *chametz* in an open and visible place, this commandment prohibits *chametz* that is hidden and not apparent to an outsider.[273]

The disposal of *chametz* could produce serious financial hardship when large quantities of foodstuffs are involved, or where *chametz* is used for business purposes. To alleviate this problem, the rabbis devised the legal formula of "selling" the *chametz* (*mechirat chametz*) to a non-Jew before Passover and then "buying" it back after the festival has concluded. This applies only to foods; utensils used for *chametz* need only be stored separately.

Initially, the selling of *chametz* involved the physical transfer from Jew to non-Jew "in the market place" (Pes. 13a), though soon there developed the mutual understanding that the Jew would buy it back after Passover. To preclude the need for having to physically transfer the property, today the seller merely writes down the type of *chametz* without specifying the precise amount or exact location. The parties agree on a price and a down payment made by the non-Jew, who theoretically could choose to pay the purchase price and keep the *chametz*. Because a formal legal document is required, the sale usually is done through a rabbi, who is empowered to act as the agent in the transaction. After Passover, the agent buys back the *chametz* and restores it to the original owners.

Laws of the Nazirite (202-209)

The Nazirite was a person who voluntarily undertook austere modes of self-dedication beyond the obligatory commandments in order to reach an elevated state of holiness (Pos. Comm. 92-93). The Torah (Num. 6:1-21) indicates the specific activities forbidden to the Nazirite.

The Nazirite was forbidden to drink wine or eat any grape products. The primary prohibition (**202**) was the drinking of wine, even for *Kiddush* and *Havdalah*, in conjunction with sanctifying the Sabbath (Pos. Comm. 155). However, the Torah added provisions against any grape products, lest the Nazirite be in the proximity of foods that might tempt him to drink the forbidden beverage.[274] Thus, there are separate commandments prohibiting the consumption of (**203**) fresh grapes, (**204**) dried grapes (raisins), (**205**) kernels of grapes, and (**206**) husks of grapes. According to *Sefer ha-Chinuch*, the reason for the multiple prohibitions with respect to grapes is to safeguard the Nazirite from sin, "since every part of the grape has its power to increase the evil inclination in man. This is well known to students of nature."[275] Another explanation is that these prohibitions avoid giving others a wrong impression. People who see a Nazirite eating grapes might suspect that he or she would drink grape wine as well. As the Midrash states (Num. R. 19:8), "Avoid unseemliness and the appearance of unseemliness."[276]

The Nazirite was prohibited from rendering himself ritually unclean by having any contact with a human corpse (**207**), or even by entering a house containing a corpse (**208**). This ritual defilement was forbidden even in relation to the deaths of a father, mother, or sibling. The reason given by the Torah is "because the *nezer* [crown] of God is upon his head." Ibn Ezra explained that, "All people are slaves of their desires. The monarch who wears the true crown of royalty on his head is therefore the man who frees himself from his worldly desires."[277] The only exception to this prohibition of ritual defilement from contact with the dead was the case of the *met mitzvah*. According to the Talmud (Nazir 47a), if both the *Kohen Gadol* and a Nazirite (both of whom were forbidden to come in contact with the dead) came upon a neglected corpse (*met mitzvah*), the Nazirite should attend to the burial, since his sanctity was temporary and not lifelong like that of the *Kohen Gadol*.[278] If the Nazirite inadvertently came into contact with a corpse (either accidentally or carelessly by negligence), the days already counted were forfeited, a sacrificial ritual was performed, and a new term of Nazirism began. The sacrifices included a sin offering to provide atonement, which the Rabbis considered was required either because of the failure of the Nazirite to take better precautions to avoid becoming contaminated, or because of having deprived himself of the pleasure of drinking wine (Rashi). [279]

The Nazirite was prohibited from shaving (**209**) during the course of his vow. Both the shaver and the shaved were considered equally guilty. According to Sforno, the long, wild hair of the Nazir that resulted from his being forbidden to cut it served to protect his mind from vain thoughts so that he could concentrate on his life of consecration.[280] This was the most striking characteristic of the most famous biblical Nazirite, Samson, whose supernatural strength was attributed to his unshorn hair (Judg. 13-16).

The Nazirite who failed to fulfill his vow was not only guilty of violating one of the above negative commandments, but also the general prohibition against infringing any oral obligation (Neg. Comm. 157).

The Rabbis debated whether the assumption of the Nazirite vow was a praiseworthy act. Maimonides[281] maintained that it could be commended "only if the intention of the person who took the vow was to reform his conduct and to discipline his thoughts, as for example if one had contracted the habit of drinking to excess, or had become conceited because of his physical appearance. Only in circumstances such as these does the Nazirite vow constitute a mode of service to the Lord."

Failure to Leave Produce for the Poor (210-214)

These five commandments are the negative correlates of the positive commandments (120-124) that require farmers to leave certain produce of the fields and vineyards for the poor. According to Menachem Hababli, providing for the impoverished at harvest time mitigates the bitterness some poor people feel toward their Divinely decreed fate. In this way, the owner of the field helps to preserve peace between the poor and God, while at the same time being reminded that all he possesses is ultimately the property of the true Owner of everything.[282]

Therefore, it was forbidden for the farmer to (210) reap all the harvest, (211) gather ears of corn that fell during the harvest, (212) gather the whole produce of the vineyard at vintage time, and (213) gather single fallen grapes during the harvest (Lev. 19:9-10), as well as to (214) return for a forgotten sheaf of grain (Deut. 24:19).

The law of forgotten produce teaches that charity, even when not given intentionally, benefits the donor. "If a coin falls out of one's hand and a poor man finds it and supports himself by it, one will be blessed on that account" (Sifre).[283]

Forbidden Mixtures (215-218)

Jewish law forbids human beings from interfering with the Divine design of creation. God commanded each species of plant and animal to reproduce "after its kind," and thus Jews are prohibited from violating this decree and mixing them.[284]

"You shall not sow your field with two kinds of seed" (Lev. 19:19) is the commandment (**215**) forbidding the sowing of a mixture of seeds (*kilayim*). However, this was permitted if the different varieties were separated by a fence or planted far enough apart so that each could extract nutrients from the soil without interfering with the other.[285] Maimonides[286] noted that this commandment only applied to seeds of edible plants and not to herbs used mainly for medicinal purposes. Similarly, it was forbidden (**216**) to sow grain or vegetables in a vineyard (*kelai ha-kerem*, see Neg. Comm. 193), which was derived from the verse *"You shall not sow your vineyard with two kinds of seeds"* (Deut. 22:9).

"You shall not mate your animal with another species" (Lev. 19:19) is the commandment (**217**) prohibiting the mating of any two different species of animal, whether domestic or wild. Maimonides[287] believed that "animals of different species do not copulate together, unless by force," and thus the Torah "objected to any person degrading himself by doing these things, which require so much vulgarity and indecency." Nachmanides maintained that attempts to crossbreed plants and animals were effectively arrogant human assertions that they were permitted to produce new creatures, a right that belongs only to God.[288]

Working with two different kinds of animals together was also forbidden (**218**), derived from the verse *"You shall not plow with an ox and a donkey together"* (Deut. 22:10). According to Rashi, this prohibition applied to the coupling of any two different species and to any activity, not only plowing. The ox and donkey differ greatly in temperament, size, and strength, so that it would be cruel to the weaker animal to yoke them together.[289] Maimonides, however, related this commandment to the prior one, seeing it as preventing intercourse between two species that might result from their being joined together in any work.

For the prohibition against combining fibers of linen and wool in a single garment (*sha'atnez*), see Neg. Comm. 42.

Rashi viewed the commandments against forbidden mixtures to be the ultimate *chukim*, Divine injunctions for which human beings know no reasons. Nevertheless, Nachmanides offered a rationale for forbidding *kilayim*. God created certain distinctions in the natural world, and it would be wrong for humans to obliterate them by the process of intermixing (thus demonstrating insufficient confidence in the Divine design for nature).[290] Josephus attributed the prohibition against mating different species to the fear that such deviations in the natural order might result in immoral relationships among human beings.[291]

The laws forbidding mixtures apply only to the scenarios specified in the Bible. Human beings are encouraged to use their intellectual prowess to develop alloys and other combinations of materials that improve the world, thus aiding God in "completing" the work of Creation.[292]

Preventing an Animal from Eating the Produce Amid Which it is Working (219)

"You shall not muzzle the ox when it is threshing" (Deut. 25:4) prohibits the farmer from preventing an animal from satisfying its appetite by eating of the produce with which it is working. This prohibition extends to all animals employed in any type of labor. As *Sefer ha-Chinuch* observed, this and other regulations forbidding cruelty to animals (Pos. Comm. 148; Neg. Comm. 218, 306) develop an attitude of kindness and compassion that human beings can use when interacting with each other.[293]

Limitations for the Sabbatical Year
(220-223, 230-231)

"But the seventh year shall be a complete rest for the land, (a Sabbath for the Lord); you shall neither sow your field nor prune your vineyard. That which grows by itself of the harvest you shall not reap, and the grapes of your untrimmed vine you shall not gather" (Lev. 25:4-5) is the source of several of the negative commandments relating to the prohibition of planting, pruning, and gathering in the Sabbatical Year (*Shemittah*). During this seventh year the land was to lie fallow and be freed from cultivation (Pos Comm. 135). The rabbis of the Talmud regarded the Sabbatical Year (and Jubilee Year) as applying only to the Land of Israel, based on the introductory verse "When you come into the land that I give you ..." (Lev. 25:2).

During the Sabbatical Year, it was forbidden to (**220**) cultivate the soil, (**221**) prune trees, (**222**) reap anything that grows by itself, and (**223**) gather fruit in the same manner as in an ordinary year. According to the *Sifra* (Lev. 25:5), this final prohibition meant that "seventh-year figs may not be cut with a [special] fig-knife, but may be cut with an ordinary knife; grapes may not be trodden in a wine-press, but they may be trodden in a vat; and olives could may not be prepared in an olive-press or with an olive crusher, but may be crushed and put into a small press."

Rashi defines the phrase anything that "grows by itself" as referring to the crops that developed from seeds that fell on the soil while harvesting the sixth year's crop and had not be planted intentionally. During the Sabbatical Year, it was forbidden for people to treat their fields as their own and prevent others from enjoying the harvest (Pos. Comm. 134). The produce could be eaten by everyone (owners, gentile laborers, and wild animals alike) and used exclusively for food (not commerce).[294]

As the need for Jews to grow food in Israel became an acute issue in modern times, the observance of the Sabbatical Year became a problem. To cope with this situation, most rabbinic authorities have permitted Jewish farmers (via a legal fiction) to sell their land to non-Jews for the *Shemittah* period. In this way, they can cultivate the land as non-owners.[295]

"Every creditor shall release that which he has lent his neighbor; he shall not exact it of his neighbor or his kinsman" (Deut. 15:2) is the commandment (**230**) forbidding the demanding of payment of debts during the Sabbatical Year and causing them to be entirely canceled (Pos. Comm. 141). This remission of debts in the seventh year did not apply to gentiles living in the Land. With respect to Jews, only personal loans were canceled, not those secured by collateral.[296] The Torah recognized that financial concerns might lead one to refuse to give a loan to a needy fellow-Jew, especially as the Sabbatical Year approached. Therefore, it warned *"Beware that there not be a base thought in your heart saying: 'the seventh year, the year of release, is approaching' ... and you give him nothing"* (Deut. 15:9)—the commandment (**231**) forbidding one from withholding a loan to a fellow-Jew solely on the basis that it would be canceled by the Sabbatical Year.

Limitations for the Jubilee Year (224-227)

"You shall not sow, you shall not reap that which grows by itself, and you shall not gather the grapes of untrimmed vines" (Lev. 25:11) is the source of several of the negative commandments relating to the Jubilee Year. In common with the Sabbatical Year, it was forbidden to (**224**) cultivate the soil, (**225**) reap anything that grows by itself, or (**226**) gather fruit in the same manner as in an ordinary year (see Neg. Comm. 220-223).

According to Kli Yakar, sanctifying the Sabbatical Year was to remind us that the earth belonged to God. Sanctifying the 50th year was to stress that "there is a limit to our earthly toil, since a man living the ordinary span of life spends 50 years of it (from ages 20 to 70) in work. Thus the laws of the Jubilee Year remind man that he is but a sojourner on the face of the earth."[297]

"The land shall not be sold in perpetuity" (Lev. 25:23) is the commandment (227) prohibiting the permanent selling of one's holdings in the Land of Israel, since every 50 years all land was to revert to its original owner (Pos. Comm. 138). Such a transaction was invalid, and both the buyer and the seller were guilty of violating the commandment.[298] The reason for this prohibition appears in the second half of the verse, "for the land is Mine." As the Psalmist wrote, "The earth is the Lord's" (24:1), with humans having only temporary custody of it. Rather than the land itself, what could be sold was what the human labor could harvest from it.[299]

Selling the Open Lands of the Levites (228)

"The fields of the open land about their cities may not be sold; (for it is an eternal heritage for them)" (Lev. 25:34) is the commandment prohibiting the permanent selling of the fields of the Levites. Although the fields could be sold, all levitical property reverted to its original owner in the Jubilee Year. This was in contrast to the situation of an ordinary Israelite, who could lose ownership right to property forever by consecrating a field to the Temple treasury and either not redeeming it or having the Temple treasurer sell it before the original owner or a relative redeemed it. In both of these cases, the field would not revert back to the Israelite owner in the Jubilee Year, but instead would be divided among the Kohanim (Rashi).[300]

According to Maimonides, the Tradition read the verse as meaning that the property of the Levites may not "change" (rather than "change ownership"). Thus, *Sefer ha-Chinuch* observed that God had prescribed the precise design in which these cities were to be laid out (Num. 35:2-5), so that they would be an appropriate home for the students and teachers of Torah. Any change in this plan, such as converting open lands into urban areas and vice versa, would deviate from the Divine concept and thus destroy the intended effect.[301]

Forsaking the Levites (229)

"Be sure not to neglect the Levite, (all your days on your Land)" (Deut. 12:19) is the commandment prohibiting the Israelites from neglecting to give the Levites their due portions in full or to gladden their hearts on the festivals. This was important because the Levites never received a portion in the Land (Neg. Comm. 169). Hirsch notes that among a population engaged in farming and raising cattle, such "unproductive" members of society could easily become neglected and even resented. Therefore, it was essential that the people provide for the Levites in recognition of the vital role that the Levites played in preserving the spiritual and moral welfare of the community.[302] Rashi maintained that the final phrase of the verse implies that there is no special obligation to support the Levites in the Diaspora, other than the general obligation to support any poor person.[303]

Failure to Give Charity to Our Needy Brethren (232)

"Do not harden your heart, nor shut your hand from your needy kinsman" (Deut. 15:7) is the commandment forbidding the withholding of charity and relief from a fellow Jew (Pos. Comm. 195).

The first half of the verse is a warning to the person debating whether he or she can afford to give charity or make a loan. The remainder is addressed to one who decides to give but reneges at the last moment. Both of these behaviors can have dire consequences; as Rashi observed, failing to help one's needy kinsman may result in a person joining him in poverty.

The order of priority in dispensing charity was derived from the opening of the verses, "If there be a destitute person among you, any of your brethren in any of your cities, in the Land that the Lord your God gives you," and "If you lend money to My people, to the poor among you..." (Exod. 22:24). Based on the latter verse, the Rabbis drew several inferences (BM 71a): "Between a Jew and a gentile, My people come first; .... between your poor [members of your family] and the [general] poor of your town, your poor come first; between the poor of your city and of another city, the 'poor among you' [of your city] come first." Nevertheless, according to the *Shulchan Aruch*, this rule does not apply to the poor of the Land of Israel, who have priority over all. The Rabbis maintained that charity should be given to the non-Jewish poor "to preserve good relations," though they strongly urged Jews not to accept financial assistance from non-Jews unless absolutely necessary.

Sending Away a Hebrew Bondman Empty-Handed (233)

"When you set him free, do not send him away empty-handed" (Deut. 15:13) is the commandment prohibiting a person from permitting a departing Hebrew bondman or bondwoman to leave one's service without assets. Instead, the master was commanded to give generous gifts when the Hebrew bondman or bondwoman became free, so that he or she could make a fresh start in life following the six years of service (Pos. Comm. 196). As *Sefer ha-Chinuch* noted: "The pride and glory of our moral qualities is to show compassion towards one who has worked for us, to give him of our own as an act of lovingkindness, beside the reward that is due to him for his labor."[304]

The Torah provides a reason for this commandment by stressing the need for Jews to remember that they also were once slaves in the Land of Egypt (Deut. 15:15). When God redeemed the people and they went free, God caused the Egyptians to give them abundant gifts (Rashi).

Demanding Payment from a Debtor Known to be Unable to Pay (234)

"(When you lend money to My people...), do not act toward him as a creditor" (Exod. 22:24) is the commandment prohibiting a person from demanding money from a debtor who is known to be unable to pay. Although the lender has a right to have his money returned, he may not embarrass the borrower by harassing him.[305] The lender is forbidden to seize the debtor's land or to sell him or his family into slavery to secure payment.[306]

Conversely, Jewish law condemns the person who has the means to repay a debt but refuses to do so, based on the verse: "The wicked man borrows and does not repay; the righteous is generous and keeps giving" (Ps. 37:21).[307]

Lending or Borrowing at Interest (235-237)

Jews are forbidden to (235) lend at interest (Lev. 25:36-37) or (236) borrow at interest from a fellow-Jew (Deut. 23:20). In addition, Jews are forbidden (237) to even take part in a transaction between borrower and lender involving a loan at interest – whether as surety, witness, or notary drawing up the contract between them for payment of the interest on which they have agreed (Exod. 22:24). Maimonides maintained that it was a *command* to exact interest from non-Jews to whom one lends money (Pos. Comm. 198), while virtually all other commentators believed it was merely *permitted* to do so.

The Torah strictly forbids lending money to a fellow Jew at interest, even though such payments might be regarded as no more than a "rental charge" for the use of the money. Giving a loan without any expectation of profit was considered one of the highest forms of charity, because it preserved the self-respect of the borrower and allowed him to rebuild his own financial stability, so that he would no longer be dependent on others.[308] Kli Yakar observed that the lender actually derives a greater benefit from his generosity than the borrower does from the loan. The borrower is helped only in this world; however, by generously helping the poor on earth, the lender receives a reward in the World to Come.[309] The Talmud considered lending money at interest to be like both murder (BM 61b) and doubting the Divine wisdom and origin of the Torah (BM 75b).

In addition to direct and fixed interest payments (lending four coins and receiving five in return), the Talmud prohibited a broad spectrum of "indirect benefits" that could be offered in lieu of interest. These included offering a gift when asking for a loan or giving a gift when repaying it (pre- and post-paid interest, respectively); allowing the lender to live on the borrower's premises rent-free or at a reduced rent (BM 64b); and a borrower giving a lender valuable information or even "extending a greeting to him if that is not his usual practice" (BM 75b). If two people agreed to do work for each other in turn, they had to make certain that the values were identical (since in different seasons the work may be of unequal difficulty), lest the more valuable work be construed as containing a component of forbidden interest (BM 5:10).

As the agrarian society of the biblical Land of Israel was transformed into a more urban economy, lending money at interest became necessary to preserve the financial well-being of the Jewish community. Consequently, the Rabbis developed a variety of techniques for circumventing the prohibition against lending at interest. The simplest method was to lend money at interest to a non-Jew, who in turn would lend the money to a Jew (BM 61b). A more ingenious approach was the *hetter iskah* (permission to form a partnership). Using a standardized and witnessed legal form, the "lender" would agree to provide a specified amount of money to the "borrower" as a "joint venture." The "borrower" alone would operate the business, pledging to pay a fixed minimum profit (i.e., interest) and guaranteeing the "lender's" capital against all loss. At the agreed time of maturity, the "lender" would recover the initial investment ("loan") plus the promised minimum profit as stipulated in the deed. Today, making an interest-bearing business transaction comply with Jewish law merely requires adding the words *al-pi hetter iskah* to the legal document.

Oppressing an Employee by Delaying Payment of Wages (238)

"You shall not withhold a worker's wage with you until morning" (Lev. 19:13) is the commandment prohibiting one from injuring a laborer by delaying payment of his wages (Pos. Comm. 200; Neg. Comm. 247). As the talmud (BM 110b) explains, "A worker engaged by the day can collect [his wages] any time during the [following] night; one engaged by the night can collect [his wages] any time during the [following] day." This means that an employer has until the next morning to pay a day worker and until the following evening to pay a person who works at night. This rule comes into effect once the wage is due to be paid, so that a worker hired on a weekly basis must be paid at the end of the week, rather than a portion each day.

Law of Pledges of Debtors (239-242)

The Torah was deeply concerned with preserving the dignity of a debtor and preventing the creditor from taking as pledges items that were desperately needed by their impoverished owner for making his living or for his bare necessities.

"You shall not enter into his house to seize his pledge" (Deut. 24:10) is the commandment (**239**) forbidding taking a pledge

(security for a loan) from a debtor by force, "except by order of a judge and through his emissary." Neither the creditor nor the agent of the Court was permitted to go into the debtor's house to collect the pledge, since this would humiliate the debtor and his family and might lead to a violent confrontation; instead, they were required to wait outside and allow the debtor to bring the security to them. An emissary of the Court who met the debtor in the street was empowered to take the pledge from him by force. However, this right did not extend to the creditor, who had to wait until the debtor freely gave the pledge to him.[310]

"You shall not sleep with his pledge" (Deut. 24:12) is the commandment (**240**) forbidding a creditor from keeping a pledge from its owner who was in need of it (Pos. Comm. 199).

If a borrower did not pay back a loan by the stipulated date, the lender could ask the court to order that personal effects of the borrower be given to him as collateral. In this case, however, the lender was required to return them to the borrower at those times when they would be needed. If the item was something the borrower needed during the day, such as a tool for his trade or occupation, it must be held as security only at night and promptly restored to him by morning so as not to deprive him of its use. Conversely, an item that was needed at night, such as bedding or a garment in which he slept, had to be restored to him before nightfall.[311]

"Nor shall you take the garment of a widow as a pledge" (Deut. 24:17) is the commandment (**241**) forbidding a creditor from taking a pledge from a widow, regardless of whether she was poor or rich. Although the garments of other debtors may be seized and returned at night, if necessary, the garments of a widow may not be taken at all to compel payment of a loan.[312] Some commentators have maintained that a pledge could not be taken from any woman, arguing that the Torah only men-

tioned the widow because she is most likely to take part in business activities.[313]

"One shall not take an upper or lower millstone as a pledge; for that would be taking a life as a pledge" (Deut. 24:6) is the commandment (242) forbidding a creditor to take in pledge "utensils that are used in the preparation of food, such as vessels for grinding, kneading, or cooking; implements for slaughtering cattle; and all other objects categorized as 'utensils with which necessary food is prepared'." Deeming that preventing someone from earning a living was almost like taking his life, the Rabbis extended this commandment to prohibit the creditor from taking anything that the debtor needed for his livelihood, such as a portion of the millstone that would render it useless.[314]

Abducting an Israelite (243)

"You shall not steal" (Exod. 20:13), the eighth of the Ten Commandments, was interpreted by the Rabbis as applying specifically to only one kind of thief—a kidnapper who forced his victim to work for him and then sold him into slavery (Sanh. 86a). As the first two prohibitions in this verse were against the capital offenses of murder and adultery, they reasoned that "you shall not steal" must refer to kidnapping, the only theft for which the perpetrator was liable to the death penalty.[315]

The commandment against ordinary theft (Neg. Comm. 244) is based on Leviticus 19:11.

Stealing Money (244)

"You shall not steal" (Lev. 19:11) is the commandment forbidding the stealing of money or property. The prohibition also applies to any person who assists a theft, sees a theft but does not report it, or falsely claims money that is not owed him (Ibn Ezra). Maimonides[316] noted that a person who receives stolen property

can never fully repent, "because he does not know who is the owner of the stolen property, since the thief steals from many persons and brings him the stolen articles; and also because the receiver encourages the thief and induces him to sin."

The Rabbis extended this prohibition to forbid the stealing of things other than property. Failure to respond to a greeting was considered the theft of a fellow man's self-respect. Especially reprehensible was winning someone's gratitude or favorable regard through misrepresentation, flattery, or other forms of deceit.[317] The Mechilta added another aspect to this prohibition — "stealing the hearts of people" — giving such examples as asking a friend to be a guest when not really wanting to invite him, or offering a gift knowing that it will not be accepted.[318]

The law concerning the restitution for various types of theft is given in Pos. Comm. 239.

Committing Robbery (245)

"You shall not commit robbery" (Lev. 19:13) is considered by Maimonides as the commandment forbidding a person from taking by force and violence any item that is not rightfully his. In the context of the verse, however, this prohibition refers specifically to not depriving a worker of his earnings (Rashi), or to fraudulently or forcibly keeping something belonging to another, such as an article that was left for safekeeping (Maimonides).[319]

Fraudulently Altering Land Boundaries (246)

"You shall not remove the boundary marker of your neighbor" (Deut. 19:14) is the commandment prohibiting the stealthy moving of a landmark with the intent to fraudulently enlarge one's property at the expense of a neighbor.

Bahya ben Asher and Abravanel observed that infringing on the property rights of others shows contempt for God's grand design. Just as God apportioned the Promised Land among the Twelve Tribes of Israel, so all individual holdings of land are ultimately Divine gifts that may not be seized covertly or by force.[320]

The Rabbis extended this commandment to forbid any unfair encroachment on the honor or livelihood of another person. They also applied it to attributing the opinion of one person to another.[321] In modern times, this commandment also prohibits copyright and patent violations.[322]

Failure to Repay Debts (247-249)

Dealing honestly with others is an essential aspect of a successful society. Therefore, the Torah prohibited the Israelites from attempting to deceive others in business (Neg. Comm. 250, 252, 271), to deny obligations that could not be proven, to invoke God's name to convince others that lies are true (Neg. Comm. 62), to underpay laborers, and to seek personal gain through unctuous flattery (Neg. Comm. 244). Such conduct is wrong, even though the courts may not be able to effectively deal with it.

"You shall not defraud your neighbor" (Lev. 19:13) is the commandment (**247**) forbidding one from retaining money or property owed to someone else. In context, it primarily applies to "oppressing" a hired servant (as in Deut. 24:14), taking advantage of his vulnerability by either withholding his wages (Pos. Comm. 200, Neg. Comm. 238) or paying him less than what he is owed for his work.

"(You shall not steal,) you shall not deny falsely, and you shall not lie to one another" (Lev. 19:11) is the verse underlying the commandments forbidding a person from (**248**) repudiating monetary debts or denying having possession of any item deposited with him for safekeeping and then (**249**) falsely swearing about it under oath. Under biblical law, a defendant who completely denied the monetary claim against him was exempt

from payment and from taking an oath. However, because it appeared unlikely that the plaintiff would come to court without a plausible claim, the Rabbis ruled that the defendant should be required to take an oath. If the defendant made a partial admission, he must swear that he did not owe the rest of the amount. If even a single witness came forward to corroborate the plaintiff's claim, the defendant was required to take an oath to be absolved from payment.[323]

According to Rashi, the sequence of transgressions cited in this verse may overwhelm a person after he commits the initial sin. One who steals will attempt to defend himself by denying that he took anything, even going so far as to swear falsely to conceal his guilt.[324]

Wronging One Another in Business (250)

"When you sell anything to your neighbor, or make a purchase from the hand of your fellow, you shall not wrong one another" (Lev. 25:14) is the commandment prohibiting one person from cheating another in business dealings (Pos. Comm. 245). In the verse, this rule specifically applied to real estate sales, but was expanded by the Talmud (BM 47b) to include all commercial transactions. Thus substantial overcharging is grounds for canceling a business agreement.[325]

Jewish ethics attaches great significance to this commandment. As the Mechilta notes, "If one is honest in his business dealings, and the spirit of his fellow-creatures takes delight in him, it is accounted to him as though he had fulfilled the whole Torah."[326]

Wronging One Another by Speech (251)

"Do not wrong one another, but fear your God" (Lev. 25:17) is interpreted by the Rabbis as the commandment prohibiting one from saying things that would wound or humiliate another person

or cause him unbearable pain. This includes reminding people of their previous transgressions, making insensitive references to their distressing physical defects, or even knowingly giving bad advice. Lest one believe that he could hide his malicious intentions from others, Rashi notes that the verse concludes by stressing that God knows what is truly in a person's heart.[327] A person also is forbidden to feign interest in a purchase, such as by asking a merchant the price of an article or requesting to taste some food, when he has no money or knows that he will not buy it.

Verbal insults cause severe pain and elicit intense prayers to God, who quickly answers them by punishing the transgressor (Bahya ben Asher). According to the Talmud (BM 58b), hurting someone personally is worse than injuring him financially, for while money can be replaced, humiliation and disgrace may persist indefinitely. A person who publicly embarrasses another is considered to be like a murderer, who has no share in the World to Come.[329]

Wronging a Proselyte (252-253)

"You shall not taunt or oppress a ger, (for you were strangers in the land of Egypt)" (Exod. 22:20) is the source of the commandments forbidding the wronging of a proselyte. (The injunction to love the *ger* is Pos. Comm. 207.)

The commandment (252) prohibiting wronging a proselyte by speech was interpreted by the Rabbis as forbidding the taunting of a convert by reminding him of his non-Jewish past and suggesting that this makes him unfit to study God's Torah (Rashi). As the *Sifra* states: "Do not say to him, 'Yesterday you worshiped idols, and now you have come under the wings of the *Shechinah* (Divine Presence)'." *Or ha-Chaim* warns that Jews should not feel superior to converts, because they are not direct descendants of the patriarchs. Indeed, Jews-by-Birth must remember that, while enslaved in Egypt, they had descended to the lowest stage of spiritual contamination and thus they were at no higher level than a convert before conversion.[330]

In a responsum to the question whether a convert could use the term "God of Our Fathers" in prayer, Maimonides replied that not only was he permitted to do so, seeing that Abraham was the father of all those who believe in the Unity of God, but that his status as a Jew was even superior to that of an Israelite. Although Israel's lineal descent is from the Patriarchs, that of the proselyte is from God, based on the verse (Isa. 44:5), "One shall say: 'I am the Lord's; and another shall call himself by the name of Jacob'."[331]

In context, the prohibition of wronging a *ger* by speech applies to any stranger, even a fellow Jew who has recently moved to a new neighborhood or is attending a new school and feels anxious or uncomfortable in unfamiliar surroundings.[332]

The commandment (**253**) prohibiting wronging in business forbids one from causing a proselyte to suffer a loss in buying and selling.

The reason for these prohibitions against mistreating a stranger is given in the second half of the verse, "for you were strangers in the Land of Egypt." In light of their own history, Jews should be especially sensitive to the plight of strangers in their midst.

Laws Relating to the Fugitive Slave (254-255)

"You shall not turn over a slave [who has escaped] to his master. He shall dwell with you in your midst ... you must not ill-treat him" (Deut. 23:16-17) is the source for the commandments prohibiting one from (**254**) handing over or (**255**) wronging a fugitive slave. These commandments applied to a fleeing non-Israelite slave seeking refuge in the Land from the harsh treatment of an unjust master (Jew or non-Jew) outside it.[333] Unlike the Hammurabi code, in which aiding and abetting the escape of a runaway slave was a crime punishable by death, the Torah

teaches that the Jew should always be merciful in protecting and assisting those who are in need of help.[334] As with the proselyte (Neg. Comm. 252), it was forbidden to taunt the runaway slave by mocking his past.

Slaves and prisoners escaping from a besieged enemy city must be given their freedom and allowed to settle wherever they wish in the Land of Israel. Sending a man seeking his freedom back to a life of idolatry would be inconsistent with ideal of sanctity permeating the Israelite camp. Indeed, asylum seekers often provided information that was valuable in permitting the conquest of the territory of the slave's former master (Nachmanides).[335]

Dealing Harshly with Orphans and Widows (256)

"You shall not ill-treat any widow or orphan" (Exod. 22:21) is the commandment prohibiting one from dealing harshly with orphans and widows, who have no human protector, lack the physical force to defend their rights, and are likely to become the victims of exploitation – like the ancestors of the Jews in Egypt.

Maimonides[336] wrote that one should "show them unvarying courtesy, not hurt them physically with hard toil, nor wound their feelings with harsh speech. One must take greater care of their property than of one's own. Whoever irritates them, provokes them to anger, pains them, tyrannizes over them, or causes them loss of money, is guilty of a transgression, and still more so, if one beats them or curses them."

Specifically referring to orphans, Maimonides[337] urged their teachers to "not treat them like others, but to make a distinction in their favor. He should guide them gently, with the utmost tenderness and courtesy."

As indicated in the two verses that follow in the biblical

text, anyone who violated this commandment should expect severe retribution from the Father of orphans and the Judge of widows. Because the first of these verses is in the plural while the second is in the singular, Ibn Ezra concluded that if a single individual afflicted a widow or orphan and the community as a whole did not intervene to protect them, God would punish them all.[338]

Laws Relating to Hebrew Bondmen/ Bondwomen (257-262)

Rather than a "slave," a Hebrew bondman was an indentured servant, like a laborer hired for a specified period of time (Pos. Comm. 232). It was forbidden (**257**) to employ a Hebrew bondman in degrading menial tasks (Lev. 25:39), which could be performed by a Canaanite bondman. A Hebrew bondman could not be forced to bring his master's toiletries and clothes to the bathhouse, wash or put shoes on his master's feet, or carry him in a litter or chair. Instead, he was to be assigned to skilled work or field labor, like hired help.

It was forbidden (**259**) to break the body or spirit of a Hebrew bondman by ruling over him "with rigor" (Lev. 25:43), the same word used to describe the hardship of Israel's bondage in Egypt (Exod. 1:13). The master was prohibited from ordering a Hebrew bondman to perform tasks that had no useful purpose (like boiling water when there was no need for it) or whose duration was ill-defined (such as to continue digging around a tree until his master returned). As Maimonides noted, one was prohibited from having a Hebrew bondman work just to "keep him busy."[339] Because a Hebrew bondman and his master were ultimately kin, he could not be given food or accommodation inferior to that of his master. Kindness and humanity were to characterize the bearing of the Israelite towards his less fortunate brother.[340] In view of all these limitations upon the buyer of a Hebrew bondman, the Talmud (Kid. 15a) observed: "One who buys a Hebrew slave buys himself a master."

It was forbidden (258) to sell a Hebrew bondman (as Canaanite bondmen were sold) by public auction in the slave-market (Lev. 25:42). A Jew is ultimately owned by God, and thus it would be blasphemous to attempt to sell him at auction (Rashi). Instead, a Hebrew bondman must be sold in private so that he can maintain at least of modicum of dignity (Maimonides).[341]

It was forbidden (260) to permit a heathen dwelling in the Land of Israel to maltreat "with rigor" a Hebrew bondman who had sold himself to him (Lev. 25:53). This verse ends with the phrase "in your sight," which the Rabbis interpreted as meaning that an Israelite was not obliged to supervise how the heathen was treating the Hebrew bondman when in his own home. However, an Israelite could not permit a fellow Jew to be publicly treated in a harsh manner (Ibn Ezra).[342]

It was forbidden (261) for the owner of a Hebrew bondwoman (Pos. Comm. 233, 234) to sell her to anyone, whether an Israelite or a heathen (Exod. 21:8). The Rabbis interpreted this prohibition as referring to both her father and the master. Because the initial sale was supposed to result in her marrying the owner or his son, after this "betrayal" neither subsequently had the right to sell a Hebrew bondwoman to anyone else (Rashi).[343]

It was forbidden (262) for the owner (or his son) who married his Hebrew bondwoman to treat her any differently than a free woman (Exod. 21:10). Despite her effectively being "purchased" as a wife, she had the same rights to food, clothing, and marital relations as a woman from the highest stratum of Israelite society. These obligations to the former bondwoman persisted even if he later took another wife.[344]

According to Jewish law, a man who marries incurs seven obligations to his wife in addition to the three listed above.

Of rabbinic origin, these include: "to treat her if she falls ill; to ransom her if she is captured; to bury her if she dies; to provide for her maintenance out of his estate after his death; to let her dwell in his house after his death for the duration of her widowhood; to let the daughters sired by him receive their maintenance out of his estate until they become espoused; to let her male children sired by him inherit her *ketubah* (marriage contract), in addition to their share with their half brothers in his estate."[345]

Selling/Enslaving a Captive Woman (263-264)

An Israelite warrior who was attracted to a beautiful woman among the enemy captives was not permitted to make her his wife until she had remained in his house for at least a month in a state of mourning and general dishevelment (Pos. Comm. 221). If, as the Rabbis hoped, the Israelite had a change of heart and no longer wished to marry her, he was required to set her completely free. He was forbidden to (263) sell her or (264) make her his slave (Deut. 21:14).

Though the Israelite was permitted to convert a captive woman to his faith and marry her, the Rabbis strongly discouraged this practice because it amounted to a forced conversion rather than one undertaken of her own free.[346]

Coveting Another's Property (265-266)

"You shall not covet ... anything that belongs to your neighbor" (Exod. 20:14) is the last of the Ten Commandments. According to Maimonides, this verse (and the repetition of the Decalogue in Deut. 5:18, which uses a different Hebrew word) gives rise to the commandments forbidding both (266) having the desire for what belongs to another (wife, home, riches, etc.) and (265) occupying one's mind with schemes to acquire it. Because the

sin of coveting is the source of the urge to commit robbery (Neg. Comm. 265-266), which is forbidden to non-Israelites as one of the seven Noahide laws, these commandments prohibiting the coveting of the belongings of another must also apply to every person (*Sefer ha-Chinuch*).[347]

Ibn Ezra observed that one who has complete faith in God should realize that the property of his neighbor was not Divinely intended to be his.[348] As noted in *Pirkei Avot* (4:1), "Who is rich? One who is happy with his lot."

Limitations on a Hired Laborer (267-268)

"(*When you enter another man's vineyard, you may eat as many grapes as you want, until you are full,*) *but you must not put any in your vessel.* (*When you enter another man's field of standing grain, you may pluck ears with your hand;*) *but you must not put a sickle to your neighbor's grain*" (Deut. 23:25-26) are the verses dealing with the rights and limitations of a hired farm laborer.

The owner of an orchard or vineyard must permit workers to eat as much as they wish of the fruit they are harvesting (Pos. Comm. 201) without chastising them or deducting the value of the fruit from their wages. However, this rule applies only to those harvesting crops from the soil; a worker milking a cow is not allowed to drink any of it. Interrupting the harvesting is not permitted, and the farm laborer can only eat while he is actually working (such as after emptying his basket and while walking back to reap more crops).[349]

However, a farm worker was forbidden (**268**) to take more of the harvested crops than he needed for his meal. The laborer was prohibited from taking home any of the produce for his wife and children or giving it to someone who was not personally entitled to take it.

Maimonides derived from the phrase "*but you must not put a sickle to your neighbor's grain*" the commandment (**267**) prohibiting a hired laborer working on growing crops, such as in reaping or cutting, from eating of them until after his work was finished. Other commentators have attempted to resolve the apparent contradiction with the previous commandment, suggesting that since a sickle cuts several stalks at once, using it could yield more than the laborer could eat at that moment (which was all that he was entitled to take).[350]

Ignoring Lost Property (269)

"You shall not hide yourself [remain indifferent]" (Deut. 22:3) is the commandment prohibiting one from shutting his eyes to the lost property of another. Instead, one is required to pick it up and return it to its owner (Pos. Comm. 204).

Although in context the verse refers to a lost animal, the Rabbis extended the commandment to apply to any case in which one can prevent someone from suffering by a loss either by performing some action or even merely by speaking out.[351] For example, one who sees that an overflowing river is about to destroy the home of another must work hard to avoid a disaster by trying to construct a dam or dike.[352] The Rabbis (Sanh. 73a) interpreted this commandment as also prohibiting one from passing by a lost child or any person who has lost his way.[353]

Leaving a Trapped Person (270)

"(If you see the donkey of someone you hate lying under its burden) and would refrain from helping him, (you shall surely raise it with him)" (Exod. 23:5) is the source of the commandment prohibiting one from leaving a person "who is trapped under his burden and delayed on the road" (or whose donkey has fallen under its burden). One must assist by relieving him or his donkey of the burden until he can adjust it (Pos. Comm. 202), and must

help him lift it either onto his back or that of his animal (Pos. Comm. 203).

False Weights and Measures (271-272)

"You shall not falsify measures of length, weight, or volume" (Lev. 19:35) is the commandment (**271**) forbidding a person from cheating in measuring land or from using false measures and weights (Pos. Comm. 208). On Rosh Hashanah, God decides each individual's income for the year. By using false weights, a person unfairly increases his income and thus interferes with the Divine plan (Alshekh). Weights should be made of materials that cannot rust, because rust adds weight.[354] A grain merchant was required to wipe his measuring vessels clean at least once every 30 days, so that he always sold the exact amount and not less (BB 88a).

"You shall not have in your pouch diverse weights, one large and one small" (Deut. 25:13) is the commandment (**272**) forbidding a person from keeping false weights in his possession or his home (Deut. 25:14), "even though he does not use them for purposes of trade." As Sforno observed, "God abhors not only the actual practice of dishonesty, but also the instruments that enable one to commit it."[355] Rashi noted that the verses regarding weights and measures immediately precede the commandment to wipe out the memory of Amalek, the arch-enemy of Israel. He concluded that it was because the Jews failed to be scrupulously honest in their business dealings that God sent enemies against them.

Limitations on Judges (273-281, 283, 286-287)

Establishing fair and impartial courts of justice is one of the seven Noahide laws and a basic requirement for any civilized ociety. The Torah strictly prohibits anything that perverts justice, or even gives the appearance of injustice (Pos. Comm 177).

It is forbidden (**273**) for a judge to commit unrighteousness in judgment (Lev. 19:15). He must be scrupulously fair and honorable to preserve the integrity of the judicial system, not departing from the Torah-mandated principles of guilt and innocence. "He who does not deliver judgments in perfect truth causes the Divine Presence [*Shechinah*] to depart from the midst of Israel" (Sanh. 7a).

It is forbidden (**274**) for a judge to accept gifts (bribes) from litigants (Exod. 23:8), even if he renders a judgment that "acquits the innocent and condemns the guilty" (*Sifre*). Even the mere suspicion of injustice damages the integrity of the judicial system. However, a judge who was not paid by the community for his services and was forced to take time off from his usual occupation to preside over a court was permitted to accept a fee, as long as it was paid equally by both parties in the litigation (i.e., considered as just compensation rather than a bribe) (*Sefer ha-Chinuch*).[356]

It is forbidden (**275**) for a judge to favor one of the litigants in a trial (Lev. 19:15). Absolute equality before the law must be maintained, even as regards the personal status of the litigants. Even if one litigant is a man of high rank and distinction, the judge is prohibited from showing him any special honor or treating him with more deference and respect (Shev. 30a-31a).

It is forbidden (**276**) for a judge to be deterred by fear from rendering a correct judgment (Deut. 1:17). The judge must always rule fairly, even if a litigant threatens him with bodily injury or financial harm. As the agent of God in the administration of justice, nothing but the fear of Heaven may enter into his deliberations.[357] Analogous to this, a student who is convinced that his teacher is about to rule incorrectly on a case must immediately inform him, rather than waiting until after a wrong decision has been delivered in court (Shev. 31a).[358]

It is forbidden (**277**) for a judge to decide in favor of a poor man because of pity and compassion for him (Exod, 23:3; Lev.

19:15). Despite the temptation to render a verdict that would allow a poor person to receive money from a rich man, who would not miss it, one cannot pervert the law regardless of how admirable the purpose.

It is forbidden (278) for a judge to pervert judgment against a litigant whom he knows to be a wicked sinner (Exod. 23:6). A judge must render justice with complete impartiality to all who come before him, whether the person is "rich or poor, sinner or saint."[359] Similarly, a judge must not allow his decision to be influenced by the past criminal record of the defendant. The defendant must be judged for the crime for which he is now being tried, not for any past transgressions. Only God may judge all the actions of men, both past and present.

It is forbidden (279) for a judge to pity one who has slain a man, or caused him the loss of a limb, in fixing the penalty (Deut. 19:13, 21). A judge should not say "One person was already killed, what is the point of killing a second – so that two Jews will be killed?" (Rashi). According to Nachmanides, compassion for a murderer only leads to further bloodshed, both because it frees the person to commit more crimes himself and because it encourages others who may be tempted to follow his example.[360]

It is forbidden (280) for a judge to pervert the justice that is due to gerim ("strangers" or proselytes) or orphans (Deut. 24:17), the most vulnerable and defenseless members of society.

It is forbidden (281) for a judge to listen to one litigant in the absence of the other (Exod. 23:1). Such a private conference generally results in the litigant presenting false evidence that, since the other party is not present to contradict it, will lead the judge to form an inaccurate or untrue view of the case.

It is forbidden (283) for a judge to rely on the opinion of a fellow judge in convicting the guilty or acquitting the innocent (Exod. 23:2). Each judge must come to his own conclusion based on his understanding of the evidence and the law. According to Rashi, a judge must not alter his opinion merely to agree with the majority of his colleagues if he thinks they either are in error or are intentionally misinterpreting the law.[361] Indeed, a judge who cannot justify his decision on the basis of his own learning and reasoning ability is guilty of rendering a "false judgment" (Sanh. 4:6).[362]

It is forbidden (286) for a judge to receive and act in accordance with the testimony of a wicked man (Exod. 23:1). Under rabbinic law, ten types of witnesses were disqualified from testifying in court. They included: (a) women (whose emotions might overrule their judgment); (b) slaves (who never think independently); (c) minors (intellectually immature); (d) imbeciles (incapable of thinking); (e) deaf-mutes; (f) the blind (incapable of being "eyewitnesses"); (g) relatives of the parties involved in the case (biased testimony); (h) those personally involved in the case (biased testimony); (i) the "shameless" (who could not appreciate the need to tell the truth in court); and (j) a variety of "wicked" persons (e.g., compulsive gamblers, thieves, usurers).[363]

It is forbidden (287) for a judge to receive testimony from relatives of a litigant, whether for or against him (Deut. 24:16). In context, the verse deals with individual responsibility and prohibits fathers or children from being put to death for the evil deeds of the other. The Rabbis interpreted it as referring to witnesses, so that no person can be found guilty based on the testimony of relatives (Rashi).[364] In cases involving monetary claims, however, one of the parties may agree to be bound by such evidence.[365]

Laws Relating to Capital Punishment
(282, 290-291)

Capital cases were tried by a court of 23 judges. If there was a division of opinion among these judges, it was forbidden (282) to convict by a majority of one, based on the verse *"You shall not follow a multitude to do evil"* (Exod. 23:2). Maimonides noted that "in inflicting the death penalty you are not to follow any chance majority;" although a verdict of acquittal needs only a majority of one, a verdict of condemnation needs a majority of two. *Sefer ha-Chinuch* observed that since a mistaken decision in a capital case cannot be rectified, the Court must do everything possible to obtain an acquittal.[366]

It was forbidden (**290**) to inflict capital punishment based on circumstantial evidence, even if it was virtually conclusive of guilt. Maimonides presented the scenario of a man who pursued his enemy with intent to kill him and chased him into a house. Another person, who had previously given a legal warning, then entered the house and found the pursuer standing over the dead man with a bloodstained knife in his hand. Even in this case, the pursuer was not to be put to death by the Court, since there were no witnesses to testify that they had actually seen the murder committed. He based this conclusion on the verse, *"Do not execute those who are innocent or in the right, for I will not exonerate the wicked"* (Exod. 23:7). Maimonides feared that, had the Torah permitted conviction in a capital case on the basis of circumstantial evidence, the probability of guilt required would slowly decrease. Eventually, people would be put to death because of unwarrantable presumptions according to the caprice of the judges. He believed that it was better and more satisfactory to acquit a thousand guilty persons than to put a single innocent man to death. Once a defendant had been acquitted in a capital case because there was only circumstantial evidence against him, he could not be brought to trial again for the same offense, even if direct evidence had turned up in the meantime to prove his guilt.[367]

The prohibition against the use of circumstantial evidence extended to the situation in which two witnesses testified that a man had committed two transgressions (for each of which the penalty was death), but each witness had only seen him commit one transgression. Because a conviction required the testimony of two witnesses on each count, the person would not have been proven guilty.

In connection with this verse, Ibn Ezra observed that even if the judge knew that this defendant was an evil person who deserved to be executed because of other crimes he had committed, it was forbidden to find him guilty of a capital crime that he did not commit. Even if the death of such a wicked person resulted in an overall benefit for the community, God would never forgive the judge for making such a decision.[368]

It was forbidden (**291**) for a witness in a capital case to also act as a judge or advocate. This prohibition was derived from the verse, "*(The testimony of) a single witness shall not be sufficient for a sentence of death*" (Num. 35:30), by interpreting "testimony" as meaning "pleading." Once a witness had finished testifying about what he had seen, he was required to remain silent and allow the judges to decide how much weight to give his evidence. In a case involving monetary claims, however, a testifying witness was allowed to act as an advocate, though he was prohibited from presiding as a judge.[369]

(The specific forms of capital punishment are discussed in Pos. Comm. 226-230.)

Appointing an Unlearned Judge (284)

"*You shall not respect persons in judgment*" (Deut. 1:17) was considered by Maimonides as the source for the commandment prohibiting the appointment of a judge who is not learned in the wisdom of Torah, even if he possesses other good qualities (Pos. Comm. 176). He interpreted the verse as referring to those whose function it was to appoint judges – the Great Court and the Exilarch (head of the Babylonian Jewish community). The *Sifre* observed that one should not say "I will appoint so-and-so a judge because he is handsome, or because he is rich, or because he is my relative, or because he has lent me money, or because he knows many languages. [If you do that], the result will be that he will acquit the guilty and condemn the innocent, not because he is wicked, but because he lacks knowledge."[370]

Sefer ha-Chinuch extended this commandment by requiring that the community only appoint qualified people for specific tasks and not be afraid to refuse appointment to those who are unqualified.[371]

Bearing False Witness (285)

"You shall not bear false witness against your neighbor" (Exod. 20:13) is the ninth of the Ten Commandments. The Rabbis extended this injunction to prohibit testimony even in cases when a witness was convinced that something took place but did not actually see it. A person may not present hearsay (not personally witnessed) testimony even if he heard it from an apparently impeccable source. The Talmud (Shev. 31a) offers a scenario in which a renowned teacher had one valid witness and asked a disciple to join him at court and "stand there" and not say anything, so that he would not be uttering a lie. In this way, the disciple would "appear" to be the second witness needed to support his claim and might trick the defendant into admitting the truth. However, the Rabbis ruled that the disciple was forbidden to comply, based on the verse, "from a false matter keep far" (Exod. 23:7).

In addition to the literal meaning of giving false testimony in court, this passage also prohibits gossip, slander, and misrepresentation – whether of an individual, a group, a people, a race, or a faith.[372] Analogizing this to the Fourth Commandment concerning the Sabbath, the Mechilta suggested that one who lies in court may eventually deny that God created the world in six days and rested on the seventh.[373]

As for the punishment of the person who violated this commandment, "You shall do to him as he conspired to do to his fellow" (Deut. 19:19) (Pos. Comm. 180).

Convicting on the Testimony of a Single Witness (288)

"*A single witness shall not stand up against a man for any iniquity or for any sin*" (Deut. 19:15) is the commandment prohibiting the infliction of physical punishment (such as death or lashes) based on the testimony of a single witness, "even though he be perfectly trustworthy." As Abravanel noted, because one man is on trial, logic would dictate that more than one man is required to prove his guilt, lest it merely be the word of one against another.[374] In a monetary case, however, if a single witness testified in favor of the plaintiff, the defendant was obligated to take an oath that he was not liable. This oath was the strictest in Jewish law, with the defendant required to hold a Torah scroll and invoke the name of God. Taking the oath effectively freed the defendant from all liability; if he refused to take the oath, he was required to pay the claim.[375]

The testimony of a single person, man or woman, is sufficient to decide whether something is ritually permitted or forbidden. This enables a determination whether an item is kosher by either a *mashgiach* (*kashrut* supervisor) in a factory or restaurant, or even an individual homemaker in a private kitchen.[376]

Murdering a Human Being (289)

"*You shall not murder*" (Exod. 20:13) is the sixth of the Ten Commandments. Although often incorrectly translated as "You shall not kill," Jewish law recognized that there were situations in which it was required to take a human life. These included the obligatory war (Pos. Comm. 187), the infliction of capital punishment based on judicial decree (Pos. Comm. 226-229), and the requirement to kill a pursuer (*rodef*) if there was no other way to save the person being pursued (Pos. Comm. 247).

The Rabbis extended this commandment by describing many things as equivalent to murder, although they did not warrant the death penalty. Rather than cause immediate bloodshed or death, these created situations that could ultimately result in physical or psychological destruction. These include shaming a fellow human being in public (lit., "makes [his face] pale;" BM 58b); failing to provide food and safety for travelers; causing loss of livelihood; and withholding charity from the poor. According to Ibn Ezra, "One may murder with the hand or with the tongue, by talebearing or by character assassination. One may murder also by carelessness, by indifference, or by failure to save human life when it is in your power to do so." [377, 378]

The infinite worth of human life is based on man being created "in the image of God." God alone gives life, and God alone may take it away.[279] According to the Mishnah (Sanh. 37a), "Whoever destroys a single soul, Scriptures regards him as though he had destroyed a whole world." Correlating the first commandments on each of the two tablets, the Mechilta maintains that a person who believes in God as the Creator of human life (first tablet) could never commit murder (second tablet).[380]

Killing a Murderer Without Trial (292)

"That the one who has killed shall not die until he stands trial before the assembly" (Num. 35:12) is the commandment prohibiting "the slaying of a perpetrator, whom one has seen doing something punishable by death, before he is brought to trial." Every individual has to be accorded "due process of law." Consequently,

a person could only testify against the perpetrator in court, leaving it to the judges to condemn him for any crime he has committed and to decree the appropriate punishment.

According to *Sefer ha-Chinuch*, one who violates this commandment (even a witness to the actual crime) and takes the law into his own hands is considered a murderer, and he himself is liable to death.

Sparing the Life of a Pursuer (293)

"You shall cut off her hand, your eye shall not show pity" (Deut. 25:12) is the commandment prohibiting one from sparing the life of a pursuer (*rodef*), a person who is running after another with the intent to commit murder or rape (Pos. Comm. 247). This is different from the previous commandment (Neg. Comm. 292) – which forbids witnesses of a crime from slaying a criminal before he is properly convicted by the Court, and only applies when the perpetrator has already completed the deed for which he is liable for the death penalty. When a person is still engaged in trying to commit the crime, one is required to do whatever is necessary to prevent him from carrying out his evil intentions. This may entail cutting off one of her limbs (as in the context of the biblical verse), blinding her, or even killing her.

Punishing a Person for a Sin Commited Under Duress (294)

"But you shall do nothing to the girl" (Deut. 22:26) is the basis for the commandment prohibiting the punishment of a person who has committed a sin under duress. In context, this refers to one of two situations described in which a man has sexual intercourse with a virgin who is betrothed. If a man finds her in the city and lies with her, both are condemned to death – the

man because he "afflicted the wife of a fellow," and the woman because she did not cry out. Since the attack occurred in the city, where there presumably would be other people around who would have heard her shouts and saved her, the Torah attaches some degree of complicity to her failure to scream for help. However, if a man discovers her in the field and attacks her, only he is executed. The text states that the woman "has committed no capital sin," giving her the benefit of the doubt that "the betrothed girl cried out, but she had no savior."

According to Maimonides,[381] "the penalty of death or of whipping is inflicted only on one who committed a transgression of his own free will, in the presence of witnesses and after due warning… [Even] in the case of idolatry, which is the gravest of offenses, one who sins under compulsion does not incur the penalty of [spiritual] extinction or … death by judicial sentence."

Accepting a Ransom from One Who Has Commited Murder (295-296)

"You shall not accept a ransom for the life of a murderer who is guilty of a capital crime; he must be put to death. Nor shall you accept a ransom for one who fled to a city of refuge" (Num. 35:31-32) are the commandments forbidding the acceptance of ransom from someone who has, respectively, committed willful (**295**) or unintentional (**296**) murder. The same term "ransom" (lit., "atonement money") was previously used in the context of a man whose ox killed another (Exod. 21:29-30), where the Torah decreed that the ox is stoned while the owner pays a specific sum "as a redemption for his life." Therefore, these commandments are necessary to indicate unequivocally that a murderer does not have this same option (*Sifre*). [382]

As Maimonides noted,[383] "even if the murderer is prepared to give all the treasure in the world, and even if the next of kin of the murdered man is willing to absolve him, the Court is forbidden to accept the ransom. For the soul of the murdered man belongs not to the next of kin, but to God." *Sefer ha-Chinuch* added: "If men in power were permitted to take ransom for intentional or unintentional murder, the strong and the rich would kill their opponents and then offer their ransom; thus men would be in constant warfare, and society would be destroyed." [384]

Neglecting to Save an Israelite in Danger of His Life (297)

"You shall not stand idly by the blood of your neighbor" (Lev. 19:16) is the commandment prohibiting a person from failing to attempt to save the life of a fellow Jew in danger (although one is not required to endanger his own life). As the Talmud says (Sanh. 73a), "if a man sees his fellow drowning, mauled by beasts, or attacked by robbers, he is bound to save him." To protect the life of one in danger, a person is even permitted to take the life of another, who is treated as a "pursuer" (Pos. Comm. 247; Neg. Comm 292).

The Rabbis extended this principle to forbid a person from withholding evidence, if he was in a position in which he could restore his friend's lost money by simply telling the truth (Pos. Comm. 178). Menachem Hababli deduced from this commandment the principle that one is forbidden to isolate himself from the community in which he lives.[385] A person who sees another traveling down a self-destructive path (whether physical or spiritual) is duty bound to "rebuke" him (Pos. Comm. 205), tactfully criticizing his behavior and urging him to select a more appropriate course of action.

Leaving Obstacles on Public or Private Domain (298)

"(When you build a new house, you shall make a parapet for your roof), so that you will not place blood guilt upon your house (if anyone should fall from it)" (Deut. 22:8) is the source for the commandment forbidding one "to leave an obstacle or hindrances on public or

private property, so as not to cause [preventable] fatal accidents" (Pos. Comm. 184). As Maimonides[386] observed, "Whoever keeps on his premises anything dangerous, such as a vicious dog or an unsafe ladder, is put under a ban until he removes the nuisance."

Giving Misleading Advice (299)

"You shall not put a stumbling block before the blind" (Lev. 19:14) is the commandment prohibiting one from giving misleading advice to an unsuspecting or uninformed person, especially if you may benefit from his error.

This commandment was extended to include causing someone to sin, especially the young and innocent and the morally weak. Among the numerous violations of this ethical precept are: offering forbidden food to an unsuspecting individual; tempting the Nazirite to break his oath by holding out a cup of wine (Pes. 22b; Av. Zar, 6b); offering "the limb of a living animal to the children of Noah [thus enticing him to violate one of the seven Noahide laws];" ibid.); a man administering corporal punishment to his grown-up son, lest it lead him to rebel and forget his filial duty (MK 17a; Pos. Comm. 319); a borrower offering interest to appeal to the greed of a creditor (BM 75b); and selling a knife or other lethal weapon to a person of dubious or dangerous character.[387] The overall import of this commandment is to stress that each person is responsible for the welfare of others and may not do anything to endanger it.[388] *Sefer ha-Chinuch* observes that the three pillars on which the world is established are truth, shared confidence, and mutual trust.[389]

Inflicting Excessive Corporal Punishment (300)

"(If the guilty one is to be flogged, the judge shall cause him to lie down and be given lashes in his presence) according to the measure of his wickedness. He may be given up to forty lashes, but no more" (Deut.

25:2-3) is the commandment prohibiting a judge from inflicting on a wrong-doer corporal punishment so severe as to cause permanent injury. According to tradition, the maximum number of strokes that could be inflicted on a man liable to whipping was 39 (Pos. Comm. 224). However, no person was subjected to corporal punishment until an estimate was made of the number of strokes he could bear (based on his age, temperament, and physique); in no case was it less than three. Rather than the infliction of pain, the goal of lashes was to allow the guilty party to atone for past transgressions and to discourage him from engaging in similar activity in the future. In support of this view, the Rabbis taught that the official who administered the lashing was to be "superior in wisdom but deficient in strength."[390]

This commandment also was interpreted by the Rabbis as prohibiting striking or wounding oneself[391] and giving an unprovoked slap to another.[392]

Bearing Tales (301)

"You shall not be a tale-bearer among your people" (Lev. 19:16) is the commandment prohibiting one from *lashon ha-ra* (lit., "evil speech," often translated as "gossip"). This refers to any derogatory or damaging statement against an individual–even when the slanderous or defaming remarks are true–which if publicized to others would cause the subject physical or monetary damage, anguish, or fear.

Ibn Ezra noted that the Torah follows this commandment with a verse warning against standing idly by the blood of your neighbor (Neg. Comm. 297), indicating that slander is considered tantamount to murder.[393] Indeed, the Rabbis deemed the slanderer worse than a murderer, "since he destroys a man's reputation, which is more precious than his life."[394] Ecclesiasticus (28:18) observed that, "Many have been killed by the sword, but not so many as by the tongue."

The Talmud (Git. 55b-56a) declared that the destruction of Jerusalem resulted from false charges brought to the Roman authorities by a disgruntled individual who was insulted by his neighbor. Those making false accusations to a ruling authority were placed in the category of persons who commit assault with intent to kill, and putting them to death was authorized. The extent to which Jewish communities were endangered throughout the centuries led to the inclusion in the daily *Amidah* of the prayer, "And for slanderers (*malshinim*), let there be no hope." The dangerous temptation of *lashon ha-ra* is also emphasized in the concluding paragraph of the Amidah, which begins, "My God, guard my tongue from evil and my lips from speaking falsely" (Ps. 34:14).

Hating One Another (302)

"You shall not hate your kinsman in your heart" (Lev. 19:17) is the commandment prohibiting a person from nursing a grievance against one's fellow man, even without giving it outward expression.[395]

In order to prevent smoldering enmity, Maimonides[396] said that when a man sins against another, "the injured party should not hate the offender and keep silent." Instead, he should ask the reason for the sin. "If the offender repents and pleads for forgiveness, he should be forgiven." Rather than hate a person who caused injury or offense, one should still think of him as a "brother" (Hirsch).[397] Ibn Ezra and *Sefer ha-Chinuch* taught that the proper functioning of society requires that people be completely honest, for the most grievous transgression is to secretly hate another and wait for an opportunity to attack him.[398]

The Rabbis maintained that the Second Temple was destroyed by causeless hatred (*sinat chinam*), even though at the time the study of Torah and the performance of good deeds flourished, and God's commandments were obeyed.[399]

Putting One to Shame (303)

"You shall surely admonish your neighbor, and not bear a sin [incur any guilt] because of him" (Lev. 19:17) is the commandment forbidding putting another person to shame. Although the verse requires one to rebuke a sinner (Pos. Comm. 205), it must be done tactfully and in a kind and gentle manner, without using unduly disrespectful terms, so as not to cause him public embarrassment. Failure to reprove a person in a correct manner would result in one's "bearing sin because of him."

One who rebukes a person in a friendly manner for an alleged transgression, giving the other party an opportunity to explain the reasons for his action or statement, may discover that the other was justified and free from guilt (Ibn Ezra, Hizzekuni).[400]

Taking Revenge/Bearing a Grudge (304-305)

"You shall not take revenge or bear a grudge" (Lev. 19:18) are the commandments forbidding one from displaying these specific reactions to a person who has wronged or displeased him. The Jew is forbidden either to (304) take revenge, by repaying evil with evil, or (305) bear a grudge.

The Rabbis offer the following illustration of these two commandments. A asks B to lend him a sickle, but B refuses. The next day, B asks to borrow A's hatchet. If A replies, "I *will not* lend it to you, just as you refused to lend me your sickle," that is taking revenge. If A replies, "I *will* lend it to you, even though yesterday you refused to lend me your sickle," that is bearing a grudge.[401] Maimonides[402] explained that, "One should rather practice forbearance in all secular matters, for the intelligent realize that these are vain things and not worth taking vengeance for. As long as one nurses a grievance and keeps it in mind, he may come to take vengeance. The Torah therefore emphatically warns us not to bear a grudge, so that the impression of wrong shall be obliterated and be no longer remembered. This is the right principle, for it alone makes civilized life and social intercourse possible."

Taking the Entire Bird's Nest (306)

"You shall not take the mother together with her young" (Deut. 22:6) is the commandment forbidding one from taking the entire nest of an ownerless bird when it is sitting on eggs or tending its young. Instead, he must send the mother bird away (Pos. Comm. 148)—even many times if she continually returns to the nest—before being permitted to take the eggs or the young.

Limitations of One with *Tzara'at* (307-308)

"Beware of a tzara'at *affliction"* (Deut. 24:8) is the commandment (**308**) forbidding an affected person from "cutting out or cauterizing the [physical] signs of *tzara'at* [a skin condition often mistranslated as "leprosy"] so as to change its appearance." *Tzara'at* was a punishment for slander, gossip, and other forms of selfish and antisocial behavior (Pos. Comm. 101-103). The next verse says, "Remember what the Lord your God did to Miriam," whose entire body became covered with *tzara'at* for slandering her brother Moses "because of the Cushite woman he had married" (Num. 12:1–15).

"He shall not shave the netek *(scall)"* (Lev. 13:33) is the commandment (**307**) forbidding one afflicted with *tzara'at* of the scalp or beard to shave all the way to it. (He could not shave the *netek* itself, since it was already hairless.) According to Rashi, he must leave a surrounding circle of hair (at least two hairs thick), so that the Kohen can assess whether the *netek* has spread.[403]

Sefer ha-Chinuch maintains that these commandments teach that, rather than rebelling against it, suffering should be borne without complaining since it atones for sin.[404]

Plowing a Valley in Which the Rite of the Axed Heifer Has Been Performed (309)

"*(The elders of that city shall bring the heifer down to a harsh valley), which cannot be tilled nor sown*" (Deut. 21:4) is the commandment prohibiting plowing or cultivating in the area where the rite of the axed heifer (*eglah arufah*) had been performed. This ritual was required in response to the discovery of the corpse of an unwitnessed murder lying in the open (Pos. Comm. 181).

Maimonides[405] declared that forbidding the land from being worked would ultimately help to solve the crime, since "the owner of the land will use all means possible to search and to find the murderer, in order that the heifer not be killed and his land not made useless to him."

Permitting a Sorcerer to Live (310)

"*You shall not permit a sorceress to live*" (Exod. 22:17) is the commandment predicated on the severe spiritual harm that potentially could be caused by this individual. Rashi noted that the verse uses the feminine gender because women were the primary practitioners of this activity, although both male and female sorcerers were liable to the death penalty.[406]

The special severity of the phrase "not permit ... to live" (rather than merely "incurs the death penalty") was understood by the Rabbis as reflecting the extreme danger that this activity posed to the Jewish community by misleading the people into believing in various baseless superstitions. Therefore, it was the task of Israel to identify and ruthlessly remove all sorcerers from its midst.[407]

Taking a Bridegroom Away from His Home (311)

"(When a man marries a new wife), he shall not go out with the army, nor shall he be responsible for any service; he shall be exempt and remain at home (for one year, to give happiness to the woman he has married)" (Deut. 24:5) is the commandment prohibiting taking a bridegroom away from his home for any kind of military (even non-combatant) or civil service during the first year after his marriage. Instead, he was to be relieved from all public duties and responsibilities that would require his absence from his new wife (Pos. Comm. 214).

Differing From Traditional Authorities (312)

"You shall not deviate from the word that they will tell you, (either to the right or left)" (Deut. 17:11) is the commandment prohibiting one from "differing from the authorized bearers of the Tradition" handed down from Moses, or deviating from whatever the Rabbis ordain in matters of Torah.

During the course of Jewish history, there have been heretics (apikorsim) who rejected the authority of the Written Torah, or who accepted the Written Torah but denied the authority of the Oral Law (such as the Karaites). Because the existence of any society requires obedience to accepted law, it is incumbent on Jews to comply with the decisions of the duly constituted rabbinical authorities.[408] As Maimonides noted,[409] "if every scholar had the power to make modifications on the Law, the multitude of disputes and differences of opinion would have produced an injurious effect." Therefore, only the Great Sanhedrin was given this power, and anyone who opposed their decision was subject to the death penalty.

Maimonides maintained that this commandment meant that a Jew must accept the traditional (Masoretic) text of the Torah;

all laws derived from the Bible by the 13 hermeneutic rules of Rabbi Ishmael; and the decrees (*gezerot*), ordinances (*takanot*), and customs (*minhagim*) established by the rabbis. Nachmanides disagreed, regarding only the first two categories as included in this commandment and arguing that laws of rabbinic origin did not have the same sanctity as those expressly stated in the Torah or directly derived from it.[410]

Adding to/Detracting from the Written or Oral Law (313-314)

"(Be careful to observe only that which I command you;) do not add to nor subtract from it" (Deut. 13:1) is the source of these commandments to observe the entire Torah exactly as it was transmitted. The Torah is complete and perfect as is ("The Torah [law] of the Lord is perfect, restoring the soul;" Ps. 19:8), and any attempt to "improve" it by using human intelligence to add or subtract commandments may only detract from the original Divine meaning of the text and be repugnant to God.[411] As Rashi observed, Israel was not to invent new additions to the laws, nor arbitrarily diminish them, such as by using five species instead of four in the command of the *lulav* on Sukkot (Pos. Comm. 169) or leaving out one of the three priestly blessings (Pos. Comm. 26).

In the Introduction to his *Mishneh Torah*, Maimonides noted that the Oral Tradition of the Torah, which is found in the Talmud and its commentaries, "received the assent of all Israel, and those Sages who instituted the ordinances, issued the decrees, introduced the customs, gave the decisions and taught which rulings were correct, constituted the whole body or the majority of Israel's wise men. They were the leaders who received from each other the traditions concerning the fundamentals of Judaism, in unbroken succession back to Moses, our teacher."[412]

Maimonides stressed that "constant changes would tend to

disturb the whole system of the law, and would lead people to believe that the Torah is not of Divine origin." Nevertheless, permission is "given to the wise men (i.e., Great Court of every generation) to make 'fences' around the Torah statutes to ensure that they are kept." Thus the sages have the power "temporarily to dispense with some religious act prescribed in the Torah, or to allow that which is forbidden, if exceptional circumstances and events require it." However, none of the laws can be canceled for all time.[413]

The laws of the Talmud have been codified many times. In the Middle Ages, by far the greatest of these legal codes was the *Mishneh Torah* of Maimonides, a massive 14-volume work (also known as the *Yad*, since the numerical value of these Hebrew letters equals 14) that discusses every conceivable topic of Jewish law in an immensely logical sequence. The most influential code in modern Jewish life, and the last comprehensive one to be written, is the *Shulchan Aruch* (Set Table) of Yosef Karo, which is divided into four major sections—*Orach Hayim* (OH), concerning the daily commandments, Sabbaths, and festivals; *Yoreh De'ah* (YD), dealing with various subjects such as dietary laws, interest, purity, and mourning; *Even ha-Ezer* (EH), on marriage, divorce, and related topics; and *Hoshen Misphat* (HM), dealing with civil and criminal law. Reflecting Karo's Sephardic background, the *Shulchan Aruch* did not gain universal acceptance until the addition of the *Mappah* (Tablecloth) by Moses Isserles (mid-16th century; known as the "Rema"), which included the distinctive customs of the Jews of Eastern Europe. This composite work has become the functioning code for observant Jews to the present day.

Cursing Another (315-318)

In ancient times, a curse was more than an expressed wish for evil. Often pronounced in the name of a pagan god or demon, a curse was considered a method of making a potential harm become a reality.

Many of the Rabbis interpreted the verse *"You shall not curse 'elohim'"* (Exod. 22:27), as referring to God and prohibiting blasphemy. The cosmopolitan Josephus and Philo interpreted this as not blaspheming the gods of fellow citizens, implying that one should not speak disrespectfully of the religious beliefs of the followers of other faiths.[414] Because the Torah specifically forbids blaspheming the Name of God elsewhere and labels it a capital crime warranting death by stoning (Neg. Comm. 60), Maimonides preferred to translate the word *"elohim"* as "judges" (as in Exod. 21:6 and 22:7), so that this verse prohibits the cursing of a judge (**315**). The most likely violator of this commandment would be a litigant who lost a case and refused to admit that he was wrong.

"You shall not curse a leader among your people" (Exod. 22:27) forbids the cursing of a ruler (**316**). In the Bible, the word *"nasi"* used in this verse was the title given to the chief of a clan or a tribe in the period before the monarchy.[415] In later biblical books, the term referred to a king who held the power of government, while in later talmudic literature it applied to the Chief of the Great Sanhedrin. Therefore, it was forbidden to curse anyone who holds a position of supreme authority, whether secular or religious. The Rabbis stated that a religious leader could forego the honor due him while a king could not; however, a religious leader could not pardon one who cursed him.[416]

"You shall not curse the deaf" (Lev. 19:14) is the source of the commandment prohibiting the cursing of any Israelite (**317**). If a person is forbidden to curse one who cannot hear it, and thus would not be angered or embarrassed by these words, how much more is it forbidden to curse one who would react with anger or shame and might even resort to violence in a moment

of uncontrollable passion. Maimonides observed that this commandment also forbids a person from being hot-tempered and vindictive toward others. The Rabbis (Ned. 22a) stated, "He who loses his temper is exposed to all the torments of Gehenna (Hell)." They also maintained, "To allow oneself to be carried away by wrath is as bad as worshiping idols."[417]

"One who curses his father or mother shall surely be put to death" (Exod. 21:17) is the commandment prohibiting cursing a parent (**318**). The Hebrew word could also be translated as "to treat with contempt," the direct opposite of the "honor" due parents in the Fifth Commandment.[418] For capital punishment to be incurred, the Rabbis declared that the son must have used the Divine Name itself in cursing his parents. The death sentence could only be pronounced by a court of law after a judicial trial and not by the parents themselves. This was unlike ancient Rome, where a father could have his grown son put to death, even without a specific reason.[419] Maimonides[420] wrote that severe punishment is warranted not only for cursing a parent, but also for any act of contempt for one's father or mother, "even by mere words or by the slightest hint."

According to *Da'at Zekenim*, because God is an equal partner with the mother and the father in the birth of each child, a child who curses his parents also curses God. This is substantially different from striking one's parents (Neg. Comm. 319), since it is impossible to physically injure the Divine. Consequently, the child who *cursed* his father or mother was liable to what the Rabbis considered more severe punishment (stoning) than one who *struck* his parent (strangling).[421]

Striking Parents (319)

"One who strikes his father or mother shall surely be put to death" (Exod. 21:15) is the commandment prohibiting a person from

striking his parents. The Rabbis ruled that capital punishment could be inflicted only if the blow left a bruise or drew blood. This is in contrast to an ordinary assault, for which the perpetrator would be liable for damages regardless of whether he caused a bruise.[422]

According to Maimonides,[423] "He who strikes his father or mother is put to death on account of his great audacity, and because he undermines the constitution of the family, which is the foundation of the state."

The Rabbis discussed two variations on this theme. It was forbidden for a man employed by the court to administer floggings to inflict that punishment on his father; instead, he was required to find another to replace him. A surgeon was not permitted to operate on his parent (since it would cause loss of blood), unless there was no other qualified physician available.[424]

Working on the Sabbath (320)

"(But the seventh day is Sabbath to the Lord your God;) you shall not do any type of work" (Exod. 20:10) is the commandment forbidding work on the Sabbath. The Bible does not specifically list those labors that are prohibited on the Sabbath, although it alludes to field labor (Exod. 34:21; Num. 15:32–36), treading in a winepress and loading animals (Neh. 13:15–18), doing business and carrying (Isa. 58:13; Jer. 17:22; Amos 8:5), traveling (Exod. 16:29–30), and kindling fire (Exod. 35:2–3) as forbidden work. In the Mishnah, the Rabbis enumerated 39 major categories of labor that were forbidden (*avot melachah*), based on those types of work that were related to the construction of the Tabernacle in the wilderness and ceased on the Sabbath (Shab. 7:2). Those activities that cannot be performed on the Sabbath are: basic tasks connected with preparing the Show-bread (sowing, plowing, reaping, binding, threshing, winnowing, selecting, grinding, sifting, kneading, baking); work related to making

the coverings in the Tabernacle and the vestments used by the Kohanim (shearing [sheep], bleaching, carding [changing tangled or compressed material into separate fibers], dyeing, spinning, stretching [material], making two loops [meshes], threading needles, weaving, separating, tying [a knot], untying [a knot], sewing, tearing); activities concerned with writing, including the preparation of parchment from animal skin (trapping or hunting, slaughtering, flaying [skinning], treating skins [curing hides], scraping pelts, marking out [to make ready for cutting], cutting [to shape], writing, erasing); construction (building, demolishing); kindling a flame (lighting, extinguishing); carrying (from private to public domain, and vice versa), and putting the finishing touches to a piece of work already begun before the Sabbath.[425]

The Rabbis decreed that one should not only avoid forbidden acts but also must not do anything that (1) resembles a prohibited act or could be confused with it, (2) is a habit linked with a prohibited act, or (3) usually leads to performing a prohibited act. The rabbinic enactment of measures to prevent these possibilities was termed "putting a fence around the Torah" (Avot 1:1). For example, ripping up a piece of paper was forbidden since it resembles "cutting to shape" or could be confused with it. Similarly, agreeing to buy something was prohibited, because most agreements are confirmed in "writing"; climbing a tree is forbidden, because it may lead to breaking twigs or tearing leaves, which could be construed as "reaping" (i.e., separating part of a growing plant from its source).[426]

For an activity to be considered as work forbidden on the Sabbath, the violation must be intentional. Therefore, moving a chair from one place to another is permissible, even though it may produce an impression on the ground. Similarly, walking on the grass is allowed, even though this may result in some of it being crushed underfoot and thus technically constitute the prohibited activity mentioned above or the forbidden cutting of blades of grass. One has not violated the Sabbath as long as the original purpose was solely to move the chair or to walk on the grass. In contrast, one is not permitted to engage in a task that always results in forbidden work Thus washing oneself on a lawn is prohibited because it inevitably will result in watering the grass, which is forbidden on the Sabbath.[427]

Any items that may not be used on the Sabbath may not even be handled on that day, lest one unintentionally perform one of the forbidden types of work. These objects are termed *muktzeh,* meaning to "set aside" or "store away." Among the many things considered *muktzeh* are money and checks; scissors, hammers, and saws; pencils and pens; battery-operated toys and flashlights; radios and CDs; telephones and computers; and religious objects such as a shofar, tefillin, and *lulav.* Even the Sabbath candlesticks are *muktzeh* and thus should not be moved on the Sabbath after the candles have been lit.[428]

In addition to the general forbidding of all manner of work on the Sabbath, there is a special prohibition against making a fire (Exod. 35:3). The Rabbis considered this to include everything that pertains to the kindling of light, even if no actual work is involved. In modern times, there is a controversy regarding whether the switching on of electric lights and appliances is equivalent to making a fire There are two reasons to think that switching on an electric light may not be considered kindling. For one, switching on a light does not create electric power; the power exists already. In addition, there is no combustion in the filament of an electric light. Nevertheless, Orthodox Jews do not directly use electrical appliances on the Sabbath, believing that the prohibition against kindling a fire was not based on the physical effort involved in rubbing two stones together to produce a spark, but rather on the thought and planning that resulted in its generation. For the Hazon Ish, the activation of an electric current and its transmission to sources of power, heat, and light that is produced by turning on a switch is forbidden because it falls under the category of "building"—intentionally causing something to happen. An exception is the refrigerator, which may be opened and closed because any electrical current that this produces is incidental and without conscious intent. However, many observant Jews unscrew the refrigerator bulb for the Sabbath. A light that has been kindled before the Sabbath, such as the Sabbath candles, is allowed, as are an oven for keeping previously cooked food warm and a burner to keep water warm for coffer or tea. Similarly, it is permitted to leave an electrical appliance running during the Sabbath and to use a timer to automatically turn an appliance on or off, as long as the timer is set before the Sabbath begins.

One mechanism to ease the difficulty of complying with the prohibition against work on the Sabbath was the concept of the *Shabbos goy*—a non-Jew hired by an observant family to perform certain activities forbidden to Jews on the Sabbath, such as starting a fire and turning lights on and off.[429] However, the proliferation of electronic timers has virtually eliminated the need for the *Shabbos goy*.

All of the Sabbath restrictions may be violated in order to preserve life (*pekuach nefesh*). As Maimonides noted,[430] "The commandments of the Sabbath, like all other commandments, may be set aside if human life is in danger," based on the verse "You shall keep my laws and ordinances, through which a man shall live [and not die]" (Lev. 18:5). Even if one is in doubt as to whether a life will be saved, a person is permitted to violate the Sabbath, "for the mere possibility of danger to human life overrides the Sabbath." As the Talmud concluded, "Violate one Sabbath [in order that someone may live] to observe many Sabbaths" (Yoma 85b). Thus the deliberate desecration of the Sabbath to save a life is more than outweighed by the potential for future sanctification of the Sabbath and God's Name.

Journeying on the Sabbath (321)

"Let no one leave his place on the seventh day" (Exod. 16:29) is the commandment forbidding one to journey on the Sabbath. The Rabbis interpreted the verse prohibiting the gathering of manna on the seventh day (Exod. 16:29) as forbidding one from journeying on the Sabbath. Unlike the Karaites, who took the verse "let no person go out of his place on the seventh day" literally and did not allow anyone to leave home on the Sabbath, the Rabbis did not restrict movement within one's town. However, they prohibited Jews from walking more than two thousand cubits (approximately a half mile) beyond the town boundaries on the Sabbath, "because traveling interrupts the rest of both man and beast."[431] As Menachem Hababli observed, because Jews have an "extra soul" on the Sabbath, they must devote their free time to Torah study rather than waste the day going from place to place.[432]

As with all of the negative commandments, the prohibition against journeying on the Sabbath is overridden when a life is in danger, or even if there is only possible or potential danger to life. Maimonides[433] noted that it was permissible and even mandatory to exceed the 2000 cubit limit to rescue one or more Israelites whose lives were in danger from heathens, a flooding river, a collapsed building, or physical or mental illness.

Orthodox rabbis forbid driving an automobile on the Sabbath, based on the fact that it involves turning on the ignition, which in turn ignites sparks—an act that violates the Torah law against making a fire on the Sabbath (Exod. 35:3). Conservative rabbis generally permit Jews to drive on the Sabbath, but only to synagogue. This ruling was made in response to the migration of Jews to the suburbs, where most no longer live within walking distance of a synagogue. Continuing to forbid driving on the Sabbath would have forced many congregants to remain at home or to pursue nonreligious activities. Fearing an erosion of Jewish identity if synagogue attendance dropped precipitously, these rabbis permitted driving as the lesser of two evils. Orthodox rabbis denounced this decision, arguing that Conservative rabbis should instead encourage their congregants to live within walking distance of their synagogues.[434]

In Israel, public transport does not operate on the Sabbath in Jerusalem and Tel Aviv, but it does run in Haifa. Except for specifically non-Jewish sections of the country, the Sabbath is the official day of rest on which all businesses and stores must close.

Punishing on the Sabbath (322)

"You shall kindle no fire in any of your dwellings on the Sabbath day" (Exod. 35:3) was considered by Maimonides as forbidding the "carrying out of the punishment of a wrong-doer on the Sabbath." He interpreted this verse to mean that one cannot "burn the culprit who is liable for burning." The Rabbis extended this injunction to prevent all four forms of judicial execution (Pos. Comm. 226-229) on the Sabbath.

As *Sefer ha-Chinuch* observed, "The Sabbath being God's gift to man as a day of rest, it is His desire that the gift be extended even to those who have acted against His will." Menachem Hababli noted that although desecration of the Sabbath is required to save human life (*pekuach nefesh*), it is strictly forbidden in the context of taking human life.[435]

Working on the Festivals (323-329)

The prohibition against working on the first (**323**) and seventh (**324**) days of Passover, Shavuot (**325**), Rosh Hashanah (**326**), Yom Kippur (**329**), the first day of Sukkot (**327**), and Shemini Atzeret (**328**) is derived from the phrase that accompanies each festival, *"You shall do no laborious work"* (cited, respectively, in Lev. 23:7; 23:8; 23:21; 23:25; 26:31; 23:35, and 23:36).

No English translation can capture the sense of the term *m'lechet avodah*, which is generally rendered as "laborious or servile work," in contrast to the more restrictive prohibition "you shall do no work" that applies to the Sabbath and Yom Kippur. According to Rashi, *m'lechet avodah* means "essential work that will cause a significant loss if it is not performed." Nachmanides considers it "burdensome" work, such as ordinary farm or factory labor; in contrast, a person may engage in "pleasurable work," such as the preparation of food.[436] Whatever the interpretation of the term, all agree that the preparation of food—including such labors as slaughtering, cooking, and baking—is permitted on festivals (other than Yom Kippur) that fall on a weekday, based on the verse "only what every person is to eat, that alone may be prepared for you" (Exod. 12:16).

While preparation of holiday meals is permitted on festivals, it is forbidden to prepare food for another day. Strictly speaking, if a festival occurs on Friday, one would not be permitted to prepare food for the Sabbath. To overcome this problem, the Rabbis instituted the *eruv tavshilin*. On the day before the festival, one prepares a special dish consisting of two items of food (such as bread and a piece of fish) for the Sabbath. In this way, a "blending" (*eruv*) of the Sabbath and festival foods occurs, making it permissible to prepare food on Friday for the Sabbath.[437] According to another talmudic view, the prohibition against preparing food for the Sabbath without an *eruv tavshilin* was intended to stress the importance of the ban against working on a festival to prepare for the subsequent weekdays.[438]

Maimonides deemed the injunction to rest (abstain from work) on the festivals as positive commandments (159-160, 162-163, 165-167), while actually performing work on the festival was a violation of these negative commandments.

Forbidden Relationships (330-345)

The laws governing sexual relationships are the key to Jewish holiness. The concept of the sacred bond between a man and wife is clearly expressed in the first step of a Jewish marriage, in which the groom betroths his bride and says, "You are consecrated to me."[439]

All the forbidden relationships, whether temporary or permanent, are termed "incestuous." The two people could not be considered married under Jewish law, no *get* (document of divorce) would be required for the dissolution of their relationship, and any children would be considered *mamzerim* (see Neg. Comm. 354)

According to the Rabbis, before the Revelation at Sinai, the only relationships that were prohibited were those between a man and his mother, his father's wife, a married woman, and a sister on his mother's side. Therefore, Abraham was permitted to marry his half-sister Sarah (the daughter of his father, according to Gen. 20:12); Jacob could wed two sisters, Rachel and Leah; and Amram was allowed to marry his aunt Yocheved (the parents of Aaron, Moses, and Miriam).

Leviticus 18 (6-17) specifically prohibits a man from having sexual intercourse with his (330) mother; (331) father's wife (step-mother); (332) sister (whether born of a legal marriage or out of wedlock); (333) half-sister; (334, 335) granddaughter; (336) daughter; (337) wife and her daughter; (338) wife and her son's daughter; (339); wife and her daughter's daughter; (340) father's sister (aunt); (341) mother's sister (aunt); (342) father's brother's wife (aunt); (343) son's wife (daughter-in-law, either after divorce or his son's death); (344) brother's wife (sister-in-law); or (345) wife's sister (during the former's lifetime).

A few of these forbidden relationships deserve further study. In the Near East, it was a regular practice for an heir-apparent to take possession of his father's wife to assert his right to the throne and to become identified with the ruler's personality in the eyes of the people.[440] This explains Reuben's conduct in bedding Bilhah, the concubine of his father, Jacob (Gen. 35:22), which resulted in Reuben earning the unending wrath of his father, thus forfeiting his privilege as the firstborn.

The prohibition against having a sexual relationship with one's brother's wife did not apply to the situation in which he died childless, where there was the obligation of levirate marriage or the alternative of *chalitzah* (Pos. Comm. 216-217).

Marriage to his wife's sister was forbidden as long as his wife was alive (even if they had been divorced), lest the two sisters become "rivals" (Lev. 18:18). Ironically, after his wife's death, marriage to the surviving sister was not only permitted, but even deemed praiseworthy by the Rabbis, who maintained that no other woman would show the same deep affection for the orphaned children of the deceased sister.

The Rabbis expanded the primary forbidden relationships in the ascending and descending line. Known as "secondary" prohibited marriages, this meant that just as a man was forbidden to have relations with his mother, so was he forbidden to marry his grandmother or great-grandmother. Similarly, since his step-mother was forbidden, so was his grandfather's wife; as his daughter-in-law was prohibited, so was his grandson's wife. Marriages of the secondary prohibited degree had to be dissolved by a divorce, and the children were legitimate.

The forbidden relationships and the immoral sexual practices (Pos. Comm. 346-353) constitute the Torah reading for the afternoon service on Yom Kippur. This reflects the days of the Temple, when Yom Kippur had a festive character. Following the announcement of forgiveness by the *Kohen Gadol*, the young maidens danced in the vineyards and betrothals were announced. This Torah reading was selected to impress upon the young people the need for maintaining Israel's high standard of chastity and family morality. Impurity in marriage, incestuous promiscuity among near relations, and other abominations were unequivocally condemned and regarded as unpardonable sins. This portion is still read today in traditional synagogues to inculcate the critical duties of self-control and marital fidelity and purity that have proven to be potent factors in the survival of the Jewish people.[441]

Having Intercourse With a Menstruant (346)

"You shall not approach a woman during her period of impurity, to uncover her nakedness" (Lev. 18:19) is the commandment prohibiting intercourse with a menstruating woman. It is the negative commandment that corresponds to the law of the menstruant (Pos. Comm. 99). Marital intercourse was prohibited during menstruation (*niddah*) as well as for an additional seven days (*taharah*), and could only be resumed after the wife immersed herself in a ritual bath (*mikveh*) (Pos. Comm. 109).

Maimonides viewed this prohibition as designed to curb a man's natural passions, lest he spend all his time with women. Nachmanides maintained that since the Torah deemed the purpose of sex to be procreation, forbidding marital relations during menstruation was logical because a woman cannot conceive during that time.[442]

Having Intercourse with Another Man's Wife (347)

"You shall not lie carnally with your neighbor's wife" (Lev. 18:20) is the commandment related to the prohibition of adultery, the seventh of the Ten Commandments (Exod. 20:13). The Mechilta considered adultery to be parallel to the second commandment forbidding idolatry, reasoning that a person who fails to honor the marriage vows is likely also to be unfaithful to God. This

prohibition was extended to include most contact with the opposite sex, which the Rabbis feared could lead to a level of passionate lust that was virtually equivalent to adultery itself.[443]

Termed a "great sin" in the Bible (Gen. 20:9) and simply "the sin" in the Talmud (Sanh. 74a), adultery was one of the three transgressions, along with idolatry and murder, that a Jew must avoid at all costs, even on pain of death. In addition to posing a threat to the purity and honor of the family, a major value in Judaism, *Sefer ha-Chinuch* noted that children born of an adulterous relationship would never be able to completely perform the mitzvah of honoring their parents, and that adultery may lead to murder if a jealous husband killed his wife's lover.

Lying With Animals (348-349)

"Do not lie with an animal" (Lev. 18:23) and *"A woman shall not stand before an animal for mating (it is a perversion)"* (Lev. 18:23) are the commandments prohibiting sexual intercourse with animals by men (**348**) and women (**349**). Unlike almost all of the other forbidden relationships, which involve natural activity, though with prohibited mates, bestiality is an unnatural and perverse practice that is termed "an abomination." The Hebrew word *tevel* (perversion) is derived from a root meaning "to mix," implying that sexual relations with beasts is a forbidden "mixture" of species (Neg. Comm. 217).[444]

A Man Lying Carnally with a Man (350)

"You shall not lie with a man as one lies with a woman; it is an abomination" (Lev. 18:22) is the commandment forbidding male homosexuality. This verse comes at the conclusion of the list of prohibited sexual relationships, but is the only one, other than bestiality, that uses the harsh term "abomination."

The Rabbis offered three basic reasons for the strict ban on homosexuality. They considered it an unnatural perversion, defying the very structure of the anatomy of the sexes (which they deemed to be obviously designed for heterosexual relationships) and thus debasing the dignity of human beings created in the image of God. Homosexuality frustrates the procreative purpose of sex, just as does masturbation and other forms of "spilling the seed in vain." Finally, a homosexual might abandon his wife and severely disrupt the integrity of the family, a core principal in Jewish life. For all these reasons, traditional Jewish law utterly rejects the concept that homosexuality is to be regarded as morally neutral. It is unwilling to countenance the increasingly prevalent "politically correct" view that homosexual acts are acceptable as long as they are between two consenting adults and merely constitute an alternative lifestyle.

Since the 1980s, the rise of the gay pride movement has forced the Jewish community to confront the issue of homosexuality. Synagogues have been established by and for homosexuals. Requests have been made to accept homosexuality as an alternative lifestyle and for rabbinic sanctification of homosexual commitment ceremonies, based on the argument that procreation is the primary but not the only purpose of Jewish marriage.[445] It is interesting that the question of gay marriage was addressed in talmudic times, when the Rabbis stated that even those gentiles who engage in homosexual practices "do not draw up a *ketubah* for males"—that is, they do not write a marriage deed for gay couples (Hul. 92b).[446]

Barry Freundel, a prominent Orthodox rabbi, has argued that, "we cannot close our eyes and pretend that a problem of this magnitude will go away. It is our task to present a legitimate Jewish response, balancing our opposition to homosexual activity with our concern for the human beings involved." He urged the traditional Jewish community to motivate homosexuals to change their orientation, stressing that gays should be kept within the Torah community by the creation of a situation that "offers a positive alternative to the gay synagogue and to the even worse choices of complete abandonment and assimilation."[447]

The marginalization of gays exists to a much lesser degree in the other denominations within Judaism. Reform rabbis endorsed same-sex civil marriages in 1996, and the movement recently voted to allow rabbis to conduct same-sex marriages and to permit the ordination of admittedly gay men (and women).[448] While the Conservative movement does not ordain openly gay men or women as rabbis and officially prohibits same-sex commitment ceremonies, this latter policy is being increasingly flouted.

The Torah does not mention female homosexuality, either because lesbianism was not widely practiced or because it was considered merely a minor offense. Maimonides[449] maintained that this lenient approach reflected the belief that lesbianism does not involve genital intercourse. He argued that, although prohibited, a married woman guilty of female homosexuality did not become automatically forbidden to her husband. Nevertheless, he stated that a husband should object to his wife indulging in such activities by preventing her from associating with women known to engage in lesbian practices. In addition, he urged a court dealing with a case of lesbianism to apply the punishment of flogging prescribed for rebelliousness, since the women had performed a forbidden act.[450]

A Man Lying Carnally with his Father or Father's Brother (351-352)

"You shall not uncover the nakedness of your father" (Lev. 18:7) and *"You shall not uncover the nakedness of your father's brother"* (Lev.

18:14) are the commandments prohibiting, respectively, sexual relations with one's father (**351**) and uncle (**352**).

Intimacy with a Close Relative (353)

"You shall not approach any close relative to uncover their nakedness" (Lev. 18:6) is the commandment forbidding one from seeking pleasurable contact with any relative within the prohibited degrees of marriage, even though it does not go beyond such endearments as embracing and kissing. In the Hebrew text, this injunction is written in the plural, indicating that it applies equally to men and women (Rashi).[451] However, Maimonides[452] and all other authorities excluded from this ban the kissing of one's mother, daughter, sister, and aunt.

Maimonides[453] urged each person to "accustom oneself to refrain from light-hearted conversation, drunkenness, and all manner of lewd talk, for all these constitute great causes [of actual unchastity]. His solution was for a man to "devote himself and his mind to study of Torah, seeking always to broaden his knowledge of its wisdom, since thoughts of lewdness arise only in a heart that is turned away from the pursuit of wisdom."[454]

A *Mamzer* Marrying a Jew (354)

"A mamzer *shall not enter the congregation of the Lord"* (Deut. 23:3) is the commandment prohibiting marriage between a *mamzer* and a Jew. Contrary to popular misconception, a *mamzer* (often mistranslated as "bastard") is not someone born out of wedlock. Rather it is the child of a sexual relationship between a man and woman whose marriage could never be valid under Jewish law (Kid. 3:12). Examples include the offspring of a union between a brother and sister or other incestuous relationship, a child born to a married woman by some man other than her

lawful husband (adultery), and a child born of a woman who had remarried without having obtained a valid divorce (*get*) from her first husband. According to the Bible, a *mamzer* and all of his or her descendants may never marry a Jew. However, a marriage between two *mamzerim* is permitted. Addressing the issue of why the child was penalized for the immoral action of his parents, Maimonides viewed it as a deterrent against such behavior, for "in order to create a horror of illicit marriages, a *mamzer* was not allowed to marry an Israelite woman; the adulterer and the adulteress were thus taught that by their act they bring upon their seed irreparable injury."[455] Realizing that this law was overly harsh and unfair to both the *mamzer* and his or her descendants, the Rabbis eventually allowed a *mamzer* to marry a convert as a way of becoming more quickly integrated into the Jewish community. They believed that the offspring of a *mamzer* who had married a convert would, within a generation or so, begin to be referred to as a descendant of the convert (not the *mamzer*) and become fully accepted.

Except in regard to marriage, the personal status of a *mamzer* is not adversely affected in any way. He can be called up to the Torah, has equal rights of inheritance as other heirs, and can hold public office. The Mishnah even states: "a *mamzer* who is a scholar (*talmid hacham*) takes precedence over a *Kohen Gadol* who is an ignoramus (*am ha-aretz*)" (Hor. 3:8).

Having Intercourse Without Marriage (355)

"*There shall not be a harlot [promiscuous woman] among the daughters of Israel, and there shall not be a male prostitute (promiscuous man) among the sons of Israel*" (Deut. 23:18) is the commandment that Maimonides interpreted as forbidding premarital sexual relations. Maimonides related this to the verse "Do not profane your daughter to make her a harlot" (Lev. 19:29), which he stated referred either "to one who gave his unmarried daughter for unchastity, or to a woman who voluntarily consorted with a man without the benefit of a legal marriage." The Rabbis (Sanh. 76a) added that this also prohibited giving one's daughter in marriage to an old man, since this might tempt her to adultery.

According to Biale,[456] the biblical prohibitions that form the basis of the sexual codes in the *halachah* prohibit only incestuous and adulterous relations. When polygamy was permissible, as during biblical times, a married man was not forbidden from having sexual relations with an unmarried woman as long as he could theoretically marry her. If he did not attempt to marry her, the man would be condemned and even flogged in some communities, but he was not guilty of a sexual transgression. Similarly, an unmarried and not betrothed woman who had sexual relations with a man did not violate any explicit sexual prohibition.

Nevertheless, the *halachah* condemns non-marital sexuality as "promiscuity" (*zenut*). The Talmud uses the term in multiple ways to refer to a spectrum of relationships such as professional prostitution; sexual relations of an unmarried woman not in the pursuit of marriage but merely for pleasure; any type of illicit sexual relationship, including adultery; and a specific type of woman whom a Kohen is forbidden to marry (*zonah*; Neg. Comm. 158) but who is permitted to all other men.

Remarrying One's Divorced Wife After She Had Remarried (356)

"Her former husband who divorced her, shall not again take her to be his wife, after she has been defiled" (Deut. 24:4) is the commandment prohibiting a man from remarrying his divorced wife who has remarried and had her second marriage also terminated by divorce or death. If this were not the case, people

may feel free to divorce one another at will to sample other mates, before subsequently getting together again. Abravanel (citing Ralbag) suggested that this prohibition was intended to prevent the possibility of a man conspiring with his wife to leave him, marry another man, and make life so miserable for her second husband that he would agree to make a cash settlement and divorce her, thus enabling her to then return to her first husband with a financial windfall.[457]

The Rabbis (Yev. 11b) noted that the phrase "after she has been defiled" is the source of the prohibition against a man having intercourse with his wife after she has committed adultery.[458]

Having Intercourse with a Woman Subject to Levirate Marriage (357)

"*The wife of the deceased shall not marry a stranger outside the family*" (Deut. 25:5) is the commandment prohibiting a widow subject to a levirate marriage (Pos. Comm. 216) from marrying anyone other than her brother-in-law.

If the rite of *chalitzah* (Pos. Comm. 217) is performed, the widow is permitted to marry any other man, except a Kohen.

Limitations on Divorce (358-359)

"*He may never divorce her all his days*" (Deut. 22:29) is the commandment (**358**) forbidding a man from ever divorcing a woman he had raped and been compelled to marry (Pos. Comm. 218). The same phrase in a different verse (Deut. 22:19) is the commandment (**359**) prohibiting a man from ever divorcing his wife if he had defamed her by falsely accusing her of committing adultery between the time of their betrothal and the marriage ceremony (Pos. Comm. 219).

A Man Incapable of Procreation Marrying a Jewess (360)

"A man with crushed testicles or a severed organ shall not enter the congregation of the Lord" (Deut. 23:2) is the commandment prohibiting a man from marrying a Jewish woman if his reproductive organs have been so severely damaged that he has become impotent. If, however, the disability arose through natural means (such as birth defect or illness), it was considered an "act of God" and this prohibition does not apply. One who was voluntarily sterilized or castrated was subject to this injunction, since this action indicated that he had no intention of fathering children.[459]

Maimonides and Abravanel argue that the major reason for this prohibition is that there is no real purpose to marriage other than procreation, totally ignoring the importance of warm companionship that this relationship can provide. They also make the questionable claim that a man who fails to disclose his impotence will lead his wife to engage in immoral relationships with other men.[460]

Castration (361)

"(One whose testicles are squeezed, crushed, torn, or cut, you shall not offer to the Lord;) nor shall you have such practices in your Land" (Lev. 22:24) is the commandment forbidding the castration of a male of any species, whether man or beast. The end of the verse indicates that it is forbidden to castrate any animal, regardless of whether it can be used as an offering or is kosher as food.[461]

Limitations Relating to a King (362-365)

The king was to be a constitutional monarch who governed in accordance with the Torah. *"You may not set a foreigner over you, who is not your kinsman"* (Deut. 17:15) is the commandment

(362) prohibiting the appointment of a king who was not an Israelite by birth. Although no reason is given, the underlying rationale was presumably the danger that the people could be led into idolatry by a foreigner would was not a faithful adherent of the monotheistic worship of God.[462]

"He shall not have too many horses for himself" (Deut. 17:16) is the commandment **(363)** prohibiting the king from having an excessive number of horses. Ibn Ezra and *Sefer ha-Chinuch* noted that, after leaving Egypt, the Israelites were forbidden to ever settle there again (Neg. Comm. 46). Egypt was a major source of horses in ancient times. If permitted to purchase horses without restriction, a king would send agents for this purpose to Egypt, thus setting up an Israelite settlement there.[463] Rashi saw this verse as a warning to the king not to cherish military ambitions. Maimonides maintained that, although the king could keep horses in his stable for his army to ride in wars, for personal use he was only permitted the single horse on which he rode.

"He shall not have too many wives" (Deut. 17:17) is the commandment **(364)** that was interpreted as prohibiting the king from having "more than 18 wives by duly contracted marriage." The danger of foreign wives was that they might "turn his heart astray" toward their idolatrous practices.

"He shall not amass [lit., greatly increase silver and gold for himself" (Deut. 17:17) is the commandment **(365)** forbidding the king to amass great personal wealth. The king was only permitted sufficient funds "for the upkeep of his army and his personal attendants." According to Ibn Ezra, the desire to accumulate wealth would impel the king to impose excessive taxes on his people, which could become so burdensome and oppressive that they would overthrow him.[464]

Despite these admonitions, Solomon felt no qualms about violating these restrictions on the royal privileges because he was certain that his incomparable wisdom would protect him from the consequences indicated in the biblical verses. However, Solomon was mistaken. Filling his large stables brought the people back to Egypt, his foreign wives led the people to idol worship, and the heavy taxes he imposed led to a split of his realm into the Kingdoms of Judah and Israel after his death.[465]

Bibliography

ArtScroll Siddur. Brooklyn: Mesorah Publications, 1986.

Biale, Rachel. *Women and Jewish Law*. New York: Schocken, 1984.

Chill, Abraham. *The Mitzvot*. New York: Bloch, 1974.

Etz Hayim. Philadelphia: Jewish Publication Society, 2001.

Frankel, Ellen and Teutsch, Betsy Platkin. *The Encyclopedia of Jewish Symbols*. Northvale (NJ): Jason Aronson, 1992.

Hertz, J.J. *The Pentateuch and Haftorahs*. London: Soncino Press, 1978.

Ibn Ezra, Abraham. *Commentary on the Torah*, translated by H. Norman Strickman and Silver, Arthur M. New York: Mesorah, 1996.

Isaacs, Ronald H. Mitzvot: *A Sourcebook for the 613 Commandments*. Northvale (NJ): Jason Aronson, 1996.

Kolatch, Alfred J. *The Jewish Book of Why*. Middle Village (NY): Jonathan David, 1981.

Kolatch, Alfred J. *The Second Jewish Book of Why*. Middle Village (NY): Jonathan David, 1985.

Levine, Baruch A. *The JPS Torah Commentary: Leviticus*. Philadelphia: Jewish Publication Society, 1996.

Maimonides, Moses. *The Commandments*, translated by Charles Chavel, London and New York: Soncino Press, 1967.

Maimonides, Moses. *The Guide of the Perplexed*, translated by Shlomo Pines. Chicago and London: University of Chicago Press, 1963.

Maimonides, Moses. *Mishneh Torah*, translated by Philip Birnbaum. New York: Hebrew Publishing Corp., 1974.

Millgram, Abraham. *Jewish Worship*. Philadelphia: Jewish Publication Society, 1971.

Nachmanides. *Commentary on the Torah*, translated by Charles Chavel. New York: Shilo, 1974.

Sefer ha-Chinuch, translated by Charles Wengrov. New York: Feldheim, 1978.

Sforno, Obadiah ben Jacob: *Commentary on the Torah*. Brooklyn: Mesorah, 1987.

Stone Chumash. Brooklyn: Mesorah, 1994.

Strassfeld, Michael. *The Jewish Holidays: A Guide and Commentary*. New York: Harper & Row, 1985.

Telushkin, Joseph. *Jewish Literacy*. New York: William Morrow, 1991.

Tigay, Jeffrey H. *The JPS Torah Commentary: Deuteronomy*. Philadlephia: Jewish Publication Society, 1996.

Witty, Abraham B. and Witty, Rachel. *Exploring Jewish Tradition*. New York: Doubleday, 2001.

Textual Sources
Positive Commandments

1. Belief in the existence of God (Exod. 20:2)
2. Unity of God (Deut. 6:4)
3. Love of God (Deut. 6:5)
4. Fear of God (Deut. 6:13; 10:20)
5. Serving (worshiping) God (Exod. 23:25; Deut. 6:13, 11:13, 13:15)
6. Cleaving to God (Deut. 6:13; 10:20)
7. Swearing in God's name (Deut. 10:12)
8. Walking in God's ways (Deut. 28:9)
9. Sanctifying God's name (*Kiddush ha-Shem*) (Lev. 22:32)
10. Reading the *Shema* (Deut. 6:7)
11. Teaching and studying the Torah (Deut. 6:7)
12-13. Wearing tefillin (Deut. 6:8)
14. Fringes (tzitzit) (Num. 15:38)
15. Affixing a mezuzah (Deut. 6:9; 11:20)
16. The Assembly during the feast of Tabernacles (Deut. 31:12)
17. A king to write a scroll of Law (Deut. 17:18)
18. Writing a Torah scroll (Deut. 31:19)
19. Grace after meals (*Birkat ha-Mazon*) (Deut. 8:10)
20. Building a Sanctuary (*Mishkan*) (Exod. 25:8)
21. Revering the Sanctuary (Lev. 19:30)
22. Guarding the Sanctuary (Num. 18:4)
23. Levitical services in the Sanctuary (Num. 18:23)
24. Ablutions of the Kohanim (Exod. 30:19)
25. Kindling the Menorah in the Sanctuary (Exod. 27:21)
26. Priestly blessing (Num. 6:23-26)
27. The Show-bread (Exod. 25:30)
28. Burning the incense (Exod. 30:7)
29. Keeping a fire continually on the Altar (Lev. 6:6)
30. Removing the ashes from the Altar (Lev. 6:3)
31. Removing the ritually unclean (Num. 5:2-3)
32. Honoring the Kohanim (Lev. 21:8)
33. Priestly garments (Exod. 28:2)
34. Kohanim bearing the Ark (Num. 7:9)
35. Oil of anointment (Exod. 30:31; Lev. 21:10)
36. Kohanim ministering in courses (Deut. 18:6-8)
37. Kohanim defiling themselves for close relatives (Lev. 21:2-3)
38. *Kohen Gadol* marrying only a virgin (Lev. 21:13-14)
39. Daily burnt offering (Exod. 29:38-39; Num. 28:3)
40. Daily meal offering of the *Kohen Gadol* (Lev. 6:13)
41. Additional offering for Sabbath (Num. 28:9-10)
42. Additional offering for New Moon (Num. 28:11-15)
43. Additional offering for Passover (Num. 28:16-25)
44. Meal offering of new barley (Lev. 23:10)

45. Additional offering for Shavuot (Num. 28:26-31)
46. Bringing of the two loaves on Shavuot (Lev. 23:17)
47. Additional offering for the New Year (Num. 29:1-6)
48. Additional offering for the Day of Atonement (Num. 29:7-11)
49. Service of the Day of Atonement (Lev. 16:1-34)
50. Additional offering for Sukkot (Num. 29:12-34)
51. Additional offering for Shemini Atzeret (Num. 29:35-38)
52. Three annual Pilgrimage Festivals (Exod. 23:14)
53. Appearing before the Lord during the festivals
     (Exod. 34:23; Deut. 16:16)
54. Rejoicing on the festivals (Deut. 16:14)
55. Slaughtering the Passover offering (Exod. 12:6)
56. Eating the Passover offering (Exod. 12:8)
57. Slaughtering the second Passover offering (Num. 9:10-12)
58. Eating the second Passover offering (Num. 9:10-12)
59. Blowing the trumpets in the Sanctuary (Num. 10:10)
60. Offering cattle of a minimum age (Exod. 22:29; Lev. 22:27)
61. Offering only unblemished sacrifices (Lev. 22:21)
62. Bringing salt with every offering (Lev. 2:13)
63. Burnt offering (Lev. 1:1-17)
64. Sin offering (Lev. 4:1 - 5:13)
65. Guilt offering (Lev. 5:14-26)
66. Peace offering (Lev. 3:1-17)
67. Meal offering (Lev. 2:1-16)
68. Offering of a Court that has erred (Lev. 4:13)
69. Fixed sin offering (Lev. 4:27-35)
70. Suspensive guilt offering (Lev. 5:17-19)
71. Unconditional guilt offering (Lev. 5:15-16)
72. Offering of a higher or lower value (Lev. 5:1-4)
73. Making confession (Num. 5:6-7)
74. Offering brought by a *zav* (Lev. 15:13-15)
75. Offering brought by a *zavah* (Lev. 15:29-30)
76. Offering after childbirth (Lev. 12:6)
77. Offering brought by one with *tzara'at* (Lev. 14:10)
78. Tithe of cattle (Lev. 27:32)
79. Sanctifying the firstborn (Exod. 13:2)
80. Redeeming the firstborn (Exod. 22:28; Num. 18:15)
81. Redeeming the firstborn donkey (Exod. 13:13)
82. Breaking the neck of the firstborn donkey (Exod. 13:13)
83. Bringing due offerings on the first festival (Deut. 12:5-6)
84. All offerings to be brought to the Sanctuary (Deut. 12:14)
85. All offerings due from outside the Land of Israel to be brought to
     the Sanctuary (Deut. 12:26)
86. Redeeming blemished offerings (Deut. 12:15)
87. Holiness of a substituted offering (Lev. 27:10)
88. Kohanim eating the residue of the meal offerings (Lev. 8:9)
89. Kohanim eating the meat of consecrated offerings (Exod. 29:33)
90. Consecrated offerings that have become unclean to be burnt (Lev. 7:19)

91. Remnant of consecrated offerings to be burnt (Lev. 7:17)
92. Nazirite to let his hair grow (Num. 6:5)
93. Nazirite obligations on completion of vow (Num. 6:13-21)
94. All oral commitments to be fulfilled (Deut. 23:24)
95. Revocation of vows (Num. 30:3)
96. Defilement through carcasses of animals (Lev. 11:24)
97. Defilement through carcasses of certain creeping creatures (Lev. 11:29-30)
98. Defilement of food and drink (Lev. 11:34)
99. The menstruant (Lev. 15:19-24)
100. Offerings after childbirth (Lev. 12:2-8)
101. *Tzara'at* (Lev. 13:3)
102. Garments contaminated by *tzara'at* (Lev. 13:47-59)
103. *Tzara'at* of a house (Lev. 14:33-53)
104. *Zav* (Lev. 15:2)
105. Semen (Lev. 15:16)
106. *Zavah* (Lev. 15:25-28)
107. Uncleanness of a corpse (Num. 19:14)
108. Law of the water of sprinkling (Num. 19:1-22)
109. Immersing in a ritual bath (Lev. 15:16)
110. Cleansing from *tzara'at* (Lev. 14:1-7)
111. Person with *tzara'at* to shave his head (Lev. 14:9)
112. Person with *tzara'at* to be made distinguishable (Lev. 13:45)
113. Ashes of the red heifer (Num. 19:1-22)
114. Valuation of a person (Lev. 27:2-8)
115. Valuation of animals (Lev. 27:9-13)
116. Valuation of houses (Lev. 27:14-15)
117. Valuation of fields (Lev. 27:16-25)
118. Restitution for sacrilege (Lev. 5:16; 22:14)
119. Fruits of fourth-year plantings (Lev. 19:24)
120. *Pe'ah* for the poor (Lev. 19:9)
121. Gleanings for the poor (Lev. 19:9)
122. Forgotten sheaf for the poor (Deut. 24:19)
123. Defective grape clusters for the poor (Lev. 19:10)
124. Grape gleanings for the poor (Lev. 19:10)
125. First fruits to be brought to the Sanctuary (Exod. 23:19)
126. Great heave offering (Deut. 18:4)
127. First tithe (Num. 18:21)
128. Second tithe (Deut. 14:22)
129. Levites' tithe for the Kohanim (Num. 18:26)
130. Poor man's tithe (Deut. 14:28)
131. Avowal of the tithe (Deut. 26:13-15)
132. Recital on bringing the first fruits (Deut. 26:5-10)
133. Dough offering (*challah*) (Num. 15:20)
134. Renouncing as ownerless produce of the Sabbatical Year (Exod. 23:11)
135. Resting the land during the Sabbatical Year (Exod. 34:21; Lev. 25:2, 4)
136. Sanctifying the Jubilee Year (Lev. 25:10)
137. Blowing the shofar on Tishre 10 in the Jubilee Year (Lev. 25:9)
138. Reversion of land in the Jubilee Year (Lev. 25:13)

139.   Redemption of property in a walled city (Lev. 25:29-30)
140.   Counting the years to the Jubilee (Lev. 25:8)
141.   Canceling claims in the Sabbatical Year (Deut. 15:2)
142.   Exacting debts from idolaters (Deut. 15:3)
143.   Kohen's due in the slaughter of every clean animal (Deut. 18:3)
144.   First of the fleece to be given to the Kohen (Deut. 18:4)
145.   Devoted things (Lev. 27:21)
146.   *Shechitah* (Deut. 12:21)
147.   Covering the blood of slain birds and animals (Lev. 17:13)
148.   Not taking the mother bird with its young (Deut. 22:7)
149.   Searching for prescribed tokens in cattle and animals (Lev. 11:2)
150.   Searching for prescribed tokens in birds (Deut. 14:11)
151.   Searching for prescribed tokens in grasshoppers (Lev. 11:21)
152.   Searching for prescribed tokens in fishes (Lev. 11:9)
153.   Determining the New Moon (Exod. 12:2)
154.   Resting on the Sabbath (Exod. 23:12; 34:21)
155.   Proclaiming the sanctity of the Sabbath (Exod. 20:8)
156.   Removal of leaven (Exod. 12:15)
157.   Recounting the departure from Egypt (Exod. 13:8)
158.   Eating unleavened bread on the evening of Nisan 15 (Exod. 12:8)
159.   Resting on first day of Passover (Lev. 23:7)
160.   Resting on seventh day of Passover (Lev. 23:8)
161.   Counting the Omer (Lev. 23:15-16)
162.   Resting on Shavuot (Lev. 23:21)
163.   Resting on Rosh Hashanah (Lev. 23:24)
164.   Fasting on Yom Kippur (Lev. 16:29)
165.   Resting on Yom Kippur (Lev. 16:31)
166.   Resting on first day of Sukkot (Lev. 23:35)
167.   Resting on Shemini Atzeret (Lev. 23:36)
168.   Dwelling in a booth during Sukkot (Lev. 23:42)
169.   Four species (taking the lulav) on Sukkot (Lev. 23:40)
170.   Hearing the shofar on Rosh Hashanah (Num. 29:1)
171.   Giving a half-shekel annually (Exod. 30:13)
172.   Heeding the prophets (Deut. 18:15)
173.   Appointing a king (Deut. 17:15)
174.   Obeying the Great Court (Deut. 17:11)
175.   Abiding by a majority decision (Exod. 23:2)
176.   Appointing judges and officers of the court (Deut. 16:18)
177.   Treating litigants equally before the law (Lev. 19:15)
178.   Testifying in court (Lev. 5:1)
179.   Inquiring into the testimony of witnesses (Deut. 13:15)
180.   Condemning witnesses who testify falsely (Deut. 19:19)
181.   The axed heifer (Deut. 21:4)
182.   Establishing six cities of refuge (Deut. 19:2-3)
183.   Assigning cities to the Levites (Num. 35:7)
184.   Removing sources of danger from our habitations   (Deut. 22:8)
185.   Destroying all idol worship (Exod. 34:13; Deut. 7:5, 12:2)
186.   Law of the apostate city (Deut. 13:17)

187. Law of the Seven Nations (Deut. 20:17)
188. Extinction of Amalek (Deut. 25:19)
189. Remembering the nefarious deeds of Amalek (Deut. 25:17)
190. Law of the non-obligatory war (Deut. 20:10)
191. Appointing a Kohen for war (Deut. 20:2)
192. Preparing a place beyond the camp (Deut. 23:13)
193. Including a paddle among war implements (Deut. 23:14)
194. A robber to restore the stolen article (Lev. 5:23)
195. Charity (Lev. 25:35; Deut. 15:11)
196. Lavishing gifts on a Hebrew bondman on his freedom (Deut. 15:14)
197. Lending money to the poor (Exod. 22:24)
198. Interest (Deut. 23:21)
199. Restoring a pledge to a needy owner (Exod. 22:25; Deut. 24:13)
200. Paying wages on time (Lev. 9:13; Deut. 24:15)
201. Allowing an employee to eat of the produce among which he is
     working (Deut. 23:25-26)
202. Unloading a tired animal (Exod. 23:5)
203. Assisting the owner in lifting up his burden (Deut. 22:4)
204. Returning lost property to its owner (Exod. 23:4; Deut. 22:1)
205. Rebuking a sinner (Lev. 19:17)
206. Love your neighbor (Lev. 19:18)
207. Loving the stranger (Deut. 10:19)
208. The law of weights and balances (Lev. 19:36)
209. Honoring scholars and the aged (Lev. 19:32)
210. Honoring parents (Exod. 20:12)
211. Respecting parents (Lev. 19:3)
212. Be fruitful and multiply (Gen. 1:28)
213. The law of marriage (Deut. 24:1)
214. Bridegroom devoting himself to his wife for one year (Deut. 24:5)
215. Law of circumcision (Gen. 17:10)
216. Law of levirate marriage (Deut. 25:5)
217. *Chalitzah* (Deut. 25:9)
218. Violator must marry the maiden he has violated (Deut. 22:29)
219. Law of the defamer of a bride (Deut. 22:19)
220. Law of the seducer (Exod. 22:15-16)
221. Law of the captive woman (Deut. 21:11)
222. Law of divorce (Deut. 24:1)
223. Law of a suspected adulteress (Num. 5:12-15)
224. Whipping transgressors of certain commandments (Deut. 25:2)
225. Law of manslaughter (Num. 35:24)
226. Transgressors of certain commandments to be beheaded (Exod. 21:20)
227. Transgressors of certain commandments to be strangled (Lev. 20:10)
228. Transgressors of certain commandments to be put to death by
     burning (Lev. 20:14)
229. Transgressor of certain commandments to be stoned (Deut. 22:24)
230. Bodies of certain transgressors to be hanged after execution
     (Deut. 21:22)
231. Law of burial (Deut. 21:23)

232. Law of a Hebrew bondman (Exod. 21:2)
233. Hebrew bondwoman to be married by her master or his son (Exod. 21:8)
234. Redemption of a Hebrew bondwoman (Exod. 21:8)
235. Law of a Canaanite bondman (Lev. 25:46)
236. Penalty for inflicting injury (Exod. 21:18-19)
237. Law of injuries caused by an ox (Exod. 21:28)
238. Law of injuries caused by a pit (Exod. 21:33)
239. Law of theft (Exod. 22:3)
240. Law of damage caused by a beast (Exod. 22:4)
241. Law of damage by a fire (Exod. 22:5)
242. Law of an unpaid bailee (Exod. 22:6)
243. Law of a paid bailee (Exod. 22:9)
244. Law of a borrower (Exod. 22:13)
245. Law of buying and selling (Lev. 25:14)
246. Law of litigants (Exod. 22:8)
247. Saving the life of the pursued (Deut. 25:12)
248. Law of inheritance (Num. 27:8-11)

Negative Commandments

1.   Believing in a deity other than the One God (Exod. 20:3)
2.   Making images for the purpose of worship (Exod. 20:4)
3.   Making an idol for others to worship (Lev. 19:4)
4.   Making figures of human beings (Exod. 20:20)
5.   Bowing down to an idol (Exod. 20:5)
6.   Worshiping idols (Exod. 20:5)
7.   Handing over some of your offspring to Molech (Lev. 18:21)
8.   Practicing the sorcery of the *Ob* (Lev. 19:31)
9.   Practicing the sorcery of the *Yid'oni* (Lev. 19:31)
10. Studying idolatrous practices (Lev. 19:4)
11. Erecting a pillar which people will assemble to honor (Deut. 16:22)
12. Making figured stones upon which to prostrate ourselves (Lev.26:1)
13. Planting trees within the Sanctuary (Deut. 16:21)
14. Swearing by an idol (Exod. 23:13)
15. Summoning people to idolatry (Exod. 23:13; Deut. 13:12)
16. Seeking to persuade an Israelite to worship idols (Deut. 13:12)
17. Loving the person who seeks to mislead him into idolatry (Deut. 13:9)
18. Relaxing one's aversion to the misleader (Deut. 13:9)
19. Saving the life of the misleader (Deut. 13:9)
20. Pleading for the misleader (Deut. 13:9)
21. Suppressing evidence which is unfavorable to the misleader (Deut. 13:9)
22. Benefiting from ornaments which have adorned an idol   (Deut. 7:25)
23. Rebuilding an apostate city (Deut. 13:17)
24. Deriving benefit from the property of an apostate city (Deut. 13:18)
25. Increasing our wealth from anything connected with idolatry
        (Deut. 7:26)
26. Prophesying in the name of an idol (Deut. 18:20)
27. Prophesying falsely (Deut. 18:20)

28. Listening to the prophesy of one who prophesizes in the name of an idol (Deut. 13:4)
29. Having pity on a false prophet (Deut. 18:22)
30. Adopting the habits and customs of unbelievers (Lev. 18:3)
31. Practicing divination (Deut. 18:10)
32. Regulating our conduct by the stars (Deut. 18:10)
33. Practicing the art of the soothsayer (Deut. 18:10)
34. Practicing sorcery (Deut. 18:10)
35. Practicing the art of the charmer (Deut. 18:10)
36. Consulting a necromancer who uses the *Ob* (Deut. 18:10)
37. Consulting a sorcerer who uses the *Yid'oni* (Deut. 18:10)
38. Seeking information from the dead (Deut. 18:10)
39. Women wearing men's clothes or adornments (Deut. 22:5)
40. Men wearing women's clothes or adornments (Deut. 22:5)
41. Imprinting any tattoos upon our bodies (Lev. 19:28)
42. Wearing a garment of wool and linen (*sha'atnez*) (Deut. 22:11)
43. Shaving the temples of our heads (Lev. 19:27)
44. Shaving the beard (Lev. 19:27)
45. Making cuttings in our flesh (Lev. 19:28; Deut. 14:1)
46. Settling in the land of Egypt (Deut. 17:16)
47. Accepting opinions contrary to those taught in the Torah (Num 15:39)
48. Making a covenant with the Seven Nations of Canaan (Deut. 7:2-3)
49. Failing to observe the law concerning the Seven Nations (Deut. 20:16)
50. Showing mercy to idolaters (Deut. 7:2)
51. Suffering idolaters to dwell in our land (Exod. 23:33)
52. Intermarrying with the heretics (Deut. 7:3)
53. Intermarrying with a male Ammonite or Moabite (Deut. 23:4)
54. Excluding descendants of Esau (Deut. 23:8)
55. Excluding descendants of Egyptians (Deut. 23:8)
56. Offering peace to Ammon or Moab (Deut. 23:7)
57. Destroying fruit trees during a siege (Deut. 20:19)
58. Fearing the heretics in time of war (Deut. 7:21)
59. Forgetting what Amalek did to us (Deut. 25:19)
60. Blaspheming the great Name (Lev. 24:16)
61. Violating a *shevuat bittui* (Lev. 19:12)
62. Swearing a *shevuat shav* (Exod. 20:7)
63. Profaning the Name of God (Lev. 22:32)
64. Testing God's promises and warnings (Deut. 6:16)
65. Breaking down houses of worship (Deut. 12:4)
66. Leaving the body of a criminal hanging overnight after execution (Deut. 21:23)
67. Interrupting the watch over the Sanctuary (Num 18:5)
68. *Kohen Gadol* entering the Sanctuary at any but the prescribed time (Lev. 16:2)
69. A Kohen with a blemish entering any part of the Sanctuary (Lev. 21:23)
70. A Kohen with a blemish ministering in the Sanctuary (Lev. 21:17)
71. A Kohen with a temporary blemish ministering in the Sanctuary (Lev. 21:18)

72. Levites and Kohanim performing each other's allotted services (Num 18:3)
73. Entering the Sanctuary or giving a decision on any law of the Torah while intoxicated (Lev. 10:8-11)
74. A *zar* ministering in the Sanctuary (Num 18:4)
75. An unclean Kohen ministering in the Sanctuary (Lev. 22:2)
76. A Kohen who is *tevel yom* ministering in the Sanctuary (Lev. 21:6)
77. Any unclean person entering any part of the Sanctuary (Num. 5:3)
78. Any unclean person entering the camp of the Levites (Deut. 23:11)
79. Building an altar of stones which have been touched by iron (Exod. 20:22)
80. Ascending the Altar by steps (Exod. 20:23)
81. Extinguishing the Altar fire (Lev. 6:6)
82. Offering any sacrifice on the Golden Altar (Exod. 30:9)
83. Making oil like the oil of anointment (Exod. 30:32)
84. Anointing anyone except the *Kohen Gadol* and kings with the oil of anointment (Exod. 30:32)
85. Making incense like that used in the Sanctuary (Exod. 30:37)
86. Removing the staves from their rings in the Ark (Exod. 25:15)
87. Removing the Breastplate from the Ephod (Exod. 28:28)
88. Tearing the edge of the robe of the *Kohen Gadol* (Exod. 28:32)
89. Offering any sacrifice outside the Sanctuary Court (Deut. 12:13-14)
90. Slaughtering any of the holy offerings outside the Sanctuary Court (by inference)
91. Dedicating blemished animals to be offered upon the Altar (Lev. 22:20)
92. Slaughtering blemished animals for sacrifice (Lev. 22:22)
93. Dashing the blood of blemished animals upon the Altar (Lev. 22:24)
94. Burning the sacrificial portions of a blemished animal upon the Altar (Lev. 22:22)
95. Sacrificing an animal with a temporary blemish (Deut. 17:1)
96. Offering blemished sacrifices of a gentile (Lev. 22:25)
97. Causing an offering to become blemished (Lev. 22:21)
98. Offering leaven or honey upon the Altar (Lev. 2:11)
99. Offering a sacrifice without salt (Lev. 2:13)
100. Offering on the Altar the hire of a harlot or the price of a dog (Deut. 23:19)
101. Slaughtering the mother and her young on the same day (Lev. 22:28)
102. Putting olive oil on the meal offering of a sinner (Lev. 5:11)
103. Bringing frankincense with the meal offering of a sinner (Lev. 5:11)
104. Mingling olive oil with the meal offering of a suspected adulteress (Num. 5:15)
105. Putting frankincense on the meal offering of a suspected adulteress (Num. 5:15)

106.   Changing an animal that has been consecrated as an offering (Lev. 27:10)
107.   Changing one holy offering for another (Lev. 27:26)
108.   Redeeming the firstling of a clean animal (Num 18:17)
109.   Selling the tithe of cattle (Lev. 27:33)
110.   Selling devoted property (Lev. 27:28)
111.   Redeeming devoted land without any specific statement of purpose (Lev. 27:28)
112.   Severing the head of the bird of a sin offering during *melikah* (Lev. 5:8)
113.   Doing any work with a dedicated animal (Deut. 15:19)
114.   Shearing a dedicated animal (Deut. 15:19)
115.   Slaughtering the Passover offering while leavened bread remains in our possession (Exod. 23:18)
116.   Leaving the sacrificial portions of the Passover offering overnight (Exod. 23:18)
117.   Allowing any of the meat of the Passover offering to remain until morning (Exod. 12:10)
118.   Allowing any of the meat of the Festival offering of Nisan 14 to remain until the third day (Deut. 16:4)
119.   Allowing any of the meat of the Second Passover offering to remain until morning (Num 9:12)
120.   Allowing any of the meat of a thanksgiving offering to remain until morning (Lev. 22.30)
121.   Breaking any of the bones of the Passover offering (Exod. 12:46)
122.   Breaking any of the bones of the Second Passover offering (Num 9:12)
123.   Removing the Passover offering from where it is eaten (Exod. 2:46)
124.   Baking the residue of a meal offering with leaven (Lev. 6:10)
125.   Eating the Passover offering boiled or raw (Exod. 12:9)
126.   Allowing a *ger toshav* to eat the Passover offering (Exod. 12:45)
127.   An uncircumcised person eating the Passover offering (Exod. 12:48)
128.   Allowing an apostate Israelite to eat the Passover offering (Exod. 12:43)
129.   An unclean person eating hallowed food (Lev. 12:4)
130.   Eating meat of consecrated offerings which have become unclean (Lev. 7:19)
131.   Eating *nothar* (Lev. 19:6-8)
132.   Eating *piggul* (Lev. 7:18)
133.   A *zar* eating *terumah* (Lev. 22:10)
134.   A Kohen's tenant or hired servant eating *terumah* (Lev. 22:10)
135.   An uncircumcised Kohen eating *terumah* (Lev. 22:10)
136.   An unclean Kohen eating *terumah* (Lev. 22:4)
137.   A *chalalah* eating holy food (Lev. 22:12)
138.   Eating the meal offering of a Kohen (Lev. 6:16)
139.   Eating meat of sin-offerings whose blood has been brought within the Sanctuary (Lev. 6:23)
140.   Eating invalidated consecrated offerings (Deut. 14:3)
141.   Eating the unredeemed second tithe of corn outside Jerusalem (Deut. 12:17)

142. Consuming the unredeemed second tithe of wine outside Jerusalem
      (Deut. 12:17)
143. Consuming the unredeemed second tithe of oil outside Jerusalem
      (Deut. 12:17)
144. Eating an unblemished firstling outside Jerusalem
      (Deut. 12:17)
145. Eating the sin offering and the guilt offering outside the Sanctuary
      Court (Deut. 12:17)
146. Eating the meat of a burnt offering (Deut. 12:17)
147. Eating lesser holy offerings before dashing their blood on the Altar
      (Deut. 12:17)
148. A Kohen eating first fruits outside Jerusalem (Deut. 12:17)
149. A *zar* eating first fruits outside Jerusalem (Exod. 29:33)
150. Eating an unredeemed unclean second tithe, even in
      Jerusalem (Deut. 26:14)
151. Eating the second tithe during mourning (Deut. 26:14)
152. Spending the redemption money of the second tithe except on food
      and drink (Deut. 26:14)
153. Eating *tevel* (Lev. 22:15)
154. Altering the prescribed order of harvest tithing (Exod. 22:28)
155. Delaying payment of vows (Deut. 23:22)
156. Appearing on a festival without a sacrifice (Exod. 23:15; Deut. 16:16)
157. Infringing any oral obligation, even if undertaken without an oath
      (Num 30:3)
158. A Kohen marrying a *zonah* (Lev. 21:7)
159. A Kohen marrying a *chalalah* (Lev. 21:7)
160. A Kohen marrying a divorced woman (Lev. 21:7)
161. A *Kohen Gadol* marrying a widow (Lev. 21:14)
162. A *Kohen Gadol* having intercourse with a widow (Lev. 21:15)
163. Kohanim with disheveled hair entering the Sanctuary (Lev. 10:6)
164. Kohanim wearing rent garments entering the Sanctuary (Lev. 10:6)
165. Ministering Kohanim leaving the Sanctuary (Lev. 10:7)
166. A common Kohen defiling himself for any dead person except those
      prescribed in Scripture (Lev. 21:1)
167. A *Kohen Gadol* being under one roof with a dead body (Lev. 21:11)
168. A *Kohel Gadol* defiling himself for any dead person (Lev. 21:11)
169. Levites acquiring a portion in the Land of Israel (Deut. 18:1)
170. Levites sharing in the spoil on the conquest of the Land of Israel
      (Deut. 18:1)
171. Tearing out hair for the dead (Deut. 14:1)
172. Eating any unclean animal (Deut. 14:7)
173. Eating any unclean fish (Lev. 11:11)
174. Eating any unclean fowl (Lev. 11:13)
175. Eating any swarming winged insect (Deut. 14:19)
176. Eating anything which swarms upon the earth (Lev. 11:41)
177. Eating any creeping thing that breeds in decayed matter (Lev. 11:44)
178. Eating living creatures that breed in seeds or fruit (Lev. 11:42)
179. Eating any swarming thing (Lev. 11:43)

180. Eating *nevelah* (Deut. 14:21)
181. Eating *terefah* (Exod. 22:30)
182. Eating a limb of a living creature (Deut. 12:23)
183. Eating *gid ha-nasheh* (sinew of thigh vein) (Gen 32:33)
184. Eating blood (Lev. 3:17; 7:26; 17:14)
185. Eating the fat of a clean animal (Lev. 7:23)
186. Cooking meat in milk (Exod. 23:19, 34:26; Deut. 14:21)
187. Eating meat cooked in milk (Exod. 23:19, 34:26; Deut. 14:21)
188. Eating the flesh of a stoned ox (Exod. 21:28)
189. Eating bread made from the grain of the new crop (Lev. 23:14)
190. Eating roasted grain of the new crop (Lev. 23:14)
191. Eating fresh ears of grain (Lev. 23:14)
192. Eating *orlah* (Lev. 19:23)
193. Eating *kelai ha-kerem* (Deut. 22:9)
194. Drinking *yain nesech* (Exod. 34:15)
195. Eating and drinking to excess (Lev. 19:26; Deut. 21:20)
196. Eating on Yom Kippur (Lev. 23:29)
197. Eating *chametz* during Passover (Exod. 13:3)
198. Eating anything containing *chametz* during Passover (Exod. 12:20)
199. Eating *chametz* after the middle of Nisan 14 (Deut. 16:3)
200. *Chametz* being seen in our habitations during Passover (Exod. 13:7)
201. Possessing *chametz* during Passover (Exod. 12:19)
202. A Nazirite drinking wine (Num 6:3)
203. A Nazirite eating fresh grapes (Num 6:3)
204. A Nazirite eating dried grapes (Num 6:3)
205. A Nazirite eating the kernels of grapes (Num 6:4)
206. A Nazirite eating the husks of grapes (Num 6:4)
207. A Nazirite rendering himself unclean for the dead (Num 6:7)
208. A Nazirite rendering himself unclean by entering a house containing a corpse (Lev. 21:11)
209. A Nazirite shaving (Num 6:5)
210. Reaping all the harvest (Lev. 19:9)
211. Gathering ears of corn that fell during the harvest (Lev. 19:9)
212. Gathering the whole produce of the vineyard at vintage time (Lev. 19:10)
213. Gathering single fallen grapes during the vintage (Lev. 19:10)
214. Returning for a forgotten sheaf (Deut. 24:19)
215. Sowing *kelayim* (Lev. 19:19)
216. Sowing grain or vegetables in a vineyard (Deut. 22:9)
217. Mating animals of different species (Lev. 19:19)
218. Working with two different kinds of animals together (Deut. 22:10)
219. Preventing an animal from eating the produce amid which it is working (Deut. 25:4)
220. Cultivating the soil in the seventh year (Lev. 25:4)
221. Pruning trees in the seventh year (Lev. 25:4)
222. Reaping a self-grown plant in the seventh year as in an ordinary year (Lev. 25:5)

223. Gathering a self-grown fruit in the seventh year as in an ordinary
      year (Lev. 25:5)
224. Cultivating the soil in the Jubilee Year (Lev. 25:11)
225. Reaping the aftergrowth of the Jubilee Year as in an
      ordinary year (Lev. 25:11)
226. Gathering fruit in the Jubilee Year as in an ordinary year (Lev. 25:11)
227. Selling our holdings in Israel in perpetuity (Lev. 25:23)
228. Selling the open lands of the Levites (Lev. 25:34)
229. Forsaking the Levites (Deut. 12:19)
230. Demanding the payment of debts after the Sabbatical Year (Deut. 15:2)
231. Withholding a loan to be cancelled by the Sabbatical Year (Deut. 15:9)
232. Failure to give charity to our needy brethren (Deut. 15:7)
233. Sending away a Hebrew bondman empty-handed (Deut. 15:13)
234. Demanding payment from a debtor known to be unable to pay (Exod.
      22:24)
235. Lending at interest (Lev. 25:37)
236. Borrowing at interest (Deut. 23:20)
237. Participating in a loan at interest (Exod. 22:24)
238. Oppressing an employee by delaying payment of wages (Lev. 19:13)
239. Taking a pledge from a debtor by force (Deut. 24:10)
240. Keeping a needed pledge from its owner (Deut. 24:12)
241. Taking a pledge from a widow (Deut. 24:17)
242. Taking in pledge food utensils (Deut. 24:6)
243. Abducting an Israelite (Exod. 20:13)
244. Stealing money (Lev. 19:11)
245. Committing robbery (Lev. 19:13)
246. Fraudulently altering land boundaries (Deut. 19:14)
247. Usurping our debts (Lev. 19:13)
248. Repudiating our debts (Lev. 19:11)
249. Swearing falsely in repudiating a debt (Lev. 19:11)
250. Wronging one another in business (Lev. 25:14)
251. Wronging one another by speech (Lev. 25:17)
252. Wronging a proselyte by speech (Exod. 22:20)
253. Wronging a proselyte in business (Exod. 20:20)
254. Handing over a fugitive bondman (Deut. 23:16)
255. Wronging a fugitive bondman (Deut. 23:17)
256. Dealing harshly with orphans and widows (Exod. 22:21)
257. Employing a Hebrew bondman in degrading tasks (Lev. 25:39)
258. Selling a Hebrew bondman by public auction (Lev. 25:42)
259. Employing a Hebrew bondman on unnecessary work (Lev. 25:43)
260. Allowing the maltreatment of a Hebrew bondman (Exod. 25:53)
261. Selling a Hebrew bondwoman (Exod. 21:8)
262. Afflicting one's espoused Hebrew bondwoman (Exod. 21:10)
263. Selling a captive woman (Deut. 21:14)
264. Enslaving a captive woman (Deut. 21:14)
265. Coveting another's belongings (Exod. 20:14; Deut. 5:18)
266. Planning to acquire another's property (Exod. 20:14; Deut. 5:18)
267. Hired laborer eating growing crops (Deut. 23:26)

268. Hired laborer putting of the harvest in his own vessel (Deut. 23:25)
269. Ignoring lost property (Deut. 22:3)
270. Leaving a trapped person (Exod. 23:5)
271. Cheating in measurements and weights (Lev. 19:35)
272. Keeping false weights and measures (Deut. 25:13)
273. A judge committing unrighteousness (Lev. 19:15)
274. A judge accepting gifts from litigants (Exod. 23:8)
275. A judge favoring a litigant (Lev. 19:15)
276. A judge being deterred by fear from giving a just judgment (Deut. 1:17)
277. A judge deciding in favor of a poor man through pity (Exod. 23:3; Lev. 19:15)
278. A judge perverting judgment against a person of evil repute (Exod. 23:6)
279. A judge pitying one who has slain a man (Deut. 19:13)
280. A judge perverting justice due to proselytes or orphans (Deut. 24:17)
281. A judge listening to one of the litigants in the absence of another (Exod. 23:1)
282. A Court convicting in a capital case by a majority of one (Exod. 23:2)
283. A judge relying on the opinion of a fellow-judge (Exod. 23:2)
284. Appointing an unlearned judge (Deut. 1:17)
285. Bearing false witness (Exod. 20:13)
286. A judge receiving a wicked man's testimony (Exod. 23:1)
287. A judge receiving testimony from a litigant's relative (Deut. 24:16)
288. Convicting on the testimony of a single witness (Deut. 19:15)
289. Murdering a human being (Exod. 20:13)
290. Capital punishment based on circumstantial evidence (Exod. 23:7)
291. A witness acting as an advocate (Num 35:30)
292. Killing a murderer without trial (Num 35:12)
293. Sparing the life of a pursuer (Deut. 25:12)
294. Punishing a person for a sin committed under duress (Deut. 22:26)
295. Accepting a ransom from one who has committed willful murder (Num 35:31)
296. Accepting a ransom from one who has committed murder unwittingly (Num 35:32)
297. Neglecting to save an Israelite in danger of his life (Lev. 19:16)
298. Leaving obstacles on public or private domain (Deut. 22:8)
299. Giving misleading advice (Lev. 19:14)
300. Inflicting excessive corporal punishment (Deut. 25:2)
301. Bearing tales (Lev. 19:16)
302. Hating one another (Lev. 19:17)
303. Putting one to shame (Lev. 19:17)
304. Taking vengeance on one another (Lev. 19:18)
305. Bearing a grudge (Lev. 19:18)
306. Taking the entire bird's nest (Deut. 22:6)
307. Shaving the scall (Lev. 13:33)
308. Cutting or cauterizing signs of *tzara'at* (Deut. 24:8)
309. Plowing a valley in which the rite of the axed heifer has been performed (Deut. 21:4)
310. Permitting a sorcerer to live (Exod. 22:17)
311. Taking a bridegroom away from his home (Deut. 24:5)
312. Differing from traditional authorities (Deut. 17:11)

313. Adding to the Written or Oral Law (Deut. 13:1)
314. Detracting from the Written or Oral Law (Deut. 13:1)
315. Cursing a judge (Exod. 22:27)
316. Cursing a ruler (Exod. 22:27)
317. Cursing an Israelite (Lev. 19:14)
318. Cursing parents (Exod. 21:17)
319. Striking parents (Exod. 21:15)
320. Working on the Sabbath (Exod. 20:10)
321. Journeying on the Sabbath (Exod. 16:29)
322. Punishing on the Sabbath (Exod. 35:3)
323. Working on the first day of Passover (Lev. 23:7)
324. Working on the seventh day of Passover (Lev. 23:8)
325. Working on Shavuot (Lev. 23:21)
326. Working on Rosh Hashanah (Lev. 23:25)
327. Working on the first day of Sukkot (Lev. 23:35)
328. Working on Shemini Atzeret (Lev. 23:36)
329. Working on Yom Kippur (Lev. 23:31)
330. Having intercourse with one's mother (Lev. 18:7)
331. Having intercourse with one's father's wife (Lev. 18:8)
332. Having intercourse with one's sister (Lev. 18:9)
333. Having intercourse with the daughter of one's father's wife if she be his sister (Lev. 18:11)
334. Having intercourse with one's son's daughter (Lev. 18:10)
335. Having intercourse with one's daughter's daughter (Lev. 18:10)
336. Having intercourse with one's daughter (Lev. 18:10)
337. Having intercourse with a woman and her daughter, (Lev. 18:17)
338. Having intercourse with a woman and her son's daughter (Lev. 18:17)
339. Having intercourse with a woman and her daughter's daughter (Lev. 18:17)
340. Having intercourse with one's father's sister (Lev. 18:12)
341. Having intercourse with one's mother's sister (Lev. 18:13)
342. Having intercourse with the wife of one's father's brother (Lev. 18:14)
343. Having intercourse with one's son's wife (Lev. 18:15)
344. Having intercourse with a brother's wife (Lev. 18:16)
345. Having intercourse with a sister of his wife during the latter's lifetime (Lev. 18:18)
346. Having intercourse with a menstruant (Lev. 18:19)
347. Having intercourse with another man's wife (Exod. 20:13; Lev. 18:20)
348. Men lying with animals (Lev. 18:23)
349. Women lying with animals (Lev. 18:23)
350. A man lying carnally with a man (Lev. 18:22)
351. A man lying carnally with his father (Lev. 18:7)
352. A man lying carnally with his father's brother (Lev. 18:14)
353. Intimacy with a close relative (Lev. 18:6)
354. A *mamzer* marrying a Jew (Deut. 23:3)
355. Having intercourse without marriage (Deut. 23:18)
356. Remarrying one's divorced wife after she had remarried (Deut. 24:4)

357.   Having intercourse with a woman subject to levirate
        marriage (Deut. 25:5)
358.   Divorcing a woman he has raped and been compelled to marry (Deut.
        22:29)
359.   Divorcing a woman after having falsely brought an evil name upon
        her (Deut. 22:19)
360.   A man incapable of procreation marrying a Jewess (Deut. 23:2)
361.   Castration (Lev. 22:24)
362.   Appointing a king not born an Israelite (Deut. 17:15)
363.   A king owning many horses (Deut. 17:16)
364.   A king taking many wives (Deut. 17:17)
365.   A king amassing great personal wealth (Deut. 17:17)

Commandments by Parshiyot

Genesis

Bereishit (1:1 – 11:32)

1:28   Be fruitful and multiply (PC 212)

Lech Lecha (12:1 – 17:27)

17:10   Law of circumcision (PC 215)

Va-yishlach (32:4 – 36:43)

32:33   Eating *gid ha-nasheh* (sinew of the thigh vein)

         (NC 183)

Exodus

Bo (10:1 – 13:16)

12:2   Determining the New Moon (PC 153)
12:6   Slaughtering the Passover offering (PC 55)
12:8   Eating unleavened bread on the evening of Nisan 15 (PC 158)
12:9   Eating the Passover offering boiled or raw (NC 125)
12:15   Removal of leaven (PC 156)
12:18   Eating the Passover offering (PC 56)
12:19   Possessing *chametz* during Passover (NC 201)
12:20   Eating anything containing *chametz* during Passover (NC 198)
12:43   Allowing an apostate Israelite to eat the Passover offering (NC 128)
12:45   Allowing a *ger toshav* to eat the Passover offering (NC 126)
12:46   Breaking any of the bones of the Passover offering (NC 121)
12:46   Removing the Passover offering from where it is eaten (NC 123)
12:48   An uncircumcised person eating the Passover offering (NC127)
13:2   Sanctifying the firstborn (PC 79)
13:3   Eating *chametz* during Passover (NC 197)
13:7   *Chametz* being seen in our habitations during Passover (NC 200)
13:8   Recounting the departure from Egypt (PC 157)
13:13   Redeeming the firstborn donkey (PC 81)
13:13   Breaking the neck of the firstborn donkey (PC 82)

Beshalach (13:17 – 17:16)

16:29   Journeying on the Sabbath (NC 321)

Yitro (18:1 – 20:23)

20:2   Belief in the existence of God (PC 1)
20:3   Believing in a deity other than the One God (NC 1)
20:4   Making images for the purpose of worship (NC 2)
20:5   Bowing down to an idol (NC 5)
20:5   Worshiping idols (NC 6)
20:7   Swearing a *shevuat shav* (NC 62)
20:8   Proclaiming the sanctity of the Sabbath (PC 155)
20:10   Working on the Sabbath (NC 320)
20:12   Honoring parents (PC 210)
20:13   Abducting an Israelite (NC 243)
20:13   Bearing false witness (NC 285)
20:13   Murdering a human being (NC 289)
20:13   Having intercourse with another man's wife (NC 347)
20:14   Coveting another's belongings (NC 265)
20:14   Planning to acquire another's property (NC 266)
20:20   Making figures of human beings (NC 4)
20:20   Wronging a proselyte in business (NC 253)
20:22   Building an altar of stones which have been touched by iron (NC 79)
20:23   Ascending the Altar by steps (NC 80)

Mishpatim (21:1 – 24:18)

21:2   Law of a Hebrew bondman (PC 232)
21:8   Hebrew bondwoman to be married by her master or his son (PC 233)
21:8   Redemption of a Hebrew bondwoman (PC 234)
21:8   Selling a Hebrew bondwoman (NC 261)
21:10   Afflicting one's espoused Hebrew bondwoman (NC 262)
21:15   Striking parents (NC 319)
21:17   Cursing parents (NC 318)
21:18-19   Penalty for inflicting injury (PC 236)
21:20   Transgressors of certain commandments to be beheaded (PC 226)
21:28   Law of injuries caused by an ox (PC 237)
21:28   Eating the flesh of a stoned ox (NC 188)
21:33   Law of injuries caused by a pit (PC 238)
22:3   Law of theft (PC 239)
22:4   Law of damage caused by a beast (PC 240)
22:5   Law of damage by a fire (PC 241)
22:6   Law of an unpaid bailee (PC 242)
22:8   Law of litigants (PC 246)
22:9   Law of a paid bailee (PC 243)
22:13   Law of a borrower (PC 244)
22:15-16   Law of the seducer (PC 220)
22:17   Permitting a sorcerer to live (NC 310)
22:20   Wronging a proselyte by speech (NC 252)
22:21   Dealing harshly with orphans and widows (NC 256)
22:24   Lending money to the poor (PC 197)
22:24   Demanding payment from a debtor known to be unable to pay (NC 234)
22:24   Participating in a loan at interest (NC 237)

22:25	Restoring a pledge to a needy owner (PC 199)

22:25   Restoring a pledge to a needy owner (PC 199)
22:27   Cursing a judge (NC 315)
22:27   Cursing a ruler (NC 316)
22:28   Altering the prescribed order of harvest tithing (NC 154)
22:29   Offering cattle of a minimum age (PC 60)
22:30   Eating *terefah* (NC 181)
23:1   A judge listening to one of the litigants in the absence of another (NC 281)
23:1   A judge receiving a wicked man's testimony (NC 286)
23:2   Abiding by a majority decision (PC 175)
23:2   A Court convicting in a capital case by a majority of one (NC 282)
23:2   A judge relying on the opinion of a fellow-judge (NC 283)
23:3   A judge deciding in favor of a poor man through pity (NC 277)
23:4   Returning lost property to its owner (PC 204)
23:5   Unloading a tired animal (PC 202)
23:5   Leaving a trapped person (NC 270)
23:6   A judge perverting judgment against a person of evil repute (NC 278)
23:7   Capital punishment based on circumstantial evidence (NC 290)
23:8   A judge accepting gifts from litigants (NC 274)
23:10   Allowing any of the meat of the Passover offering to remain until morning (NC 117)
23:11   Renouncing as ownerless produce of the Sabbatical Year (PC 134)
23:12   Resting on the Sabbath (PC 154)
23:13   Swearing by an idol (NC 14)
23:13   Summoning people to idolatry (NC 15)
23:14   Three annual Pilgrimage Festivals (PC 52)
23:15   Appearing on a festival without a sacrifice (NC 156)
23:18   Slaughtering the Passover offering while leavened bread remains in our possession (NC 115)
23:18   Leaving the sacrificial portion of the Passover offering overnight (NC 116)
23:19   First fruits to be brought to the Sanctuary (PC 125)
23:19   Cooking meat in milk (NC 186)
23:19   Eating meat cooked in milk (NC 187)
23:25   Serving (worshiping) God (PC 5)
23:33   Suffering idolaters to dwell in our land (NC 51)

Terumah (25:1 – 27:29)

25:8   Building a Sanctuary (*Mishkan*) (PC 20)
25:15   Removing the staves from their rings in the Ark (NC 86)
25:30   The Show-bread (PC 27)
25:53   Allowing the maltreatment of a Hebrew bondman (NC 260)

Tetzaveh (27:20 – 30:10)

27:21   Kindling the Menorah in the Sanctuary (PC 25)
28:2   Priestly garments (PC 33)
28:28   Removing the Breastplate from the Ephod (NC 87)
28:32   Tearing the edge of the robe of the *Kohen Gadol* (NC 88)

29:33	Kohanim eating the meat of consecrated offerings (PC 89)
29:33	A *zar* eating first fruits outside Jerusalem (NC 149)
29:38-39	Daily burnt offering (PC 39)
30:7	Burning the incense (PC 28)
30:9	Offering any sacrifice on the Golden Altar (NC 82)

Ki Tissa (30:11 – 34:35)

30:13	Giving a half-shekel annually (PC 171)
30:19	Ablutions of the Kohanim (PC 24)
30:31	Oil of anointment (PC 35)
30:32	Making oil like the oil of anointment (NC 83)
30:32	Anointing anyone except the *Kohen Gadol* and kings with the oil of anointment (NC 84)
30:37	Making incense like that used in the Sanctuary (NC 85)
34:13	Destroying idolatry (PC 185)
34:15	Drinking *yain nefesh* (NC 194)
34:20	Redeeming the firstborn donkey (PC 81)
34:21	Resting the land during the Sabbatical Year (PC 135)
34:22	Resting on the Sabbath (PC 154)
34:23	Appearing before the Lord during the festivals (PC 53)
34:26	Cooking meat in milk (NC 186)
34:26	Eating meat cooked in milk (NC 187)

Va-yachel (35:1 – 38:20)

| 35:3 | Punishing on the Sabbath (NC 322) |

Leviticus

Vayikra (1:1 – 5:26)

1:1-17	Burnt offering (PC 63)
2:1-16	Meal offering (PC 67)
2:11	Offering leaven or honey upon the Altar (NC 98)
2-13	Bringing salt with every offering (PC 62)
2:13	Offering a sacrifice without salt (NC 99)
3:1-17	Peace offering (PC 66)
3:17	Eating blood (NC 184)
4:1-5:13	Sin offering (PC 64)
4:13	Offering of a Court that has erred (PC 68)
4:27-35	Fixed sin offering (PC 69)
5:1	Testifying in court (PC 178)
5:1-4	Offering a higher or lower value (PC 72)
5:8	Severing the head of the bird of a sin offering during *melikah*(NC 112)
5:11	Putting olive oil on the meal offering of a sinner (NC 102)
5:11	Bringing frankincense with the meal offering of a sinner (NC 103)
5:14-26	Guilt offering (PC 65)
5:15-16	Unconditional guilt offering (PC 71)
5:16	Restitution for sacrilege (PC 118)
5:17-19	Suspensive guilt offering (PC 70)

| 5:21-27 | Unconditional guilt offering (PC 71) |
| 5:23 | A robber to restore the stolen article (PC 194) |

Tzav (6:1 – 8:36)

6:3	Removing the ashes from the Altar (PC 30)
6:6	Keeping a fire continually on the Altar (PC 29)
6:6	Extinguishing the Altar fire (NC 81)
6:10	Baking the residue of a meal offering with leaven (NC 124)
6:13	Daily meal offering of the *Kohen Gadol* (PC 40)
6:16	Eating the meal offering of a Kohen (NC 138)
6:23	Eating meat of sin offerings whose blood has been brought within the Sanctuary (NC 139)
7:17	Remnant of consecrated offerings to be burnt (PC 91)
7:18	Eating *piggul* (NC 132)
7:19	Consecrated offerings that have become unclean to be burnt (PC 90)
7:19	Eating meat of consecrated offerings which have become unclean (NC 130)
7:23	Eating the fat of a clean animal (NC 185)
7:26	Eating blood (NC 184)
8:9	Kohanim eating the residue of the meal offerings (PC 88)

Shemini (9:1 – 11:47)

10:6	Kohanim with disheveled hair entering the Sanctuary (NC163)
10:6	Kohanim wearing rent garments entering the Sanctuary (NC 164)
10:7	Ministering Kohanim leaving the Sanctuary (NC 165)
10:8-11	Entering the Sanctuary or giving a decision on any law of the Torah while intoxicated (NC 73)
11:2	Searching for the prescribed tokens in cattle and animals (PC 149)
11:9	Searching for prescribed tokens in fishes (PC 152)
11:11	Eating any unclean fish (NC 173)
11:13	Eating any unclean fowl (NC 174)
11:21	Searching for prescribed tokens in grasshoppers (PC 151)
11:24	Defilement through carcasses of animals (PC 96)
11:29-30	Defilement through carcasses of certain creeping creatures (PC 97)
11:34	Defilement of food and drink (PC 98)
11:41	Eating anything which swarms upon the earth (NC 176)
11:42	Eating living creatures that breed in seeds or fruit (NC 178)
11:43	Eating any swarming thing (NC 179)
11:44	Eating any creeping thing that breeds in decayed matter (NC 177)

Tazria (12:1 – 13:59)

12:2-8	Offerings after childbirth (PC 100)
12:4	An unclean person eating hallowed food (NC 129)
12:6	Offering after childbirth (PC 76)

13:3	*Tzara'at* (PC 101)
13:33	Shaving the scall (NC 307)
13:45	Person with *tzara'at* to be made distinguishable (PC 112)
13:47-59	Garments contaminated by *tzara'at* (PC 102)

Metzora (14:1 – 15:33)

14:1-7	Cleansing from *tzara'at* (PC 110)
14:9	Person with *tzara'at* to shave his head (PC 111)
14:10	Offering brought by one with *tzara'at* (PC 77)
14:33-53	*Tzara'at* of a house (PC 103)
15:2	*Zav* (PC 104)
15:13-15	Offering brought by a *zav* (PC 74)
15:16	Semen (PC 105)
15:16	Immersing in a ritual bath (PC 109)
15:19-24	The menstruant (PC 99)
15:25-28	*Zavah* (PC 106)
15:29-30	Offering brought by a *zavah* (PC 75)

Acharei Mot (16:1 – 18:30)

16:1-34	Service of the Day of Atonement (PC 49)
16:2	*Kohen Gadol* entering the Sanctuary at any but the prescribed time (NC 68)
16:19	Fasting on Yom Kippur (PC 164)
17:13	Covering the bird of slain birds and animals (PC 147)
17:14	Eating blood (NC 184)
18:3	Adopting the habits and customs of unbelievers (NC 30)
18:6	Intimacy with a close relative (NC 353)
18:7	Having intercourse with one's mother (NC330)
18:7	A man lying carnally with his father (NC 351)
18:8	Having intercourse with one's father's wife (NC 331)
18:9	Having intercourse with one's sister (NC 332)
18:10	Having intercourse with one's son's daughter (NC 334)
18:10	Having intercourse with one's daughter's daughter (NC 335)
18:10	Having intercourse with one's daughter (NC 336)
18:11	Having intercourse with the daughter of one's father's wife if she be his sister (NC 333)
18:12	Having intercourse with one's father's sister (NC 340)
18:13	Having intercourse with one's mother's sister (NC 341)
18:14	Having intercourse with the wife of one's father's brother (NC 342)
18:14	A man lying carnally with his father's brother (NC 352)
18:15	Having intercourse with one's son's wife (NC 343)
18:16	Having intercourse with a brother's wife (NC 344)
18:17	Having intercourse with a woman and her daughter (NC 337)
18:17	Having intercourse with a woman and her son's daughter (NC 338)
18:17	Having intercourse with a woman and her daughter's daughter (NC 339)

18:18	Having intercourse with a sister of his wife during the latter's lifetime (NC 345)
18:19	Having intercourse with a menstruant (NC 346)
18:20	Having intercourse with another man's wife (NC 347)
18:21	Handing over some of your offspring to Molech (NC 7)
18:22	A man lying carnally with a man (NC 350)
18:23	Men lying with animals (NC 348)
18:23	Women lying with animals (NC 349)

Kedoshim (19:1 – 20:27)

19:3	Respecting parents (PC 211)
19:4	Making an idol for others to worship (NC 3)
19:4	Studying idolatrous practices (NC 10)
19:6-8	Eating *nothar* (NC 131)
19:9	*Pe'ah* for the poor (PC 120)
19:9	Gleanings for the poor (PC 121)
19:9	Reaping all the harvest (NC 210)
19:9	Gathering ears of corn that fell during the harvest (NC 211)
19:10	Defective grape clusters of the poor (PC 123)
19:10	Grape gleanings for the poor (PC 124)
19:10	Gathering the whole produce of the vineyard at vintage time (NC 212)
19:10	Gathering single fallen gapes during the vintage (NC 213)
19:11	Stealing money (NC 244)
19:11	Repudiating our debts (NC 248)
19:11	Swearing falsely in repudiating a debt (NC 249)
19:12	Violating a *shevuat bittui* (NC 61)
19:13	Paying wages on time (PC 200)
19:13	Oppressing an employee by delaying payment of wages (NC 238)
19:13	Committing robbery (NC 245)
19:13	Usurping our debts (NC 247)
19:14	Giving misleading advice (NC 299)
19:14	Cursing an Israelite (NC 317)
19:15	Treating litigants equally before the law (PC 177)
19:15	A judge committing unrighteousness (NC 273)
19:15	A judge favoring a litigant (NC 275)
19:15	A judge deciding in favor of a poor man through pity (NC 277)
19:16	Neglecting to save an Israelite in danger of his life (NC 297)
19:16	Bearing tales (NC 301)
19:17	Rebuking a sinner (PC 205)
19:17	Hating one another (NC 302)
19:17	Putting one to shame (NC 303)
19:18	Loving your neighbor (PC 206)
19:18	Taking vengeance on one another (NC 304)
19:18	Bearing a grudge (NC 305)
19:19	Sowing *kelayim* (NC 215)
19:19	Mating animals of different species (NC 217)
19:20-21	Unconditional guilt offering (PC 71)
19:23	Eating *orlah* (NC 192)

19:24	Fruits of fourth-year plantings (PC 119)
19:26	Eating and drinking to excess (NC 195)
19:27	Shaving the temples of our heads (NC 43)
19:27	Shaving the beard (NC 44)
19:28	Imprinting any tattoos upon our bodies (NC 41)
19:28	Making cuttings in our flesh (NC 45)
19:30	Revering the Sanctuary (PC 21)
19:32	Honoring scholars and the aged (PC 209)
19:31	Practicing the sorcery of the *Ob* (NC 8)
19:31	Practicing the sorcery of the *Yid'oni* (NC 9)
19:35	Cheating in measurements and weights (NC 271)
19:36	The law of weights and balances (PC 208)
20:1	Making figured stones upon which to prostrate ourselves (NC 12)
20:10	Transgressors of certain commandments to be strangled (PC 227)
20:14	Transgressors of certain commandments to be put to death by burning (PC 228)

Emor (21:1 – 24:23)

21:1	A common Kohen defiling himself for any dead person except those prescribed in Scripture (NC 166)
21:2-3	Kohanim defiling themselves for close relatives (PC 37)
21:6	A Kohen who is *tevel yom* ministering in the Sanctuary (NC 76)
21:7	A Kohen marrying a *zonah* (NC 158)
21:7	A Kohen marrying a *chalalah* (NC 159)
21:7	A Kohen marrying a divorced woman (NC 160)
21:8	Honoring the kohanim (PC 32)
21:10	Oil of anointment (PC 35)
21:11	A *Kohen Gadol* being under one roof with a dead body (NC 167)
21:11	A *Kohen Gadol* defiling himself for any dead person (NC 168)
21:11	A Nazirite rendering himself unclean by entering a house containing a corpse (NC 208)
21:13-14	*Kohen Gadol* marrying only a virgin (PC 38)
21:14	A *Kohen Gadol* marrying a widow (NC 161)
21:15	A *Kohen Gadol* having intercourse with a widow (NC 162)
21:17	A Kohen with a blemish ministering in the Sanctuary (NC 70)
21:18	A Kohen with a temporary blemish ministering in the Sanctuary (NC 71)
21:23	A Kohen with a blemish entering any part of the Sanctuary (NC 69)
22:2	An unclean Kohen ministering in the Sanctuary (NC 75)
22:4	An unclean Kohen eating *terumah* (NC 136)
22:10	A zar eating *terumah* (NC 133)
22:10	A Kohen's tenant or hired servant eating *terumah* (NC 134)
22:10	An uncircumcised Kohen eating *terumah* (NC 135)
22:12	A *chalalah* eating holy food (NC 137)
22:14	Restitution for sacrilege (PC 118)
22:15	Eating *tevel* (NC 153)

22:20   Dedicating blemished animals to be offered upon the Altar (NC 91)
22:21   Offering only unblemished sacrifices (PC 61)
22:21   Causing an offering to become blemished (NC 97)
22:22   Slaughtering blemished animals for sacrifice (NC 92)
22:22   Burning the sacrificial portions of a blemished animal upon the
            Altar (NC 94)
22:23   Dashing the blood of blemished animals upon the Altar (NC 93)
22:24   Castration (NC 361)
22:25   Offering blemished sacrifices of a gentile (NC 96)
22:27   Offering cattle of a minimum age (PC 60)
22:28   Slaughtering the mother and her young on the same day (NC
            101)
22:30   Allowing any of the meat of a thanksgiving offering to remain
            until morning (NC 120)
22:32   Sanctifying God's name (*Kiddush ha-Shem*) (PC 9)
22:32   Profaning the Name of God (NC 63)
23:7   Resting on the first day of Passover (PC 159)
23:7   Working on the first day of Passover (NC 323)
23:8   Resting on the seventh day of Passover (PC 160)
23:8   Working on the seventh day of Passover (NC 324)
23:10   Meal offering of new barley (PC 41)
23:14   Eating bread made from the grain of the new crop (NC 189)
23:14   Eating roasted grain of the new crop (NC 190)
23:14   Eating fresh ears of grain (NC 191)
23:15-16   Counting the Omer (PC 161)
23:17   Bringing of the two loaves on Shavuot (PC 46)
23:21   Working on Shavuot (NC 325)
23:21   Resting on Shavuot (PC 162)
23:24   Resting on Rosh Hashanah (PC 163)
23:25   Working on Rosh Hashanah (NC 326)
23:29   Eating on Yom Kippur (NC 196)
23:31   Resting on Yom Kippur (PC 165)
23:31   Working on Yom Kippur (NC 329)
23:35   Resting on Sukkot (PC 166)
23:35   Working on the first day of Sukkot (NC 327)
23:36   Resting on Shemini Atzeret (PC 167)
23:36   Working on Shemini Atzeret (NC 328)
23:40   Four species (taking the *lulav*) on Sukkot (PC 168)
23:42   Dwelling in a booth during Sukkot (PC 166)
24:16   Blaspheming the great Name (NC 60)

Behar (25:1 – 26:2)

25:2   Resting the land during the Sabbatical Year (PC 135)
25:4   Resting the land during the Sabbatical Year (PC 135)
25:4   Cultivating the soil in the seventh year (NC 220)
25:4   Pruning trees in the seventh year (NC 221)
25:5   Reaping a self-grown plant in the seventh year as in an ordinary
            year (NC 222)

25:5	Gathering a self-grown fruit in the seventh ear as in an ordinary year (NC 223)
25:8	Counting the years to the Jubilee (PC 140)
25:9	Blowing the shofar on Tishre 10 in the Jubilee Year (PC 137)
25:10	Sanctifying the Jubilee Year (PC 136)
25:11	Cultivating the soil in the Jubilee Year (NC 224)
25:11	Reaping the aftergrowth of the Jubilee Year as in an ordinary year (NC 225)
25:11	Gathering fruit in the Jubilee Year as in an ordinary year (NC 226)
25:13	Reversion of land in the Jubilee Year (PC 138)
25:14	Law of buying and selling (PC 245)
25:14	Wronging one another in business (NC 250)
25:17	Wronging one another by speech (NC 251)
25:23	Selling our holdings in Israel in perpetuity (NC 227)
25:29-30	Redemption of property in a walled city (PC 139)
25:34	Selling the open lands of the Levites (NC 228)
25:3	Charity (PC 195)
25:37	Lending at interest (NC 235)
25:39	Employing a Hebrew bondman in degrading tasks (NC 257)
25:42	Selling a Hebrew bondman by public auction (NC 58)
25:43	Employing a Hebrew bondman on unnecessary work (NC 259)
25:46	Law of a Canaanite bondman (PC 235)

Bechukotai (26:3 – 27:34)

27:2-8	Valuation of a person (PC 114)
27:9-13	Valuation of animals (PC 115)
27:10	Holiness of a substituted offering (PC 87)
27:14-15	Valuation of houses (PC 116)
27:16-25	Valuation of fields (PC 117)
27:21	Devoted things (PC 145)
27:26	Changing one holy offering for another (NC 107)
27:28	Selling devoted property (NC 110)
27:28	Redeeming devoted land without any specific statement of purpose (NC 111)
27:32	Tithe of cattle (PC 78)
27:33	Selling the tithe of cattle (NC 109)

Numbers

Naso (4:21 – 7:89)

5:2-3	Removing the ritually unclean (PC 31)
5:3	An unclean person entering any part of the Sanctuary (NC 77)
5:6-7	Making confession (PC 73)
5:12-15	Law of a suspected adulteress (PC 223)
5:15	Mingling olive oil with meal offering of a suspected adulteress (NC 104)
5:15	Putting frankincense on meal offering of a suspected adulteress (NC 105)

5:18   Coveting another's belongings (NC 265)
5:18   Planning to acquire another's property (NC 266)
6:3   A Nazirite drinking wine (NC 202)
6:3   A Nazirite eating fresh grapes (NC 203)
6:3   A Nazirite eating dried grapes (NC 204)
6:4   A Nazirite eating the kernels of grapes (NC 205)
6:4   A Nazirite eating the husks of grapes (NC 206)
6:5   Nazirite to let his hair grow (PC 92)
6:5   A Nazirite shaving (NC 209)
6:7   A Nazirite rendering himself unclean for the dead (NC 207)
6:13-21   Nazirite obligations on completion of vow (PC 93)
6:23-26   Priestly blessing (PC 26)
7:9   Kohanim bearing the Ark (PC 34)

Beha'alotcha (8:1 – 12:16)

9:10-12   Slaughtering the second Passover offering (PC 57)
9:10-12   Eating the second Passover offering (PC 58)
9:12   Allowing any of the meat of the second Passover offering to
            remain until morning (NC 119)
9:12   Breaking any of the bones of the second Passover offering (NC
            122)
10:10   Blowing the trumpets in the Sanctuary (PC 59)

Shelach Lecha (13:1 – 15:41)

15:20   Dough offering (*challah*) (PC 133)
15:38   Fringes/tzitzit (PC 14)
15:39   Accepting opinions contrary to those taught in the Torah (NC 47)

Korach (16:1 – 18:32)

18:3   Levites and Kohanim performing each other's allotted services
            (NC 72)
18:4   Guarding the Sanctuary (PC 22)
18:4   A *zar* ministering in the Sanctuary (NC 74)
18:5   Interrupting the watch over the Sanctuary (NC 67)
18:15   Redeeming the firstborn (PC 80)
18:17   Redeeming the firstling of a clean animal (NC 108)
18:21   First tithe (PC 127)
18:23   Levitical services in the Sanctuary (PC 23)
18:26   Levites' tithe for the Kohanim (PC 129)

Chukat (19:1 – 22:1)

19:1-22   Ashes of the red heifer (PC 113)
19:1-22   Law of water of sprinkling (PC 108)
19:14   Uncleanness of a corpse (PC 107)

Pinchas (25:10 – 30:1)

27:8-11   Law of inheritance (PC 248)
28:3   Daily burnt offering (PC 39)
28:9-10   Daily meal offering of the *Kohen Gadol* (PC 41)

28:11-15   Additional offering for New Moon (PC 42)
28:16-25   Additional offering for Passover (PC 43)
28: 26-31   Additional offering for Shavuot (PC 45)
29:1   Hearing the shofar on Rosh Hashanah (PC 170)
29:1-6   Additional offering for the New Year (PC 47)
29:7-11   Additional offering for the Day of Atonement (PC 48)
29:12-34   Additional offering for Sukkot (PC 50)
29:35-38   Additional offering for Shemini Atzeret (PC 51)

Mattot (30:2 – 32:42)

30:3   Revocation of vows (PC 95)
30:3   Infringing any oral obligation, even if undertaken without an
            oath (NC 157)

Masei (33:1 – 36:13)

35:7   Assigning cities to the Levites (PC 183)
35:12   Killing a murderer without trial (NC 292)
35:24   Law of manslaughter (PC 225)
35:30   A witness acting as an advocate (NC 291)
35:31   Accepting a ransom from one who has committed willful murder
            (NC 295)
35:32   Accepting a ransom from one who has committed murder un-
            wittingly (NC 296)

Deuteronomy

Devarim (1:1 – 3:22)

1:17   A judge being deterred by fear from giving a just judgment
            (NC 276)
1:17   Appointing an unlearned judge (NC 284)

Va-etchanan (3:23 – 7:11)

5:18   Coveting another's belongings (NC 266)
6:4   Unity of God (PC 2)
6:5   Love of God (PC 3)
6:7   Reading the *Shema* (PC 10)
6:7   Teaching and studying Torah (PC 11)
6:8   Wearing tefillin (PC 12, 13)
6:9   Affixing a mezuzah (PC 15)
6:13   Fear of God (PC 4)
6:13   Serving (worshiping) God (PC 5)
6:13   Swearing in God's name (PC 7)
6:16   Testing God's promises and warnings (NC 64)
7:2-3   Making a covenant with the Seven Nations of Canaan (NC48)
7:2   Showing mercy to idolaters (NC 50)
7:3   Intermarrying with the heretics (NC 52)
7:5   Destroying all idol worship (PC 185)

Ekev (7:12 – 11:25)

7:21	Fearing the heretics in time of war (NC 58)
7:25	Benefiting from ornaments which have adorned an idol (NC 22)
7:26	Increasing our wealth from anything connecting with idolatry (NC 25)
8:10	Grace after meals (*Birkat ha-Mazon*) (PC 19)
10:12	Walking in God's ways (PC 8)
10:19	Loving the stranger (PC 207)
10:20	Fear of God (PC 4)
10:20	Cleaving to God (PC 6)
10:20	Swearing in God's name (PC 7)
11:13	Serving (worshiping) God (PC 5)
11:20	Affixing a mezuzah (PC 15)

Re-eh (11:26 – 16:17)

12:2	Destroying all idol worship (PC 185)
12:4	Breaking down houses of worship (NC 65)
12:5-6	Bringing due offerings on the first festival (PC 83)
12:9	Forsaking the Levites (NC 229)
12:13-14	Offering any sacrifice outside the Sanctuary Court (NC 89)
12:14	All offerings to be brought to the Sanctuary (PC 84)
12:15	Redeeming blemished offerings (PC 86)
12:17	Eating the unredeemed second tithe of corn outside Jerusalem (NC 141)
12:17	Consuming the unredeemed second tithe of wine outside Jerusalem (NC 142)
12:17	Consuming the unredeemed second tithe of oil outside Jerusalem (NC 143)
12:17	Eating an unblemished firstling outside Jerusalem (NC 144)
12:17	Eating the sin offering and the guilt offering outside the Sanctuary Court (NC 145)
12:17	Eating the meat of a burnt offering (NC 146)
12:17	Eating lesser holy offerings before dashing their blood on the Altar (NC 147)
12:17	A Kohen eating first fruits outside Jerusalem (NC 148)
12:21	*Shechitah* (PC 146)
12:23	Eating a limb of a living creature (NC 182)
12:26	All offerings due from outside the Land of Israel to be brought to the Sanctuary (PC 85)
13:1	Adding to the Written or Oral Law (NC 313)
13:1	Detracting from the Written or Oral Law (NC 314)
13:4	Listening to the prophesy of one who prophesies in the name of an idol (NC 28)
13:7	Law of the apostate city (PC 186)
13:9	Loving the person who seeks to mislead him into idolatry (NC 17)
13:9	Relaxing one's aversion to the misleader (NC 18)
13:9	Saving the life of the misleader (NC 19)
13:9	Pleading for the misleader (NC 20)

13:9	Suppressing evidence which is unfavorable to the misleader (NC 21)
13:12	Summoning people to idolatry (NC 15)
13:12	Seeking to persuade an Israelite to worship idols (NC 16)
13:15	Serving (worshiping) God (PC 5)
13:15	Inquiring into the testimony of witnesses (PC 179)
13:17	Rebuilding an apostate city (NC 23)
13:18	Deriving benefit from the property of an apostate city (NC 24)
14:1	Tearing out hair for the dead (NC 171)
14:3	Eating invalidated consecrated offerings (NC 140)
14:7	Eating any unclean animal (NC 172)
14:11	Searching for prescribed tokens in birds (PC 150)
14:11	Making cuttings in our flesh (NC 45)
14:19	Eating any swarming winged insect (NC 175)
14:21	Eating *nevelah* (NC 180)
14:21	Cooking meat in milk (NC 186)
14:21	Eating meat cooked in milk (NC 187)
14:22	Second tithe (PC 128)
14:28	Poor man's tithe (PC 130)
15:2	Canceling claims in the Sabbatical Year (PC 141)
15:2	Demanding the payment of debts after the Sabbatical Year (NC 230)
15:3	Exacting debts from idolaters (PC 142)
15:7	Failure to give charity to our needy brethren (NC 232)
15:9	Withholding a loan to be canceled by the Sabbatical Year (NC 231)
15:11	Charity (PC 195)
15:13	Sending away a Hebrew bondman empty-handed (NC 233)
15:14	Lavishing gifts on a Hebrew bondman on his freedom (PC 196)
15:19	Doing any work with the dedicated animal (NC 113)
15:19	Shearing a dedicated animal (NC 114)
16:3	Eating *chametz* after the middle of Nisan 14 (NC 199)
16:4	Allowing any of the meat of the Festival offering of Nisan 14 to remain until the third day (NC 118)
16:14	Rejoicing on the festivals (PC 54)
16:16	Appearing before the Lord during festivals (PC 53)
16:16	Appearing on a festival without a sacrifice (NC 156)

Shoftim (16:18 – 21:9)

16:18	Appointing judges and officers of the court (PC 176)
16:21	Planting trees within the Sanctuary (NC 13)
16:22	Erecting a pillar which people will assemble to honor (NC 11)
17:1	Sacrificing an animal with a temporary blemish (NC 95)
17:11	Obeying the Great Court (PC 174)
17:11	Differing from traditional authorities (NC 312)
17:15	Appointing a king (PC 173)
17:15	Appointing a king not born an Israelite (NC 362)
17:16	Settling in the land of Egypt (NC 46)
17:16	A king owning many horses (NC 363)
17:17	A king taking many wives (NC 364)

17:17	A king amassing great personal wealth (NC 365)
17:18	A king to write a scroll of Law (PC 17)
18:1	Levites acquiring a portion in the Land of Israel (NC 169)
18:1	Levites sharing in the spoils on the conquest of the Land of Israel (NC 170)
18:3	Kohen's due in the slaughter of every clean animal (PC 143)
18:4	Great heave offering (PC 126)
18:4	First of the fleece to be given to the Kohen (PC 144)
18:6-8	Kohanim ministering in courses (PC 36)
18:10	Practicing divination (NC 31)
18:10	Regulating our conduct by the stars (NC 32)
18:10	Practicing the art of the soothsayer (NC 33)
18:10	Practicing sorcery (NC 34)
18:10	Practicing the art of the charmer (NC 35)
18:10	Consulting a necromancer who uses the *Ob* (NC 36)
18:10	Consulting a sorcerer who uses the *Yid'oni* (NC 37)
18:10	Seeking information from the dead (NC 38)
18:15	Heeding the prophets (PC 172)
18:20	Prophesying in the name of an idol (NC 26)
18:20	Prophesying falsely (NC 27)
18:22	Having pity on a false prophet (NC 29)
19:2-3	Establishing six cities of refuge (PC 182)
19:13	A judge pitying one who has slain a man (NC 279)
19:14	Fraudulently altering land boundaries (NC 246)
19:15	Convicting on the testimony of a single witness (NC 288)
19:19	Condemning witnesses who testify falsely (PC 180)
20:2	Appointing a Kohen for war (PC 191)
20:10	Law of the non-obligatory war (PC 190)
20:16	Failing to observe the law concerning the Seven Nations (NC 49)
20:17	Law of the Seven Nations (PC 187)
20:19	Destroying fruit trees during a siege (NC 57)
21:4	The axed heifer (PC 181)
21:4	Plowing a valley in which the rite of the axed heifer has been performed (NC 309)

Ki Teitzei (21:10 – 25:19)

21:11	Law of the captive woman (PC 220)
21:14	Selling a captive woman (NC 263)
21:14	Enslaving a captive woman (NC 264)
21:20	Eating and drinking to excess (NC 195)
21:22	Bodies of certain transgressors to be hanged after execution (PC 230)
21:23	Law of burial (PC 231)
21:23	Leaving the body of a criminal overnight after execution (NC 66)
22:1	Returning lost property to its owner (PC 204)
22:3	Ignoring lost property (NC 269)
22:4	Assisting the owner in lifting up his burden (PC 203)
22:5	Women wearing men's clothes or adornments (NC 39)
22:5	Men wearing women's clothes or adornments (NC 40)

22:6	Taking the entire bird's next (NC 306)
22:7	Not taking the mother bird with its young (PC 148)
22:8	Removing sources of danger from our habitations (PC 184)
22:8	Leaving obstacles on public or private domain (NC 298)
22:9	Eating *kelai ha-kerem* (NC 193)
22:9	Sowing grain or vegetables in a vineyard (NC 216)
22:10	Working with two different kinds of animals together (NC 218)
22:11	Wearing a garment of wool and linen (*sha'atnez*) (NC 42)
22:19	Law of the defamer of a bride (PC 219)
22:19	Divorcing a woman after having falsely brought an evil name upon her (NC 359)
22:24	Transgressors of certain commandments to be stoned (PC 229)
22:26	Punishing a person for a sin committed under duress (NC 294)
22:29	Violator must marry the maiden he has violated (PC 218)
22:29	Divorcing a woman he has raped and been compelled to marry (NC 358)
23:2	A man incapable of procreation marrying a Jewess (NC 360)
23:3	A *mamzer* marrying a Jew (NC 354)
23:4	Intermarrying with a male Ammonite or Moabite (NC 53)
23:7	Offering peace to Ammon or Moab (NC 56)
23:8	Excluding descendants of Esau (NC 54)
23:8	Excluding descendants of Egyptians (NC 55)
23:11	Interest (198)
23:11	Any unclean person entering the camp of the Levites (NC 78)
23:13	Preparing a place beyond the camp (PC 192)
23:14	Including a paddle among war implements (PC 193)
23:16	Handing over a fugitive bondman (NC 254)
23:17	Wronging a fugitive bondman (NC 255)
23:18	Having intercourse without marriage (NC 355)
23:19	Offering on the Altar the hire of a harlot or the price of a dog (NC 100)
23:20	Borrowing at interest (NC 236)
23:22	Delaying payment of vows (NC 155)
23:24	All oral commitments to be fulfilled (PC 94)
23:25-26	Allowing an employee to eat of the produce among which he is working (PC 201)
23:25	Hired laborer putting of the harvest in his own vessel (NC 268)
23:26	Hired laborer eating growing crops (NC 267)
24:1	The law of marriage (PC 213)
24:1	Law of divorce (PC 222)
24:4	Remarrying one's divorced wife after she had remarried (NC 356)
24:5	Bridegroom devoting himself to his wife for one year (PC 214)
24:5	Taking a bridegroom away from his home (NC 311)
24:6	Taking a pledge in food utensils (NC 242)
24:8	Cutting or cauterizing signs of *tzara'at* (NC 308)
24:10	Taking a pledge from a debtor by force (NC 239)
24:12	Keeping a needed pledge from its owner (NC 240)
24:13	Restoring a pledge to a needy owner (PC 199)
24:15	Paying wages on time (PC 200)
24:16	A judge receiving testimony from a litigant's relative (NC 287)
24:17	Taking a pledge from a widow (NC 241)
24:17	A judge perverting justice due to proselytes or orphans (NC 280)

24:19	Forgotten sheaf for the poor (PC 122)
24:19	Returning for a forgotten sheaf (NC 214)
25:2	Whipping transgressors of certain commandments (PC 224)
25:2	Inflicting excessive corporal punishment (NC 300)
25:4	Preventing an animal from eating the produce amid which it is working (NC 219)
25:5	Law of levirate marriage (PC 216)
25:5	Having intercourse with a woman subject to levirate marriage (NC 357)
25:9	*Chalitzah* (PC 217)
25:12	Saving the life of the pursued (PC 247)
25:12	Sparing the life of a pursuer (NC 293)
25:13	Keeping false weights and measures (NC 272)
25:17	Remembering the nefarious deeds of Amalek (PC 189)
25:19	Extinction of Amalek (PC 188)
25:19	Forgetting what Amalek did to us (NC 59)

Ki Tavo (26:1 – 29:8)

26:5-10	Recital on bringing the first fruits (PC 132)
26:13-15	Avowal of the tithe (PC 131)
26:14	Eating an unredeemed unclean second tithe, even in Jerusalem (NC 150)
26:14	Eating the second tithe during mourning (NC 151)
26:14	Spending the redemption money of the second tithe except on food and drink (NC 152)

Va-yelech (31:1 – 31:30)

31:12	*The Assembly during the feast of Tabernacles (PC 16)*
31:19	*Writing a Torah scroll (PC 18)*

Notes

Positive Commandments

[1] Etz Hayim, 442.
[2] Stone Chumash, 973.
[3] Donin. *To Pray as a Jew*, 150.
[4] *ArtScroll Siddur*, 92.
[5] Etz Hayim, 1025.
[6] Ibid.
[7] Stone Chumash, 973.
[8] Dosick, 173.
[9] Chill, 372.
[10] Mishneh Torah, Tefillah 4:15-16.
[11] Guide of the Perplexed 3:54.
[12] Sherwin. *Beyond Human Perfection*, 140.
[13] Chill, 388.
[14] Mishneh Torah, Yesodei ha-Torah 5:11.
[15] Hammer. *Entering Jewish Prayer*, 122, 131-132.
[16] Some cover their eyes with the *edges* of their fingers when reading the first verse of the *Shema* and then kiss the fingers when finished. The index, middle, and ring fingers are flexed to form the letter *shin*; the thumb is bent to form the letter *daled*; and the fifth finger is bent to form the letter *yud*, thus producing the word *Shaddai*, a name of God (Gelbard, 45).
[17] Mishneh Torah, Keri'at Shema 2:2.
[18] Donin. *To Pray as a Jew*, 147-148.
[19] Ibid., 341.
[20] Stone Chumash, 975.
[21] Mishneh Torah, Aboth, Kinyan Torah 6:1.
[22] Chavel, 18.
[23] Chill, 374-375.
[24] ArtScroll Siddur, 6.
[25] Mishneh Torah, Tefillin, 4:25.
[26] Chavel, 19.
[27] Lau, 46.
[28] Chavel, 21.
[29] Ibid., 22.
[30] Mishneh Torah, Tzitzit 3:9.
[31] Frankel and Teutsch, 170.
[32] Kolatch. *The Jewish Book of Why*, 105.
[33] Stone Chumash, 1095.
[34] Mishneh Torah, Chagigah 3:3
[35] Stone Chumash, 1096.
[36] Ibid., 1029-1030.
[37] Kolatch. *This is the Torah*, 91.
[38] Millgram. *Jewish Worship*, 295.
[39] Chill, 118.
[40] Ibid., 247.
[41] Ibid., 343.
[42] Guide of the Perplexed 3:45
[43] Mishneh Torah, K'lei ha-Mikdash 3:7
[44] Chavel, 33.
[45] Chill, 121.
[46] Ibid.
[47] Hertz, 594.
[48] Ibid., 329.
[49] Chill, 120.
[50] Ibid., 128.
[51] Hertz, 349.
[52] Donin. *To Pray as a Jew*, 331.
[53] Millgram. *Jewish Worship*, 300.
[54] Hertz, 430.
[55] Ibid., 429.
[56] Ibid., 334.
[57] Contrary to popular misconception, a *mamzer* (often mistranslated as "bastard") is not someone born out of wedlock. Rather, it is the child of a sexual relationship between a man and woman whose marriage could never be valid under Jewish law (Kid. 3:12).
[58] Chill, 132.

[59] Hertz, 513.
[60] Chavel 47.
[61] Stone Chumash, 481.
[62] Donin, *To Pray as a Jew*, 12-14.
[63] Etz Hayim, 615.
[64] Stone Chumash, 571.
[65] Ibid., 896-897.
[66] Hammer. *Entering Jewish Prayer*, 87.
[67] Hammer. *Entering the High Holy Days*, 157.
[68] Millgram. *Jewish Worship*, 254.
[69] Steinsaltz, 206.
[70] Chavel, 61.
[71] Chill, 421.
[72] Mishneh Torah, Yom Tov 6:18.
[73] Chill, 421.
[74] Stone Chumash, 783.
[75] Chill, 336.
[76] Chavel, 69.
[77] Etz Hayim, 820-821.
[78] Stone Chumash, 545.
[79] Etz Hayim, 593.
[80] Stone Chumash, 553.
[81] ArtScroll Siddur, 443b.
[82] Etz Hayim, 595-596.
[83] Ibid., 596.
[84] Stone Chumash, 555.
[85] Ibid., 679.
[86] Guide of the Perplexed, 3:46.
[87] Mishneh Torah, Me'ilah 8:8.
[88] Chavel, 74.
[89] Kolatch. *The Jewish Book of Why*, 173.
[90] Chill, 138.
[91] Ibid.
[92] Stone Chumash, 752.
[93] Etz Hayim, 794.
[94] Mishneh Torah, Mada, Hilchoth Teshubah 1:1.
[95] Chavel, 85.
[96] Hertz, 459.
[97] Chill, 199.
[98] Ibid.
[99] Etz Hayim, 650.
[100] Stone Chumash, 608.
[101] Ibid., 609.
[102] Ibid., 621.
[103] Ibid.
[104] Hertz 465.
[105] Ibid., 473.
[106] Ibid., 550.
[107] Chill, 24.
[108] Kadden and Kadden, 5.
[109] Stone, 365.
[110] Etz Hayim, 393.
[111] Hertz, 801.
[112] Guide of the Perplexed, 3:32
[113] Chavel, 97.
[114] Ibid., 98.
[115] Ibid., 95.
[116] Mishneh Torah, Temurah 4:13.
[117] Chavel, 99-100.
[118] Chill, 125-126.
[119] Ibid., 125.
[120] Chavel, 104.
[121] Chill, 166.
[122] Hertz, 592.
[123] Stone Chumash, 759.
[124] Hertz, 592-593.
[125] Stone Chumash, 761.
[126] Etz Hayim, 800.
[127] Stone Chumash, 761.
[128] Witty and Witty, 248.
[129] Trepp, 113.
[130] Stone Chumash, 901.
[131] Ibid.
[132] Ibid., 902.
[133] Chavel, 109.
[134] Guide of the Perplexed 3:47
[135] Telushkin, 617.
[136] Dosick, 272.
[137] Telushkin, 618.
[138] Hertz, 652.
[139] Etz Hayim, 880.
[140] Stone Chumash, 839.
[141] Hertz, 655.
[142] Etz Hayim, 880.
[143] Dosick, 270.
[144] Ibid.
[145] Telushkin, 619.
[146] Stone Chumash, 718.
[147] Ibid., 719.
[148] Ibid.
[149] Chill, 308.
[150] Ibid., 309-310.
[151] Ibid., 313-314.
[152] Ibid., 239.
[153] Chavel, 129.
[154] Stone Chumash, 663.
[155] Chill, 111,
[156] Stone Chumash, 1069.
[157] Guide of the Perplexed 3:39.
[158] Chavel 140.
[159] Stone Chumash, 837.
[160] Mishneh Torah, Ma'aser 1:2.
[161] Ibid., Terumot 6:5-6.
[162] Stone Chumash, 1014-1015.

163 Guide of the Perplexed 3:39.
164 Hertz, 811.
165 Mishneh Torah, Ma'aser Sheni
    v'Nata Revai 11:5-6.
166 Hertz, 632.
167 Chill, 337-338.
168 Hertz, 632.
169 Chavel, 143.
170 Ibid., 149.
171 Etz Hayim, 740.
172 Ibid., 738.
173 Stone Chumash, 698.
174 Hertz, 812.
175 Stone, 1031.
176 Chill, 432.
177 Chavel, 152.
178 Stone, 722-723.
179 Mishneh Torah, Arakin v'Charamin
    7:4.
180 Hertz, 803.
181 Ibid., 487.
182 Stone Chumash, 648.
183 Chavel, 156.
184 Guide of the Perplexed, 3:48.
185 Isaacs. *Animals*, 82.
186 Stone Chumash, 1051.
187 Hertz, 254.
188 In the 3rd, 6th, 8th, 11th, 14th, 17th,
    and 19th years of the cycle.
189 Millgram. *Jewish Worship*, 263.
190 Frankel and Teutsch, 141.
191 Guide of the Perplexed 2:31.
192 Hertz, 367.
193 Chavel, 164.
194 Ibid., 165.
195 Mishneh Torah, Shabbat 30:15.
196 Heschel. *The Sabbath*, 1966.
197 Ahad Ha-Am, *Al Parashat Derakhim*
    3:30
198 Mishneh Torah, Chametz u-Matzah
    2:2.
199 Witty and Witty, 288-289.
200 Rabbinical Assembly Haggadah, 15.
201 Strassfeld, 12
202 ArtScroll Haggadah Treasury, 104.
203 Chavel, 170.
204 Hertz, 524.
205 Maimonides, Yom Tov 7:1-4.
206 Guide of the Perplexed 3:43.
207 Frankel and Teutsch, 123.
208 www.torahtots.com/holidays/yomki-
    pur/yomkstr.htm (accessed.11/16/03).
209 ArtScroll Yom Kippur Reader, 67.
210 Hertz, 484.
211 Steinsaltz, 169.
212 Frankel and Teutsch, 164.
213 Hertz, 525.
214 Lau, 252.
215 Chill, 294.
216 Ibid., 293.
217 Mishneh Torah, Teshuvah 3:4.
218 Hammer. *Entering the High Holidays*,
    70-71.
219 Ibid., 38.
220 Stone Chumash, 485.
221 Sperling, 265.
222 Hertz, 353.
223 Stone Chumash, 1033.
224 Hertz, 828.
225 Mishneh Torah, Yesodei ha-Torah 9.
226 Chavel, 182.
227 Stone Chumash, 1034.
228 Chill, 428-429.
229 Chavel, 174-176.
230 Stone Chumash, 1028.
231 Chill, 105.
232 Ibid., 106.
233 Chavel, 187.
234 Mishneh Torah, Sanhedrin 2:1-7.
235 Chavel, 187-188.
236 Stone Chumash, 1024.
237 Chill, 226.
238 Stone Chumash, 661.
239 Mishneh Torah, Edut 17:7.
240 Chavel, 192.
241 Ibid., 193.
242 Stone Chumash, 1043-1045.
243 Chill, 445-446.
244 Stone Chumash, 1043.
245 Chill, 445.
246 Hertz, 722.
247 Ibid., 843.
248 Mishneh Torah, Rotzeach u'Shimirat
    Nefesh 11:8.
249 Chill, 456-457.
250 Mishneh Torah, Rotzeach u'Shimirat
    Nefesh 11:6.
251 Hertz, 843.
252 Guide of the Perplexed 3:29.
253 Stone Chumash, 978.
254 Mishneh Torah, Avodat Kochavim 5:6.
255 Chavel, 199.
256 Stone, 1041.
257 Telushkin, 51.
258 Etz Hayim, 1136.
259 Stone, 1039.

260 Chill, 471.
261 Chavel, 207.
262 Ibid., 208.
263 Stone Chumash, 565.
264 Mishneh Torah, Matanot Aniyim
    10:7-14.
265 Stone Chumash, 703.
266 Mishneh Torah, Matanot Aniyim
    9:1-3.
267 Stone Chumash., 419.
268 Mishneh Torah, Avadim 4:2.
269 Stone Chumash, 419.
270 Ibid., 1018.
271 Chavel, 211.
272 Stone Chumash, 431.
273 Chavel, 213.
274 Hertz, 849.
275 Ibid.
276 Ibid., 500.
277 Guide of the Perplexed 3:42.
278 Chavel, 215.
279 Stone Chumash, 1058.
280 Etz Hayim, 471.
281 Hertz, 316.
282 Guide of the Perplexed 3:17.
283 Chill 108.
284 Mishneh Torah, Rotzeach u-Shemir-
    at Nefesh 13:13.
285 Chavel, 218.
286 Etz Hayim, 1115.
287 Mishneh Torah, Teshuvah 4:2.
288 Ibid., Ohel 14:1.
289 Stone Chumash, 661.
290 Ibid.
291 Hertz, 505.
292 Chill, 251-252.
293 Etz Hayim, 700.
294 Stone Chumash, 665.
295 Chill, 44.
296 Hertz, 498.
297 Etz Hayim, 10.
298 Chavel, 228.
299 Chill, 3.
300 Mishneh Torah, Ishut 12:1.
301 Stone Chumash, 1059.
302 Ibid., 1064.

303 Ibid., 1065.
304 Mishneh Torah, Yibum v'Chalitzah
    1:3,6,7.
305 Stone Chumash, 429-430.
306 Telushkin, 613.
307 Stone Chumash, 1053.
308 Ibid., 1046-1047.
309 Ibid., 1047.
310 Hertz, 850.
311 Telushkin, 621.
312 Biale, 78.
313 Telushkin, 622.
314 Ibid.
315 Ibid.
316 Ibid., 623.
317 Kadden and Kadden, 69.
318 Stone Chumash, 755.
319 Ibid., 755-758.
320 Hertz, 589.
321 Chavel, 237.
322 Chill, 483.
323 Stone Chumash, 1063.
324 Mishneh Torah, Sanhedrin 15:9.
325 Chavel, 244.
326 Mishneh Torah, Avadim 9:8.
327 Chavel, 247.
328 Ibid.
329 Ibid., 248.
330 Guide of the Perplexed 3:40.
331 Chavel, 251.
332 Ibid., 250.
333 Stone Chumash, 427.
333 Chill, 47.
335 Stone Chumash, 425-426.
336 Ibid., 427.
337 Ibid., 429.
338 Ibid., 428.
339 Ibid., 699.
340 Ibid., 429.
341 Chavel, 255.
342 Chill, 227-228.
343 Guide of the Perplexed, 3:40.
344 Chill, 228.
345 Hertz, 692.
346 Ibid.

Negative Commandments

[1] Hertz, 295.
[2] Mishneh Torah, Teshuvah 3:15.
[3] Stone Chumash, 408.
[4] Ibid.
[5] Chavel, 3.
[6] Chill, 33.
[7] Ibid.
[8] Chavel, 3.
[9] Mishneh Torah, Avodat Kochavim 3:10-11.
[10] Eight Chapters, 5.
[11] Stone Chumash, 408-409.
[12] Chavel, 7.
[13] Ibid., 8-9.
[14] Stone Chumash, 653.
[15] Mishneh Torah, Avodat Kochavim 6:1.
[16] Chavel, 9-10.
[17] Stone Chumash, 665.
[18] Chill, 215.
[19] Stone Chumash, 657.
[20] Chill, 216.
[21] Mishneh Torah, Avodat Kochavim 6:7.
[22] Hertz, 775.
[23] Chill, 423-424.
[24] Mishneh Torah, Avodat Kochavim 6:10.
[25] Ibid., Sanhedrin 11:5.
[26] Chavel, 17-18.
[27] Stone Chumash, 1009.
[28] Ibid.
[29] Mishneh Torah, Avodat Kochavim 8:7.
[30] Guide of the Perplexed 3:37.
[31] Stone Chumash, 982.
[32] Mishneh Torah, Avodat Kochavim 4:7-8.
[33] Ibid.
[34] Hertz, 826.
[35] Mishneh Torah, Yesodei ha-Torah 10:4.
[36] Chavel, 25.
[37] Mishneh Torah, Abovat Kochavim 5:7.
[38] Stone Chumash, 649.
[39] Etz Hayim, 688.
[40] Chavel, 30.
[41] Eight Chapters, 8.
[42] Mishneh Torah, Teshuvah 5.
[43] Chavel, 33.
[44] Mishneh Torah, Avodat Kochavim 11:5.
[45] Hertz, 826.
[46] Mishneh Torah, Avodat Kochavim 11:11-12.
[47] Ibid., Yesodei ha-Torah 10:3.
[48] Chill, 244.
[49] Stone Chumash, 1033.
[50] Chill, 454-455.
[51] Guide of the Perplexed 3:37.
[52] Mishneh Torah, Tzitzit 3:9.
[53] Frankel and Teutsch, 170.
[54] Kolatch. *The Jewish Book of Why*, 105.
[55] Chill, 246.
[56] Mishneh Torah, Avodat Kochavim 12:11.
[57] Kolatch. *The Second Book of Why*, 286.
[58] Guide of the Perplexed, 3:37.
[59] Chill, 237.
[60] Hertz, 844.
[61] Werblowsky, R.J. Zwi, and Geoffrey Wigoder, eds. *Oxford Dictionary of the Jewish Religion*. Oxford: Oxford University Press, 1997.
[62] Ibid.
[63] Stone Chumash, 664.
[64] Dosick, 251.
[65] Chill, 247.
[66] Chavel, 45-46.
[67] Mishneh Torah, Avodat Kochavim, 2:3.
[68] Chavel, 46-47.
[69] Mishneh Torah, Avodat Kochavim 10:7.
[70] Chavel, 50.
[71] Mishneh Torah, Melachim 10:12.
[72] Chavel, 49.
[73] Stone Chumash, 1054.
[74] Chavel, 52.
[75] Stone Chumash, 1055.
[76] Hertz, 846.
[77] Mishneh Torah, Isurei Bi'ah 12:25.
[78] Tigay, 212.
[79] Stone Chumash, 1055.
[80] Chavel, 52.
[81] Tigay, 212.
[82] Stone Chumash, 1055.
[83] Mishneh Torah, Melachim 6:6.
[84] Tigay, 190.
[85] Chavel, 56.
[86] Mishneh Torah, Avodat Kochavim 2:6.

[87] Ibid., 2:10.
[88] Chavel, 61.
[89] Hertz, 519.
[90] Stone Chumash, 681.
[91] Ibid., 975.
[92] Ibid., 976.
[93] Hertz, 772.
[94] Chavel, 64.
[95] Hertz, 800.
[96] Mishneh Torah, Yesodei Ha-Torah 6:8.
[97] Millgram. *Jewish Worship*, 340.
[98] Hertz, 800.
[99] Tigay, 198.
[100] Hertz, 842.
[101] Stone Chumash, 1049.
[102] Guide of the Perplexed 3:45.
[103] Etz Hayim, 719.
[104] Mishneh Torah, Biat ha-Mikdash 8:16.
[105] Chavel, 70.
[106] Chill, 263.
[107] Chavel, 68.
[108] Guide of the Perplexed 3:45.
[109] Stone Chumash, 594.
[110] Hertz, 446-447.
[111] Mishneh Torah, Biat ha-Mikdash 9:6-7.
[112] Hertz, 515.
[113] Chavel, 75.
[114] Stone Chumash, 751.
[115] Guide of the Perplexed 3:45.
[116] Chavel, 79.
[117] Etz Hayim, 614.
[118] Stone Chumash, 414.
[119] Hertz, 301.
[120] Stone Chumash, 415.
[121] Ibid.
[122] Ibid.
[123] Chavel, 81.
[124] Stone Chumash, 483.
[125] Guide of the Perplexed 3:45.
[126] Hertz, 354.
[127] Stone Chumash, 489.
[128] Chill, 133.
[129] Chavel, 83.
[130] Stone Chumash, 447.
[131] Chavel, 84-85.
[132] Stone Chumash, 470.
[133] Ibid., 469-470.
[134] Stone Chumash, 472.
[135] Ibid.
[136] Chill, 205.
[137] Chavel, 88.
[138] Mishneh Torah, Isurei Mizbe'ach 2:1-6.
[139] Stone Chumash, 680.
[140] Hertz, 517.
[141] Mishneh Torah, Ma'aseh ha-Korbanot 3:4.
[142] Ibid., Bi'at ha-Mikdash 9:13
[143] Hertz, 517.
[144] Chill, 268.
[145] Hertz, 414.
[146] Chavel, 96.
[147] Stone Chumash, 551.
[148] Hertz, 414.
[149] Chill, 146.
[150] Stone Chumash, 553.
[151] Hertz, 848.
[152] Ibid.
[153] Stone Chumash, 1057.
[154] Etz Hayim, 1125.
[155] Stone Chumash, 1057.
[156] Chavel, 98.
[157] Guide of the Perplexed 3:48
[158] Chill 274.
[159] Stone Chumash, 565.
[160] Chavel, 100.
[161] Hertz, 589.
[162] Stone Chumash, 755.
[163] Hertz, 590.
[164] Stone Chumash, 755.
[165] Hertz, 548.
[166] Chavel, 102.
[167] Stone Chumash, 722.
[168] Hertz, 647.
[169] Chavel, 103.
[170] Stone Chumash, 723.
[171] Chavel, 105-106.
[172] Ibid., 107.
[173] Ibid., 106.
[174] Ibid.
[175] Stone Chumash, 437.
[176] Chavel, 110.
[177] Hertz, 255.
[178] Chavel, 111.
[179] Guide of the Perplexed 3:46.
[180] Chavel, 113.
[181] Ibid., 114.
[182] Hertz, 255.
[183] Stone Chumash, 360.
[184] Hertz, 430.
[185] Stone Chumash, 577.
[186] Chavel, 121.
[187] ibid., 122.

[188] Ibid., 122-123.
[189] Ibid., 124.
[190] Ibid., 125.
[191] Guide of the Perplexed 3:46.
[192] Stone Chumash, 572.
[193] Etz Hayim, 616.
[194] Stone Chumash, 573.
[195] Ibid., 1011.
[196] Chavel, 132.
[197] Ibid., 146-147.
[198] Ibid., 136.
[199] Ibid., 137.
[200] Ibid., 138.
[201] Ibid.
[202] Hertz, 861.
[203] Chavel, 142.
[204] Hertz, 849.
[205] Stone Chumash, 1057.
[206] Chill, 396.
[207] Ibid., 397.
[208] Chavel., 148.
[209] Etz Hayim, 941.
[210] Mishneh Torah, Beit ha-Mikdash 6:9.
[211] Stone Chumash, 673.
[212] Ibid., 674.
[213] Chavel, 150.
[214] Guide of the Perplexed 3:49.
[215] Hertz, 514.
[216] Stone Chumash, 675.
[217] Chavel, 156-157.
[218] Mishneh Torah, Beit ha-Mikdash 2:6.
[219] Stone Chumash, 672-673.
[220] Mishneh Torah, Avel 3:8.
[221] Ibid., 7:6.
[222] Chavel, 162-163.
[223] Etz Hayim, 1094.
[224] Stone Chumash, 1031.
[225] Chavel, 165-166.
[226] Stone Chumash, 1011.
[227] Chavel, 166.
[228] Hertz, 453.
[229] Guide of the Perplexed 3:48.
[230] Chavel, 169.
[231] Chill, 177.
[232] Guide of the Perplexed 3:48.
[233] Chavel, 170.
[234] Guide of the Perplexed 3:48.
[235] Stone Chumash, 599.
[236] Chill, 176-177.
[237] Stone Chumash, 599.
[238] Ibid.
[239] Ibid., 605.
[240] Ibid., 1013.
[241] Guide of the Perplexed 3:48.
[242] Chill, 411.
[243] Chavel, 178.
[244] Mishneh Torah, Shechitah 10:9.
[245] Chill, 93.
[246] Guide of the Perplexed 3:48.
[247] Chill, 8.
[248] Stone Chumash, 647.
[249] Chill, 169.
[250] Ibid., 168.
[251] Stone Chumash, 578
[252] Hertz, 433.
[253] Chill, 168.
[254] Dosick, 264.
[255] Telushkin, 636.
[256] Guide of the Perplexed 3:48.
[257] Hertz, 318.
[258] Chill, 75.
[259] Guide of the Perplexed 3:40.
[260] Chavel, 186.
[261] Chill, 280.
[262] Guide of the Perplexed 3:37.
[263] Chavel, 188.
[264] Guide of the Perplexed 3:37.
[265] Chavel, 191.
[266] Stone Chumash, 663.
[267] Guide of the Perplexed 3:33.
[268] Stone Chumash, 1048.
[269] Strassfeld, 219.
[270] ArtScroll Yom Kippur Reader, 67.
[271] Chavel, 197.
[272] Ibid., 198.
[273] Ibid., 201.
[274] Stone Chumash, 759.
[275] Chavel, 202.
[276] Etz Hayim, 800.
[277] Chavel, 203.
[278] Ibid.
[279] Stone Chumash, 760-761.
[280] Chill, 327.
[281] Mishneh Torah, Nedarim 13:23.
[282] Chavel, 205.
[283] Ibid., 209.
[284] Chill, 235.
[285] Stone Chumash, 663.
[286] Mishneh Torah, Kelaim 1:4.
[287] Ibid.
[288] Chill 236.
[289] Hertz, 844.
[290] Stone Chumash, 662.
[291] Hertz, 502
[292] Stone Chumash, 662.
[293] Chavel, 213.

294 Stone Chumash, 697.
295 Kolatch. *Second Book of Why*, 321.
296 Stone Chumash, 1015-1016.
297 Chavel, 217.
298 Ibid., 218.
299 Hertz, 534.
300 Stone Chumash, 702-703.
301 Chavel, 219.
302 Etz Hayim, 1066.
303 Stone Chumash, 1004.
304 Chavel, 222.
305 Stone Chumash, 431.
306 Hertz, 314.
307 Chavel, 223.
308 Stone Chumash, 703.
309 Chill, 87.
310 Chavel, 228.
311 Stone Chumash, 1061.
312 Etz Hayim, 1131.
313 Chavel, 229-230.
314 Stone Chumash, 1059.
315 Ibid., 412.
316 Mishneh Torah, Teshuvah 4:5.
317 Stone Chumash, 659.
318 Chavel, 233.
319 Stone Chumash, 660.
320 Chill, 438.
321 Chavel, 235.
322 Etz Hayim, 1100.
323 Chavel, 237.
324 Stone Chumash, 659.
325 Etz Hayim, 740.
326 Chavel, 238.
327 Stone Chumash, 699.
328 Chill, 301-302.
329 Stone Chumash, 699.
330 Ibid., 431.
331 Chavel, 241.
332 Stone Chumash, 431.
333 Hertz, 848.
334 Chavel, 243.
335 Stone Chumash, 1056.
336 Mishneh Torah, De'ot 6:10.
337 Ibid.
338 Stone Chumash, 431.
339 Ibid., 705.
340 Hertz, 537.
341 Stone Chumash, 704-705.
342 Ibid., 707.
343 Ibid., 419.
344 Ibid..
345 Mishneh Torah, Ishut 12:1-4.
346 Chavel, 250.

347 Ibid., 252.
348 Chill, 54.
349 Chill, 474.
350 Tigay, 220.
351 Stone Chumash, 1049.
352 Chill, 453.
353 Chavel, 254.
354 Chill, 251-252.
355 Chavel, 257.
356 Chill, 97.
357 Stone Chumash, 943.
358 Chill, 101
359 Chavel, 261.
360 Stone Chumash, 1036.
361 Ibid., 433.
362 Chavel, 265.
363 Chill, 103.
364 Stone Chumash, 1061.
365 Chavel, 268.
366 Chill, 105.
367 Ibid., 96.
368 Stone Chumash, 435.
369 Chavel, 271.
370 Ibid., 265.
371 Ibid., 265-266.
372 Hertz, 300.
373 Stone Chumash, 412.
374 Chill, 368.
375 Chavel, 268.
376 Stone Chumash, 1037.
377 Chill 46.
378 Etz Hayim, 447.
379 Hertz, 299.
380 Stone Chumash, 411.
381 Mishneh Torah, Yesodei ha-Torah
    5:4.
382 Stone Chumash, 932.
383 Mishneh Torah, Rotzeach u-Shemir-
    at Nefesh 1:4.
384 Chavel, 275-276.
385 Ibid., 277.
386 Mishneh Torah, Talmud Torah 6:14.
387 Hertz, 500.
388 Stone Chumash, 660.
389 Chill, 225.
390 Stone Chumash, 1063.
391 Chavel, 279.
392 Chill, 483.
393 Ibid., 228.
394 Hertz, 501.
395 Ibid.
396 Mishneh Torah, De'ot 6:6, 9.
397 Stone Chumash, 661.

[398] Chill, 229.
[399] Hertz, 501.
[400] Chill, 231.
[401] Ibid., 232.
[402] Mishneh Torah, De'ot 7:7-8.
[403] Stone Chumash, 615.
[404] Chavel, 284.
[405] Guide of the Perplexed 3:49.
[406] Stone Chumash, 430.
[407] Ibid.
[408] Chill, 424-425.
[409] Guide of the Perplexed 3:41
[410] Chill, 425.
[411] Stone Chumash, 1007.
[412] Chavel, 289.
[413] Ibid., 288.
[414] Hertz, 315.
[415] Etz Hayim, 470.
[416] Chavel, 290.
[417] Ibid., 292-293.
[418] Etz Hayim, 460.
[419] Hertz, 308.
[420] Mishneh Torah, Mamrim 6:15.
[421] Chill, 70-71.
[422] Stone Chumash, 421.
[423] Guide of the Perplexed 3:41.
[424] Chill, 70.
[425] Lau, 194.
[426] Witty and Witty, 187.
[427] Chill, 38.
[428] Witty and Witty, 193.
[429] Kolatch. *The Jewish Book of Why,* 166.
[430] Mishneh Torah, Shabbat 1.
[431] Hertz, 277.
[432] Chavel, 296.
[433] Mishneh Torah, Shabbat 27:17.

[434] Telushkin, 484.
[435] Chavel, 297.
[436] Stone Chumash, 683.
[437] Chavel, 300.
[438] Chill, 278.
[439] Stone Chumash, 651.
[430] Hertz, 490.
[431] Silverman Machzor, 409.
[432] Chill, 212.
[433] Stone Chumash, 411.
[434] Etz Hayim, 691.
[435] Kolatch. *The Second Jewish Book of Why,* 151.
[436] Gross, 381.
[437] Grossman. The Gay Orthodox Underground
(Moment Magazine, April 2001, 56-58, 97.
[438] Ibid., 57.
[439] Mishneh Torah, Issurai Bi'ah 21:8.
[440] Biale, 195.
[441] Stone Chumash, 651.
[442] Mishneh Torah, Issurei Bi'ah, 21:1, 6.
[443] Ibid., 22:21.
[444] Chavel, 231.
[445] Guide of the Perplexed 3:49.
[446] Biale, 190–192.
[447] Chill, 478.
[448] Chavel, 324.
[449] Chill, 465.
[450] Ibid., 466.
[451] Stone Chumash, 681.
[452] Etz Hayim, 1092.
[453] Chill, 429.
[454] Ibid.
[455] Stone Chumash, 1029.

Index

ABOUT THE AUTHOR

Ronald L. Eisenberg has been a student of Jewish law, history, and culture for many years. In addition of this volume, he is also the author of *The Jewish World in Stamps*, *Dictionary of Jewish Terms*, *The JPS Guide to Jewish Traditions*, and *The Streets of Jerusalem*.

An internationally-renowned radiologist, who has authored 20 books in his medical specialty, Dr. Eisenberg is also a non-practicing attorney.